THE **Building Christian English** SERIES

Building

Christian English

Communicating Effectively

Grades 9 and 10

Book One

Rod and Staff Publishers, Inc.
P.O. Box 3, Hwy. 172
Crockett, Kentucky 41413
Telephone: (606) 522-4348

Acknowledgments

We are indebted first and most of all to God, whose blessing made possible the writing and publishing of this book.

We express gratitude to each one who was involved in this work. Bruce Good wrote the text. Marvin Eicher and Ernest Wine were the editors, and various other brethren were reviewers. Simon Myers supplied the photograph on page 91, and Corel Corporation supplied the photograph on page 242. The engraving on page 163 is from the *Martyrs Mirror*. Lester Miller did most of the hand drawings. Samuel Hoover provided the rest of the illustrations and photographs. We are also indebted to the teachers who used the material on a laboratory basis in their classrooms, as well as to numerous people who assisted along the way by providing finances, by encouraging those directly involved in the work, and by interceding in prayer for the work.

Various reference books were consulted in accomplishing this task, such as English handbooks, other English textbooks, encyclopedias, and dictionaries. For these too we are grateful. We have chosen to favor the more conservative schools of thought that are considered authoritative in correct English usage.

—The Publishers

Copyright 2003

by

Rod and Staff Publishers, Inc.
Crockett, Kentucky 41413

Printed in U.S.A

ISBN 0-7399-0539-2

Catalog no. 12901.3

2   3   4   5   6   —   16   15   14   13   12   11   10   09   08   07

Table of Contents

(Stars indicate lessons on editing skills, writing style, or speaking style.)

Chapter 5   Glossary of Usage

Chapter 6   Writing an Argumentative Essay

Chapter 7   Substantives

Chapter 8   Paragraphs That Build an Essay

Chapter 13 Connecting Words, Interjections, and Idioms

Chapter 14 Letters and Special Short Compositions

Year-end Reviews

Introduction

New Features in Grades 9 and 10 of *Building Christian English*

Welcome to a new level in the study of English. In previous years of the *Building Christian English* series, you focused mainly on grammar—things like sentence structure and parts of speech. Now in Books One and Two, you will find several things that are different from the earlier books in the series.

One difference is that Books One and Two place a stronger emphasis on composition than the earlier books did. Instead of studying several lessons on grammar and then one on composition, you will have entire chapters on composition (alternating with chapters on grammar). The lessons in these chapters will give you practical help in effective listening, speaking, reading, and writing.

Another difference is that Books One and Two are parallel rather than consecutive. That is, Book Two does not build on Book One. Instead, each book reviews grammar concepts from grade 8 and previous years, and each book deals with different kinds of composition. For this reason, you may study either Book One or Book Two first, and grades 9 and 10 can be in the same English class.

A third difference is the three new kinds of lessons distributed throughout Books One and Two. They are called "Improving Your Writing Style," "Improving Your Speaking Style," and "Improving Your Editing Skills." These lessons will give you regular practice with writing, public speaking, and proofreading. In the writing and speaking lessons, the focus is on the style rather than the mechanics of a written or an oral presentation. That is, instead of teaching you how to gather and organize information, these lessons will teach you how to make your oral and written compositions more interesting and effective.

May God bless your study of English this year.

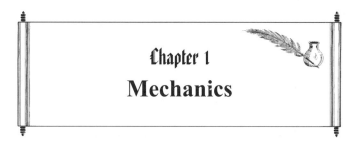

Chapter 1
Mechanics

1. Capitalization and End Punctuation

The mechanics of English relate primarily to the rules of capitalization and punctuation. Like road signs, these rules help a reader to understand where the road of thought turns, pauses, or stops.

Capitalization

1. *Capitalize the first word of every sentence, direct quotation, and line of poetry.*

Before us lies a year of study and learning.
Grandfather remarked quietly, "We must always cultivate patience."

Thou lowly mortal, wouldst thou rise
To set thy name above the skies?
    Know this: The self-exalted must
    By God's own hand be brought to dust.

2. *Capitalize all proper nouns.*
    a. Names of persons, including titles, abbreviations, and initials. Capitalize a title only if it is used as part of the name or in place of a name. Capitalize the word *president* when it refers to the current president of the United States.

    Mr. Clymer   Clair Eby, Jr.
    Uncle Ira; my uncle   saw the President; met former presidents

    b. Names that refer to God, and words that refer to the Bible or to parts of it. Also capitalize personal pronouns that refer to God.

    the Lord God; the gods of Canaan
    Jesus Christ; false christs
    the Law; the Gospel; a social gospel
    the Book of Genesis; a book written by Moses

    c. Names of geographical features, such as rivers, lakes, and mountains; and of political units, such as cities, states, provinces, and nations. Capitalize words like *north* and *southwest* only when they name specific geographical regions, not when they name directions.

    Mississippi River; large river systems   Ireland
    lived in the West; drove west all day   Missouri

d. Titles of stories, poems, songs, and publications. Capitalize the first and last words and other important words. Do not capitalize articles, coordinating conjunctions, and prepositions of fewer than four letters.

"A Rock to Stand On" (story)   *The Way of the Cross* (book)

e. Names of specific organizations, businesses, institutions, groups, races, and languages.

Cloverdale Mennonite School	Hispanics and Eskimos
Greenville Savings and Loan	American Medical Association
the House of Representatives	Chinese culture

f. Names of specific ships, airplanes, trains, buildings, monuments, natural phenomena, and heavenly bodies.

the *Mayflower*	the Gateway Arch
the *Concorde*	Hurricane Agnes
the Empire State Building	Mercury; Venus; Earth

Note: Capitalize *earth* only if you use it as a proper noun to name the planet on which we live. Omit the article *the* in such a case.

The planet making the closest approach to Earth is Venus. (proper noun)
The earth and Venus are almost identical in size. (common noun)

g. Names of parks, historic sites, events, eras, and documents.

Banff National Park	the Ten Plagues; the Exodus
the Industrial Revolution	the Edict of Milan

h. Brand names and registered trademarks. Do not capitalize a common noun that follows the brand name or trademark, even if it is capitalized in a label.

Parson's ammonia	Nabisco shredded wheat
Keri lotion	Wolverine shoes

i. Names of school subjects derived from proper nouns or followed by numbers.

Anabaptist history	Algebra I	spelling class

j. Calendar items, but not the names of seasons.

January	Independence Day
Wednesday	summer

3. *Capitalize most words derived from proper nouns.* A word may become so common that it is no longer capitalized. Check a dictionary if you are not sure.

Italian seasoning	Roman law	davenport

4. *Capitalize the pronoun* I *and the interjection* O. The word *O* occurs mainly in poetry and in archaic English, such as that in the King James Bible. In modern prose,

it signifies a solemn appeal and always precedes a noun of direct address. Do not confuse *O* with the interjection *oh*.

"Unto thee will I cry, O L<small>ORD</small> my rock."
Let us pray, O brethren, for help from God; oh, how we need His aid.

5. *Capitalize the greeting, closing, and signature of a letter.*

Dear Grandma,

. . . .

Your grandson,
Brendon Showalter

6. *Capitalize abbreviations of proper nouns and of many other common terms.* Check a dictionary or an English handbook when you are not sure.

8:30 P.M.   A.D. 70

End Punctuation

7. *Use a period after a declarative sentence, an indirect question, and an imperative sentence.*

One good example is worth more than many words.
Brother Clair asked if we had considered the power of our influence.
Guard carefully the influence of your life.

8. *Use periods with initials and with many abbreviations.* Common exceptions include the two-letter abbreviations for states and provinces and the abbreviations for organizations and government agencies. Check a dictionary or an English handbook when you are not sure. Avoid most abbreviations in formal writing.

Mr. John G. Woods	e.g. (for example)
4 in.	CT (Connecticut)
2 tsp.	FHA (Federal Housing Administration)

9. *Use a question mark after an interrogative sentence or quotation.* For emphasis, you may use question marks between items in a series within an interrogative sentence.

"Are you doing your best?" asked Father.
Do you know the reference for the Lord's Prayer? the Great Commission? the Love Chapter?

10. *Use a question mark within parentheses to indicate uncertainty about the preceding information.*

The Seminole Indian chief Osceola lived from 1800 (?) until 1838.

11. *Use an exclamation point after a strong interjection and after an exclamatory sentence or quotation.*

Hallelujah! The Saviour has risen!

Applying the Lesson

A. Write correctly each word or abbreviation that has a capitalization error.

1. our sovereign lord has revealed himself through the scriptures.
2. the new testament warns against the folly of rejecting jesus christ and following false christs.
3. consider well, o Youth, the godly examples of joseph, miriam, and daniel.
4. "have you considered, o people," questioned brother Leon, "how very thankful we should be despite the drought this Summer?"
5. We sang "in thy holy place" and "walk in the light" from the *church hymnal.*
6. Did grandfather enjoy the story "i will be with thee" and the poem "in his hands" in the *christian example?*
7. When i dropped the pyrex dish and the china cup on the macadam, they broke.
8. Classes on friday afternoon include anabaptist history, typing I, and Art.
9. The *great eastern,* a british steam and sail vessel, laid the first cable across the atlantic ocean.
10. The president has requested the fbi to investigate the disaster.
11. Timothy asked, "do you know, father, who was President when you were born?"
12. The *stourbridge lion,* built in england in 1829, was the first locomotive used in america.
13. Before a new Drug is sold without prescription, the fda must approve it.
14. The students of the watson mennonite school sang at the ashbury rest home.
15. "go South on bird road," said mr. lodge, "until you come to a broad River."
16. Many portions of the east were paralyzed by a Blizzard in 1996.
17. The highest point in the Great Smoky Mountains national park is clingmans dome.
18. For Science class, I wrote a report about the planet venus.
19. In History class we learned that king John signed the magna carta at runnymede in june 1215.
20. These western family plastic strips are cheaper than band-aids.
21. We observe easter on the first sunday after the first full moon after the first day of Spring.
22. The treaty of Versailles, signed on june 28, 1919, ended world war I.
23. Among the german settlers were many mennonites as well as lutherans.
24. The netherlands museum in holland, michigan, displays many dutch relics.

B. Copy each word that should be followed by end punctuation, and add the correct mark.

1. Have you considered how your actions influence your friends determine your reputation set your course of life
2. What fools men make of themselves when they forget God
3. If only all men would love and obey the Lord
4. Did you pray this morning for protection and safety for wisdom to perform your duties for courage to resist temptation
5. "Why would any Christian want to copy the world's ways" asked Lee

6. Lowell wondered why we often find it easier to learn nonsense rhymes than to memorize wholesome poems
7. Melinda asked what we can do to help Mother
8. Sharon responded, "Has the kitchen floor been swept"

C. Write a correct abbreviation for each word or phrase.

1. Fahrenheit
2. after midday *(post meridiem)*
3. verses
4. Incorporated
5. Thursday

6. dozen
7. Mountain Standard Time
8. southwest
9. Manitoba (two letters)
10. and so forth

Review Exercises

Copy each numbered word, and write the abbreviation for the part of speech that it is.

noun—n.   adjective—adj.   conjunction—conj.
pronoun—pron.   adverb—adv.   interjection—interj.
verb—v.   preposition—prep.

A [1]large bird [2]with brown-checked wings [3]swept down [4]toward the [5]lake. [6]Splash! [7]It [8]snatched up a fish.

[9]"Oh, Joshua," [10]Alice exclaimed, [11]"get the camera! [12]Quick!"

Her [13]brother dropped [14]his sandwich [15]and grabbed the camera. [16]"Is [17]that an osprey [18]or some kind of hawk?" he asked. [19]He took a picture just [20]as the bird [21]swiftly flew [22]off [23]with its [24]flopping prey.

---

2. Commas

1. *Use a comma before the coordinating conjunction that joins the clauses of a compound sentence.* (The common coordinating conjunctions are *and, but, or, for, nor, yet,* and *so.*) If the clauses are very short and closely related, you may omit the comma. If one or both of the clauses are long and already contain several commas, the comma between the clauses is often changed to a semicolon to make the division between the clauses more clear.

> The Bible is God's inspired Word, yet many people ignore its principles.
> God loves us and we love Him.
> When a person fears the Lord, he will depart from evil; [or evil,] for he serves a holy God that hates all sin.

2. *Use commas to separate items in a series.*

a. A series of words, phrases, or clauses. If a pair within the series is joined by a conjunction (as *ham and eggs* in the second example below), no comma is used between those two items. If a writer wishes to emphasize the number and variety of the things listed, he may connect all the items with conjunctions and omit the commas.

Before the overnight guests arrive, we need to make the beds, clean the house, and plan several meals.

We had toast, ham and eggs, orange juice, and yogurt for breakfast.

All summer we hoed and staked and pruned and watered and fertilized those tomatoes.

b. A series of descriptive adjectives that have equal rank. When two adjectives have equal rank, (1) you generally pause as you read them, (2) you could place *and* between them, and (3) you generally could switch their order. Sometimes the adjective immediately before the noun is closely related to the noun (almost like a compound noun) and should not be preceded by a comma.

A border of bright, cheery spring flowers welcomed us.
> (*Bright* and *cheery* have equal rank, but *spring* is closely related to *flowers*.)

3. *Use commas to set off certain introductory material.*
   a. Words of response and mild interjections.

   Yes, we are ready to go.   Well, I didn't see anyone.

   b. Verbal phrases.

   Purring softly, Tabby rubbed against my leg.

   c. Long prepositional phrases or a series of prepositional phrases. Do not use a comma, however, if a sentence has inverted word order.

   In the shade of the big oak tree, we spread a picnic lunch.
   In the shade of the big oak tree sat three tired boys.
   > (inverted word order—no comma)

   d. Adverb clauses.

   Although the sun glared upon us, a slight breeze moderated the heat.

4. *Use commas to set off nonrestrictive and parenthetical elements.*
   a. Nonrestrictive words, phrases, and clauses used as adjectives. Whereas a restrictive adjective limits the meaning of a substantive by telling *which one,* a nonrestrictive adjective merely gives additional information. Because it is not needed to make the meaning of the sentence clear, it is set off with commas.

   Glade Valley, peaceful and verdant, welcomed the weary pioneers.
   > (words are nonrestrictive—set off with commas)
   The valley <u>below</u> was shrouded in the early morning mist.
   > (word is restrictive—no commas)

   Winding Creek, meandering through our pasture, was well named.
   > (phrase is nonrestrictive—set off with commas)
   The creek <u>meandering through our pasture</u> was named Winding Creek.
   > (phrase is restrictive—no commas)

b. Nonrestrictive appositives. Like an adjective phrase, an appositive is nonrestrictive if it merely gives additional information about the substantive it follows. It is restrictive if it is necessary to the meaning of a sentence and restricts that substantive. A restrictive appositive generally consists of only one or two words and is closely related to the substantive it follows.

Mrs. Roberts, our next-door neighbor, appreciates our help.
   (appositive is nonrestrictive; set off with commas)
My sister Jane often helps her with the cleaning and washing.
   (appositive is restrictive—no commas)

c. Titles of family relationship or of professional rank that follow names.

Henry C. Shertzer, Sr., owns this business.
I needed the services of Dr. Brent Hershey, D.D.S.

d. Nouns of direct address.

Susan, Mother is calling you.
This paper, Jason, looks neat.

e. Parenthetical expressions such as explanatory words, transitional expressions, and contrasting ideas.

In any event, we are thankful to be home safely.
The cold wind, however, came right through our clothes.
Summer, not winter, is my favorite season.

5. *Use commas in certain conventional situations.*
   a. To separate the parts of addresses and dates.

Route 2, Box 21
Martinsburg, PA 16662
August 25, 1996

On April 19, 1990, we moved to 7498 Marion Road, Newark, Ohio, to help care for my grandmother.

b. To separate large numerals into periods of thousands, millions, and so forth.

3,850 miles
$453,000,000

c. To follow the greeting of a friendly letter and the closing of any letter.

Dear Grandmother,
Sincerely,

d. To separate a direct quotation from the rest of the sentence unless some other punctuation is used.

"That pair of house wrens must be building a nest," announced Joyce.
"They are making it," she continued, "in the old apple tree."

6. *Use a comma if it is needed to prevent misunderstanding.* Only rarely should you use a comma that is not clearly required by one of the basic rules. Using too many commas is just as undesirable as omitting necessary commas.

> After all, his efforts have been deeply appreciated.
> (comma needed to prevent reading *After all his efforts* as a phrase)

Applying the Lesson

A. Write the number and letter of the rule illustrated by each comma. If two commas have the same letter, one rule applies to that pair.

1. Because friends influence us greatly,[a] we must choose friends who have integrity of character,[b] respect for authority,[b] and reverence for the Lord.
2. By their good example,[a] I'm sure you agree,[b] true friends help us understand what are noble,[c] worthwhile actions.
3. No,[a] a popular,[b] fun-loving person is not always the best friend.
4. The Lord God,[a] who is gracious and merciful,[a] seeks man's good,[b] yet many ignore Him.
5. Speaking with firm conviction,[a] Nevin Watson declared,[b] "I want to be true to the Lord."
6. My friend,[a] if you take your burdens to the Lord,[b] you need not bear them alone.
7. I have an appointment with M. R. Davids,[a] M.D.,[a] on May 3,[b] 20—.
8. "Ann,[a] May,[a] and Vera may plan the bulletin board,"[b] stated Brother Mark.
9. On the other side of town,[a] a farm sold for $450,000[b] last week,[c] but it will soon be growing houses instead of crops.
10. Standing at the window,[a] we watched the snowplow,[b] a large Payloader with a V-plow,[b] struggling through the huge drift.
11. Inside,[a] the barn was cold,[b] not cozy.
12. Marlin M. Fisher,[a] Jr.,[a] of Ephrata,[b] Pennsylvania,[b] has a flock of 60,000[c] chickens.
13. Rhonda,[a] have you ever met Wilma Mast,[b] my cousin from Wisconsin?
14. Well,[a] from the garage,[b] doors open into the house and into the shop.

B. Copy each word or number with which a comma should be used, and put the comma where it belongs.

1. Lo God has given us many principles warnings and promises in His Word which He has preserved to this day.
2. Men of a carnal worldly outlook reject truth however because it conflicts with human reasoning.
3. "Given by God Himself the Bible is authoritative and it contains the answers to all man's problems Mr. Ludwig" answered Brother Leon.
4. Well Mother the snow sleet and rain must be over for today.
5. In the old church building the new Sunday school rooms is scheduled to begin on July 14 2002.
6. "In our school reference books may not be taken home without permission" said Anita "and that is only given for special occasions."

7. In the dense thicket at the edge of the pasture many wild animals no doubt are making their homes.
8. Bleating softly Frisky our pet ewe trotted over to the fence.
9. "Before the epidemic could be controlled over 80000 cows in the region were afflicted" reported Dean L. Gray D.V.M.
10. In the enclosed porch of his cottage Arnold L. Kauffman Jr. is opening a clock repair shop.
11. Mr. Kinnick's house a small bungalow stands along a narrow dusty dirt road.
12. On March 23 2002 the Wilcox Homestead sold for $325000.

Review Exercises

Write *yes* or *no* to tell whether the underlined words should be capitalized. [1] (Turn to the lesson number in brackets if you need help.)

1. Abraham Lincoln was <u>president</u> of the United States during the <u>civil war</u>.
2. Civil <u>war</u> has brought heart-rending tragedy in many African <u>countries</u>.
3. I thought that <u>brother</u> Henry gave an interesting assignment in American <u>history</u>.
4. The <u>book</u> of Genesis describes the <u>fall</u> and its effect on man.
5. The <u>earth</u> and most other planets rotate toward the <u>east</u>.
6. On the first <u>friday</u> of each <u>month,</u> all the students gather together for chorus.
7. The <u>school</u> at Locust Dale begins on the day after <u>labor day</u>.
8. In closing we sang the song "Lord, <u>it</u> Belongs Not <u>to</u> My Care."

3. Improving Your Writing Style, Part 1: Originality

Originality
Exact Words
Active Voice
Figurative Lang.
Triplets

You have had many lessons on writing with good content and organization. This is important, for writing must say something meaningful and say it logically if readers are to understand it.

But content and organization alone do not produce effective writing. How many times have you started to read something, decided it was not interesting, and laid it aside without finishing it? You can be assured that people will do the same thing with your writing if it fails to capture their interest. The challenge is to write in a way that gets and keeps the reader's attention.

How can we accomplish this? These lessons on writing style will give a number of helps for making our writing more interesting and enjoyable to read.

A major element of an effective and forceful style is **originality.** Do not always settle for the first thing that comes to your mind. Seek rather to be creative, to express your ideas in a way that is fresh, a way that the reader will enjoy. For example, in saying that your summer vacation was a time of hard work, you could write the following sentence.

I spent many hours working in the bean patch.

This sentence expresses its thought clearly. Anyone who knows English should be able to understand it. But stop and think. Can you say this in a more appealing way, a way deliberately designed to be interesting? One student emphasized that his summer vacation was not a vacation from work by writing something like this:

I spent many hours of my vacation in the bean patch.

Connecting *vacation* with many hours in the bean patch is a surprising twist that we can hardly fail to notice—and enjoy. So this was the writer's vacation? He has effectively made his point, and we want to read on to see what else he will tell us. The writer's originality has provided a spark that ignites our interest.

Consider another example, written by a person leaving the hospital after an accident.

Sadder but wiser, I hobbled out of the hospital on crutches.

Apparently, the writer landed in the hospital because of a careless mistake, and he has learned something from the experience. We understand what he means. But compare the following way of saying the same thing.

Wearing the evidence of my painful education, I hobbled out of the hospital on crutches.

Which way of writing is more forceful and interesting? Most people will agree that the second example is better for two reasons. First, to call the incident a painful education shows clever thinking. Since the writer learned something, he did receive an education; and since he was hobbling on crutches, the education was obviously painful. Second, *wearing the evidence* of his education is an apt description of his cast or bandages. We enjoy this kind of writing because the writer has given careful thought to expressing himself creatively.

The second example is also better because the phrase *sadder but wiser* is an old expression that we have heard many times before. Even though it expresses the thought clearly, it lacks force because it has been used so often. A phrase like this is a *cliché* (klē·shā′). You have heard many such expressions.

He had <u>bitten off more than he could chew</u>.
She turned <u>as white as a sheet</u>.
That's <u>as old as the hills</u>.
We got up <u>bright and early</u>.

Clichés are common in speech, when people have little time to think of original expressions. But in writing you usually have plenty of time to express yourself creatively. Put that time to good use, and let your readers enjoy the results.

In striving for originality, you need to beware of two pitfalls. One of these is the temptation to step over the bounds of propriety. You must never stoop to using slangy expressions or expressions that treat sacred subjects lightly or irreverently. This kind of originality cheapens your work and weakens its power to convey a worthwhile message.

The other pitfall is to try so hard to be original that your writing sounds strained. If a student writes expressions that he would consider too pretentious for speech, he has probably fallen into this trap. You do not need to write something unusual in every other sentence. Originality is truly effective only when it flows from an active, imaginative mind.

No originality:

> Rover had a hard problem to solve. How could he tell his master about the fire? He could bark and howl, but that might not be understood.

Strained:

> Rover faced a difficulty that taxed the powers of his canine constitution. How could he inform his master about the conflagration? His language was limited to barking and howling, which might not communicate effectively.

Creative:

> Rover had a serious problem on his paws. How could he warn his master about the danger? He could bark and howl, but no word in his canine vocabulary would remotely suggest the human word for *fire*.

For these lessons on writing style, you will write various compositions that your teacher will likely evaluate by using the chart below. The element introduced in this first lesson is *Originality*, so this assignment will be evaluated only for that point of emphasis. The element introduced in the next writing style lesson will be *Exact Words*, and then you will be evaluated on both originality and exactness.

Each of the third through fifth writing style lessons will introduce another point of emphasis, and each will add one more item to the number of points on which your writing is evaluated. The last lesson is a review of the five elements of effective writing style.

Evaluation of Writing Style

Part	*Points of Emphasis*			
Originality	*Exact Words*	*Active Voice*	*Figurative Language*	*Triplets*
1. ————	·······	·······	·······	·······
2. ————	————	·······	·······	·······
3. ————	————	————	·······	·······
4. ————	————	————	————	·······
5. ————	————	————	————	————
6. ————	————	————	————	————

G = Good   **F** = Fair   **P** = Poor

Now read the following sample compositions. Especially compare the underlined words in the first one with the way the same thought is expressed in the second one. Can you appreciate the originality that is evident in the second composition? Do you see how a writer's thought and effort can greatly improve the style of his composition?

"I Forgot"

Lacks originality:

Father's instructions were <u>very clear</u>. I knew exactly what I was supposed to do. But I forgot.

All morning and afternoon, <u>we had to hurry</u>. First we needed to bale the hay that Father had mowed the day before. Then we had to start the evening chores early because Father was scheduled to speak at a school meeting at Centerville. About that time the heifers <u>thought the grass was greener on the other side of the fence</u> and <u>went over to the neighbors' lawn</u>.

When we finally <u>got the heifers back into their pen</u>, it was milking time. Father said, "Bradley, when you finish feeding the heifers, give round bales to the milk cows. That way Allen can help with the milking the whole time."

Six hours later, our family pulled up to the house. As I sleepily opened the van door, <u>I heard the cows bawling loudly</u>. "The round bales!" I gasped. "I forgot all about them!"

Illustrates originality:

Father's instructions were <u>as simple as a first grade math problem</u>. I knew exactly what I was supposed to do. But I forgot.

All morning and afternoon, <u>our work urged us on</u>. First we needed to bale the hay that Father had mowed the day before. Then we had to start the evening chores early because Father was scheduled to speak at a school meeting at Centerville. About that time the heifers <u>decided to investigate the neighborhood</u> and <u>turned the neighbors' lawn into a playground</u>.

When we finally <u>persuaded the heifers to go home</u>, it was milking time. Father said, "Bradley, when you finish feeding the heifers, give round bales to the milk cows. That way Allen can help with the milking the whole time."

Six hours later, our family pulled up to the house. As I sleepily opened the van door, <u>a loud bawling from the barnyard jolted me wide awake</u>. "The round bales!" I gasped. "I forgot all about them!"

Applying the Lesson

Write a composition of 150–200 words about a real-life lesson you have learned, using the title "If Only I Had Listened!" or "A Lesson I Learned From a Mistake." Do your best to incorporate originality and creativity that will make your writing interesting to read.

———————————————

4. Colons, Semicolons, and Ellipsis Points

Colons

1. *Use a colon to separate the numbers in Scripture references and in expressions of time.*

   2 Timothy 2:15   8:30 A.M.

2. *Use a colon after the salutation of a business letter.*

   Dear Sirs: Dear Mr. Broyhill: Gentlemen:

3. *Use a colon to introduce something that is to follow.* What follows may be a list, an explanation, a question, an appositive, or a formal quotation. In this use, the colon is a literary arrow: it points to the information that follows, directing the reader's attention there.

> The sad course of Demas is traced in the following Scripture verses: Colossians 4:14, Philemon 24, and 2 Timothy 4:10.
> One thing kept Demas from remaining faithful: love for the world.

If a complete sentence follows a colon, that sentence may begin with a capital letter, especially if it is long.

> The Bible calls us to a heavenly conversation: Our entire manner of life must reflect heavenly values.

A formal quotation is a notable statement made by a respected or high-ranking person. If it is introduced by a colon, it must be written with quotation marks and proper capitalization.

> Henry Ward Beecher made this interesting observation about diligence: "In the ordinary business of life, industry can do anything which genius can, and very many things which it cannot."

The words before a colon must express a complete thought. Therefore, a colon should never separate a verb from its complement or a preposition from its object.

> **Incorrect:** The books of the Pentateuch are: Genesis, Exodus, Leviticus, Numbers, and Deuteronomy.
> **Correct:**   The books of the Pentateuch are Genesis, Exodus, Leviticus, Numbers, and Deuteronomy.
> **Correct:**   The Pentateuch includes the following books: Genesis, Exodus, Leviticus, Numbers, and Deuteronomy.

Semicolons

4. *Use a semicolon to join independent clauses in certain cases.*
   a. When no conjunction is used.

   > The rain poured down all day; by evening the creeks were flooded.

   b. When a conjunctive adverb is used.

The rain poured down all day; therefore, by evening the creeks were flooded.

    c. When commas are already used in one or more of the clauses. Sometimes either a comma or a semicolon is correct, depending on the degree of separation intended by the writer.

The rain poured down, the winds blew, and lightning sliced the sky; and by evening the creeks were flooded, some roads were closed, and several houses needed to be evacuated.

If you need help, let me know, [*or* ;] and I'll do what I can.

    5. *Use a semicolon to separate items in a series when individual items contain commas.*

Before moving to our community, the Gibbs family had lived near Allentown, Pennsylvania; Boerne, Texas; and Brighton, Colorado.

Ellipsis Points

    6. *Use ellipsis points to show an omission within a quotation.* Such an omission may be desirable when space is limited or when the omitted words do not apply specifically to the subject under discussion. But you need to guard against changing the meaning of a quotation by a careless omission. And you must *never* change the meaning deliberately by omitting certain words.

Original:

Servants, be obedient to them that are your masters according to the flesh, with fear and trembling, in singleness of your heart, as unto Christ. [Ephesians 6:5]

Unacceptable quotation:

"Servants, be obedient... unto Christ."

(May suggest that servants can ignore their masters' wishes.)

Acceptable quotation:

"Servants, be obedient to them that are your masters according to the flesh,... as unto Christ."

When omitting words within a sentence, you may choose to retain or omit the punctuation immediately before or after the omission. If you retain punctuation, place it directly after the first part (before the ellipsis points). Study the following example, which shows three possible ways to punctuate the same quotation.

Original:

And let the peace of God rule in your hearts, to the which also ye are called in one body; and be ye thankful. [Colossians 3:15]

Quotations:

"And let the peace of God rule in your hearts,... and be ye thankful." (comma retained)

"And let the peace of God rule in your hearts;... and be ye thankful." (semicolon retained)

"And let the peace of God rule in your hearts... and be ye thankful." (no punctuation retained)

When you quote two sentences and omit the ending of the first sentence, place the appropriate end punctuation directly after the first part if it makes a complete sentence. Then use ellipsis points to show the omission, and continue with the quotation.

Original:

Who hath directed the Spirit of the LORD, or being his counsellor hath taught him? With whom took he counsel, and who instructed him, and taught him in the path of judgment, and taught him knowledge, and shewed to him the way of understanding? [Isaiah 40:13, 14]

Quotation:

"Who hath directed the Spirit of the LORD?... With whom took he counsel, and who instructed him?"

Do not use ellipsis points at the beginning or end of a quotation. Remember: Ellipsis points indicate an omission *within* a quotation. They are not necessary at the beginning or the end.

Incorrect quotations:

"Who hath directed the Spirit of the LORD, or being his counsellor hath taught him?..."

"...With whom took he counsel, and who instructed him, and taught him in the path of judgment... ?"

Correct quotation:

"With whom took he counsel, and who instructed him, and taught him in the path of judgment?" (No ellipsis points are needed even though the beginning and ending of the verse are omitted.)

7. *Use ellipsis points to indicate that a sentence trails off without a proper ending.* Do not use any end punctuation with these ellipsis points.

The frost killed most of the tomato plants, so now...

Applying the Lesson

A. Write the number and letter of the rule illustrated by each colon, semicolon, or set of ellipsis points.

1. In the description of the Christian's armor, only one weapon is listed:[a] "the sword of the Spirit, which is the word of God" (Ephesians 6:17[b]).

2. If we would overcome, we must "take...[a] the whole armour of God";[b] moreover, we must pray for wisdom to use it properly.

3. This fact is clear:[a] God expects us to face the foe;[b] therefore, He provides no armor for the back.

4. Thank God for His provision:[a] without it we would have no power at all for victory;[b] we could do nothing.

5. The fact that "we wrestle...[a] against the rulers of the darkness of this world" is a sobering reality;[b] however, we must trust God to aid us.

6. My brothers and I mowed grass for Mr. Gratz, an elderly neighbor;[a] Mrs. White, a victim of a recent accident;[b] and Sister Anna, a widow with four young children.
7. Yes, I had looked forward to helping Aunt Betty;[a] but now with a broken leg...[b]
8. Our flight was scheduled to arrive at 1:30[a] P.M.;[b] but because of a storm, we were delayed.
9. The three visitors at school today were Marcus Sensenig, a teacher at Morris Mennonite School;[a] Linda Graybill, Lucy Graybill's cousin;[b] and Faye Oberholtzer, Sister Norma's mother.
10. "We've tried hard to follow Romans 12:21[a]," Henry sighed, "but so far..."[b]

B. Copy each word or number with which there is a punctuation error. Place the correct mark where it belongs, or omit the unnecessary mark.
1. One fact explains all the evil in the world, man is sinful by nature.
2. Three Bible heroes are: Joseph, Jacob's son, Samuel, Hannah's son, and Daniel, whose parents are not named.
3. To be truly wise, we must reject the wisdom of this world, furthermore, we must apply our hearts to divine wisdom.
4. "Hath not God made foolish the wisdom of this world?" (1 Corinthians 120).
5. I have uncles living at: Phoenix, Arizona, Salem, Ohio, and Burns Lake, B.C.
6. I was born in Rockingham County, Virginia, but when I was twelve years old, our family moved to Illinois.
7. We had planned to be home before supper, because of bad weather, we did not arrive until 920 P.M.
8. We trimmed trees all day, nevertheless, the job still is not finished.
9. When we started in the morning, the air was cool and fresh, but by late afternoon, the air had become hot, still, and sultry.
10. Oranges are nutritious, they are especially rich in Vitamin C.

C. Copy these quotations, using ellipsis points correctly to indicate omissions.
1. "Let every one of us please his neighbour. For even Christ pleased not himself" (Romans 15:2, 3).
2. "Put on therefore humbleness of mind, meekness" (Colossians 3:12).
3. "But continue thou in the things which thou hast learned, knowing of whom thou hast learned them" (2 Timothy 3:14).
4. "We shall not all sleep, but we shall all be changed, at the last trump" (1 Corinthians 15:51, 52).

Review Exercises
For each underlined word, write *yes* or *no* to tell whether it should be followed by a comma. [2]
1. Our small army of <u>workers</u> hoed row after row of <u>potatoes</u> beans, and corn.
2. The evening was <u>sultry</u> the sun was <u>setting</u> and we were all weary.
3. Just one more <u>row</u> Glenda, and <u>then</u> we will be finished.
4. <u>Oh</u> I see a <u>row</u> that we missed.

5. Though we had planned to leave <u>promptly</u> our <u>neighbors</u> the Moores, had other ideas.
6. "In a few <u>minutes</u>" said Mr. <u>Moore</u> "we'll have a snack."
7. Soon mounds of <u>fresh</u> delectable homemade ice <u>cream</u> were set before us.
8. Strangely <u>enough</u> our hurry to <u>leave</u> evaporated immediately.
9. We all <u>relaxed</u> on the breezy <u>patio</u> chattering and eating.
10. Feeling full and <u>satisfied</u> we climbed into the <u>car</u> and headed for home.

---

5. Quotation Marks and Italics

Quotation Marks

1. *Enclose a direct quotation in quotation marks.* In a divided quotation, capitalize the second part only if it begins a new sentence.

> "Hankering after worldly things," commented Father, "has no place in the lives of God's people."
> "Satan dominates the system of this world," he continued. "Eventually he gains full control of all who feed a love for this world."

In a quotation of more than one paragraph, place quotation marks at the beginning of each paragraph. Do not place quotation marks at the end of a paragraph, except the last one.

2. *Enclose a quotation from a printed source in quotation marks.*

> In the preface to *Martyrs Mirror,* T. J. Van Braght writes this about freedom from persecution: "These are sad times, in which we live; nay, truly, there is more danger now than in the time of our fathers, who suffered death for the testimony of the Lord."

If a quotation is long, it may be printed in smaller type as an indented block without quotation marks.

3. *Enclose the title of a minor work in quotation marks.* Minor works include songs, short stories, sections of books, and poems less than book length. Generally, a comma is unnecessary before such a title.

> I found some interesting facts in the article "Commerce" in *Unger's Bible Dictionary.*

4. *Use single quotation marks for a quotation within a quotation.* For the rare occasion when another quotation occurs within the inner quotation, use another set of double quotation marks.

> "Jesus said, 'It is more blessed to give than to receive,'" reminded John.
> "Did Mrs. Long say, 'You people should sing "Praise to God, Immortal Praise" before you leave'?" asked Aaron.

5. *You may use quotation marks to enclose an expression you wish to call into question.* If you use *so-called,* however, do not also use quotation marks.

> Much evil abounds in this "Christian" nation.
> Much evil abounds in this so-called Christian nation.

Be careful not to overuse quotation marks for this purpose. They tend to make writing look cluttered.

Other Punctuation With Quotation Marks

6. *If a quotation is followed by a comma or period, place that mark inside the quotation marks.*

> "For an opening song," announced Brother Leon, "we will sing 'O Worship the Lord.'"

Note this exception to the rule above: If a reference follows a quotation from a written source, place the reference in parentheses after the quotation marks, and place the comma or period after the parentheses.

> "The tongue can no man tame" (James 3:8), so we must ask God to tame it for us.

7. *If a quotation is followed by a colon or semicolon, place that mark outside the quotation marks.*

> Mr. Hart obviously appreciated the words of "What a Friend We Have in Jesus"; indeed, he asked that we pray for him.

8. *If a quotation is followed by a dash, a question mark, or an exclamation point, place that mark inside the quotation marks if it applies to the quotation, and outside the quotation marks if it applies to the whole sentence.*

> The twins shouted, "What a pleasant surprise!"
> (The exclamation point applies to the quotation.)
> Do you know the song "Shine Where You Are"?
> (The question mark applies to the whole sentence, not to the quotation.)
> Last week we learned "Remember Thy Mother"—quite a challenging song.
> (The dash applies to the whole sentence, not to the quotation.)

9. *If a sentence contains a quotation within a quotation, place the question mark or exclamation point with the part of the sentence that is a question or an exclamation.*

> "Did you hear Grandmother say, 'I'm getting tired'?" asked Sharon.
> (The inner quotation is not a question, so the question mark is outside the single quotation mark. But Sharon's words are a question, so the question mark is inside the double quotation marks.)
> "Did you hear Grandmother ask, 'What time is it?'" asked Sharon.
> (Both the inner quotation and Sharon's words are questions, so the mark is inside both the single and the double quotation marks.)

Italics

Italics are not actually punctuation marks. But since they help us to communicate clearly, they are part of the mechanics of English just as capitalization and punctuation are. In handwritten or typewritten material, italics are indicated by underlining.

10. *Use italics for the title of a major work.* Major works include books, newspapers, pamphlets, book-length poems, and periodicals such as church papers, magazines, and newsletters. Italicize and capitalize an article (*a, an, the*) when it begins a book title, but not when it begins the title of a newspaper or periodical.

> I enjoyed the book *The Man in Bearskin*.
> I read "The Missing Ice Chest" in the *Christian Pathway*.
>> (not *The Christian Pathway,* even though that is the actual title of this periodical)

11. *Use italics for the specific name of a ship, an airplane, a train, or another vehicle.*

> Father drove the car onto the *River Maid,* a rickety ferry.
> (*The* is usually not part of the specific name.)

12. *Use italics for a word, phrase, letter, number, or symbol that is the subject of discussion.* Such an item is not being used in its normal sense, but is being discussed as a word, phrase, letter, or other symbol.

> You wrote your *d* so carelessly that the word *dock* looks like *clock*.
> When you use *of course* as a parenthetical element, set it off with commas.
> The teacher deducted several points because the *$* symbols were missing.

13. *Italicize foreign words that have not been adopted into the English language.*

> In the expression "10:00, D.V.," the abbreviation stands for the Latin words *Deo volente,* which mean "God willing."

14. *You may occasionally use italics for emphasis.* Use italics sparingly for this purpose; otherwise, they will lose their effectiveness.

> Do not be satisfied with *good* work; strive to make it your *best*.

Applying the Lesson

A. If the underlined part of the sentence has a punctuation error, write it correctly. If it is correct, write *correct*.

1. "Do these mountains remind you of the psalmist's words, 'I will lift up mine eyes unto the hills, from whence cometh my <u>help?'"</u> asked Father.
2. The Bible commands us, "Keep yourselves from <u>idols:"</u> we must not allow any person or thing to come between us and God.
3. The Bible declares that "safety is of the <u>Lord";</u> therefore, we trust Him, not insurance companies.
4. "How often I have encouraged myself with the words, 'My help cometh from the <u>Lord!'"</u> testified Brother Clyde.

5. Brother Amos said, "This week our theme song will be 'What Did He <u>Do?'"</u>
6. "Benjamin Franklin well <u>said, 'He</u> that is good for making excuses is seldom good for anything else,'" commented Father.
7. Aldine Kieffer, who died in 1904, wrote the words of "Twilight Is <u>Stealing".</u>
8. "Didn't you hear Karen ask, 'What time does church <u>start'?"</u> asked Heidi.
9. Twila exclaimed, "Imagine our surprise when the little boy shouted, 'That's not <u>fair!'"</u>
10. "You would enjoy the story 'Can You Do <u>It'?"</u> replied Carol.
11. "Matthew Prior once <u>wrote they</u> always talk who never think, and who have the least to say,'" said Brother Thomas.
12. Thomas O. Chisholm penned lofty thoughts in "O to Be Like <u>Thee."</u>

B. Copy the words with which there are errors in the use of punctuation or italics (underlining), and put the missing marks where they belong. Do not punctuate words as a direct quotation unless the sentence has explanatory words.
  1. Does Praises We Sing have the song Brighten the Corner? asked Harvey.
  2. Love thy neighbour as thyself, even when you know that your neighbor probably does not love you.
  3. The holy war to free Jerusalem from Turkish control was far from holy.
  4. How can I tell asked Brother Zehr if each of these marks represents an r or an n?
  5. On the back of the Great Seal of the United States are the words annuit coeptis, meaning He has smiled on our undertakings.
  6. The scribes were to copy the parchments verbatim ac litteratim, that is, word for word and letter for letter.
  7. The second vowel in prosperity sounds the same as in severity and sincerity.
  8. This book, The Marvels of Light, has an interesting chapter titled How Does Light Travel? said Tina.
  9. Mr. Schmidt has many interesting stories, said Father, about his travels on the Arcadia as the ship physician.
  10. We enjoyed a ride on Mr. Grassley's old sleigh, the Snow Beauty.

Review Exercises

Write *yes* or *no* to tell whether the underlined words should be capitalized. [1]
1. Mr. H. G. Spafford lost all his possessions in the great <u>fire</u> that destroyed much of <u>chicago</u>.
2. This fire started on a <u>sunday</u> in <u>october</u> 1871.
3. About two years later, Mr. Spafford put his wife and four daughters aboard a <u>french</u> ship, expecting to join them in France that <u>winter</u>.
4. On November 22, 1873, this ship was rammed by an <u>english</u> vessel, the <u>lochearn</u>.
5. Within two hours the huge <u>liner</u> sank, taking the Spafford children and 222 other <u>passengers</u> to their deaths.
6. Nine days later, <u>mrs. spafford</u>, along with other survivors, reached <u>wales</u>.
7. From a <u>telegraph</u> office, she cabled two sad words to her husband: "<u>saved</u> alone."

8. His response to a <u>friend</u> was, "I am glad to trust the <u>lord</u> when it will cost me something."
9. While sailing across the Atlantic <u>ocean</u> on another ship, he was shown the place in the <u>sea</u> where his children had perished.
10. That night, sleepless and grief-stricken, Mr. Spafford wrote the hymn "It Is Well <u>with</u> <u>my</u> Soul."

---

6. Dashes, Parentheses, Brackets, Apostrophes, and Hyphens

Dashes

1. *Use a dash to show a sudden interruption or change in thought.*
   a. A sudden break in thought.

   "Tell the boys—oh, what was that!" Mother ran to the door.

   b. Parenthetical matter that is abrupt or that has commas within it.

   Little Timmy knocked the vase—the one that Grandmother Snyder gave—off the shelf.
   My father could fix your car—he's an experienced mechanic, you know—in a short time.

   c. Interrupted speech. Ellipsis points can also indicate interrupted speech. Ellipsis points suggest hesitancy or uncertainty; a dash shows abruptness.

   "No, I don't want—" Glancing up, Joan blushed as she saw Father's stern look.

Parentheses

2. *Use parentheses to enclose a parenthetical element that is relatively unimportant.*

   Last summer we visited relatives and friends in Lebanon County, Pennsylvania (where my parents grew up).

Note: Commas, dashes, and parentheses are all used to set off parenthetical elements. You must choose which to use according to the meaning you want to convey.
   a. Commas make the parenthetical element a part of the sentence. Therefore, they cannot set off elements that are complete sentences or that have other punctuation. Of these three marks, commas are by far the most common in normal writing.

   Aunt Edna's garden, which she keeps very neat, is much smaller than ours.

   b. Dashes sharply emphasize the parenthetical element. Sometimes they set
off an exclamation or a question.

>   Aunt Edna's flower beds—very pleasant places—contain a wide variety
>   of flowers.
>   Aunt Edna's flower beds—how I enjoy helping her with them!—contain
>   a wide variety of flowers.

   c. Parentheses minimize the importance of the parenthetical element, making
it somewhat beside the point of the sentence.

>   Aunt Edna (she's not really my aunt) will be seventy years old this week.

   3. *Use parentheses to enclose supplementary or illustrative matter, such as a
Scripture reference or a short explanation.*

>   "Pray without ceasing" (1 Thessalonians 5:17).
>   Mr. Hendrickson attended the Lancaster (Ohio) High School.
>   This issue of the *Homes and Lands of Earl County* (June 20—) lists a prom-
>   ising farm.

   4. *Use parentheses to enclose figures or letters used for enumeration within a
sentence. If letters are used for this purpose, they should be italicized.*

>   Before starting the tour, our guide requested that we (1) stay together as a
>   group, (2) pay attention to him, and (3) obey all printed signs.

Brackets

   5. *Use brackets to enclose a comment or correction within a quotation.*

>   "See then that ye walk circumspectly [precisely; particularly], not as fools, but
>   as wise" (Ephesians 5:15).

   6. *Use brackets as parentheses in material already enclosed by parentheses.*

>   The ancient country of Gaul (also called Gallia [gŏl′·ē·ä]) covered primarily
>   the areas of modern France and Belgium.

   7. *Learn the correct use of other punctuation marks with dashes, parentheses,
and brackets.*

   a. If a dash ends a sentence fragment, omit any end punctuation.

>   "How can we—" Darren whirled around in dismay as several heifers
>   dashed through the open gate.

   b. Place other punctuation marks inside these marks if they apply to the
enclosed matter, and outside if they apply to the whole sentence.

>   I read *The Man in Bearskin*—what a captivating story!—for my book
>   report. (exclamation point inside dashes because the enclosed matter
>   is an exclamation)

What book are you reporting on (if I may ask)?
(question mark outside parentheses because the whole sentence is a question)

Apostrophes

8. *Use an apostrophe to form the possessive case of a noun or an indefinite pronoun.* For specific rules and examples, see Lessons 55 and 57.

9. *Use an apostrophe to show an omission in a contraction or other shortened form.* Contractions are acceptable for informal writing, such as friendly letters and the dialogue in stories. You should generally avoid them in formal writing.

aren't   won't   let's   a '76 Dodge

10. *Use an apostrophe to form the plural of a letter, a figure, an abbreviation followed by a period, or a word used as the subject of discussion.* No apostrophe is needed in the plural form of a number with several digits or of an abbreviation with several capital letters (1800s, IOUs). Remember to italicize (underline) such an item when it is the subject of discussion, but do not italicize the *'s*.

His *5*'s look too much like *S*'s.
Too many *uh*'s in a report may show poor preparation.
Some of the POWs were men with Ph.D.'s.

Hyphens

11. *Use a hyphen to join some compound words.* Pay special attention to the following groups of compound words.

a. Compound number words from twenty-one through ninety-nine.

thirty-four   two hundred sixty-nine

b. A fraction written in words. (A hyphen joins the numerator and denominator unless either one already has a hyphen.)

two-thirds   sixty-one hundredths   three and one-sixth

c. Words ending with -*in-law*.

father-in-law   sister-in-law

d. Compound words beginning with *great-* that refer to relatives, those beginning with *self-,* and many beginning with *all-*.

great-grandfather   self-disciplined   all-day meeting

e. Many compound adjectives, in which two or more words form a unit that modifies a substantive.

a two-cycle engine   a never-to-be-forgotten trip

f. A proper noun or adjective with a prefix.

the post–World War II era   anti-Christian attitudes

12. *In a series of hyphenated adjective–noun combinations, with the noun included in only the last one, use a hyphen after each adjective.*

   two- and three-year-old children   six-, eight-, and ten-foot posts

13. *Use a hyphen to divide a word between syllables at the end of a line.* Observe these three rules: (1) divide only between syllables, (2) never leave a single letter at the beginning or end of a line, and (3) divide a hyphenated word only at the existing hyphen. The following words illustrate permissible divisions.

   al-a-bas-ter   alac-ri-ty   shrub-bery

14. *Use a hyphen to show a series of connected numbers, as in Scripture references or dates.*

   Mark 11:12–14, 20–26   1985–1995

Applying the Lesson

A. Copy enough words to show where commas, dashes, parentheses, and brackets are needed, and add the missing marks. Some sentences have notes telling you how to treat the parenthetical elements.
   1. The Beatitudes how contrary to human nature! describe essential inner qualities for the Christian. (sharp emphasis)
   2. The Lord's Prayer which Jesus gave as a model prayer is rich with meaning. (part of the sentence)
   3. Jesus taught that wrong motives which God, of course, clearly sees can make good actions evil in God's sight. (somewhat beside the point)
   4. His teaching on nonresistance ridiculed and rejected by many "Christians" must govern our daily relationships with others. (sharp emphasis)
   5. "Whosoever shall say to his brother, Raca worthless one, shall be in danger of the council" Matthew 5:22.
   6. "And why beholdest thou the mote speck that is in thy brother's eye, but considerest not the beam large timber that is in thine own eye?" Matthew 7:3.
   7. In the story of the wise and the foolish man which ends the Sermon on the Mount Jesus emphasized the importance of doing what we know. (part of the sentence)
   8. This rolling countryside are there any large towns near? seems fairly fertile. (somewhat beside the point)
   9. "I think we'll stop well, Brother Gerald's are at this picnic area too," declared Father.
   10. "I wish the sun would no, I want to be thankful even if it's cloudy," said Carl.

B. Write correctly the items that have errors in the use of apostrophes or hyphens. If an item needs to be italicized, show it by underlining.
   1. God is all powerful and self existing; He isnt threatened by any opponent.
   2. The sixty six books of the Bible comprise the all encompassing, written revelation of God to man.
   3. Jesus shed His blood to redeem sin cursed mankind.

4. In the pre Flood days, the world was filled with anti God attitudes.
5. We helped Great aunt Lydia freeze fifty five quarts of peaches.
6. Dont make your &s look like capital Ss.
7. My brother in law uses a 59 Chevrolet pickup around the farm.
8. Theyll need some four, six, and eight inch lengths of yarn for the project.
9. About one fourth of the men wrote their 4s without lifting their pencils.
10. Brother Waynes sisters in law put up a three dimensional bulletin board display.
11. One week in mid August, we sold over seventy five dozen ears of corn per day.
12. Two thirds of the buns made with this self rising flour did not rise normally.
13. Three and one half miles down the road is a small museum that displays a variety of external and internal combustion engines.
14. The two boxes weighed eighteen and three fourths pounds and twenty one pounds.
15. When you see wherefores and therefores in the Bible, look to see what they are there for.
16. A two faced person is hard to deal with, for his yess and nos mean nothing.
17. During the two world wars, anti German feeling ran strong, and some bad tempered patriots persecuted nonresistant plain people who were of German descent.
18. Mr. Kline, who had only five years of schooling, is a self educated man.
19. Your essay has too many ands and too many two, three, and four sentence paragraphs.
20. The brown sugar is available in five, ten, or twenty pound bags.

Review Exercises

Write the letter of the sentence in which the boldface part is correct. [4, 5]

1. a. Many people in Romania lack the basic **necessities:** adequate food, clothing, and shelter.
   b. Many people in Romania lack the basic **necessities;** adequate food, clothing, and shelter.
2. a. We usually have family worship at **7:30** A.M.
   b. We usually have family worship at **7;30** A.M.
3. a. Here are your jobs: Janet, **dusting, Linda, sweeping,** and Amy, mopping.
   b. Here are your jobs: Janet, **dusting; Linda, sweeping;** and Amy, mopping.
4. a. We canned our green beans and **applesauce;** however, we put our peas and corn into the freezer.
   b. We canned our green beans and **applesauce,** however, we put our peas and corn into the freezer.
5. a. Carol said, "Look in **the . . .** No, I think it's on the shelf."
   b. Carol said, "Look in **the,** No, I think it's on the shelf."
6. a. **". . . In every thing by prayer . . .** with thanksgiving let your requests be made known unto God."
   b. **"In every thing by prayer . . .** with thanksgiving let your requests be made known unto God."

7. a. Have you ever sung "Who Is on the Lord's **Side?**"
    b. Have you ever sung "Who Is on the Lord's **Side**"?
8. a. The martyr Jim Elliot made this notable **statement;** "A man is no fool who gives what he cannot keep in order to gain what he cannot lose."
    b. The martyr Jim Elliot made this notable **statement:** "A man is no fool who gives what he cannot keep in order to gain what he cannot lose."
9. a. In my father's book ***The Pursuit of God,*** **the chapter "Meekness and Rest"** was especially inspiring.
    b. In my father's book **"The Pursuit of God,"** the chapter *Meekness and Rest* was especially inspiring.
10. a. My grandfather's favorite song was **"The Love of God."**
    b. My grandfather's favorite song was *The Love of God.*

---

7. Improving Your Editing Skills, Part 1

When you have completed the first writing of an essay or a story, is it ready to be printed? No, you have learned in previous years that revising is an essential part of the writing process. As you revise and proofread, you can mark your changes clearly and simply by using the standard symbols that most publishers use.

Throughout this textbook, you will find a series of lessons entitled "Improving Your Editing Skills." These lesson exercises are printed both in this textbook and in a separate booklet of tests and editing sheets, on which you can easily make your proofreading marks. The editing lessons have the following three general purposes.

1. To stimulate critical reading so that you will be able to catch errors in grammar, mechanics, and spelling.
2. To give practice in correct usage of grammar and mechanics.
3. To give practice in the use of proofreading marks.

Study the following table of proofreading marks. The sample manuscript below the table shows how the marks are used.

Marks Used in Editing and Proofreading

$\vee$ or $\wedge$ insert (caret)	⟑ delete	. . . . stet (let it stand)
¶ begin new paragraph	*ℓc* change to lowercase (small letter)	*uc* change to uppercase (capital letter)

Explanations	Sample Manuscript
Delete symbol has loop so that deletion is not overlooked.	The Bible was written over a period of
Caret shows exact point of insertion.	about 1,600 years by about forty authors. These
Comma after *experience* is unnecessary.	writers represent a wide scope of experience,
Any inserted punctuation is marked by a caret. Question mark or exclamation point is inserted above the caret.	and background. Why do we say this? They ranged from highly educated Moses and Paul to a herdsman named Amos and a fisherman named
Loop of delete symbol may curve down, especially if deleted item is replaced by item above.	Peter, David and Solomon were Kings of God's
Kings is a common noun here.	people, while Matthew, a despised tax collector,
Comma or period is inserted below the caret.	also made his contribution. To this company stet add Daniel, prime minister of a foreign
The word *stet* and the dots mean deleted item is to be retained.	nation, and the physician Luke. Only an all-
Caret helps to assure that inserted hyphen is not overlooked.	knowing God could have used such diverse
Apostrophe or quotation marks are inserted above inverted caret.	authors' work, written over many centuries and in scattered places, to produce a book
Book is to be capitalized because it refers to the Bible.	that agrees perfectly in even its smallest details. We say with the songwriter, "How great Thou art!"

Observe carefully how the proofreading marks are made, and pattern your marks after them. In this way, both you and others can easily tell what changes you intended.

Editing Practice

A. Use the proper proofreading marks to correct the errors in the sentences below. Each sentence needs one insertion and one deletion or replacement.

1. Did you know you that over eight hundred verses in the Bible speak of the heart

2. The wise man wrote, "Keep thy hart with all diligence; fore out of it are the issues of life."

3. The Bible mentions wisdom of heart uprightness of heart, integrity of a heart, and pureness of heart.

4. A selfish heart, of course will bring you many troubbles.

5. You shouldnt have a heart that is the proud and stubborn.

6. Psalm 51:10 says, Create in me a clean heart, O God;

   and renew a rite spirit within me."

B. Use the proper proofreading marks to correct the errors in capitalization. In each sentence, one letter should be changed to uppercase and one to lowercase.

1. Singing is an excellent Source of encouragement for the

   people of god.

2. When you are tempted to do Wrong, you can sing "Yield

   Not to temptation."

3. When you are Rejoicing, you can sing a song like "halle-

   lujah, Praise Jehovah."

4. Many songs are based on Poetry from the bible.

5. Psalms is a book of songs that the israelites used in

   Worship services.

C. Now try your editing skills on the selection below. You will need to do the following things.
   a. Make six insertions.
   b. Make five deletions or replacements. (Be sure to read the note following the selection.)
   c. Make five corrections in capitalization.
   d. Mark one place where a new paragraph should begin.
   e. Show that one word already deleted should be retained.

   This means that eighteen corrections are needed. Can you find them all?

1. Niagara falls is one of the most spectacular ~~beautiful~~

2. Natural wonders in north America It consists of two

3. Falls: the Horseshoe falls on the Canadian side and the

4. American Falls on the American ~~side~~. Two cities called

5. Niagara Falls have groan up near the falls, one on ether

6. side of the Niagara River. Do you know which of of the

7. two waterfalls is larger Canadas Horseshoe Falls is 185

8. feet high (56 meters) and 2,600 feet wide (792 meters);

9. the American Falls is 190 feet high (58 meters) and the

10. 1000 feet wide (303 meters). What a trimendous amount of

11. watter flows these falls!

Note: In the editing lessons, you will proofread a number of paragraphs about waterfalls. Dictionaries indicate that a singular or plural verb is correct with the noun *falls* ("falls is" or "falls are"). You will not need to check for verb agreement with *falls* or *waterfall* in any proofreading exercise of this course. Neither will you be expected to check the spelling of proper nouns or to verify technical information, such as the height of a waterfall.

---

8. Chapter 1 Review

A. Use proofreading marks to correct the errors in capitalization and end punctuation.

1. in Bible Class we studied about ruth, the moabitess who became the Great-grandmother of king David

2. for this week's bible lesson, we are to study "the day of rest and worship" in <u>doctrines of the bible</u>

3. "do you know, o youth," said brother Amos, "That your commitment to gospel principles can be a strong testimony to the World"

4. If only i had taken father's advice last Spring

5. To prepare for Reading class, Charlotte must practice reading the last three paragraphs in the story "in that bottom drawer"

B. Use proofreading marks to add the missing commas.

1. "Young people if you expect to be godly adults" admonished Brother Silas "you must begin now to develop godly habits attitudes and values."

2. Knowing man's need for guidance God provided His Word which is a road map to glory.

3. Bradley R. Gascho Jr. boarded with us for two years but now he is teaching school at Duchess Alberta.

4. Almost 6100000 passenger cars in fact were manufactured in the United States during the year 1990.

5. In the new school desks were arranged in straight even rows.

C. Use proofreading marks to correct the errors in the use of colons, semicolons, and ellipsis points. Place ellipsis points below the caret, and colons and semicolons above the caret.

1. Outstanding Christian women of the early church included: Mary, who chose to sit at Jesus' feet, Lydia, who opened her house to the missionaries, and Eunice, whose faith inspired faith in her son Timothy.

2. "Be of the same mind one toward another. Be not wise in your own conceits" (Romans 12:16).

3. Before school started, the sun was shining brightly, but by noon there was a gentle rain, which later became a steady downpour.

4. Whenever we discuss history or current events, we should remember this basic principle, God is sovereign over the affairs of men.

5. "I thought I understood the lesson, but these questions," Clara threw up her hands.

D. Use proofreading marks to correct the errors in capitalization, punctuation, and italics.

1. In the book Good Grapes Guaranteed, I found some good suggestions in the chapter Proper Pruning Father remarked.

2. Grandpa asked if the boys may go with him to Point Clare on the Charlotte Lake Express this afternoon, stated Mother.

3. Do you know the words of the song Someone to Thank? asked Diane.

4. Brother Mervin often tells us, The t in epistle is silent; but often I forget his admonition.

5. What a surprise to hear Father say, You may have the rest of the afternoon to explore in the woods!

E. Use proofreading marks to add the missing dashes, parentheses, and brackets.

1. "Oh, I'm so sorry; I just" Norma burst into tears.

2. "And as he passed over Penuel the sun rose upon him, and he halted limped upon his thigh" (Genesis 32:31).

3. Our ponds one natural and one artificial provide a habitat for much wildlife. (minor importance)

4. Several kinds of wild ducks mallards, mergansers, and canvasbacks come to these ponds. (minor importance)

5. Rocky the rooster what a proud fellow he is! likes to chase unwary little children. (sharp emphasis)

F. Copy each phrase, using apostrophes and hyphens correctly. If a word needs to be italicized, show it by underlining.
1. didnt find a rose colored vase
2. self employed brother in law
3. my great uncle Harvey
4. hasnt quit before six oclock
5. twenty five thens in the story
6. six, ten, and twelve inch snows
7. an all purpose tool
8. a mid May thunderstorm

G. Write the correct word for each blank.
1. A good writing style helps to capture and hold the reader's ———.
2. If writing has originality, it contains creative expressions that come from an ——— mind.
3. A ——— is a descriptive phrase that lacks its original force because it has been used so often.
4. In striving for originality, one pitfall is the temptation to use slang or expressions that treat ——— subjects lightly.
5. A second pitfall is to try so hard to be original that the writing sounds ———.
6. You should generally avoid an expression in writing if you would not consider using it in ———.

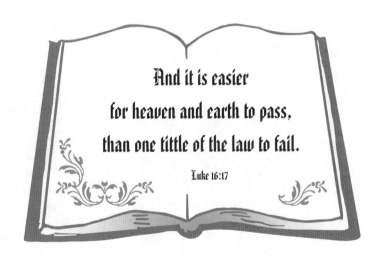

And it is easier
for heaven and earth to pass,
than one tittle of the law to fail.

Luke 16:17

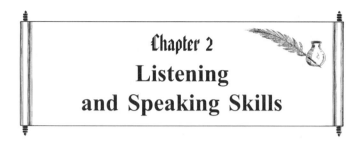

Chapter 2

Listening
and Speaking Skills

9. Cultivating Attitudes for Good Listening

Hearing is a physical activity. The ear receives sound waves and transforms them into electrical impulses that the brain interprets. *Listening,* however, involves more than your physical organs. It involves your mental powers and your will. Listening requires deliberate effort.

Surely you have had the experience of hearing someone talking when you really were not paying attention to what he was saying. Then suddenly you heard something that caught your attention. Maybe he said your name. What happened? You pricked up your ears. Your *hearing* suddenly turned into *listening.*

The Importance of Good Listening

The ability to listen is an important trait for God's people. Jesus said both "Take heed what ye hear" and "Take heed how ye hear." God calls us to "be swift to hear, slow to speak, slow to wrath." Why is listening so important?

You listen to learn. "The heart of the prudent getteth knowledge; and the ear of the wise seeketh knowledge" (Proverbs 18:15). How well do you listen? Being alert to everyday conversations and happenings will open the door to many kinds of information. Listening to adults' conversations can broaden your horizons.

To a large degree, how much you benefit from school life depends directly on your listening skills. You could, of course, learn quite a bit by simply reading your textbooks. But think of how much you learn from your teacher and your fellow students in class discussions.

The same principle applies to church life. In Sunday school classes, in devotionals, in topics, and in sermons, you hear the Scriptures explained. Your application of listening skills directly affects your understanding of truth and of God's will for your life. "So then faith cometh by hearing, and hearing by the word of God" (Romans 10:17).

You also listen to receive specific instructions. Your parents tell you to do some chores. Your teacher tells how he wants an assignment done. Your friend asks a favor of you. If you merely *hear* rather than *listen,* you may need to ask them to repeat their instructions. Or you may need to suffer the consequences of failing to do as you were told.

Attitudes for Good Listening

Good listening requires proper attitudes toward others and toward ourselves. What are some attitudes essential to being a good listener?

1. *Be respectful.* Other people are much like us. They talk because they have something to say that is important to them. We should listen especially to those in authority; for listening is part of the respect that we owe them, and they are responsible for teaching and directing us. Those whom we consider our equals also deserve our respect. We may think they do not know any more than we do; but they do have feelings, and they do know some things that can benefit us. We should listen even to those who are younger and less experienced than we. They too have feelings that we need to respect, and even they can teach us some things. Jesus had time for little children, and so should we.

2. *Be courteous.* Courtesy is an expression of the Golden Rule. Since we want others to listen courteously to us, we should listen courteously to them. What are some ways to show courtesy as we listen? We need to look at the speaker, giving him our full attention. Roving eyes generally indicate a roving mind. We must also avoid rudely finishing another person's sentence for him or interrupting his thoughts with our own comments.

Sometimes your courtesy will be tested. For example, an older person may be talking to you after church while your friends are visiting a short distance away. Your friends' conversation may sound so interesting that you are tempted to listen to them instead of the older person. Or there may be someone else you want to talk with, or something else you want to do. But you must exercise courtesy and continue listening.

If a speaker has difficulty expressing himself, listen patiently. Any display of impatience will make it even harder for him to express his thoughts clearly. But what if we have a legitimate reason not to listen? Then we can tell the other person that we cannot listen to him now. If appropriate, we should tell him why. Example: "I'm sorry, but I'll need to excuse myself. My family is waiting in the car."

3. *Be interested.* Avoid a know-it-all air. We can usually learn from anyone, even if we have more experience in a certain area than the other person does. Ask profitable questions. Few things are better at sparking interest and stimulating an enjoyable conversation than good questions.

Do not merely pretend to be interested. The very look on your face will tell whether you are truly interested. (This is also true when a teacher or minister is talking.) Even if you disagree with the other person, you should not block out what he is saying. Give him a fair hearing, and you may gain new insight and understanding.

In summary, we need to practice being kind to everyone as Jesus was. If we truly respect and appreciate other people, we will not view listening as a chore. Rather, we will see it as a privilege—an opportunity to learn something! The rewards of good listening are usually well worth any extra effort that is required.

Applying the Lesson

A. Answer these questions.

1. Why is listening important? Give the two main reasons presented in the lesson.
2. What part of our understanding will be weak if we fail to listen as the Scriptures are explained?
3. Why should we listen respectfully to a teacher? to a fellow classmate? to a first grader?
4. What are four ways to show courtesy when another person is speaking?

5. What are three ways to show interest in listening to another?
6. What should we be ready to do as we go to the house of God? (Ecclesiastes 5:1, 2)
7. What must we not be guilty of doing to God's words? (Proverbs 30:5, 6)
8. Whom are we told to listen to in Proverbs 23:22?
9. What kind of words must we refuse to listen to? (Proverbs 19:27)
10. What kind of person learns by listening? (Proverbs 1:5)

B. For each sentence, write the letter of the Bible reference which expresses that idea.
   a. Proverbs 12:15   d. Luke 16:31
   b. Zechariah 7:13   e. James 1:22
   c. Matthew 11:15
   1. Since God gave us ears, He expects us to use them.
   2. If we do not listen when God speaks to us, He will not listen when we speak to Him.
   3. If we think it is all right to hear the Word of God and not obey it, we only deceive ourselves.
   4. A foolish person depends on his own judgment, but a wise person listens to advice from others.
   5. If we refuse to heed the Word of God, we would not be convinced even if God spoke to us in a miraculous way.

C. Listen to someone as he talks to you, such as an older person, a classmate, or a younger brother or sister. Deliberately show respect, courtesy, and interest, as described in the lesson. Then write down something worthwhile or rewarding that you gained by listening. You may need to converse with several people before you glean material to record.

Review Exercises

For each underlined word, write *yes* or *no* to tell whether it should be followed by a comma. [2]
   1. Christopher Dock a teacher in a Mennonite school of the early 1700s, possessed a great love for children.
   2. After he had taught school at Skippack Pennsylvania, for ten years Dock turned to farming.
   3. While he was farming however Dock "felt the smiting hand of God" upon him.
   4. He returned to the classroom and continued teaching until he died thirty-three years later.
   5. Dock had serious questions about the stern harsh discipline which was often administered in his day.
   6. He did use the slap of the hand, the hazel branch or the birch rod on a student who needed it.
   7. Motivated by deep love he prayed for each of his students before he left the classroom in the evening.
   8. *Schulordnung,* a book about Dock's teaching methods was printed in 1770 by Christopher Saur Jr.

10. Exercising the Skills of Good Listening

Although good listening begins with proper attitudes, it also includes specific skills. If you would be a good listener, you must cultivate both the attitudes and the skills of good listening. Do not excuse yourself by saying that you simply are not a good listener. Everyone can improve his ability to listen by putting forth diligent effort to strengthen these skills.

The following skills apply in varying ways to the different kinds of listening you do. Some apply more obviously to the casual listening of everyday conversations. Most of them apply specifically to the more formal listening in school or at church. As you consider the skills discussed below, evaluate yourself honestly. Seek to improve in the areas where you recognize weakness.

1. *Listen Actively.* Since you can think about four times faster than someone can talk, many thoughts can pass through your mind while someone is speaking. You need to discipline your mind to stay with the speaker, or your extra thinking time will easily become an opportunity for taking mental by-paths.

For example, a speaker may mention getting lost in the woods, and that reminds you of an exciting story you have read about a boy who got lost in a cave. Before you know it, your mind is going over the details of that story; and for the next several minutes, you do not catch a word that the speaker says.

The opposite of listening actively is listening passively. "Yes, that's right.... That's also true.... I suppose that's right...." If you listen in this way, you will pause whenever the speaker pauses, and your mind will be idle as you wait for the next point. Then you are almost certain to drift into mental by-paths—if you don't drift off to sleep!

What are some practical ways to listen actively? Review what the speaker has already said. This not only prevents your mind from wandering into by-paths but also reinforces the relationship between previous comments and the present ideas. As a speaker states a new main point, think about how he might develop it. Will he use an illustration, give some reasons, or make a comparison or contrast?

One of the best ways to listen actively is to take notes. Note-taking gives you a mental activity (catching the speaker's points) as well as a physical activity (writing the points on your paper). That gives little opportunity for your mind to wander.

2. *Block out distractions.* Numerous things can distract your attention from a speaker: the temperature, other activities in the room, traffic going by outside, or even a persistent fly. Unless you as a listener block out these distractions, they will draw your mind away and you will miss at least some of what the speaker is saying.

It is usually impossible to remove all distractions, but there are a few things you can do. You might be able to move away from them. In church, for example, you could try to stay away from windows and doors and sit toward the front. By shifting your position, you may be able to block a distraction from your sight.

Of course, changing your seat during a service is often not proper or practical. And in some situations, like school, you are not free to choose your location. But you can still overcome distractions if you really want to. Above all, deliberately look at the speaker—and not at his chin, his ears, or his hands. Look at his eyes! Along with that, put all your effort into concentrating on what the speaker is saying.

3. *Listen for* **Cardinal points** *(main ideas).* If you remember the main ideas in a talk, you are more likely to remember other details too. Good listeners are not like sponges, trying to soak up every drop of information. Rather, they are like sieves, seeking to catch valuable nuggets of truth.

For example, suppose a minister preaches about "Proofs of Christ's Resurrection." The speaker points out that the main proof is the Word of God. The Bible teaches Christ's resurrection, so it must be true. Another proof is the disciples, whose outlook changed from fear and uncertainty to a courage and boldness that could not be shaken even by the threat of death. A third proof is the Jewish leaders, who never even tried to prove that Jesus was still dead. They knew He had risen! All they could do was try to make the apostles stop preaching in His Name.

In the example above, the cardinal points are the three proofs of Christ's resurrection: the Bible, the disciples, and the Jewish leaders. If you remember these three points, you should find it simple to remember the details that support each point.

Good speakers underscore a main idea by using an emphatic tone and sometimes by repeating it several times. They often signal the movement from one point to another by using transitional words like *next, furthermore,* or *moving on.*

4. *Listen for important* **Details.** Although main ideas are the most important, you should also remember certain kinds of details. One kind is details that form the "legs" on which a main idea rests. Not all details are as important as the ones noted in point 3 above. You need to sort out and remember the details that are truly important, for they will help you to see why the main points are valid. And even if you do not fully understand or agree with a certain main point, the supporting details will help you to further evaluate that idea later.

Other details should be remembered because something important depends on them. These include things such as the exact time of an appointment, the dosage of a medicine, or the way your parents want some chore done.

5. **Evaluate** *fact versus opinion.* When faithful parents, teachers, and ministers are speaking, you can listen with the confidence that you are hearing truth. But you cannot have this confidence in every person you hear. How can you tell whether a speaker is presenting facts or opinions? You can weigh the evidence that he uses. Does he give real proof to support what he says? Or does he merely try to convince you by making strong statements that appeal to your emotions? Remember, facts carry weight but opinions do not.

Salesmen in particular are skilled at using persuasive language. For example, a sweeper salesman may declare that his machine is the best one on the market. "No other cleaner gets out the deep-down dirt like this one does." He may even suggest that a woman is a poor housekeeper if she uses a different sweeper. These statements may appeal to the emotions, but they are difficult or impossible to prove. They are not based on solid facts.

You should also consider the reliability of the authorities that a speaker quotes in giving information and statistics. This is especially true if his information disagrees with that given by recognized authorities. Above all, compare what you hear with the Word of God. Be a "noble Berean" by using the Scriptures to test what you hear.

6. **Finish** *by reviewing the main ideas.* Can you recall the speaker's main points? Can you remember the significant details that he used to prove his points? If not, review your notes until this information is clear in your mind.

Applying the Lesson

A. Memorize the six points that summarize good listening skills, as given in the lesson. Then list those points from memory. (The key words start with the letters *A–F*.)

B. Answer these questions.
   1. Why must you discipline your mind to stay with a speaker?
   2. What are three ways to keep your mind active while you listen?
   3. What are three things that you can do to block out distractions?
   4. How is a good listener like a sieve?
   5. What are two kinds of important details that you need to remember?
   6. What do speakers sometimes use as a substitute for solid facts?
   7. What are three good ways to discern whether a speaker is actually presenting facts?

C. Prepare three questions similar to the following. Read them aloud, pausing about five seconds between each question for your classmates to jot down answers. When you have finished, your classmates will check their answers to see how well they have listened.
   1. In the series of words *hat, creek, fire, after,* which word is a synonym for *brook*?
   2. Suppose I saw a blue house, a white barn, and a yellow garage. What color was the barn?

D. Your teacher will read several paragraphs to you and then ask questions to see how well you listened.

E. Listen to a sermon or devotional, and take notes as you listen. Review your notes to be sure you remember the main points and important details.

Review Exercises

A. Name the punctuation that should follow each underlined word: *colon, semicolon, ellipsis points,* or *none.* [4]
   1. Two important properties of gold <u>are</u> ductility and malleability.
   2. Because of its ductility, gold can be drawn into <u>wire</u> indeed, one ounce can be drawn into a wire more than 40 miles long!
   3. When we speak of its malleability, we mean that gold can be beaten into thin <u>sheets</u> and, my friend, the sheets may be surprisingly thin.
   4. Here is an amazing <u>fact</u> the ancient Egyptians hammered gold into sheets that were a mere 1/367,000 inch thick.
   5. "I knew gold was an amazing metal," said Mary, "<u>but</u>"

B. Write the letter of the sentence in which the boldface part is correct. [5, 6]
   1. a. "While we were sleeping," said the **soldiers, "The** disciples stole His body."
      b. "While we were sleeping," said the **soldiers, "the** disciples stole His body."
   2. a. George Brunk's book **"Ready Bible Answers"** gives much clear, pointed teaching.
      b. George Brunk's book ***Ready Bible Answers*** gives much clear, pointed teaching.

3. a. Peter declared, "I will never deny **thee;" however,** he soon broke that promise.

   b. Peter declared, "I will never deny **thee"; however,** he soon broke that promise.

4. a. "Is there a Bible verse that says, 'Waste not, want **not?'** " asked Bertha.

   b. "Is there a Bible verse that says, 'Waste not, want **not'?"** asked Bertha.

5. a. I missed the word *extricate* on my vocabulary test.

   b. I missed the word **"extricate"** on my vocabulary test.

6. a. From Reddish Knob—how I enjoyed the **view!—we** could see for miles and miles.

   b. From Reddish Knob—how I enjoyed the **view! we** could see for miles and miles.

7. a. "Brian! Stop! That stove **is" Mother** never finished the sentence.

   b. "Brian! Stop! That stove **is—" Mother** never finished the sentence.

8. a. Your composition would sound better if it contained fewer ***but's.***

   b. Your composition would sound better if it contained fewer **"but's."**

9. a. Paul assured the Thessalonian believers, "We which are alive and remain unto the coming of the Lord shall not **prevent (precede)** them which are asleep."

   b. Paul assured the Thessalonian believers, "We which are alive and remain unto the coming of the Lord shall not **prevent [precede]** them which are asleep."

10. a. With calm **self assurance,** she started the engine and drove away.

    b. With calm **self-assurance,** she started the engine and drove away.

---

11. Gathering Information for an Oral Report

"Listening is the other half of speaking." The lessons on listening naturally precede those on speaking. Just as a vessel needs to be filled before it can be emptied for someone's benefit, so listening needs to come before speaking so that you are filled with something worthwhile to give to others.

Public speaking fills a vital place in God's plan for the church. How does He use this method of communication? Preaching the Word to an assembled audience is public speaking. But public speakers also include schoolteachers, Sunday school teachers, Sunday school superintendents, devotional leaders, and those who present topics at school meetings. When you take your turn in giving an oral report, you too are a public speaker.

Your speaking assignments at school are designed to help you prepare for the speaking responsibilities that you will face someday. The more diligently you apply yourself to these assignments, the better you will be prepared to communicate effectively with an audience in the future.

Choosing and Limiting a Topic

To gather information for an oral report, first choose a suitable topic. The topic you choose should be one that you are already familiar with or one that you can soon find information about. Your finished report will be most effective if the topic holds a definite interest to you. Be sure to think of your audience, and choose a topic that will be interesting and profitable to them as well.

An important part of choosing the topic is limiting its scope. You should aim for a report that you can give in six to eight minutes. Instead of speaking on "Agriculture in Ancient History," choose a topic like "Farm Animals in Bible Lands." This limited topic will be your working title. Perhaps you will keep it as your final title, and perhaps you will refine it later. Either way, your working title gives you the sense of direction you need in gathering information.

Closely related to limiting the topic is thinking about the main ideas that you will develop in your report. Doing this before you actually start gathering information will help to make your research more efficient, for you will know what kinds of information you want. For example, you could approach the topic "Farm Animals in Bible Lands" in either of the following ways, or in various other ways.

I. Providing transportation	I. General survey
II. Providing power	II. Care of farm animals
III. Providing food and clothing	III. Benefits of farm animals

As you do research, you will select only the information that relates to the main ideas you plan to cover in your report. If you do not have specific main ideas now, you will need to begin your research and later decide how to arrange your information according to main ideas.

Using Reference Sources

Use several reference sources to find information for your report. The most important source of information is the Bible, for it contains both specific information about many subjects and important principles relating to every subject. Books such as Bible dictionaries, Bible handbooks, and encyclopedias also contain much helpful information. A book on a specific subject (such as *Farming and Gardening in the Bible*) usually gives more detailed information than a general reference book can give.

To determine whether a book may contain information helpful to your research, do a quick check of the table of contents and the index. Scan through sections that look promising; read closely when you find information on your specific theme.

Using more than one source of information will help you give a better report for at least three important reasons. First, it helps to make the report balanced by giving you a wider scope of details. Second, it helps you to express your ideas in your own words, since you must blend the ideas you find. Third, it enables you to verify facts. If two or three books say the same thing, you can be fairly sure that the information is correct.

Perhaps most important, gathering information from several sources helps you to properly understand and interpret the facts. One author's way of writing will sometimes give you a wrong impression, which may be corrected by the writing of someone else. For example, one author wrote that after Ponce de León discovered Florida, he sailed to Puerto Rico in 1514, received a royal commission to colonize the new land, and returned to Florida in 1521. This gives the impression that he stayed in Puerto Rico for those seven years. A different writer gives a true impression by saying that Ponce de León sailed from Puerto Rico to Spain in 1514 to obtain the royal commission.

Taking Notes

What method should you use when you actually write your notes? Should you write each bit of information on a scrap of paper and put it in a shoebox? You are asking for trouble and frustration if you do that!

You need a well-organized system for taking notes. One good method is to use small note cards, such as three-by-five-inch index cards. On each card, write only information that comes from one reference source and that relates to one main topic of your report. Indicate exactly where you found each bit of information so that later you can check the accuracy of your notes or add other details. These small cards will be easy to shuffle when you organize your notes into an outline.

Be careful to avoid dishonesty when you take notes. Copying another person's work and passing it off as your own is plagiarism (plā′·jə·riz′·əm), a form of stealing. Your report may draw upon the *ideas* of others, but it must be expressed in your own words. Writing your notes in short phrases, rather than in sentences or paragraphs, helps to prevent dishonest copying.

Of course, if your report will include several sentences quoted directly from a reference source, you may copy those sentences. But be sure to place the material within quotation marks, and give proper credit to the source by clearly stating where the material comes from.

Preparing Visual Aids

A picture, a diagram, or a chalkboard demonstration is one of the best ways to reinforce the points of an oral report. In a report about animals of Bible lands, you will make your presentation much clearer if you show a picture of a donkey turning a millstone, than if you merely describe that in words. Of course, any visual aid you use must be large enough so that everyone can see it clearly.

Even if you discuss an abstract subject, you can often clarify it by using a chart or diagram. The following table shows some contrasts between the Old Testament and the New Testament.

Old Testament	New Testament
1. First things	1. Last things
2. Bondage	2. Liberty
3. Law of Moses	3. Gospel of Christ
4. Outward ceremonies	4. Inward experience
5. Prophecy	5. Fulfillment

Do not be afraid to gather plenty of information for your report. A broad understanding of your subject will help you to speak with confidence and effectiveness. Also, it is easier to discard some notes than to go back through the reference books looking for more information. Therefore, try to gather more information than necessary instead of getting barely enough.

Applying the Lesson

Take notes from at least two sources on a topic suitable for an oral report of six to eight minutes. Select a topic from the list below, or choose one of your own that your teacher approves. Plan for a visual aid to use along with your report, and write down what it is. Save these notes for later lessons.

1. The Climate of Jerusalem
2. Contrasts Between the Pharisees and the Sadducees
3. A Survey of the Jordan Valley
4. The Construction of a Beaver Lodge
5. The Operation of a Hydroelectric Power Plant

---

12. Improving Your Editing Skills, Part 2

The standard proofreading symbols provide a neat, efficient way to mark corrections in a manuscript. Anyone who is familiar with the marks will immediately understand what changes are intended. By contrast, look at the marks used to make changes in the following sentence.

Some <s>Oak</s> trees grow to <s>huge</s> enormous size.

It may not be clear that *Oak* is to be changed to *oak,* for uppercase and lowercase *o* both have the same form. And scribbling out an unwanted word does not look neat at all. Can you imagine the unsightly appearance of a whole page full of such sloppy corrections? Consider too that later you may change your mind about a deleted word. How will you retain a word if it has been obliterated beyond recognition? Using the standard proofreading marks is surely much better.

The following table reviews the six proofreading marks from Lesson 7 and introduces six new marks. Below the table is a sample manuscript showing how the new marks are used. The exercises call for the proper use of all these proofreading marks.

Marks Used in Editing and Proofreading
(Introduced in first proofreading lesson)

∨or∧ insert (caret)	_ℛ_ delete	. . . . stet (let it stand)
¶ begin new paragraph	_ℓc_ change to lowercase (small letter)	_uc_ change to uppercase (capital letter)

(Introduced in this lesson)

no ¶ no new paragraph	← move (arrow)	⌐∽⌐ transpose
# insert space	⌒ delete space	—————— use italics

Explanations

To move a word from one line to another, it may be simplest to circle the word and use an arrow.

The word *cold* is to be italicized for emphasis.

"Transpose" symbol is used with words, letters, or punctuation.

"No paragraph" symbol means the two paragraphs are to be joined.

Arrow indicates moving indented text left to the vertical line.

"Delete space" symbol means the two words or word parts should be joined.

Extended line of the symbol # shows exactly where the space is to be inserted.

Sample Manuscript

In Matthew 10:42 Jesus (merely) promised a reward for ⌄giving a little one "a cup of cold water⌐∽⌐ How could people keep water cold in Bible times? They this did very simply by storing water in unglazed pots. no¶

←Because the clay was porous, water could evaporate through the walls of the jar and thus cool the water within.

Modern refrigerators still use the process of evapor⌒ation to keep our food cold.

There are other proofreading marks besides the ones shown in this lesson. But these twelve are the most basic symbols, and they are the ones that best apply to your work. Learn to use them accurately.

Editing Practice

A. Use the proper proofreading marks to correct two spacing errors in each sentence.

1. The sun shine felt warm as we walked down the side walk.

2. Father wanted to buy stamps at the postoffice, but no body was there.

3. Then he remembered that itwas a holi day.

4. Some insects can jump tremendous distances inrelation to their smallsize.

5. If a five-foot person were able to jump proportionately as far as some grass hoppers, he could jump fivehundred feet!

B. Use the proper proofreading marks to indicate one use of italics and to correct one error of transposition in each sentence.

1. I thought "A Goodly Heritage" in the Christian Example was worthwhile a story.

2. You have used too many so's in these setnences.

3. Coffee is a short word with two sets of duoble letters.

4. We are using the book Mennonites in Europe to study the history the of Anabaptists.

5. Thirty-six people died when the Hindenburg, a huge German airship, cuaght fire in 1937.

C. Use the proper symbols to mark the changes indicated in parentheses.

1. Ruth declared that she would go back to the land of Israel with Naomi firmly. (Move *firmly* so that it follows *declared*.)

2. It was probably hard for Ruth to leave her homeland; because of her steadfast devotion, however, she experienced great blessings. (Move *however* and the comma after it to a position after the semicolon.)

3.   Ruth became an ancestor of Jesus Christ even though she came from the Moabites. (Use an arrow and a vertical line to move the indented text to the left.)

D. Now try your editing skills on the selection below. You will need to do the following things.
   a. Make one correction in each line. (You will use each proofreading mark at least once.)
   b. Show that one word already deleted should be retained.
   c. Show that the Indian name should be italicized since it is a foreign word.
   d. Make the second paragraph begin in line 11 rather than line 13.

Sixteen changes should be marked. Can you find them all?

1.   Yosemite Falls (yō·sem'·i·tē), located on the Western

2. slopes of the Sierra Nevada, makes a ~~truly~~ spectacular

3. sight. (The name Yosemite comes from U-za-ma-ti, the name

4. of the local Indians.) Actually, this water fall consists

5. of several sets of falls. At the Upper Yosemite falls, the

6. water plunges 1,430 feet (436 meters). That is eight over

7. times higher then Niagara Falls! The water drops another

8. 320 feet (98 meters) at the Lower Yosemite Falls. A serious

9.   of cascades in between brings the total height to 2,425

10. feet (739 meters), making the this highest waterfall in

11. North America. The marvelous beauty of these falls is best

12. appreciated from the floor of the Yosemite Valley.

13.   The water almost appears to come out of nowhere and

14. plunge over nearly vertical cliffs. In fact the water

15. flows from hanging vallyes that are obscured by the huge

16. massive granite walls which rim the mainvalley.

---

13. Outlining Your Material

The notes that you gathered in Lesson 11 represent the raw material of an oral report. Are you now ready to stand up and give your report to the class? Of course not. You must work that raw material into something you can use to make your report interesting and meaningful. One part of this work is outlining the information that you have gathered.

The first step in outlining your material is to sort your notes into groups according to main topics. If you decided on those main topics while taking notes, this step is already done. If not, you must now evaluate your notes to find some general ideas to use as main topics.

Below is a set of cards with notes for a report on "Farm Animals in Bible Lands." Notice that the notetaker has already decided on three main topics: "Providing transportation," "Providing food and clothing," and "Providing power." The main topic is written on the second line of each note. All the information obtained from one main source and relating to one specific idea is included on one card. You may have many more notes when you prepare for your report, but this example should be enough to show the steps in outlining your material. Study these sample notes.

Farm Animals in Bible Lands #1	Farm Animals in B. L. #2
Providing transportation	Providing transportation
The New Unger's Bible Dictionary, p. 67	NUBD, p. 69
Camels are large (second largest after elephant used by man), strong, have great endurance	Donkeys among most frequently mentioned animals in Bible
Well suited for sandy desert travel: broad feet, ability to go for days without food or water, ability to eat thorny desert plants	Some get almost as big as mules and carry large loads

---

Farm Animals in B. L.   #3

Providing food and clothing

NUBD. p. 77

Sheep milk a very important food
Sheep wool used much for clothing

Farm Animals in B. L.   #4

Providing transportation

Bible Plants and Animals. Vol. 1. p. 21

The larger freight camels can carry up to
    600 lb. of cargo at 3 mph
The smaller riding camels can travel up
    to 10 mph, covering over 100 mi. in a
    day

Farm Animals in B. L.   #5

Providing food and clothing

BPA. Vol. 1. p. 24

Camel milk used as beverage and to make
    cheese

Farm Animals in B. L.   #6

Providing food and clothing

BPA. Vol. 1. p. 26

Cattle an important source of food

Farm Animals in B. L.   #7

Providing power
BPA. Vol. 1. p. 27
Oxen usually used in pairs, joined with
    heavy wooden yoke (yoke became symbol
    of service)
Often used for plowing (Elisha with 12 yoke
    of oxen)
Used for threshing by direct trampling or
    hauling drag over sheaves

Farm Animals in B. L.   #8

Providing food and clothing

BPA. Vol. 1. p. 28

Cattle hides made into leather for
    harnesses, saddles, and armor

Farm Animals in B. L.   #9

Providing food and clothing

BPA. Vol. 1. p. 29

Cows an important source of milk

Farm Animals in B. L.   #10

Providing transportation

BPA. Vol. 1. p. 36

Donkeys can keep pace with camels on long
    journeys and outpace horses on rough
    ground

Farm Animals in B. L.   #11

Providing power

BPA. Vol. 1. p. 37

Donkeys' patient, plodding ways made
    them well suited to turning wheels for
    grinding grain, crushing grapes, or
    lifting water for irrigation

Farm Animals in B. L.   #12

Providing food and clothing

BPA. Vol. 1. p. 46

Kids considered a delicacy
Goats produced more milk than sheep, but
    was less rich
Goat hair was used to make coarse clothing

Farm Animals in B. L. #13 *Providing food and clothing* *BPA. Vol. 1. p. 47* *Goatskins produced fine leather. stronger than sheepskins*	*Farm Animals in B. L.* #15 *Providing food and clothing* *Manners and Customs of Bible Lands. p. 164* *Sheep milk very rich* *Most clothing made of wool*
Farm Animals in B. L. #14 *Providing food and clothing* *BPA. Vol. 1. p. 85* *Mutton was basic part of meat diet*	*Farm Animals in B. L.* #16 *Providing food and clothing* *MCBL. p. 257* *Camel hair was spun into strong thread and woven into coarse fabric* *Camel skin was made into leather for sandals. leggings. and water bottles*

The next step in outlining your material is to arrange the main topics in a logical order. Often a topic has a natural order that you can follow, such as the order of time, space, or importance. But sometimes the arrangement is arbitrary; that is, you must decide on a certain order without having a specific reason for it. The example in this lesson has no natural order, so the following order has been chosen arbitrarily.

Farm Animals in Bible Lands
I. Providing transportation
II. Providing power
III. Providing food and clothing

Now we are ready to expand the outline with the information that was gathered. From cards 1, 2, 4, and 10, we can draw information on how farm animals provided transportation, as shown by the following example. Again, the order of these points is arbitrary; there is no specific reason for it.

I. Providing transportation
 A. Donkeys
  1. Are among most frequently mentioned animals in Bible
  2. Can get almost as big as mules and carry large loads
  3. Can keep pace with camels on long journeys and outpace horses on rough ground
 B. Camels
  1. Have great size, strength, and endurance
   a. Larger freight camels can carry up to 600 lb. of cargo at 3 mph
   b. Smaller riding camels can travel up to 10 mph, covering over 100 miles in a day

2. Are well suited for sandy desert travel
   a. Broad feet
   b. Ability to go for days without food or water
   c. Ability to eat thorny desert plants

After outlining the details for the first main topic, you must do the same thing for the rest of the main topics on the outline. Prepare your outline carefully, for the quality of the outline will strongly influence the quality of your report.

Applying the Lesson

A. Using the information you gathered in Lesson 11, write a basic outline of three or four main topics. Show this outline to your teacher before you do Part B.

B. Use additional information from your notes to make a more detailed outline.

---

14. Giving an Oral Report

The Final Form of Your Notes

The outline you prepared in Lesson 13 is a bare skeleton. In itself, it does not provide everything you need to give an interesting report. If you were to stand up with only the outline, your report would likely be a boring recital of bare facts.

"Some farm animals kept in Bible lands were used to provide transportation. Donkeys are among the most frequently mentioned animals in the Bible. They can get almost as big as mules and carry large loads. They can keep pace with camels on long journeys and outpace horses on rough ground."

To prepare for an oral report, first decide how you will describe and illustrate the points on your outline. Go through the outline point by point, thinking of ideas that will add "flesh" to the skeleton.

What can be added to the details under point A (Donkeys)? You decide to find some verses about donkeys by using a concordance. (Donkeys are called asses in the King James Bible.) In reading the verses, you see that Abraham, Balaam, Abigail, and several other Bible characters rode on donkeys. Would this fit anywhere in your report? You decide to mention those characters under point 1.

One verse you read is Genesis 45:23, which speaks of the loaded donkeys that Joseph sent to Jacob. You put this information under point 2, for it fits well there. So does the information in 2 Samuel 16:1, 2, which describes a considerable load carried by some donkeys.

None of the verses you found seem to fit with point 3. Now what? You remember a story your grandfather told about donkeys, but that does not fit either. You let your mind run further, and finally you decide to look in an encyclopedia for specific information about the donkey's stamina and sure-footedness.

Now the beginning of your outline looks like the example below. Can you see how this will help to make the report much more interesting?

I. Providing transportation
    A. Donkeys
        1. Are among most frequently mentioned animals in Bible
            — Abraham used donkey for trip to Mt. Moriah
            — Balaam rode famous donkey that spoke with man's voice
            — Abigail rode donkey when appeasing David
            — Shunammite woman rode donkey to Elisha when child died
            — Jesus Himself rode into Jerusalem on donkey
        2. Can get almost as big as mules and carry large loads
            — Joseph sent ten donkeys loaded with corn, bread, and meat for his father in Canaan
            — Ziba met David with "a couple of donkeys" carrying 200 loaves of bread, 100 bunches of raisins, 100 summer fruits, and a bottle of wine

Another important part of preparing the final form of your notes is to write the exact words of the introduction and the conclusion. The introduction sets the tone for the report. For an effective introduction, you can use an interesting observation, an illustration, a thought-provoking question, a familiar quotation, or a direct statement. It should weave in the title of the report or at least mention the subject to be presented, so that your audience knows exactly what you will be talking about.

Read the following sample introductions for a report on "Farm Animals in Bible Lands." Notice how the underlined words weave the title into these introductory paragraphs.

Illustration:
Job owned 7,000 sheep, 3,000 camels, 500 yoke of oxen, and 500 female donkeys. These four species of animals are frequently mentioned in the Bible. Many people in Bible times apparently raised these and other animals. In this report on farm animals in Bible lands, we will discuss why various animals were raised.

First we will consider how these farm animals were used for transportation....

Direct statement:
As in modern times, so in Bible times, people raised various animals for a variety of purposes. In thinking about some of these farm animals, we will first consider how they were used for transportation....

An effective conclusion is just as important as an effective introduction. Without a carefully planned conclusion, you are likely to end your report either by stopping abruptly after your last point or by groping about for some suitable closing remarks. An effective conclusion should briefly summarize the main points or give a call to some response or action. The following sample conclusion is for a report on "Farm Animals in Bible Lands." It briefly summarizes the three main points and then closes with a clinching statement.

We have considered how farm animals were used to provide transportation, to provide power for various jobs, and to provide food and clothing. In a time when there was no modern machinery as we have today, these animals certainly filled a vital place in the people's lives.

A third basic step in preparing for your report is to copy your introduction, your expanded outline, and your conclusion in a form that is easy to follow. Your notes should be large enough and neat enough for you to read easily while you are up front. Writing your notes on index cards is a good practice. It is easier to handle these cards without causing distractions than to handle several large sheets of paper. Keeping your place in your notes is also easier when they are on small cards.

You also need to prepare any visual aid you plan to use. A picture or diagram must be neat and clear, and any writing must be large enough so that everyone can read it easily. If you plan a chalkboard demonstration, practice beforehand so that you can give it in a smooth, orderly manner.

The final step in this preparation is to practice giving your report. Be sure you know how to pronounce any difficult words. If possible, have some other person listen to you, and let him point out areas where you can improve. Also ask him to time you, and then increase or decrease the amount of material you cover so that your report is the proper length. But do not rely on this too much; when you give your report at school, you may be more tense and speak faster than you do at home.

Giving an Oral Report

In giving your oral report, remember these pointers. First, your appearance and speaking will be the most natural if you are relaxed. Probably the most important help for being relaxed is to be well prepared. Involve yourself so completely in your report that you forget yourself and your nervousness.

To relieve tension before you stand up, breathe deeply and evenly several times. Remember, however, that nervousness is not all bad. Even the most experienced speakers feel nervous at times. A little nervousness can even be a good thing: it can motivate you to do your best.

Another important point is that eye contact helps you to communicate effectively. Do not begin speaking before you have established eye contact with your audience. Let your eyes actually meet those of your listeners. Talk to the people, not to your outline, to the floor, or to the walls. Look at your audience as you emphasize your major points. And be sure to make eye contact as you end your report; it will help you to conclude on a strong, positive note.

Proper volume and enunciation also contribute to making your report effective. Keep the volume at a comfortable level for your audience. Open your mouth well so that you do not mumble. And finish your last sentence before you start back to your seat.

Distracting appearance and habits can weaken the effect of a report. Be neat and clean, and maintain good posture at all times. Do not fill your pauses with *uh*'s and *ah*'s, and avoid clearing your throat continually. Do not frequently adjust your glasses or your hair, put your hands into and out of your pockets, change your posture, or shuffle your notes.

As with any task of life, remember to depend on the Lord. Pray that God will help you to communicate effectively. After giving the report, resist the temptation to feel either discouraged or proud. Thank God for helping you, and remember that He simply asks you to do your best for His glory.

Your teacher may use the following evaluation chart to grade your oral report.

| Points possible | Points earned | **Evaluation of Oral Report** |

Evaluation of Oral Report

Points possible	Points earned	
_5_	___	**Introduction**

No clear introduction (3 points)
Introduction weak or poorly related to topic (4 points)
Clear, interesting introduction (5 points)

_5_ ___ **Content**
Poor organization; weak development (3 points)
Fairly good organization and development (4 points)
Clear main points; effective development (5 points)

_5_ ___ **Conclusion**
No clear conclusion (3 points)
Conclusion weak or poorly related to topic (4 points)
Clear, effective conclusion (5 points)

_5_ ___ **Eye contact**
Looked constantly at outline (3 points)
Looked up occasionally (4 points)
Looked at audience frequently (5 points)

_5_ ___ **Posture**
Slouched; head down; feet askew (3 points)
Had fairly good posture most of the time (4 points)
Stood straight; head up; feet flat on floor (5 points)

_5_ ___ **Volume and enunciation**
Many words hard to understand (3 points)
Occasional words hard to understand (4 points)
Good volume and clear enunciation (5 points)

_5_ ___ **Expression**
Voice flat and droning (3 points)
Good expression most of the time (4 points)
Meaningful, enthusiastic expression (5 points)

_5_ ___ **Preparation**
Often fumbled for words; many awkward pauses (3 points)
Occasionally hesitated for words (4 points)
Spoke with little hesitation (5 points)

_5_ ___ **Visual aid**
Too small or otherwise ineffective (3 points)
Fairly neat and beneficial (4 points)
Attractive, readable, and effective (5 points)

_5_ ___ **Mannerisms**
Distracting habits throughout report (3 points)
Occasional distracting habits (4 points)
No distracting habits (5 points)

_5_ ___ **Time**
Less than four minutes (3 points)
From four to five minutes (4 points)
From six to eight minutes (5 points)

_55_ ___ **Total points**

Applying the Lesson

A. Go through your outline from Lesson 13, adding ideas for descriptions and illustrations. Also prepare the visual aid you plan to use. Have your teacher check your materials before you do Part B.

B. Give your oral report at your teacher's direction.

---

15. Chapter 2 Review

A. List from memory the six points that summarize good listening skills, as given in Lesson 10. (The key words start with the letters *A–F*.)

B. Write *true* or *false* for each sentence.
1. The main reason we should listen well is to avoid unpleasant consequences.
2. Good listening depends on attitudes as well as specific skills.
3. Taking notes may be unwise because it can distract you from listening as well as you should.
4. Remembering the main points of a talk will help you to remember the important details.
5. Strong language and fervent emotion are reliable proof that a statement is based on fact.
6. In preparing for a report, you must wait to limit your topic until you are gathering information.
7. For detailed information, a book on a specific subject is usually better than an encyclopedia.
8. If your report includes material quoted directly from a reference book, you must give proper credit to the source of that material.
9. Eye contact involves meeting the eyes of individual listeners.
10. Eye contact is important at the beginning but not the end of your talk.

C. Answer these questions.
1. What is the relationship between hearing and listening?
2. What are three attitudes essential to good listening?
3. Why should we listen respectfully to those younger than ourselves? to those whom we consider equals? to those in authority?
4. What are four ways to show courtesy in listening to others?
5. What are three ways to show interest in what others are saying?
6. Why must you put forth special effort to have an active mind while listening?
7. What are three things you can do to keep your mind active?
8. What are three ways to block out distractions as you listen?
9. What are three good ways to discern whether a speaker is actually giving facts?
10. What is plagiarism? How can you avoid this form of dishonesty when you gather information for a report?
11. What four things should you do after you have outlined your material and before you give an oral report?

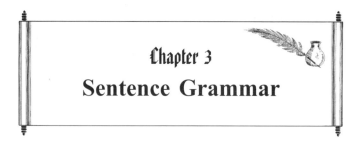

Chapter 3

Sentence Grammar

16. Complete Sentences and Sentence Skeletons

The sentence is the basic unit of language. A good grasp of sentence grammar, therefore, is essential to every kind of communication—listening, speaking, reading, and writing.

1. *A sentence is a group of words that expresses a complete thought.* It makes a statement, asks a question, gives a command, or makes an exclamation.

God is on the throne.
How can we praise Him enough?
Give all glory to His Name.
How great is our God!

2. *Every sentence can be divided into two parts: the complete subject and the complete predicate.* The complete subject tells *who* or *what* the sentence is about, and the complete predicate tells what the subject *does* or *is*.

| complete subject | complete predicate |
Simple faith in God gives a person true stability.

Sometimes the complete subject comes after the complete predicate or between parts of the complete predicate. Such a sentence is written in inverted or mixed word order, as you will see in Lesson 22. In the following sentences, the complete subject is underlined once and the complete predicate is underlined twice.

Only by faith in God comes true peace and rest.
If we live unselfishly, our lives will be a blessing to others.

3. *The sentence skeleton consists of the simple subject and the simple predicate.* The simple subject is the basic part of the complete subject. It is always a substantive: a noun or pronoun, or a word, phrase, or clause used as a noun. The simple predicate is the verb or verb phrase. Either or both of these sentence parts can be compound.

4. *A fragment does not express a complete thought.* You can correct a fragment either by joining it to another sentence or by adding words to make it a complete sentence.

Fragments:
This stream begins at Buffalo Springs. Only one mile away.
A small boat floating in the water.

Revisions:
This stream begins at Buffalo Springs, only one mile away.
This stream begins at Buffalo Springs. That is only one mile away.

We saw a small boat floating in the water.
A small boat was floating in the water.

5. *An elliptical sentence has one or more parts missing, but it expresses a complete thought because the missing parts are understood.* Most imperative sentences are elliptical because the subject *you* is understood. Also, many sentences with clauses of comparison are elliptical because parts of that clause are understood. Example: He is taller than I (am tall).

Other elliptical sentences are understandable because of the context. Elliptical sentences of this kind occur mainly in dialogue.

"Have you heard about that big hurricane?"
"What hurricane?"
"The one in Florida. Thousands of buildings have been destroyed."

6. *A run-on error occurs when two or more sentences are joined incorrectly.* You can correct a run-on error in one of the following ways.
   a. By inserting a comma and a coordinating conjunction between the two parts. (Inserting only a comma produces a comma splice.)
   b. By inserting a semicolon between the two parts.
   c. By changing one of the clauses to a dependent clause.
   d. By dividing the incorrect sentence into two or more sentences.

   Run-on error:
   Uncle Roy's family arrived at 7:00 we were soon on our way to the zoo.
   Corrections:
   (a) Uncle Roy's family arrived at 7:00, and we were soon on our way to the zoo.
   (b) Uncle Roy's family arrived at 7:00; we were soon on our way to the zoo.
   (c) After Uncle Roy's family arrived at 7:00, we were soon on our way to the zoo.
   (d) Uncle Roy's family arrived at 7:00. We were soon on our way to the zoo.

Applying the Lesson

A. Copy the complete subject, draw a vertical line after it, and copy the complete predicate. If the subject does not come first, rewrite the sentence in normal subject–predicate order before marking the division.
   1. The eternal God has existed from eternity past.
   2. The almighty Creator called the world into existence.
   3. By the skill of His hand, God fashioned man from dust.
   4. As the crowning work of creation, man bears the image of God Himself.

5. On the fence sat a pair of cardinals.
6. When the wind rose, the fire that was almost under control blazed furiously again.
7. Although he goes to church, Mr. Hock, who lives across the field, rejects many Biblical teachings.
8. Through our meadow flows a clear, sparkling stream.

B. Copy the simple subject and the simple predicate of each sentence. Draw a vertical line between the two parts. (Watch for compound parts.)
   1. A responsible person will take good care of his possessions.
   2. Good workers apply themselves diligently to their work.
   3. A mature person sees work and willingly tackles it.
   4. By exercising self-discipline, we can accomplish many hard tasks.
   5. Interest and commitment have always been essential attitudes for success.
   6. A diligent worker not only can achieve greater goals but also will find greater joy in the process.
   7. Attitudes of laziness or carelessness destroy the satisfaction of work.
   8. Even children and youth should be enjoying the pleasure of a job well done.
   9. In the heart of the diligent dwells a sense of satisfaction.
   10. Diligence and carefulness in daily chores produce a healthy outlook on work and prepare us for greater responsibilities.
   11. Under the influence of the fallen nature, men have often shirked responsibility.
   12. From the hands of the diligent have come many practical achievements.
   13. Both the present joys and the future dividends of hard work motivate and amply reward the diligent.
   14. The blessings of diligence and carefulness will surpass any supposed advantages of slothfulness.

C. The sentences below are joined or divided incorrectly. Show how to correct them by writing the words immediately before and after each mistake, and using correct capitalization and punctuation. (You may need to insert a conjunction.) If an exercise has no error, write *correct*.
   1. Learning about clouds is not only interesting but also worthwhile. Because it can help you predict the weather.
   2. The appearance of clouds varies widely, there are only three basic types of clouds.
   3. First are the familiar cumulus clouds. Which look somewhat like cotton or mashed potatoes.
   4. These clouds usually indicate fair weather, they rarely produce rain unless they develop into thunderheads.
   5. Cirrus clouds are another basic type of clouds. They have a feathery, wispy appearance.
   6. These clouds are composed entirely of ice crystals. Formed at very high altitudes.
   7. Cirrus clouds do not produce precipitation, they can only foretell precipitation.

8. It is a sign of rain when cirrus clouds become thicker and larger. Streaming out in great windblown plumes known as mare's-tails.

9. Stratus clouds, the third basic kind, form in broad layers. Covering large areas of the sky.

10. They are the clouds of overcast days, they often mean longer periods of precipitation.

D. Show how to correct the fragments and run-on errors in this dialogue, using the same method as in Part C. Do not change elliptical sentences. If a paragraph has no mistake, write *correct.*

1. "Have you seen the new calves? Father bought at the auction today?" asked Steven.

2. "No," replied Arlin. "Let's go see them now, we can name them before feeding time."

3. "Look at that mostly white one. She's a beauty!"

4. "I agree! Those black spots on her back look like pepper, let's name her Pepper."

5. "Sounds good to me," agreed Steven.

6. "Over here's another beauty. She's mostly black. With a white star on her forehead."

Review Exercises

Write correctly each word that should be capitalized. If no capital letter is needed, write *correct.* [1]

1. when the *titanic* sank
2. at wenger's feed mill
3. the book *the earth is round*
4. enjoy algebra I and science
5. just after world war II
6. visit brother john's son in vermont
7. the genesis account of the creation
8. for my mother and two of my aunts
9. found their scotch terrier on tuesday
10. our bahamian friends last winter

---

17. Sentence Complements

A *complement* is a word that *completes* the meaning of a sentence skeleton. There are three basic kinds of complements: subjective, object, and objective complements.

Subjective Complements

A *subjective complement* completes the sentence skeleton by referring to the subject. Verbs before subjective complements must be linking verbs: forms of *be* or verbs that can be replaced by them, such as *taste, look, grow, seem,* and *remain.*

1. A *predicate nominative* is a substantive that follows a linking verb and renames the subject.

> "The LORD is a great <u>God</u>."
> (*God* renames LORD.)
> Myron's dog is a <u>German shepherd</u>.
> (*German shepherd* renames *dog.*)

2. A *predicate adjective* follows a linking verb and modifies the subject.

> "The LORD is <u>righteous</u>."
> (*Righteous* modifies LORD.)
> This casserole looks <u>attractive</u> and tastes <u>delicious</u>.
> (Both *attractive* and *delicious* modify *casserole.*)
> Soon the mixture turned <u>amber</u> and <u>syrupy</u>.
> (Both *amber* and *syrupy* modify *mixture.*)

Verbs like *look, turn,* and *feel* are not always linking verbs. In some sentences they are followed by adverbs, direct objects, or other sentence parts. A sentence contains a subjective complement only if the main verb expresses being rather than action, and only if the verb is followed by a substantive that renames the subject or an adjective that modifies the subject.

> A little fawn must remain completely quiet.
> (*Must remain* expresses being; it can be replaced by *must be. Quiet* modifies *fawn. Quiet* is a predicate adjective.)
> A little fawn must remain quietly where its mother left it.
> (*Must remain* expresses action; it cannot be replaced by *must be.* Neither *quietly* nor *where its mother left it* renames or modifies *fawn;* they are adverbs.)

Object Complements

An *object complement* completes the sentence skeleton by receiving the action of a transitive verb.

1. A *direct object* is a substantive that receives the action of a transitive verb directly. In a sentence with a direct object, the subject performs the action, and the direct object receives the action. To find the direct object, say the skeleton and ask *whom* or *what.*

> "The good shepherd giveth his <u>life</u> for the sheep."
> (*Life* receives the action of *giveth.*)
> Allen closed the <u>door</u> and locked <u>it</u>.
> (*Door* receives the action of *closed,* and *it* receives the action of *locked.*)
> Lorene swept the <u>steps</u> and the <u>walks</u>.
> (Both *steps* and *walks* receive the action of *swept.*)

2. An *indirect object* is a substantive that receives the action of a transitive verb indirectly. An indirect object comes between a verb and its direct object. To find an indirect object, say the skeleton with the direct object, and ask *to whom or what* or *for whom or what.*

God gives His <u>children</u> good gifts.
(God gives gifts *to whom*? *Children* is the indirect object.)
Leslie set <u>Nathan</u> and <u>me</u> a good example.
(Leslie set example *for whom*? *Nathan* and *me* are the indirect objects.)

Objective Complements

An *objective complement* is a noun or an adjective that follows and completes the direct object of a verb which expresses the idea of "making" or "considering." If the objective complement is a noun, it renames the direct object; if it is an adjective, it modifies the direct object. An objective complement is somewhat like a subjective complement. A subjective complement relates to the subject, but an objective complement relates to the direct object. Generally, you can insert the words *to be* between the direct object and the objective complement.

God made man a <u>creature</u> of choice.
(*Creature* is a noun that renames the direct object *man*.)

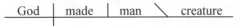

We must consider the Lord <u>worthy</u> of our loyalty.
(*Worthy* is an adjective that modifies the direct object *Lord*.)

| We | must consider | Lord \ worthy |

Use the following steps to find an objective complement.
1. Identify the sentence skeleton and the direct object.
2. Determine whether the verb has the idea of "making" or "considering." If it does not, there can be no objective complement. If it does, go to Step 3.
3. Determine whether the sentence has an indirect object. If it does, there can be no objective complement. If it does not, go to Step 4.
4. Determine whether the direct object is followed by a noun that renames the direct object or by an adjective that modifies the direct object. Also determine whether you can insert the words *to be* between the direct object and the noun or adjective.

We should consider a godly heritage very precious.
Step 1: Skeleton and direct object: *We should consider heritage.*
Step 2: The verb *should consider* has the idea of "considering."
Step 3: There is no indirect object.
Step 4: The adjective *precious* modifies *heritage*. "Consider heritage to be precious" is sensible. *Precious* is an objective complement.
We considered our options too carelessly.
Step 1: Skeleton and direct object: *We considered options.*
Step 2: The verb *considered* has the idea of "considering."
Step 3: There is no indirect object.
Step 4: *Options* is not followed by a noun or an adjective that renames or modifies *options*. There is no objective complement. (*Too* and *carelessly* are adverbs.)

Jacob made Joseph a coat of many colors.
>   *Step 1:* Skeleton and direct object: *Jacob made coat.*
>   *Step 2:* The verb *made* has the idea of "making."
>   *Step 3:* There is an indirect object, *Joseph.* There can be no objective complement.

Samuel anointed Saul king of Israel.
>   *Step 1:* Skeleton and direct object: *Samuel anointed Saul.*
>   *Step 2:* The verb *anointed* has the idea of "making."
>   *Step 3:* There is no indirect object.
>   *Step 4:* The noun *king* renames *Saul.* "Anointed Saul to be king" is sensible. *King* is an objective complement.

Are you confused by the terms *subjective complement, object complement,* and *objective complement?* Remember that a subjective complement *refers* to the subject, and an objective complement *refers* to the direct object. An object complement *is* an object—either a direct object or an indirect object. But no subject *is* a complement, so there is no such thing as a subject complement.

Applying the Lesson

A. Copy each subjective complement, and label it *PN* for predicate nominative or *PA* for predicate adjective. If a sentence has no subjective complement, write *none.*

1. The way of righteousness is seldom easy on the flesh.
2. Your greatest enemy is your own nature, bent on wrongdoing.
3. Joseph's character grew strong under severe testing.
4. Solomon's heathen wives turned his heart to idolatry.
5. Our two main produce crops were tomatoes and sweet corn.
6. The mountain path soon became rugged and steep.
7. We have never grown sweet peas to sell.
8. Carlos Monterroso has become my close friend.
9. Brother Aaron has been a teacher or a board member for thirty years.
10. I felt somewhat sick this morning and became even worse by evening.
11. My sore knee looks swollen and feels quite tender.
12. Judy's grandmother is a good writer and artist.

B. Copy each object complement, and label it *DO* for direct object or *IO* for indirect object. If a sentence has no object complement, write *none.*

1. We must anchor our faith in God and His Word.
2. The Bible contains promises for the tempted and the tested.
3. Jesus is preparing His people a wonderful home in heaven.
4. In these last days, the love of many is growing cold.
5. Glendon has been raising hamsters and gerbils.
6. Grandfather Morris gave him a pair of rare hamsters.
7. Louisa made Aunt Hettie and Aunt Loretta beautiful afghans.
8. The road workers mowed the grass and trimmed the trees along the highway.
9. Last evening we visited with the Heatwole family.

10. Sister Kaylene has written several books and many poems.
11. Father studied the map and found the way without any trouble.
12. That cow gave Curvin and me quite a chase!

C. Copy the objective complements in these sentences. If a sentence has no objective complement, write *none*.
1. Cain thought his punishment too great.
2. Youth should make the development of solid character an important goal.
3. God's people consider heavenly citizenship more valuable than earthly citizenship.
4. Repeated disobedience will make the conscience dull.
5. A person builds his reputation by many small deeds.
6. Do you esteem the Bible important above all other books?
7. Have you been making your life a blessing to others?
8. We should seek God's direction daily in our lives.
9. A mature person sees himself responsible to do his best.
10. Trustworthiness makes a person an asset in his surroundings.

D. Copy each underlined complement, and label it *PN, PA, DO, IO,* or *OC*.
1. Do you consider <u>grasses</u> rather <u>unimportant</u> to your life?
2. Some grasses, like corn and bamboo, grow very <u>tall</u>, but others, like Kentucky bluegrass and Bermuda grass, remain quite <u>short</u>.
3. The flowers on most grasses remain <u>small</u> and <u>unattractive</u>.
4. As with all flowering plants, the flowers of grasses are the seed-bearing <u>structures</u>.
5. These seeds actually become the <u>grains</u> or <u>kernels</u> that we eat.
6. God made these <u>grains</u> <u>rich</u> in starch.
7. Starch gives <u>people</u> and <u>animals</u> <u>energy</u>.
8. The leaves and stems of grasses have little food <u>value</u> for humans, but they provide <u>cattle</u> and other <u>animals</u> many <u>nutrients</u>.

Review Exercises

For each underlined word, write *yes* or *no* to tell whether it should be followed by a comma. [2]
1. The sky <u>darkened</u> distant thunder <u>rolled</u> and a strong wind began to blow.
2. Hoping to beat the <u>storm</u> we rushed to close <u>doors</u> and windows.
3. The wind grew even <u>stronger</u> and Father watched the <u>turbulent</u> inky clouds with concern.
4. Suddenly the rain began to <u>fall</u> in heavy <u>sheets</u> and jagged lightning split the sky.
5. "Thank <u>You</u> <u>Lord</u> for Your protection!" we prayed thankfully when the storm had subsided.

18. Retained Objects and Objective Complements

You know that many verbs pass their action to another word in the sentence. If the receiver of the action is an object complement, the verb is usually in the *active voice.* But if the receiver is the subject, the verb is in the *passive voice.* (You will study voice more fully in Chapter 9.) Compare the following sentences.

Active: Christ gave a new command.
  (*Command,* the receiver, is the direct object.)
Passive: A new command was given by Christ.
  (*Command,* the receiver, is the subject.)

Retained Object Complements

Can a verb in the passive voice have an object complement? Yes, it can. To show how that is possible, let us first change the sentence above so that it has a direct object and an indirect object.

Active: Christ gave the *disciples* a new command.

Now let us change this sentence to the passive voice, with the indirect object serving as the subject.

Passive: The *disciples* were given a new command by Christ.

Note that *command* still follows the verb and receives its action, the same as in the active voice. So it is still the direct object, even though the verb is in the passive voice. Since the direct object is the same as it was in the active voice, such a sentence is said to have a *retained direct object.*

We can also rewrite the original sentence in the passive voice with the direct object serving as the subject.

Passive: A new command was given the *disciples* by Christ.

Now *command,* the direct object, has become the subject; and *disciples,* the indirect object, has been retained in its original position. *Disciples* is now a *retained indirect object.*

As these examples show, either a direct object or an indirect object may be retained. In fact, only a sentence with both kinds of objects in the active voice can have a retained object in the passive voice. A sentence can even have an indirect object without a direct object!

When you need to decide whether a sentence has a retained object, use the following steps.

1. Change the sentence so that the verb is in the active voice. (You may need to supply a subject.)
2. Identify the direct object and the indirect object. If the sentence does not have two kinds of complements, there can be no retained object.
3. See if either of these complements is an object in both active and passive voice constructions.

Problem: The church has been given much severe opposition by Satan.
Step 1: Satan has given the church much severe opposition.
Step 2: Direct object: *opposition;* indirect object: *church*
Step 3: *Opposition* is a direct object in both voice constructions.
Solution: *Opposition* is a retained direct object.

Problem: Peter was put into prison by Herod.
Step 1: Herod put Peter into prison.
Step 2: Direct object: *Peter;* no indirect object
Solution: There is no retained object.

Problem: A miraculous deliverance was given Peter.
Step 1: God gave Peter a miraculous deliverance.
Step 2: Direct object: *deliverance;* indirect object: *Peter*
Step 3: *Peter* is an indirect object in both voice constructions.
Solution: *Peter* is a retained indirect object.

Retained Objective Complements

Not only object complements but also objective complements can be retained. A retained objective complement is an objective complement that is retained in a passive voice construction. Look at the following sentence. What are the direct object and the objective complement?

The wise man built his house strong.
(*house*—direct object; *strong*—objective complement)

You could rewrite this sentence in the passive voice.

The wise man's house was built strong.

With the passive voice, the direct object *house* becomes the subject. What happens to the objective complement? It is retained in its original position, so now it is a *retained objective complement.*

When you need to decide whether a sentence has a retained objective complement, use the following steps.

1. Change the sentence so that the verb is in the active voice. (You may need to supply a subject.)
2. Identify the direct object and the objective complement. If the sentence does not have both a direct object and an objective complement, there can be no retained objective complement.
3. See if the same word is an objective complement in both active and passive voice constructions.

Problem: Our neighbors have always been considered friendly.
Step 1: People have always considered our neighbors friendly.
Step 2: Direct object: *neighbors;* objective complement: *friendly*
Step 3: *Friendly* is an objective complement in both active and passive voice constructions.
Solution: *Friendly* is a retained objective complement.

Problem: Mr. Garber's request was answered quickly.
Step 1: We answered Mr. Garber's request quickly.
Step 2: Direct object: *request;* no objective complement
Solution: There is no retained objective complement.

Applying the Lesson

A. Rewrite each sentence so that the verb is in the passive voice. Follow the directions in parentheses for retaining complements. You may omit the *by* phrase at the end of your sentence unless it is needed for clarity.
1. Abram offered Lot the first choice. (Retain the indirect object.)
2. Lot did not return Abram that favor. (Retain the direct object.)
3. Lot considered the well-watered plain the better choice. (Retain the objective complement.)
4. Abram gave Melchizedek a tithe. (Retain the direct object.)
5. God gave Abraham a very difficult test of faith. (Retain the indirect object.)
6. God made the promise of an heir increasingly clear to Abraham. (Retain the objective complement.)

B. Copy each underlined complement, and label it *DO, IO,* or *OC.* Also write *ret.* after the label if the object is retained.
1. We owe the <u>Lord</u> daily <u>thanksgiving</u>.
2. Man cannot make his own <u>soul</u> <u>righteous</u> in God's sight.
3. A godly person considers God's <u>favor</u> more <u>important</u> than man's favor.
4. We are given good <u>preparation</u> for life by being faithful in small things.
5. Children can be taught many valuable <u>lessons</u> by having daily chores.
6. Your choices tell <u>others</u> a great <u>deal</u> about your character.
7. Our faith can be made <u>strong</u> through trials.
8. Courage to do right can be given <u>others</u> by one person's good example.
9. A proper perspective of life is provided <u>us</u> only by God's Word.
10. The trials of life can actually be considered a <u>blessing</u> by the man of faith.

C. Copy the retained complement in each sentence, and label it *DO ret., IO ret.,* or *OC ret.*
1. We were given a beautiful medley of notes by the mockingbird.
2. We were given a sense of satisfaction by the neatly hoed garden rows.
3. The newly fallen snow was made a sparkling blanket by the morning sun.
4. During Father's illness, our family was presented many offers of help.
5. Mr. Colby was sent a Bible by the outreach committee.
6. I was shown a good way to tie these bags by the feed man.
7. A new song was taught the students by Brother Gehman.
8. Our goals were believed too idealistic by Father.
9. The surprise was considered a good idea by Aunt Betty.
10. A forceful lesson in obedience was given the cubs by their mother.
11. Several stories were told the sick children by Grandmother.
12. Soil can be made more productive by the addition of humus.

Review Exercises

A. Name the punctuation that should follow each underlined word: *colon, semicolon,* or *ellipsis points*. [4]

1. Brian forgot to use his turn <u>signal</u> consequently, he failed his driver's examination.
2. Far too many accidents are caused by this one <u>thing</u> driver carelessness.
3. "Yes, I might be interested if <u>you</u>" Mary paused uncertainly.
4. Kenneth, Stanley, and Henry were finished with their <u>work</u> but Edward, my brother, was still busy.
5. For dinner on Sunday we have invited my cousins, James and <u>Paul</u> my friends, James and <u>Mark</u> and our schoolteacher, Brother Hershey.

B. Write the letter of the sentence in which the boldface part is correct. [5, 6]

1. a. "Who said, 'Am I my brother's **keeper?'**" asked Sharon.
   b. "Who said, 'Am I my brother's **keeper'?**" asked Sharon.
2. a. In the opening we sang "Fairest Lord **Jesus;**" then Brother Amos read from Psalm 21.
   b. In the opening we sang "Fairest Lord **Jesus**"; then Brother Amos read from Psalm 21.
3. a. "The LORD of hosts is with **us,**" (Psalm 46:7) and this gives us confidence.
   b. "The LORD of hosts is with **us**" (**Psalm 46:7**), and this gives us confidence.
4. a. In 1818 Great Britain launched the ***Vulcan,*** the first known all-iron ship.
   b. In 1818 Great Britain launched the **"Vulcan,"** the first known all-iron ship.
5. a. We found many helpful pointers in the book **"How to Train the Family Dog."**
   b. We found many helpful pointers in the book ***How to Train the Family Dog.***
6. a. Titus 2:10 tells servants to be "not purloining **[stealing]**, but shewing all good fidelity."
   b. Titus 2:10 tells servants to be "not purloining **(stealing)**, but shewing all good fidelity."
7. a. "Do you believe now that I **can—?**" The bicycle fell with a sudden crash.
   b. "Do you believe now that I **can—**" The bicycle fell with a sudden crash.
8. a. Let's all stop for a **five-minute** break.
   b. Let's all stop for a **five minute** break.
9. a. You must capitalize the word **"west"** in that sentence.
   b. You must capitalize the word ***west*** in that sentence.
10. a. **Three-fourths** of the class finished the assignment before lunch.
    b. **Three fourths** of the class finished the assignment before lunch.

19. Improving Your Writing Style, Part 2: Exact Words

Originality
Exact Words
Active Voice
Figurative Lang.
Triplets

An effective writing style requires a measure of originality. Do not always settle for the first thing that comes to your mind. Think of fresh and colorful ways to express your ideas.

Another element of good writing style is the use of *exact words*. By choosing nouns, verbs, and modifiers that say precisely what you mean, you will make your writing sharp and clear rather than vague and fuzzy. As an extreme example, contrast the following two sentences.

> At that place we saw a big thing eating some little things.
> At the zoo we watched a huge elephant eating some peanuts.

The first sentence gives only a vague impression. Even a first grader would probably do better than that! The second sentence states exactly what we saw and how we saw it (*watched*). This is the way you would write, of course. But before you smile too broadly about the "big thing" and the "little things," take a closer look at your own writing. You may be surprised at some of the *things* you find there.

Look at the nouns in your writing. Do they specifically name the things that you are writing about? Why write "the *noise* of the old *tractor*" when "the *put-put* of the old *John Deere*" describes the scene exactly? Look at your verbs. Do they state specifically what the subject does or is? Why write "Mother *put* more flour into the bread dough" when "Mother *kneaded* more flour into the bread dough" tells precisely what she did? And look at the modifiers you use. Do they describe explicitly? Why write "a *good* story" or "returned *soon*" when "a *worthwhile* story" and "returned *in five minutes*" paint sharp, clear pictures?

You can see these differences clearly when someone points them out word by word. Can you see them just as clearly on your own? Which of the underlined words in the following selection could you replace with more specific words?

> To show how mechanical was the work of a telegraph operator, Thomas Edison wrote the following story of when he worked in a telegraph office in Cincinnati, Ohio.

> > One night I noticed an <u>immense</u> crowd gathering in the street outside a <u>newspaper office</u>. I <u>made</u> the other operators aware of the crowd, and we <u>got</u> a messenger boy to go and find the cause of the excitement. He returned <u>some time later</u> and shouted, "Lincoln's shot!" <u>Instinctively</u> the operators looked from one face to the other to <u>make</u> out which man had <u>gotten</u> the news. All the faces were <u>blank</u>, and every man said he had not <u>gotten</u> a word about the shooting.

> > "<u>Search</u> your files," said the boss to the man handling the press information. For a full minute we <u>were</u> in suspense, and then the man <u>got</u> hold of a paper containing a short account of the shooting of the President. The operator had worked so <u>mechanically</u> that he had <u>gotten</u> the news without the slightest knowledge of its significance.

You will probably agree that *immense, newspaper office, Instinctively, blank, search,* and *mechanically* need no improvement. These are clear, exact words. But *some time later* is vague and should be replaced by an expression like *in a few minutes.* And *were in suspense* should definitely be changed to *waited in suspense.*

Two verbs deserve special attention: *get* and *make.* These verbs are vague because we use them so often to express so many different ideas. When we *get* sick, we *make* an appointment with the doctor. We *get* to his office, the doctor *makes* his diagnosis, and then we *get* a prescription at the drugstore. We usually *get* better if we *make* sure we follow the doctor's instructions. (You should have *gotten* the point by now.)

Did you notice all the forms of *get* and *make* in the paragraph about telegraph operators? There are seven of them! *Made* aware, *got* a messenger boy, *make* out which one, *gotten* the news, *gotten* a word, *got* hold of a paper, *gotten* the news. No, Thomas Edison did not write that way. Here are the verbs he actually used: *called* the attention, *sent* a messenger boy, *see* which one, *received* the news, *taken* a word, *held* up a paper, *handled* the news. The writer did not use *get* or *make* even one time!

Of course, the verbs *get* and *make* should not be banished from your vocabulary, for they have many worthwhile uses in everyday speech. But in writing, you should try to replace these two with verbs that communicate exactly what you mean. The following sets give several more examples.

Vague verbs:	Exact verbs:
I <u>got</u> five dollars for mowing that lawn.	I <u>earned</u> five dollars for mowing that lawn.
Two of my rabbits have <u>gotten</u> away.	Two of my rabbits have <u>escaped</u>.
We <u>made</u> it to the airport in time.	We <u>arrived</u> at the airport in time.
Our team <u>made</u> ten points.	Our team <u>scored</u> ten points.

Examine your writing with a critical eye. Whenever you spot a vague or an inexact word, replace it with a more specific word. The result will be a writing style that expresses your thoughts clearly and forcefully.

Applying the Lesson

Write a composition of 150–200 words, telling about a frightening or an exciting event. Deliberately aim for originality and exactness in your writing.

Review Exercises

Write the letters of the sentences with the better writing style. [3]
1. a. He needs to learn how to speak more kindly.
   b. He needs to study the language of gentleness.
2. a. If only he would quit parading his virtues!
   b. If only he would quit telling everyone how good he is!

3. a. Quick as a wink the cat struck with her sharp claws.
   b. Quick as a whiplash the cat struck with her sharp claws.
4. a. We got to the museum at 10:30 in the morning.
   b. We arrived at the museum at 10:30 in the morning.
5. a. The spoiled boy whined and pouted until his mother bought him some candy.
   b. The bad boy made a big fuss until his mother bought him something sweet.

---

20. Phrases and Clauses

Some sentences consist merely of a sequence of single words, but others include phrases and clauses. Study the following examples.

Ida writes stories.
Ida Nolt has written three stories that tell about her grandmother's life.

The second example has a noun phrase (*Ida Nolt*), a verb phrase (*has written*), and an adjective clause containing an adverb phrase (*that tell about her grandmother's life*). By becoming skilled in working with phrases and clauses, you will improve your ability to communicate effectively.

Phrases

A *phrase* is a group of related words without a skeleton.

1. A *prepositional phrase* begins with a preposition (like *to, for,* or *with*), it ends with an object (usually a noun), and it includes all the modifiers of the object. A prepositional phrase is usually an adjective (modifying a substantive) or an adverb (modifying a verb or another modifier). Sometimes it is a noun because it names something.

The books <u>under your bed</u> must be put away <u>before supper</u>.
   (*Under your bed* is an adjective phrase modifying the noun *books. Before supper* is an adverb phrase modifying the verb *must be put.*)
<u>Under your bed</u> is not a good place to keep your books.
   (*Under your bed* is a noun phrase that names a place. It is the subject.)

2. A *verbal phrase* contains a verb form used as another part of speech. The verbal phrase includes the verbal and all its modifiers and complements.
   a. A gerund phrase contains an *-ing* form used as a noun.

<u>Following the Golden Rule</u> is always right.
   (phrase beginning with the gerund *Following*)
I enjoy <u>reading about the pioneers</u>.
   (phrase beginning with the gerund *reading*)

b. A participial phrase contains a past form or an -*ing* form used as an adjective. It answers the question *what kind of* about a substantive.

A person <u>following the Golden Rule</u> gets along well with others.
(phrase beginning with the participle *following*)
God's people, <u>upheld by His divine power</u>, can live above sin.
(phrase beginning with the participle *upheld*)

c. An infinitive phrase contains a basic verb form preceded by *to* and is used as a noun, an adjective, or an adverb.

(1) When used as a noun, an infinitive phrase must name an action and fill a noun function in the sentence.

"I have not shunned <u>to declare unto you all the counsel of God</u>."
(phrase beginning with the infinitive *to declare* is the direct object of *have shunned*)
"The fear of the LORD is <u>to hate evil</u>."
(phrase beginning with the infinitive *to hate* is the predicate nominative renaming *fear*)

(2) When used as an adjective, an infinitive phrase immediately follows the substantive it modifies and usually answers the question *which* or *what kind of.*

There is a time <u>to keep silence</u> and a time <u>to speak</u>.
(both phrases tell *what kind of* about *time*)

(3) When used as an adverb, an infinitive phrase may modify a verb or verbal, an adjective, or another adverb. An infinitive phrase that modifies a verb or verbal almost always tells *why.* One that modifies an adjective or adverb immediately follows the word it modifies. Usually it tells *to what degree* or *how;* sometimes it does not answer any specific question but obviously adds to the meaning of an adjective or an adverb.

"He departed into a mountain <u>to pray</u>."
(tells *why* about the verb *departed*)
Striving <u>to overcome temptation</u> dare not replace dependence on the Lord.
(tells *why* about the verbal *Striving*)
"No man is able <u>to pluck them out of my Father's hand</u>."
(answers no specific question, but adds to the meaning of the predicate adjective *able*)
We pass through life too quickly <u>to learn everything by experience</u>.
(tells *to what degree* about *too quickly*)

3. A *phrase of a single part of speech* contains several nouns or verbs working together as a unit.

<u>Brother Melvin Schrock</u> <u>has moved</u> to <u>Path Valley</u>.

Clauses

A *clause* is a group of related words that contains a skeleton.

1. An *independent clause* expresses a complete thought and can stand alone as a sentence. Actually, every simple sentence is an independent clause, but this term is generally used only when a sentence has more than one clause.

> The <u>Almighty rules</u> over all.
>   (simple sentence: independent clause)
> The <u>Almighty rules</u> over all, yet <u>man</u> often <u>rebels</u> against Him.
>   (compound sentence: two independent clauses)
> Though <u>man</u> often <u>rebels</u> against Him, the <u>Almighty rules</u> over all.
>   (complex sentence: first clause is dependent; second is independent)

2. A *dependent clause* does not express a complete thought but must function within an independent clause. It may function as a noun, an adjective, or an adverb.

> <u>What the Bible says about a subject</u> is always right.
>   (dependent noun clause functioning as the subject)
> The person <u>who obeys the Bible</u> enjoys sure guidance in life.
>   (dependent adjective clause modifying *person*)
> <u>Because the Bible is God's Word</u>, we.reverence it highly.
>   (dependent adverb clause modifying *reverence*)

Applying the Lesson

A. Label each underlined phrase *prep.* (prepositional), *vb.* (verbal), or *ps.* (single part of speech). Also write the abbreviation for the part of speech that each one is.
1. Respect ^a<u>for authority</u> ^b<u>does preserve</u> youth ^c<u>from many dangers</u>.
2. ^a<u>To truly respect others</u> requires a commitment ^b<u>to reverence the Lord</u> and to remove all selfishness ^c<u>from the heart</u>.
3. ^a<u>To please the Lord</u>, we must seek ^b<u>to get along well with others</u>.
4. A person ^a<u>living under God's blessing</u> must be kind ^b<u>to all</u>.
5. ^a<u>Beyond the creek</u> is out of bounds because that land belongs to ^b<u>Morton Lee Pierce</u>.
6. ^a<u>To cheer Mrs. Troy</u>, the ^b<u>Roseview Mennonite School</u> made a scrapbook.
7. The Belgian horses ^a<u>hitched to the sleigh</u> became familiar with the trails ^b<u>in this sugar bush</u> ^c<u>in a very short time</u>.
8. ^a<u>Up this steep hill</u> is where we usually start ^b<u>gathering sap</u>.
9. ^a<u>Producing one gallon of maple syrup</u> requires gathering thirty gallons of sap ^b<u>to be evaporated</u>.
10. ^a<u>For good quality syrup</u>, the evaporation ^b<u>of the sap</u> must be done as quickly as possible.

B. Label each underlined clause *I* (independent) or *D* (dependent). If the clause is dependent, also label its part of speech.
1. "Let us therefore follow after the things <u>which make for peace</u>."
2. "<u>Whatsoever things were written aforetime</u> were written for our learning."

3. "If any man defile the temple of God, him shall God destroy."
4. "All things are lawful for me, but all things are not expedient."
5. "By the grace of God I am what I am."
6. "Now hath God set the members… in the body, as it hath pleased him."
7. "Knowledge puffeth up, but charity edifieth."
8. "His grace which was bestowed upon me was not in vain."

C. Label each underlined word group *phrase* or *clause*. Also label its part of speech.
1. True horns, ᵃfound on many ruminants, ᵇare made mostly of skin cells.
2. ᵃWhat a rhinoceros grows is not a true horn, for it consists of hair cells ᵇcemented together.
3. ᵃAlthough they may look like horns, full-grown antlers are bony structures ᵇwith no skin cells.
4. ᵃAlthough few animals shed horns, the pronghorn antelope, ᵇwhich lives in western North America, does so.
5. ᵃIn the spring, deer grow new antlers, ᵇwhich are made of bone.
6. We ᵃare planning to eat lunch in sight of ᵇTaughannock Falls.
7. A sign ᵃnear the lookout point stated ᵇthat the height of the falls is 215 feet.
8. ᵃTo attract a greater variety of birds, we hung out several feeders ᵇfilled with different kinds of bird seed.
9. ᵃTo record the different bird species at the feeders can be quite interesting ᵇas a family project.
10. The youth ᵃwho desires God's blessing throughout life must determine ᵇthat he will follow the noblest and best.
11. ᵃChoosing the noblest often requires ᵇthat one distinguishes between the merely acceptable and the best.
12. ᵃSettling for the mediocre can become a course ᵇof gradual decline.

Review Exercises

A. Copy each underlined complement, and label it *PN, PA, DO, IO,* or *OC.* [17]
1. People around the world find wheat an important part of their diet.
2. Throughout the year, one country or another is always harvesting wheat.
3. In January, farmers of Argentina and Australia are busy bringing in their wheat crop.
4. March and April are harvest months for India.
5. So things continue through the year as God gives the world this staff of life.

B. Label each underlined complement *DO ret., IO ret.,* or *OC ret.* [18]
1. Souls are made free by the truth of the Word.
2. Timothy was taught the Scriptures by his faithful mother.
3. A godly example is given us by the life of Stephen.
4. The Samaritans were considered dogs by the Jews of Jesus' day.
5. The woman at the well was offered living water by Jesus.

21. Appositives and Independent Elements

Appositives

An *appositive* is a substantive that identifies or explains another substantive. The appositive may be a substantive standing alone, or it may be a phrase that includes adjective modifiers. An appositive usually follows the substantive that it explains, but sometimes it precedes the other substantive.

> The prophet <u>Samuel</u> filled an important role in Israel's history.
> (The appositive *Samuel* identifies *prophet*.)
> Samuel, <u>a mighty prophet of the Lord</u>, filled an important role in Israel's history. (The appositive *a mighty prophet of the Lord* further explains *Samuel*.)
> <u>A mighty prophet of the Lord</u>, Samuel filled an important role in Israel's history. (The appositive precedes the substantive that it explains.)

1. A *nonrestrictive appositive* merely gives additional information about a substantive, and it is set off by commas. In the example sentences above, the second and third ones contain nonrestrictive appositives.

2. A *restrictive appositive* restricts the meaning of a substantive, and it is not set off by commas. Most restrictive appositives consist of only one or two words. In the examples above, the first sentence contains a restrictive appositive.

Independent Elements

An *independent element* is a word or word group that is not grammatically related to the rest of the sentence. Usually it is set off with commas or other punctuation.

1. A *noun of direct address* names the person or thing to whom one is speaking. It may be a single noun or a noun with modifiers.

> <u>Sarah</u>, a letter has arrived for you.
> "Hear thou, <u>my son</u>, and be wise, and guide thine heart in the way."

2. An *expletive* introduces a sentence without adding to its meaning. The two words used as expletives are *it* and *there*. You can usually reword the sentence to omit these expletives.

a. *It* is an expletive when not used as a normal pronoun. When used as a normal pronoun, *it* has an antecedent. When used as an expletive, *it* has no antecedent.

> <u>It</u> seems strange to see snow this early in the fall.
> (*It* merely introduces. The sentence can be reworded without *It:* To see snow this early in the fall seems strange.)
> <u>It</u> soon melted in the October sun.
> (*It* is the subject; the antecedent is the noun *snow* in the previous sentence. The sentence cannot be reworded without *It.*)

b. *There* is an expletive when not used as an adverb telling *where*.

> There are some ripe strawberries in the patch.
> (*There* merely introduces. The sentence can be reworded without *There:* Some ripe strawberries are in the patch.)
> There are the bowls for you children.
> (*There* is an adverb telling *where*. The sentence cannot be reworded without *There*.)

3. An *exclamation or interjection* expresses strong feeling. A few such terms are acceptable, but using them too freely can be a bad habit that mars godly speech. A mild interjection is followed by a comma; an interjection said with strong feeling is followed by an exclamation point, and the next word is capitalized.

> Well, we could not find many ripe strawberries after all.
> What! Are the birds eating them?

4. A *response* such as *yes* or *no* is sometimes used to introduce a sentence.

5. A *parenthetical expression* is a phrase such as *I believe, for example, in contrast,* or *we know.*

> Helen, I believe, saw a turtle in the patch yesterday.

6. A *nominative absolute* is an introductory phrase consisting of a substantive and a participle. Such a phrase is related to the thought of the sentence but is not grammatically tied to it. That is, a nominative absolute does not serve as a subject, an object, a modifier, or any other sentence part.

> The first bell having rung, we headed for our seats.
> (substantive *bell* + participle *having rung*)
> The sun growing quite warm, we exchanged our coats for sweaters.
> (substantive *sun* + participle *growing*)
> My chores being finished, I went to find Marcus.
> (substantive *chores* + participle *being finished*)
> My chores finished, I went to find Marcus.
> (The word *being* is often omitted from a nominative absolute.)

A nominative absolute can easily be changed to a subordinate clause, and sometimes this should be done for the clearest, most direct communication. However, the occasional use of carefully written nominative absolutes can add a special appeal to your writing. The following sentences show how the examples above can be rewritten with subordinate clauses.

> When the first bell had rung, we headed for our seats.
> Because the sun grew quite warm, we exchanged our coats for sweaters.
> When my chores were finished, I went to find Marcus.

Distinguish carefully between nominative absolutes and participial phrases. A *nominative* absolute begins with a *nominative,* but a *participial* phrase begins with a *participle.*

> <u>My chores finished</u>, I went to find Marcus.
> (nominative absolute)
> <u>Having finished my chores</u>, I went to find Marcus.
> (participial phrase modifying the subject)

A nominative absolute does not always come at the beginning of a sentence. It can also be a convenient way to add details at the end of a sentence.

> We dashed pell-mell for the house, <u>rain pouring on us, lightning flashing around us, and thunder booming in our ears</u>.

7. A *repeated word* may be used for emphasis or for poetic effect. This may be the repetition of the same word or of a word that names the same person or thing.

> <u>Loud</u>! It was so loud that we did not even try to talk.
> (*Loud* is repeated for emphasis.)
> "<u>The LORD</u>, he is the God." (*The LORD* names the same person as *he*.)

Do not confuse this repetition with an improper expression like "James he helped me today." Careless repetition of that kind merely adds clutter to a sentence. Proper repetition is deliberately planned, and it has an appealing literary effect.

Applying the Lesson

A. Copy each appositive, and label it *R* for restrictive or *N* for nonrestrictive. Commas have been omitted.
1. Character the inner core of a person's being strongly influences his reputation.
2. A man of a gracious disposition Barnabas introduced the apostle Paul to the believers at Jerusalem.
3. Nineveh the capital of the Assyrian Empire was ready to receive the message preached by the prophet Jonah.
4. The patriarch Abraham rescued Lot the nephew whom he had raised.
5. The song "I'm Pressing on the Upward Way" is one of my favorites.
6. The planet Mercury is the closest planet to the sun the center of the solar system.
7. My uncle Lamar planted this tree a silver maple when he was a boy.
8. I planned to write a report on the book *The Anabaptist Story*.

B. Copy each independent element. Include enough words to show any needed capitalization or punctuation.
1. Yes you surely made Aunt Matilda happy Lucinda with your card.
2. The guests having arrived we sat down to the meal and found it to be sure quite delicious.
3. There was nothing fancy about the meal, but it was attractive.
4. What who would have expected this much snow in October?
5. Those lovely roses how they fill the room with fragrance.
6. The geese it seems are migrating very early this fall.
7. Steam rolling from under the hood Father quickly pulled off the road.
8. The stars they shine so brilliantly tonight!

9. There is a stray dog I believe on Mr. Mackay's front porch.
10. No you have not given the heifers enough hay Stanley.
11. Well you must remember for example to plan ahead for long-term assignments.
12. Oh I forgot to copy the last row of problems.
13. Amazing how could he crawl to the truck after he had broken both legs?
14. Father will try hard no doubt to finish the hay this week the weather permitting.

C. For sentences 1–6, write whether the underlined part is a *nominative absolute,* a *participial phrase,* or a *dependent clause.* Rewrite sentences 7–10, changing each underlined part to a nominative absolute.

1. <u>Supper being ended,</u> Jesus arose and laid aside His garments.
2. <u>Having poured water into a basin,</u> He began to wash the disciples' feet.
3. <u>Jesus coming to Peter,</u> that disciple objected strongly to letting Jesus wash his feet.
4. Jesus said that Peter could have no part with Him <u>if he was not washed.</u>
5. <u>Peter hearing that,</u> he wanted Jesus to wash his hands and his head too.
6. Jesus said that one who is washed needs only to wash his feet, <u>the rest of his body being already clean.</u>
7. <u>After our preparations were finished,</u> we started on our journey.
8. <u>Because the traffic was heavy,</u> Father needed to drive with extra caution.
9. An ambulance approached from behind <u>while its lights flashed and its siren wailed.</u>
10. <u>When Father saw the ambulance,</u> he pulled over to let it pass.

Review Exercises

A. Write *true* or *false* for each sentence. [9, 10]
1. Respect for others improves our listening.
2. It is discourteous to let our minds wander when someone is speaking to us.
3. A lack of interest will make us poor listeners.
4. Nearly everyone has something worthwhile to tell us.
5. Good listening requires skills that we must learn.

B. Write the six key words that help us remember the six basic listening skills. (Remember, these words start with the letters *A–F.*)

---

22. Classes of Sentences

Classes According to Use

1. *A declarative sentence makes a statement and ends with a period.*

God is almighty.
Man was made in the image of God.

2. *An interrogative sentence asks a question and ends with a question mark.* The subject often follows the verb or comes between two parts of the verb phrase.

Have you finished your assignments?

3. *An imperative sentence gives a command or request and generally ends with a period.* The subject is always *you,* and it is usually understood rather than directly stated. Sentences with helping verbs like *shall, should,* or *must* may appear to be imperative; however, the verb in an imperative sentence never includes a helping verb.

Lord, guide me in the right way.
    (imperative; makes a request)
Every Christian must follow the right way.
    (declarative; makes a statement)

4. *An exclamatory sentence expresses strong feeling or emotion and ends with an exclamation point.* It may simply be one of the other three sentence types expressed forcefully and punctuated as an exclamation.

The cows are out!   Come quickly!

Many exclamatory sentences have a special word order. The skeleton may come at the end of the sentence so that a word like *what* or *how* can come first. Or the sentence may have the form of a dependent clause that would be a fragment if it were not exclamatory.

What a surprise you have given us!
If only I had listened to Mother's advice!

Classes According to Structure

1. *A simple sentence contains one independent clause.* Although it may have compound parts, it has only one skeleton.

Every day <u>we should read</u> the Bible and <u>pray</u>.

2. *A compound sentence contains two or more independent clauses.*

<u>We</u> <u>sang</u> several songs, and then <u>Father</u> <u>read</u> from Matthew 5.

3. *A complex sentence contains one independent clause and one or more dependent clauses.*

After <u>we</u> <u>had discussed</u> the Bible passage, <u>Father</u> <u>led</u> us in prayer.

4. *A compound-complex sentence contains at least two independent clauses and at least one dependent clause.*

<u>We</u> <u>were inspired</u> by Father's prayer, <u>which</u> <u>included</u> the mention of each person, and those <u>petitions</u> <u>lingered</u> with us through the day.

Classes According to Word Order

1. *In natural word order, the complete subject precedes the complete predicate.* This is the most common word order, which we use most naturally in forming sentences.

   A mighty tempest raged on the Sea of Galilee.

2. *In inverted word order, the complete predicate precedes the complete subject.* Do not separate these two sentence parts with a comma.

   On the Sea of Galilee raged a mighty tempest.

3. *In mixed word order, the complete subject comes between two parts of the complete predicate.* A comma often precedes the complete subject, especially if an adverb clause or a long adverb phrase begins the sentence. (The whole adverb clause is considered part of the predicate.)

   On the Sea of Galilee, a mighty tempest raged.
   When Jesus spoke, the tempest ceased.

Classes According to Style

1. *A loose sentence gives the main idea first and the details later.* Often such a sentence could end at various points, and the thought would still be complete. The following loose sentence could end after any of the underlined words.

   We should do our best and not be easily discouraged by any difficulty that we may meet along the way.

   Since loose sentences are the simplest kind to understand, most of your spoken sentences are naturally of this style. Most of your written sentences should also be of the loose variety.

2. *A periodic sentence gives the details first and saves the main idea until the end of the sentence.* A person must read to the *period* in order to get the main idea. Because the reader must wait, this sentence style helps to impress the main idea forcefully on his mind. Compare the following sentences with the example above. Do you see the increasing emphasis on the main idea?

   In spite of any difficulty, we should do our best.
   In spite of any difficulty that we may meet along the way, we should do our best.

   An inverted sentence is often short, but you must still read to the end before you get the main idea. So the inverted sentence is also periodic.

   Close beside the road stood a great oak tree.

   Used occasionally, periodic sentences can effectively emphasize key ideas in a paragraph. But too many periodic sentences will make a paragraph sound unnatural.

3. *A balanced sentence has two well-matched clauses.* One kind of balanced sentence has clauses beginning with words like "the more... the more" or "the sooner... the better." Another kind uses a slight change of wording to produce a notable or

unexpected contrast. Because of its unusual structure, a balanced sentence gives strong emphasis to the idea in focus.

> The older we grow, the wiser we should become.
> God does not call the fit; He fits the called.
> If private prayers were more sincere, public prayers would be more spontaneous.

Note the exchanging of *call* and *fit* in the second sentence. This is an example of rearranging the words to produce a striking, memorable statement. Such a sentence stands out because of its unusual structure; not many expressions can be reworded in this way. Therefore, the balanced sentence is the least common of the three sentence styles.

Changing the *style* of a sentence may have the same result as changing the *word order* of the sentence. Study the following examples.

> We need not fear man if God is with us.
> (natural word order; loose sentence)
> If God is with us, we need not fear man.
> (mixed word order; periodic sentence)

Why is the change classified in two different ways? Word order deals mainly with the mechanical arrangement of words in sentences. Its primary concern is whether the subject comes at the beginning, in the middle, or at the end. Style has more to do with the "spirit" of a sentence. Its primary concern is how the message of a sentence is affected by different word arrangements.

Applying the Lesson

A. Label each sentence according to its use (*dec., int., imp., exc.*) and its structure (*S, CD, CX, CD-CX*). End punctuation has been omitted.
  1. Guard your heart at all times
  2. Your thoughts and attitudes, which are hidden from human sight, do express themselves openly
  3. Do your words and actions reveal a godly mind, or do they suggest a love for this world
  4. How necessary it is to guard our lives diligently, yet how careless many people are
  5. When we live consistently, we maintain a clear testimony, and our lives can point others to the Lord
  6. Always seek God's blessing upon your life
  7. Live faithfully so that people can depend on you even though others fail
  8. You must first do what is right, and then you should seek to please others
  9. If we live to please God, what liberty we have
  10. Can any joy surpass that which the saints will know in heaven

B. Label the word order of each sentence *N* (natural), *I* (inverted), or *M* (mixed).
  1. Over the whole valley lay a thick mist.
  2. In the distance a panther's scream pierced the black night.
  3. A screech owl's eerie call startled us.

4. Over the wide stream bounded the frightened buck.
5. Although the skunk is not strong, he does have a powerful weapon.
6. A porcupine's weapon is quite effective too.
7. All night the friendly beams of the full moon fell upon the trail.
8. Before morning dawned, the weary refugees had reached safety.

C. Label the style of each sentence *L* (loose), *P* (periodic), or *B* (balanced).
   1. When one person has courage to stand for truth and right, others often stand with him.
   2. In spite of the failures and wrong choices of other people, you can always stand for the right.
   3. The closer you walk with Christ, the farther you will stay from temptation.
   4. God blesses the trusting heart with the assurance of His presence and His power.
   5. Reformation is turning over a new leaf; regeneration is receiving a new life.
   6. If everything seems to go wrong, do not forget to pray.
   7. Right choices set a safe course for us in this life and in eternity.
   8. It is easy to tell one lie; it is hard to tell just one lie.
   9. Though temptations may seem so severe that they seem impossible to resist, by God's grace you can overcome them.
   10. God cannot have His way when we are in the way.

D. Rewrite sentences 1–4 in mixed order and 5–8 in inverted order.
   1. We will never lose the way if we stay close to the Lord.
   2. We can find direction for every circumstance in the Bible.
   3. Those who seek happiness for themselves generally cannot find it.
   4. We find joy for ourselves if we make others happy.
   5. A vicious dog stood by the front door.
   6. The frightened squirrel scampered up the tree.
   7. The refreshing rain falls softly.
   8. The blazing sun marched westward.

E. Rewrite sentences 1–4 in the periodic style. In each of sentences 5–8, copy and complete the second clause to make a balanced sentence.
   1. Sleep was very welcome after a long, hard day of making hay.
   2. The engine suddenly sputtered and died as we were driving along a lonely stretch of road west of Prince George.
   3. We found the missing papers behind a stack of boxes in the corner of the attic.
   4. We were selling over fifty dozen ears a day during the peak of the sweet corn harvest.
   5. The atheist thinks that God is nowhere; the Christian knows that God…
   6. Faith without works is dead;… are useless.
   7. The more we concentrate on others' faults, the less we correct…
   8. The more highly we think of God, the less…

Review Exercises

Label each underlined item *nominative absolute* or *participial phrase.* [21]

1. His decision made, John immediately set to work.
2. All the cars stopped, a traffic light having turned red.
3. Brooding over your troubles, you can be confident of a successful hatch.
4. Our picnic being interrupted, we sat inside and enjoyed the refreshing rain.
5. I always like to see the cider running from the press.

---

23. Improving Your Editing Skills, Part 3

With the basic proofreading symbols that you have learned, you can mark most of the corrections commonly needed in manuscripts. However, you will soon encounter some situations where you are not sure exactly how to mark the changes. Consider the following example. Which is the best way to show the inserted dash?

```
On a tightrope over Niagara Falls^but I cannot tell you now.

On a tightrope over Niagara Falls-but I cannot tell you now.

On a tightrope over Niagara Falls^but I cannot tell you now.
```

We could use any of these ways, but we will understand one another's work more easily if we all follow the same pattern. This proofreading lesson and the next one show some specific patterns for using several of the proofreading marks. These patterns are the ones you should use throughout this course.

Marks Used in Editing and Proofreading

V or ^ insert (caret)	delete	.... stet (let it stand)	use italics
¶ begin new paragraph	no ¶ no new paragraph	lc change to lowercase (small letter)	uc change to uppercase (capital letter)
# insert space	delete space	← move (arrow)	transpose

Explanations	**Sample Manuscript**

Ellipsis points, like periods and commas, are inserted by writing them below the caret. All other punctuation is written above the caret.

Speaking of the Lord's tender care for His people, Isaiah declared, "He shall gather the lambs with his arm, and carry them in his bosom (Isaiah 40:11) Do we realize how important this is?

If there is room, these other marks may be written where they would normally go. If not, they must be written in the space above the words.

A certain farmer had an unusually fine flock of sheep. After admiring the beautiful creatures, a friend asked him this question:

Loop for delete symbol may curve up or down. Curving down often works well when deleting punctuation.

"How do you manage to raise such fine animals"

He simply said, "I take very good care of the lambs."

Inserted dash must be long enough to distinguish it from a hyphen.

God, in His wisdom, knows of the importance of giving special care care to the young.

Therefore, we rest assured of His attention— and even special interest on our behalf.

Editing Practice

A. Use proofreading marks to add the missing punctuation. In each sentence, one mark will go above the caret and one below.

1. On June 30 1859, Jean-François Gravelet (a Frenchman crossed the Niagara gorge on a tightrope.

2. He performed several stunts as he crossed lying on the rope, fishing a bottle from a boat below and doing a backward somersault.

3. Soon he was crossing the rope weekly and—to draw larger crowds of onlookers he regularly added new stunts.

4. He stood on his head, pushed a wheelbarrow, and rode a bicycle and one day he even cooked an omelet on a small stove

5. On August 17, 1859, he took a 136-pound man on his back and carried him across the rope however, I can't imagine

B. Use proofreading marks to insert one hyphen or dash and to make one deletion in each sentence. Make the loop curve down for at least two of your deletions.

1. More than seventy five years ago, Theodore Roosevelt said, said, "The most important single ingredient in the formula of success is knowing how to get along with people."

2. No one is as well able to do this as the persons who has made peace with God our loving, sovereign Creator.

3. Peace in the heart—a priceless possession preppares one to live in peace with his fellow man.

4. The time proven instructions of Jesus' Sermon on the Mounts, have guided Christians unerringly for years.

5. No rule of human relationships will ever will ever surpass the Golden Rule treating others as we would be treated.

6. He who fails to get along with the people around him suffers many self inflicted wounds..

C. Use proofreading marks to correct the fifteen errors in these paragraphs. No line contains more than one error.

1.   Iguaçú falls is located near the meeting point of three
2. South American countries: Brazil, Paraguay and Argentina.
3. This waterfall does not consist of one solid cascade,
4. rather, about 275 cascades pore over the precipice.
5. Intermingled with these cascades are many islands of
6. tropical forests. Surrounded by national parks, the falls
7. are open to the public but are not highly comercialized.
8.   With a hieght of only 237 feet (72 meters), this water-
9. fall is much more lower than Angel Falls in Venezuela, the
10. highest of all falls. Streching about 2 miles (3 kilometers)
11. from edge to edge, however, Iguaçú Falls is the widest
12. set of falls in world.
13.   If you visit the falls late in the day, you may see one
14. of most the amazing sights. Arriving at dusk, thousands of

15. swifts fly through the mist and rain bows to nest on rocky

16.   ledges behind the plunging water. Some of these birds

17. circle around the edges of the cataracts. Others zipp

18. through momentary breaksin the falls. Certainly, the

19. majestic Iguaçú Falls was made by a super natural Creator.

24. Chapter 3 Review

A. Write the words immediately before and after each mistake in this dialogue, and show how to join or divide the sentences correctly. Do not change elliptical sentences.
   1. "Can you recite by memory the Lord's Prayer? Found in Matthew 6?" asked Brother Abel.
   2. "Of course. Everyone knows that prayer, it's one of the most familiar passages in the Bible," I replied.
   3. "Maybe so. But do you actually think about the words? When you pray them?"
   4. "I know what you mean. It's easy to rush through the words. And never really pray at all."
   5. "That's right. We must concentrate on the meaning of the words, it will then be a meaningful prayer."

B. Copy the simple subject and the simple predicate of each sentence. Draw a vertical line between the two parts.
   1. The tendency to talk uncharitably about others is quite common.
   2. Though often unrecognized, the root of such talk can always be traced to pride.

3. From a humble heart come gracious words.

4. How could a truly humble person possibly belittle others or exalt himself by his speech?

5. Comments designed to make another look foolish or statements intended to insult another must be recognized as sinful.

C. Copy each complement, and label it *PN, PA, DO, IO,* or *OC.*

1. Jesus healed many sick and gave many demoniacs true liberty.

2. The common people were glad to hear Him, but many of the Jewish rulers became His bitter enemies.

3. Jesus considered every person an object of His love.

4. Jesus' cross gives you and me a glimpse of sin's awfulness.

5. Sin made the Saviour's sufferings necessary.

D. Copy each retained object, and label it *DO ret., IO ret.,* or *OC ret.*

1. Those cows are fed this older hay.

2. Several beautiful scrapbooks were given Grandmother during her illness.

3. The ground was quickly made white by the falling snow.

4. A very interesting letter was sent us by Aunt Jennifer.

E. Copy the appositives, and label them *R* (restrictive) or *N* (nonrestrictive). Commas have been omitted.

1. This book a gift from Grandfather Friesen contains the story "Roy's Goat."

2. My cousin Edna works for Hoover Foods a bulk food store and produce market.

3. Mr. Bentley still drives the first car he bought a 1948 Packard sedan.

F. Copy each independent element, and add any missing punctuation that is needed after it. Also write correctly any other word with which there is an error in capitalization or punctuation.

1. Help me Lord to do Thy will.

2. Hallelujah the Lord has answered our prayers.

3. Our hearts filled with praise every person I believe thoroughly enjoyed the song service.

4. Yes there is great joy in serving the Lord.

5. Our Saviour what blessing He brought to the world!

G. Label each underlined word group *prep.* (prepositional phrase), *vb.* (verbal phrase), *ps.* (phrase of a single part of speech), *D* (dependent clause), or *I* (independent clause). Also label the part of speech that each phrase or dependent clause is.

1. ^a<u>Before the frosts kill the stalks</u>, we try ^b<u>to harvest all the tomatoes</u>.

2. Green tomatoes ^a<u>that are properly handled and stored</u> will ripen ^b<u>after the frost</u>.

3. ^a<u>Eating green tomatoes</u> may sound unappealing to you, yet ^b<u>they can be used in many ways</u>.

4. The elderly couple ^a<u>across the road</u> said ^b<u>that they would like some green tomatoes</u> ^c<u>in the fall</u>.

5. ^a<u>To accommodate their request</u>, we are saving a basketful to give them ^b<u>on Mr.</u>
<u>Wolf's birthday</u>.
6. The tomatoes ^a<u>to take to Grandfather</u> are in those boxes ^b<u>with handles</u>.
7. These stalks, ^a<u>wilted by the frost</u>, ^b<u>should be tilled</u> into the soil.
8. ^a<u>Ernest Zook</u>, ^b<u>who works for Father</u>, is gathering up stakes.

H. Label each sentence according to its use (*dec., int., imp., exc.*) and its structure
(*S, CD, CX, CD-CX*). End punctuation has been omitted.
1. Although many people can quote the Golden Rule, few practice it daily
2. How very hard it is to truly put others first at all times
3. Do you merely know this verse, or do you strive to live it
4. If you think of others, your own life will grow richer, and you will please the
Lord
5. Do not think first about yourself, but live for others' good

I. Label the word order of each sentence *N* (natural), *I* (inverted), or *M* (mixed).
1. Through our back yard walked a skunk family.
2. Bowser was sleeping on the front porch.
3. Because he was upwind from them, he never knew they were near.
4. Thankfully, we never saw them again around the house.
5. In the back woods live quite a few skunks.

J. Label the style of each sentence *L* (loose), *P* (periodic), or *B* (balanced).
1. The more we have others' needs on our hearts, the less we will have their
faults on our tongues.
2. If you are tempted to gossip about another, pray for him.
3. Sincere intercession would stop all gossip because it casts faults in a different
light and it banishes pride and selfishness, which feed gossip.
4. A gossip is likely to harm another's reputation, but he is certain to harm his
own character.
5. In the heart that is filled with God's love is no room for a gossiping spirit.

K. Rewrite these sentences according to the directions in parentheses.
1. We can conquer every foe if we trust in the Lord. (Change to mixed word order.)
2. God's gracious love shines all around us. (Change to inverted word order.)
3. God upholds His own even in the most intense temptations and in the most
severe trials. (Change to periodic style.)
4. Christians cannot bring the whole world to Jesus, but they can spread the
Gospel. (Rewrite the second clause to make a balanced sentence.)
5. As truth is dearer to our hearts, it is clearer in our minds. (Change to a balanced
sentence beginning with "The dearer truth is…")

L. Write two exact words or phrases that could replace each underlined expression.
1. We need to develop <u>good character qualities</u>.
2. Character qualities are more important than <u>physical qualities</u>.

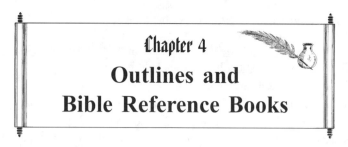

Chapter 4

Outlines and
Bible Reference Books

25. Outlining Written Material

Outlining is a valuable skill. It helps a speaker or writer to organize the material he is to present. It helps a listener or reader to comprehend the material he hears or reads.

The Form and Content of an Outline

An outline is an orderly summary of something spoken or written. It shows the title, the main topics, the subtopics, the points, and so forth. An outline may consist of a paragraph summary for each idea, though that is not common. Some outlines have complete sentences to express each idea. Most outlines are topical, with a word or phrase to express each point.

Study this topical outline, which illustrates the rules of outline form given below it.

Barnabas, "The Son of Consolation" (Acts 4:36)

I. The strength of his character
  A. Generosity (4:36, 37)
    1. Ready to share with others' needs
    2. Unpretentious in giving
  B. Vision
    1. Saw potential in Saul (9:27)
    2. Saw the reality of the work at Antioch (11:23)
    3. Saw his own limitation (11:25)
  C. Humility
    1. Was probably older than the apostle Paul
    2. Gave recognition to Paul
      a. Stood by Paul when others doubted his conversion (9:26, 27)
      b. Consulted with Paul as an equal (11:25, 26)
      c. Followed Paul as a helper (13:45–50; 14:12)
  D. Trustworthiness (11:29, 30)
II. The secret of his character (11:24)
  A. Filled with the Spirit
  B. Filled with faith

The form and structure of an outline follow a definite pattern. Notice how the sample outline above illustrates these rules.

1. Center the title above the outline.

2. Begin each line with a capital letter.
3. Indent each level equally.
4. Indent each level farther right than the previous level.
5. Put a period after each numeral or letter that marks an item. After you have used periods with *I* and *a* to mark points and subpoints, use parentheses with *I* and *a* if there are further details. On the outline above, details under "Followed Paul as a helper" would be marked *(1)* and *(2)*. And if those items also had details, they would be marked *(a)* and *(b)*.
6. Have at least two parts when subordinate points come under an item. If there is only one subordinate point, include it with the item above it.
7. Use either all paragraphs, all sentences, or all topics.
8. Use proper end punctuation with paragraph and sentence outlines. Omit end punctuation with topical outlines.
9. Use a logical progression from the beginning to the end of the outline.
10. Use headings that do not overlap in thought.
11. On a topical outline, keep the items of each level as nearly parallel as possible.

In relation to Rule 10, consider the first outline below. Some of the main topics overlap because respect for authority includes respect for parents and church leaders. The second and third items should be subordinate to "Respect for authority," as shown on the second outline.

Poor: Headings overlap
Attitudes for Godly Youth
I. Respect for authority
II. Respect for parents
III. Respect for church leaders
IV. Unselfishness

Better: Headings restructured
Attitudes for Godly Youth
I. Respect for authority
   A. Parents
   B. Church leaders
II. Unselfishness

Items that are parallel (Rule 11) are items with a basic similarity. All the items should begin with the same part of speech and be generally similar in structure. Compare the following examples.

Poor: Unparallel items
Examples of Godly Youth
I. Joseph
   A. At home
   B. When he was in Egypt
II. By Naaman's maid

Better: Parallel items
Examples of Godly Youth
I. Joseph
   A. At home
   B. In Egypt
II. Naaman's maid

On the second outline, *Joseph* and *Naaman's maid* are not perfectly parallel. But little can be done about this, since the maid's name is unknown. The outline is acceptable because these two items are as closely parallel as possible.

Outlining as a Study Aid

Outlining is an effective study aid. The very process of outlining requires you to analyze the material you are reading. You must identify the main ideas and the lesser ideas. You must consider how the various details relate to each other. Writing an accurate, thorough outline requires diligent effort and study.

An outline continues to be a valuable aid long after you have completed it. The concentration that went into making the outline impresses the details more deeply upon your mind than if you had merely read the material. The outline also provides a good source for quick review. You can usually pick out main ideas and specific details more quickly on your outline than in your book.

Here are three steps to follow in outlining a lesson.

1. *Skim the lesson to get a bird's-eye view of the main idea.* Pay special attention to the opening and the ending paragraphs of the lesson; they often introduce or summarize the main thought. Read all the main headings, boldfaced or italicized words, and lists.

2. *Read the lesson carefully, noting the major divisions.* If the lesson has main headings, they generally serve as the main topics on your outline.

3. *Go through the lesson again, finding the significant details.*

Below is an example of a short science lesson, followed by pointers to direct you through the three steps.

Producing Simple Motion With Electricity

One of the simplest ways to put electricity to practical use is with electromagnets. Since electromagnets can be turned on and off easily, we use them in devices to produce motion that can be easily controlled.

The solenoid magnet is a very simple device that uses electricity to produce motion. A solenoid magnet consists of only two main parts: an electromagnet with a hollow center and a movable iron core.

The operation of the solenoid magnet is likewise quite simple. First an electric current activates the electromagnet. The newly formed magnetic field attracts the movable core. The moving core produces the desired result: striking a door chime, activating an electrical switch, or operating electric door locks.

Another simple device using electrically produced motion is the electric bell. Every electric bell has several basic parts. One part is an electromagnet, the central feature in any electrical device that produces motion. An electric bell also includes an armature with three parts: a clapper, a contact point, and a spring. In addition, the bell must have a stationary contact point and a gong.

The operation of an electric bell can be summarized in three steps. The first step is the same as in the solenoid magnet: an electric current activates the electromagnet. In the second step, the electromagnet attracts the armature. This movement of the armature does two things. The clapper at the end of the armature strikes the gong, producing the sound of the bell; and the contact point on the armature pulls away from the stationary contact point, deactivating the electromagnet. In the final step, the spring pulls the armature back to its starting position. This brings the contact points together and starts the cycle over again.

Step 1: Skimming the paragraphs will help you to identify the main idea being discussed. That idea is electrical devices that produce motion.

Step 2: By reading the paragraphs more carefully, you should recognize the major divisions. There are two: the solenoid magnet and the electric bell.

Step 3: Another reading will help you find the details to place on the outline. The final outline should be similar to the one below.

Producing Simple Motion With Electricity

I. The solenoid magnet
   A. Its parts
      1. An electromagnet with a hollow center
      2. A movable iron core
   B. Its operation
      1. Electric current activates electromagnet
      2. Magnetic field attracts movable core
      3. Movement produces desired result
         a. Striking door chime
         b. Activating electrical switch
         c. Operating electric door locks

II. The electric bell
   A. Its parts
      1. An electromagnet
      2. An armature
         a. A clapper
         b. A contact point
         c. A spring
      3. A stationary contact point
      4. A gong
   B. Its operation
      1. Electric current activates electromagnet
      2. Electromagnet attracts armature
         a. Clapper strikes gong, producing sound
         b. Contact point on armature pulls away from stationary contact point, deactivating electromagnet
      3. Spring pulls armature back to starting position
         a. Brings contact points together
         b. Starts cycle over again

Applying the Lesson

A. Improve this outline.

First Aid for Heat-related Emergencies

I. Heat stroke
   A. Symptoms
      1. Body temperature is 106°F or higher

      2. Skin is hot, red, and dry

      3. Pulse rate is increased

      4. Unconscious

    B. What treatment to give

      1. Immediate reduction of fever, by *one* of the following methods

        a. sponge bare skin with cool water or rubbing alcohol

        b. Applying cold packs continuously

        c. By placing the victim in tub of cool water

      2. Continue to treat

        a. Repeat one of above treatments

          (1) If body temperature rises again

        b. Use fan or air conditioner to keep victim cool

      3. Seek professional medical help

II. Treating heat exhaustion

    A. What the symptoms are

      1. Near normal body temperature

      2. pale, clammy skin

      3. Perspires profusely

      4. Extremely tired and weak

      5. Intense discomfort

        a. headache

        b. Nausea

        c. Dizzy

      6. Fainting is possible

    B. Treatment

      1. cool the victim

        a. By applying cool, wet cloths

        b. by loosening the victim's clothing

        c. Fan the victim or move him to an air-conditioned room

      2. Replenish victim's water and salt

        a. mix solution of 1 teaspoon salt to 1 glass of water

        b. Give victim one-half glass every 15 minutes

        c. You should repeat this over a period of about 1 hour.

      3. Victim should lie down with feet raised 8–12 inches

      4. give further advice

        a. victim should avoid high temperatures

        b. Victim should not return to work for several days.

B. Outline the composition below according to the following directions.

    1. The outline should have these two main topics.

      I. Reasons for maintaining wholesome speech

      II. Characteristics of wholesome speech

    2. The outline should have no more than four levels of headings: Roman numerals, capital letters, Arabic numerals, and small letters.

Wholesome Speech

Speech is a wonderful gift of God to mankind. Although many other creatures can communicate, only man can use words and sentences intelligently. With such a privilege also comes the challenge to use this gift in a God-honoring way.

There are two important reasons for maintaining wholesome speech. First, a person speaks "of the abundance of the heart." What he actually says will show what his mind dwells on and reveal what he appreciates. How he says his words also reveals what is in his heart. The tone of voice, whether sweet or sour, patient or exasperated, conveys his emotions. Oftentimes it exposes the true attitudes a person has toward others.

A second reason for maintaining wholesome speech is that a person is responsible to God for his speech. Jesus said that those who use degrading words like "Thou fool" are in danger of hell fire. He also declared that men will give account of "every idle word." Indeed, Jesus declared that a person's words in general will either justify or condemn him.

What are some characteristics of wholesome speech? One that is very important is integrity. A person shows integrity by speaking the truth at all times. This includes avoiding exaggeration, which is a distortion of truth. A person of integrity also shuns rumors because he does not know whether they are true or not.

Graciousness is another characteristic of wholesome speech. One shows graciousness by using polite expressions such as "Please," "Thank you," and "Excuse me." Being just as ready to compliment as to criticize shows the graciousness of wholesome speech. A gracious person also avoids gossip. By its very nature, gossip is ruinous and hurtful—quite the opposite of graciousness.

Reverence for God characterizes wholesome speech. A person shows this virtue by expressing faith in God. A reverent person does not complain about the weather, does not make presumptuous plans, and does not become fearful, discouraged, or bitter about circumstances. Refusing profanity also shows reverence for God. The use of vulgar, unclean language is one type of profanity. Another type is the careless use of God's name (including shortened and variant forms) or of words referring to His characteristics or His works. Reverence for God further reveals itself by avoiding the lighthearted use of sacred expressions such as "Hallelujah" or "Praise the Lord."

Yet another characteristic of wholesome speech is self-control. One obviously shows self-control by limiting how much he talks. God calls His people to "be swift to hear" and "slow to speak." Self-control also means rejecting slang, even though it is catchy and appealing. Further, a self-controlled person avoids interjections that show disgust or anger. Some people surely would not swear, yet

✸✸✸

Let your speech be alway with grace, seasoned with salt, . . .

Colossians 4:6

✸✸✸

they use words like *bother* and *rats* in the same spirit as if they were profane words. This is out of place for a Christian.

Wholesome speech is not merely something nice. It is something God expects and requires of His children. Our daily prayer should echo the psalmist's words: "Let the words of my mouth, and the meditation of my heart, be acceptable in thy sight, O Lᴏʀᴅ, my strength, and my redeemer" (Psalm 19:14).

Review Exercises

Write the numbers of the statements that you should follow when gathering information for an oral report. [11]

1. Choose a broad subject that holds definite interest to you.
2. Think about possible main ideas to develop even before you start gathering information.
3. Find information from several reference sources if possible.
4. Place all the information you find about a main topic on the same note card.
5. On every note card, write the name of the source from which the information comes.
6. Consider what visual aids you could use to make your report clearer.

---

26. Outlining a Bible Passage: Finding the Main Ideas

Christians often use outlining in their Bible study. Outlining skills serve well in preparing sermons, topics, and devotional meditations; in planning articles; and in studying a Bible passage for personal benefit.

An outline of a Bible passage highlights the main teachings, ideas, or events of that passage. Not every set of verses lends itself to outlining easily. But as you grow in Bible knowledge and in outlining skill, you should be able to make at least a general outline of almost any passage. You must also realize that most Bible passages can be outlined in more than one way, depending on the main idea to be emphasized. A given outline is not necessarily the only one that is correct.

This kind of Bible study is not something you can do in a few minutes. First, you must study the Bible passage thoroughly. Read it slowly and carefully several times to determine what primary truth it is teaching. Then read the passage several more times, with your mind focused on this primary truth.

To illustrate the formation of an outline for a Bible passage, we will use a familiar Scripture—part of the Sermon on the Mount. To begin, read these verses several times. Do not allow your familiarity with the passage to cause you to read without thinking. As you read, evaluate: What is the primary truth these verses are teaching?

Matthew 6:1–18

1 ¶ Take heed that ye do not your alms before men, to be seen of them: otherwise ye have no reward of your Father which is in heaven.

2 Therefore when thou doest thine alms, do not sound a trumpet before thee, as the hypocrites do in the synagogues and in the streets, that they may have glory of men. Verily I say unto you, They have their reward.

3 But when thou doest alms, let not thy left hand know what thy right hand doeth:

4 That thine alms may be in secret: and thy Father which seeth in secret himself shall reward thee openly.

5 ¶ And when thou prayest, thou shalt not be as the hypocrites are: for they love to pray standing in the synagogues and in the corners of the streets, that they may be seen of men. Verily I say unto you, They have their reward.

6 But thou, when thou prayest, enter into thy closet, and when thou hast shut thy door, pray to thy Father which is in secret; and thy Father which seeth in secret shall reward thee openly.

7 But when ye pray, use not vain repetitions, as the heathen do: for they think that they shall be heard for their much speaking.

8 Be not ye therefore like unto them: for your Father knoweth what things ye have need of, before ye ask him.

9 After this manner therefore pray ye: Our Father which art in heaven, Hallowed be thy name.

10 Thy kingdom come. Thy will be done in earth, as it is in heaven.

11 Give us this day our daily bread.

12 And forgive us our debts, as we forgive our debtors.

13 And lead us not into temptation, but deliver us from evil: For thine is the kingdom, and the power, and the glory, for ever. Amen.

14 For if ye forgive men their trespasses, your heavenly Father will also forgive you:

15 But if ye forgive not men their trespasses, neither will your Father forgive your trespasses.

16 ¶ Moreover when ye fast, be not, as the hypocrites, of a sad countenance: for they disfigure their faces, that they may appear unto men to fast. Verily I say unto you, They have their reward.

17 But thou, when thou fastest, anoint thine head, and wash thy face;

18 That thou appear not unto men to fast, but unto thy Father which is in secret: and thy Father, which seeth in secret, shall reward thee openly.

Have you identified the primary truth this passage teaches? It could be summarized like this: We must do religious deeds out of true devotion to the Lord and not merely for a show before men. And we could use this title: "Instruction on True Devotion."

After you have determined what primary truth a passage teaches, you are ready to identify the major divisions of thought in the passage. In identifying these main points, pay close attention to the mechanical divisions of the text: chapters, verses, and paragraphs (indicated by the paragraph symbol ¶). These were not present in the original writing and are not inspired. But they were placed by Bible scholars, and they help us to know where others have sensed a division of thought.

The paragraph symbols divide Matthew 6:1–18 into three paragraphs, beginning at verses 1, 5, and 16. Each paragraph clearly emphasizes one main idea. The first paragraph relates to doing alms, the second to praying, and the third to fasting. So we could write the following outline.

Instruction on True Devotion (Matthew 6:1–18)
    I. In doing alms
    II. In praying
    III. In fasting

Also take notice of transitional expressions that indicate shifts of thought. In the passage above, verse 5 begins with *And,* which marks the shift to the topic of prayer. Verse 16 begins with *Moreover,* which introduces the topic of fasting. Note also *therefore* in verse 9. This word indicates the transition to the Lord's Prayer, which is a subtopic in the discussion of prayer.

Applying the Lesson

A. Choose one of the following passages, read it carefully several times, and try to identify its main idea. When you have decided, write down the main idea and let your teacher evaluate it before you proceed to Part B. (Hint: Both passages deal with contrasts.)

    Matthew 5:33–48   Psalm 1

B. Write an outline with three main topics for the passage you chose in Part A. Your outline should not include any subtopics at this point.

C. Write an outline with two main topics for James 2 or James 3. For either chapter, you can use the title "Exhortations for Christian Living."

Review Exercises

Write the letter of the answer that best explains how to write an outline for a report. [13]

1. Evaluate your notes and establish ᵃmain topics; ᵇan introduction—unless you have already done so.
2. Sort your notes into groups according to ᵃreference sources; ᵇmain topics.
3. Arrange the main topics in an order that is ᵃlogical; ᵇchronological.
4. If your points have no natural order, you must choose ᵃother main points; ᵇan arbitrary order.
5. Expand this basic outline by adding details from ᵃadditional research; ᵇyour notes.

---

27. Outlining a Bible Passage: Filling In the Details

The main topics of an outline give you a sense of direction as you study a Bible passage further. They highlight the main idea of each group of verses. After you have this general overview of the main teachings, you are ready to evaluate the smaller details and develop a more detailed outline. You must again read the verses that fit with each main topic, and then fill in the details as they apply to the primary truth you have identified.

Here is the outline for Matthew 6:1–18, which was given in Lesson 26.

Instruction on True Devotion
I. In doing alms
II. In praying
III. In fasting

Now read the first paragraph of that passage again, noticing the details and considering how they fit with the main idea of doing alms.

1 ¶ Take heed that ye do not your alms before men, to be seen of them: otherwise ye have no reward of your Father which is in heaven.

2 Therefore when thou doest thine alms, do not sound a trumpet before thee, as the hypocrites do in the synagogues and in the streets, that they may have glory of men.

Verily I say unto you, They have their reward.

3 But when thou doest alms, let not thy left hand know what thy right hand doeth:

4 That thine alms may be in secret: and thy Father which seeth in secret himself shall reward thee openly.

The next step is to arrange subtopics and other points under the first main topic. Notice that Jesus first said how we must *not* do alms, and then He described the right way. This can be shown by two subtopics: "How not to do alms" and "How to do alms." With these headings established, we can fill in other points from the verses as they fit under each subtopic.

Instruction on True Devotion
I. In doing alms
  A. How not to do alms
    1. Not to be seen of men
    2. Not in a showy manner
    3. Not to have glory of men
    4. Not for a mere earthly reward
  B. How to do alms
    1. Do good secretly
    2. Wait for God's reward

These same steps must be followed to fill in other points under the rest of the main topics. When that is completed, the entire outline must be written neatly in good form.

Applying the Lesson
Following the steps given in this lesson, finish the outline that you began in Part B of Lesson 26.

Review Exercises
Write *yes* or *no* to tell whether each statement is good advice for preparing and giving an oral report. [14]
1. Decide how you will describe and illustrate each point on your outline.
2. Do not write the exact words you plan to say for any part of the report.

3. Be sure that your introduction either gives the title of your report or mentions the subject it covers.

4. Conclude your report by summarizing your main points or by appealing to your audience for a response.

5. Use a full sheet of paper to write the notes that you will use in giving the report.

6. Practice giving your report, including the use of any visual aids you plan to include.

7. From the very beginning, establish eye contact with your listeners and speak clearly.

---

28. Improving Your Editing Skills, Part 4

For people to communicate successfully, they must use symbols that they understand in the same way. Misunderstandings result when a symbol means different things to different people. Some misunderstandings are humorous. Others are quite serious. For example, suppose a child has gone to the medicine cabinet to find a remedy for his upset stomach. He finds a bottle of something that might help, but the label is marked with the symbol shown at the right. Should he try it? Will it help? Understanding the meaning of this symbol could make the difference between life and death!

Failure to understand proofreading symbols could result in serious communication errors. In this lesson you will again see some specific patterns to follow in the use of these symbols.

Marks Used in Editing and Proofreading

∨or ∧ insert (caret)	ℯ delete	. . . . stet (let it stand)	——— use italics
¶ begin new paragraph	no ¶ no new paragraph	lc change to lowercase (small letter)	uc change to uppercase (capital letter)
# insert space	⌣ delete space	← move (arrow)	⌐⌐ transpose

Explanations	Sample Manuscript
	For many years an unscrupulous wood-
	cutter had been cheating his customers
	by cutting his logs a few inches under
Symbol for "transpose" may involve items in two different lines.	the required four feet. One day the went report out that he had been converted.
It may be better to delete and insert than to use the transpose or move symbol.	Indeed, lc Nobody believed the story. People thought he was too low and mean to indeed make such a change.
	While they discussed the matter, one
When a letter is deleted within a word, the symbol for "delete space" may be used to show that no space is to remain—although this is optional.	man slipped away from the group and dissappeared. He soon returned, however, and declaired confidently, "It's true! He has been converted!"
	"How can you tell?" everyone wondered.
Transpose symbol may be used with more than two words or letters.	"I measured the logs he cut yesterday," the man explained. "And they are all a long full four feet."

Editing Practice

A. Correct the two errors of transposition in each sentence. Notes in parentheses give specific instructions for correcting some errors.

1. A Christain farmer noticed that armyworms were to beginning attack the crops in one of his fields.

2. Realizing that his corps would be ruined, he was filled with despair within hours. (Use delete and insert symbols to make *within hours* come immediately after *ruined*.)

3. In faith his little daughter asked, "Father, why do'nt we ask God to drive the worms away?" (Use the transpose symbol to make *away* follow *drive*.)

4. Together they knelt in humble, fervent, silent prayer, pleading that God would remove the destrioyng worms.

   (Use the transpose symbol to make *silent* come before *humble*. Add and delete commas as required by the rearrangement.)

5. A huge cloud of blackbirds soon appeared, the hungry birds alighting on the feild where the worms were.

   (Use the transpose symbol to move *soon* to the beginning of the sentence. Correct the capitalization.)

6. When the birds disappeeard a few minutes later, not a worm single remained to harm the crop!

B. Use the "delete space" symbol twice in each sentence. Some uses will be in connection with a letter that you should delete. (Note: The word *lungfish* is a solid compound.)

1. Although many fish do nothing for their young, the lung fish provides ammazing care for its eggs.

2. First the male and the fe male lungfish dig tunnells in the mud.

3. Then, using leaves and stickes, these interesting fish build a nest in which the female de posits her eggs.

4. The male stays by the eggs as a watch man while they are incubaiting for the next eight days.

5. During this time he also agitates the watter above the nest to keep fresh water a round the eggs.

C. Use proofreading marks to correct the thirteen errors in the following paragraphs. No line has more than one error.

1.   Victoria Falls is a mighty waterfall in southern Africa.

2. The falls are found on the Zambezi River be tween Zambia

3. and Zimbabwe. Just above the falls, the river spreadsout

4. and flows among dozens of islands. Flowwing through this

5.   wide channel, the river plunges suddenly into a deep

6. chasm that is set squarely across the current.

7. The falls themselves more than are a mile wide (1.6

8. kilometers) and over 350 feet high (100 meters). This is

9. more than twice the width and height of Niagara falls in

10. in North America. The falling water produces a tremendous

11. roar can that be heard from a great distance. In fact, the

12. African name for the falls means "the smoke that thunders".

13. A great cloud of mist rises above the falls, keeping

14. near by plants green and healthy all year.

15. David Livingstone was the first Eureopan to see this

16. great handiwork of God. He discovered the Falls in 1855

17. and named it for Queen Victoria of England?

---

29. Finding Words and Topics in the Bible

The Bible is the most important library in the world. This Book provides us with the most essential facts and concepts for time and eternity. In contrast to other libraries, the information found here is always accurate and up-to-date, and it always applies to the present time.

Of course, to benefit from this library, you must "study to shew thyself approved unto God, a workman that needeth not to be ashamed, rightly dividing the word of truth" (2 Timothy 2:15). Like a master of a house, you must learn to draw from this storehouse of treasures "things new and old" (Matthew 13:52). A number of reference books offer practical help for digging into the Word. This chapter will give you directions and cautions about using some common Bible reference books.

Concordances

Many Bibles contain small concordances in the back, but these are generally too small to be very helpful in serious Bible study. For the greatest satisfaction, use a concordance described as *complete, comprehensive,* or *exhaustive.* These have an entry for every word in the Bible, with the possible exception of common words like *the, it, for,* and *was.* The most common one is *Strong's Exhaustive Concordance of the Bible.*

A concordance is like an index to the Bible. It can help you in two ways. First, it helps you find verses with which you are already familiar but whose references you cannot remember. Second, it lists all the verses that contain a certain word, including those that may not be familiar to you or that you may not have thought of.

Suppose you want to study what the Bible says about righteousness. Among the verses that come to your mind is one that says, "The work of righteousness shall be peace." But what does the rest of the verse say? And where is it found? To answer these questions, you need only open a concordance to the word *righteousness* and skim down over the verse portions until you find the one you want. You might see something like this:

righteousness
Isa   1:21 *r'* lodged in it; but now murderers.
        26 The city of *r'*, the faithful city.
        27 judgment,… her converts with *r'*
        32:17 And the work of *r'* shall be peace;

For some words, a concordance lists hundreds of references. In such a case, you can narrow your search by considering which book of the Bible probably contains the verse you want. Otherwise, it will take considerable time for you to skim the entire list. Even worse, you may overlook the verse you want and reach the end of the list without having found it.

Another way to narrow your search is to choose the least common word in the verse portion that you remember. Consider again the portion "The work of righteousness shall be peace." In *Strong's Concordance,* the entry for *righteousness* contains 301 references. However, *work* has 412 references and *peace* has 405; so *righteousness* is the best choice in this case. If we were looking for the verse that says, "Being filled with the fruits of righteousness," we could look under *filled* or *fruits.* These words have 158 and 42 references respectively. Which one would make your search easier?

Using a concordance in this way involves no human interpretation, which may be tainted with false teaching. Concordances, therefore, are an excellent resource for fruitful Bible study.

Topical Bibles

A topical Bible is an alphabetical arrangement of Bible topics with verses printed under each topic heading. This arrangement provides a Bible student with a broad range of verses about numerous subjects. Many of these topics are divided into subtopics for more detailed study.

To continue our study of righteousness, let us find this word in a topical Bible. *Nave's Topical Bible* lists three aspects of righteousness: "By faith," "Garment of," and "Imputed on account of obedience," each followed by several references. After this comes a long list of verses under the subtopic "Fruits of."

One benefit of a topical Bible over a concordance is that the topical Bible gives verses about a subject even though they do not contain a particular word. For example, under "righteousness" you will find the following verse in *Nave's:* "I will set no wicked thing before mine eyes: I hate the work of them that turn aside; it shall not cleave to me" (Psalm 101:3). This verse obviously refers to righteousness, but you would not have found it by looking up that word in a concordance.

If you want to find information on the city of Nineveh, you can look up "Nineveh" in a topical Bible. There you might find details from "Capital of the Assyrian empire (Gen. 10:11, 12)" to "Zephaniah foretells the desolation of (Zeph. 2:13–15)," with several others in between.

Chain-reference Bibles

A chain-reference Bible is a special topical Bible. The one with the most extensive chain-reference system is the *Thompson Chain-reference Bible*. In this Bible, a topic like "righteousness" is named on the margin beside the verses that deal with that topic. Beside each topic is a "pilot number" that identifies it. The verses relating to a given topic are linked together by the pilot number to form a topical chain through the Bible.

One verse that deals with righteousness is Matthew 5:20. The following illustration shows this verse as it appears in the *Thompson Chain-reference Bible*.

2991 Sanctimony.	**20 For I say unto you, That except your**
3080 Righteousness (4), Ac. 24:25.	**righteousness shall exceed the righteous-**
3165 Scribes, 7:29.	**ness of the scribes and Pharisees, ye shall**
3171 Pharisees.	**in no case enter into the kingdom of**
40 Exclusion (2), 18:3.	**heaven.**
3904 Works Insufficient (3).	

As shown on the margin, this verse deals with righteousness and five other topics. The reference after "Righteousness" (Acts 24:25) is the "forward reference" that gives the next verse in this particular chain. If we were studying the topic "Scribes," we could turn to Matthew 7:29 and read the next verse in that chain.

To find all the verses in a particular chain, we can turn to the back of the Bible and look up the pilot number for that chain in the "Condensed Cyclopedia of Topics and Texts." Here we find references for all the verses in each topical chain, with the most significant verses printed in full. Below is the first part of the entry for pilot number 3080, which is subtopic (4) under the main topic "Righteousness— Unrighteousness."

3080—(4) Enjoined,
Da. 4:27. Wherefore, O king, let my counsel be acceptable unto thee, and break off thy sins by righteousness, and thine iniquities by shewing mercy to the poor; if it may be a lengthening of thy tranquillity.
Ho. 10:12. Sow to yourselves in righteousness, reap in mercy; break up your fallow ground: for it is time to seek the LORD, till he come and rain righteousness upon you.
Mt. 5:20. For I say unto you, That except your righteousness shall exceed the righteousness of the scribes and Pharisees, ye shall in no case enter into the kingdom of heaven. (Acts 24:25)

In the example above, three verses are printed in full because they are significant Scripture verses on the topic "Righteousness, Enjoined." For one verse (Acts 24:25), only the reference is given because that verse is less significant to this particular topic.

The "Condensed Cyclopedia" shows main topics in alphabetical order. But because related topics are grouped together (such as "Righteousness—Unrighteousness"), some items are not in alphabetical order. To find a topic quickly, you should usually turn to the "General Index" just before the "Condensed Cyclopedia." This index shows all the topics and subtopics in alphabetical order, along with their pilot numbers.

Look again at the illustration showing Matthew 5:20 in the *Thompson Chain-reference Bible*. Why are no forward references given with the topics "Sanctimony," "Pharisees," and "Works Insufficient"? While those topics are suggested by Matthew 5:20, this particular verse is not actually in the topical chains for pilot numbers 2991, 3171, and 3904. To study those chains, you will need to look up those pilot numbers in the back of the Bible. Thus, the *Thompson Chain-reference Bible* is excellent for showing topics that a verse deals with directly, as well as topics that are only suggested by a verse.

Chain references in other Bibles are in the form of footnotes, each with one or two references. By following these references forward toward Revelation or backward toward Genesis, you can follow a topic through the Bible.

Cross-references

Cross-references direct a Bible student to other verses that contain ideas found in a particular verse. These are much like chain references except that they are not arranged as systematically. Many Bibles give cross-references at the bottom of each page or in the center column. *The Treasury of Scripture Knowledge* is a special cross-reference book that provides cross-references for every verse from Genesis through Revelation.

The following illustration shows Matthew 5:20 as it might appear in a center-column reference Bible.

c Ro. 10.3 *d* ch. 7.21 *e* ch. 18.3	**20 For I say unto you, That except your righteousness shall exceed the ^crighteousness of the scribes and Pharisees, ye ^eshall in no case enter into the kingdom of heaven.**

The cross-reference marked *c* (Romans 10:3) speaks of people "going about to establish their own righteousness" instead of accepting God's righteousness. The one marked *e* (Matthew 18:3) describes another case in which "ye shall not enter into the kingdom of heaven." These ideas are similar to the ones in the verse shown. (The cross-reference marked *d* is for a verse in the opposite column.)

Studying Bible topics is an enriching, valuable method of Bible study. You should remember, however, that the compilers of topical Bibles, chain references, and cross-references arrange the verses according to their own interpretation of Bible themes. Since their interpretations may be incorrect, their topical classifications are subject to error and should therefore be used with discretion.

Applying the Lesson

A. Use a concordance to do these exercises.
1. For each verse portion, write out the complete verse and the reference.
   a. "Trust not in oppression."
   b. "If we suffer, we shall also reign."
   c. "Every one could sling stones at an hair breadth."

2. How often is the word *content* used in the Old Testament? in the New Testament?
3. Write the verse and reference for the only use of *contentment* in the Bible.
4. In what three books of the Bible is the word *occupation* used?

B. Use *Nave's Topical Bible* to do these exercises.
   1. Find the entry "Horn."
      a. List two uses for horns mentioned in the Bible.
      b. List two ways in which horns are mentioned figuratively.
   2. List all the subheadings for the entry "Religion."
   3. List all the references for the topic "Duty, of Man to Man."
   4. Which book of the Bible has the most references relating to the topic "Speaking, Wisdom in"?

C. Find "Retaliation" in a topical Bible, and read the verses given for this subject. Then write a paragraph telling some things that the Bible says about retaliation. Be sure to note the difference between the teaching in the Old Testament and in the New Testament.

D. Use a *Thompson Chain-reference Bible* to do these exercises.
   1. List the pilot numbers and topics shown for Romans 14:17.
   2. Under what pilot numbers in the "Condensed Cyclopedia" can you find verses on the topic "Spiritual Mind"? (Use the index.)
   3. List the references for verses that speak about God's thoughts. Do not use abbreviations.
   4. In the "Condensed Cyclopedia," what five subtopics are listed under the topic "Sabbath"?
   5. Find "Fasting" in the "Condensed Cyclopedia."
      a. Under what main topic is it given?
      b. Into what three points is it divided?
   6. What three topics could you look up for additional verses related to the topic "Courage, Enjoined"? (See the end of that entry.)

E. List references given as cross-references for these verses.
   1. Psalm 1:6   3. Matthew 18:22
   2. Genesis 18:17   4. Colossians 2:15

Review Exercises

A. Copy each underlined complement, and label it *PN, PA, DO, IO,* or *OC.* [17]
   1. "My son, be wise, and make my <u>heart</u> <u>glad</u>, that I may answer him that reproacheth me."
   2. "But the LORD was with Joseph, and shewed <u>him</u> <u>mercy</u>."
   3. "Even so, Father: for so it seemed <u>good</u> in thy sight."
   4. "Noah was a just <u>man</u> and perfect in his generations."

B. Label each underlined complement *DO ret., IO ret.,* or *OC ret.* [18]
   1. A silver dollar was given each <u>child</u> by Grandfather.

2. The garden was made a <u>field</u> of mud by the heavy rains.
3. All men are freely sent <u>sunshine and rain</u>.
4. The students have been taught many important <u>truths</u>.

---

30. Discovering the Meanings of Bible Words

How can you find the meaning of a Bible word that you do not understand? A modern dictionary can be helpful, for many words mean the same today as when the King James Bible was produced. One example is the word *covetousness* in the following verse. This word always means "greed; improper desire for possessions, especially those of another person."

"Let your conversation be without covetousness" (Hebrews 13:5).

What about *conversation* in the verse above? This word means "dialogue" in modern usage. But as you probably realize, *conversation* in the Bible refers not to our talk but to our everyday life. How do you know this? Most likely, you have learned it from parents, teachers, and ministers as they explained the Word of God.

If you look up *conversation* in an advanced dictionary, you might find the definition "way of life" with a label like *Archaic* or *Obsolete*. A better approach is to find the meaning of the original Hebrew or Greek word from which *conversation* is translated. *Strong's Exhaustive Concordance* is probably the most common reference book that people use for this purpose.

The following illustration shows the entry for *conversation* in *Strong's Concordance,* with one verse portion from the Old Testament and one from the New Testament.

conversation
Ps   37:14 to slay such as be of upright *c*.   1870
Heb 13: 5 your *c*' be without covetousness;   *5158*

The number to the right of each verse portion is the key number for the original word from which *conversation* is translated. Numbers for Old Testament words are printed in regular type and refer to entries in the "Hebrew and Chaldee Dictionary" at the back of the concordance. Numbers for New Testament words are printed in italic type and refer to entries in the "Greek Dictionary of the New Testament." In those dictionaries, the definitions for word numbers 1870 and *5158* indicate that *conversation* refers to one's conduct or way of life.

Let us consider another example. In Colossians 2:12 we find these words: "Ye are risen with him through the faith of the operation of God." What is this *operation* of God? Under *operation* in a regular dictionary, we find definitions like "action," "process of functioning," and "surgical procedure." These definitions are of little or no value in gaining a clearer understanding of Colossians 2:12.

But if we look up *operation* in *Strong's Concordance,* we will see that in this verse the word is translated from word number *1753*. So we turn to number *1753* in the "Greek Dictionary of the New Testament." That entry is shown below, with its various parts labeled.

original Greek word   English spelling   pronunciation   root word
        ↓   ↓   ↓   ↓

1753. ἐνέργεια **ĕnĕrgĕia,** *en-erg'-i-ah;* from *1756;*
efficiency ("energy"):—operation, strong, (effectual) working.
        ↑   ↑   ↑   ↑   ↑

meaning   related English word   translations in KJV

Notice that the entry consists of several parts. First comes the original word in Hebrew or Greek letters, followed by its spelling and pronunciation in English letters. Next is the *Strong's* number for the Hebrew or Greek root word, if there is one. If we look up the root word (number *1756* in this case), we will have a broader understanding of the word we are studying. That entry is shown below.

1756. ἐνεργής **ĕnĕrgēs,** *en-er-gace';* from *1722*
and *2041; active, operative*:—effectual, powerful.

After the root word comes the meaning of the word in the original language. Actual definitions are given in italics, as *efficiency* in the entry for word *1753.* If an English word comes from the word in the original language, that word is often shown in quotation marks. The English word *energy* is derived from the Greek word *ĕnĕrgĕia.*

Finally, after the colon and dash, the entry lists all the ways that the original word is translated in the King James Version of the Bible. This entry shows that the Greek word translated *operation* in Colossians 2:12 is translated in other Scripture verses as *strong, working,* and *effectual working. (Effectual* is in parentheses because word *1753* is sometimes translated *working* and sometimes *effectual working.)*

For further study, we can look up the other ways in which this Greek word is translated. Under *strong,* we find one reference keyed to word *1753:* 2 Thessalonians 2:11. Under *working* (which includes the verses with "effectual working"), we find six references keyed to this number: Ephesians 1:19; 3:7; 4:16; Philippians 3:21; Colossians 1:29; and 2 Thessalonians 2:9. In all except the last of these verses, word *1753* clearly refers to God's power and ability. The last verse speaks of Satan's power.

Do you now have a better understanding of Colossians 2:12? This verse is not saying that a Christian must experience some unique "operation of God." Rather, by faith he rises with Christ to a new life, through the strong, effectual working of God.

Word study can be especially helpful when two verses seem to say opposite things. For example, Galatians 6:2 says, "Bear ye one another's burdens." But just a few sentences later (verse 5), we read, "Every man shall bear his own burden." We know that the Word of God never contradicts itself. Then how do these verses fit together?

By using *Strong's Concordance,* we can see that *burdens* and *burden* in these verses are translated from two different Greek words. In verse 2 the number is *922,* which refers to the Greek word *barŏs* (load, weight). In verse 5 the number is *5413,* which refers to the Greek word *phŏrtiŏn.* This word comes from *phŏrtŏs* (number *5414*), which means "something carried." In fact, word *5413* is the same one that Jesus used when He said, "My burden is light." So this kind of burden is something to carry, but it is not necessarily heavy.

Now these verses are clear. When we see someone struggling with a heavy load that he can hardly carry, we should help him to bear his burden. Yet each person has his own burden to carry, for which he alone is responsible.

We do not need to do a study like this on every word in the Bible, for most words are as simple and clear as they can be. But when we are unsure about the meaning of a Scripture passage because of the way a certain word is used, or when one verse seems to disagree with another, word study like this can be highly rewarding.

Applying the Lesson

A. In *Strong's Exhaustive Concordance,* look up the Greek word that each underlined word is translated from. Then write the English word that comes from that Greek word, choosing from the list given. You will not use all the answers.

architect	director	rabbi
catastrophe	exodus	symphony
deacon	martyr	therapy
diagnosis	medicine	zeal

1. "But he that is greatest among you shall be your <u>servant</u>" (Matthew 23:11).
2. "In the mean while his disciples prayed him, saying, <u>Master</u>, eat" (John 4:31).
3. "This Jesus hath God raised up, whereof we all are <u>witnesses</u>" (Acts 2:32).
4. "Felix… deferred them, and said, When Lysias the chief captain shall come down, I will <u>know</u> the uttermost of your matter" (Acts 24:22).
5. "As a wise <u>masterbuilder</u>, I have laid the foundation, and another buildeth thereon" (1 Corinthians 3:10).
6. "And what <u>concord</u> hath Christ with Belial? or what part hath he that believeth with an infidel?" (2 Corinthians 6:15).
7. "For I am jealous over you with godly <u>jealousy</u>" (2 Corinthians 11:2).
8. "By faith Joseph, when he died, made mention of the <u>departing</u> of the children of Israel" (Hebrews 11:22).
9. "And turning the cities of Sodom and Gomorrha into ashes condemned them with an <u>overthrow</u>" (2 Peter 2:6).
10. "And the leaves of the tree were for the <u>healing</u> of the nations" (Revelation 22:2).

B. Use *Strong's Concordance* to do these exercises.
1. Look up the word *contrary.*
   a. How many times does this word appear in the New Testament?
   b. How many different Greek words were translated *contrary?*
   c. Look up the Greek word for *contrary* in Galatians 5:17.
      (1) What is the meaning of the original Greek word?

(2) What two things in Galatians 5:17 "lie opposite" each other?

(3) This Greek word is also translated "adversary" and "opposeth." Write the references for the verses in which it is translated in those ways.

2. Look up the word *talebearer,* and research the meanings in the "Hebrew and Chaldee Dictionary."

   a. Copy the references in which *talebearer* suggests being secretive and tearing things apart.

   b. Copy the references in which *talebearer* suggests a traveling merchant, looking for slanderous tales to carry about.

3. How were the villages in 1 Chronicles 27:25 different from those in Ezekiel 38:11?

4. What relationship had apparently existed between Kenath and the other villages mentioned in Numbers 32:42?

5. Several Greek words are translated "perfection" in the New Testament. Write the correct reference for each definition.

   a. The perfection of having thorough equipment.   Luke 8:14

   b. The perfection of completeness.   2 Corinthians 13:9

   c. The perfection of bearing to maturity.   Hebrews 6:1

Review Exercises

Label each underlined item *nominative absolute* or *participial phrase.* [21]

1. Our radiator leaking, we headed for the nearest repair shop.

2. Opening the door, Mother invited our guests inside.

3. We listened to the crows screaming their disapproval at the approaching hawk.

4. Everyone headed for the basement, a funnel-shaped cloud having been sighted.

5. My English homework finished, I laid my textbook aside.

---

31. Finding Background Information on Bible Subjects

How large an area did the city of Jerusalem cover in David's time? In Jesus' time? What was linen made from? What was it used for? How far was Jerusalem from Nazareth? To find such kinds of information, you will most often turn to a Bible dictionary or a Bible atlas.

Bible Dictionaries

A Bible dictionary is a small encyclopedia of Bible knowledge. It gives valuable background information about people, places, and things mentioned in the Bible. This information can be quite helpful in gaining a full understanding of a Bible verse or passage.

For example, if you look up "Jonah" in *The New Unger's Bible Dictionary,* you will find the meaning of Jonah's name and a summary of his life. The article "Jonah, Book of" discusses the literary character of the book, its author and date, and its unity. You will also find the outline shown below. This information should be useful to you in a study of Jonah and his book.

I. The prophet's first call and disobedience (1:1–2:10)
   A. The divine commission and his flight (1:1–3)
   B. The storm (1:4–7)
   C. The confession (1:8–12)
   D. The prophet's being thrown into the sea (1:13–17)
   E. His intercession and salvation (2:1–10)
II. The prophet's second call and his obedience (3:1–4:11)
   A. He goes to Nineveh (3:1–4)
   B. The Ninevites repent (3:5–9)
   C. The city is saved (3:10)
   D. Jonah is angered (4:1–4)
   E. Jonah is reproved (4:5–11)

If you look up a place name in a Bible dictionary, you will often find a map or diagram of the place, along with information about any archaeological discoveries that have been made there. Under "Babylon" in *The New Unger's Bible Dictionary,* you can read about the size of the city and see a diagram of its layout in Nebuchadnezzar's time. Under "Capernaum" in *The Zondervan Pictorial Bible Dictionary,* you can see a photograph of the ruins of an ancient synagogue in that town. This information should help to impress upon you that these Bible locations were real places.

Bible dictionaries also have articles on doctrines such as redemption and immortality. But these articles have limited value, for Bible doctrines are taught clearly by the Bible itself. Besides, such articles often contain error, especially if they deal with doctrines like predestination and eternal security. In Lesson 32 you will learn about reference sources that are better for reading about Bible doctrines.

Bible Atlases

We usually think of an atlas as a book of maps. But a Bible atlas is much more than a collection of Bible maps. The text of *Baker's Bible Atlas* follows the course of Bible history and discusses the geographical setting of the events in each period of time. It includes maps that show the land in those different periods, as well as photographs that show how mountains, rivers, and other features look today.

For example, Chapter 7 of *Baker's Bible Atlas* begins with an explanation of why God did not lead the Israelites "through the way of the land of the Philistines" (Exodus 13:17). That route was constantly guarded by Egyptian soldiers, who would certainly have made trouble for Israel. Another place has a photograph showing how the traditional Mount Sinai looks today. These things give us a clearer understanding of the Scriptures.

Perhaps most interesting of all are the pictures and descriptions of archaeological discoveries that refer to details mentioned in the Bible. For example, Chapter 16 of *Baker's Bible Atlas* has a picture of Sennacherib's Cylinder, which bears writing that says Sennacherib shut up Hezekiah in Jerusalem "like a bird in a cage." At the end of Chapter 17 is a picture of the Cyrus Cylinder, which says that Cyrus helped captive people return to their native lands. These things confirm what we already know—that the Bible record is completely true and reliable.

In the back of *Baker's Bible Atlas* is a gazetteer, which lists and briefly describes the places mentioned in the Bible. The entries include the page numbers of maps where the places appear.

After the gazetteer is an index to the text, which gives the pages where Bible people and places are discussed. The index shows that King Mesha of Moab is discussed on pages 142 and 146.

When you use a Bible dictionary or a Bible atlas, always remember that they contain the ideas of men. Some material consists merely of facts—documented history, geographical descriptions, archaeological discoveries, and so forth. But other material is men's interpretation of the Scriptures, and it may contain false teaching. We must always test the writings of men by the Word of God to make sure we are not deceived by unsound ideas.

Applying the Lesson

A. Use a Bible dictionary to do these exercises. (They are based on *The New Unger's Bible Dictionary.*)
1. Answer these questions about the Jabbok.
    a. How far from the Jordan River does the Jabbok begin?
    b. How many miles does its winding course actually cover?
    c. Where does it flow into the Jordan River?
    d. Is it deep enough for large boats to navigate its water?
    e. At the time of the Israelite Conquest, it served as the boundary between what two kingdoms?
2. Answer these questions about Merodach-baladan.
    a. What does this name mean?
    b. Of what race was he?
    c. In what year did he first become ruler of Babylon?
    d. How long did this rule over Babylon last?
    e. To what land was he compelled to flee later in life?
3. List the main divisions suggested for the Gospel of John, as shown in the outline.
4. During what months does rain rarely fall in Palestine?
5. A number of Scripture verses refer to ashes in a figurative sense. What are three things that ashes symbolize?
6. Name three uses of lead mentioned in the Bible.
7. Briefly describe two kinds of surety mentioned in the Bible.
8. Briefly describe two possibilities for the background of the name *Maccabees.*

9. What two men translated the Scriptures into English in the fourteenth century?
10. In what year did translators begin work on the Authorized Version (King James Version)?

B. Use Chapter 14 in *Baker's Bible Atlas* to answer these questions.
1. Where does the Bible first refer to Jerusalem?
2. What name was given to Jerusalem after it was destroyed in A.D. 70?
3. How far is Jerusalem (a) from the Mediterranean Sea? (b) from the Dead Sea? (c) above the level of the Mediterranean Sea?
4. What building now stands on the site of Solomon's temple?
5. The southernmost part of the Mount of Olives is called the Mount of Offense. What is the reason for this name?
6. Jerusalem is built around what three valleys?
7. How long are the present walls of Jerusalem?
8. Why is it difficult to do archaeological work in Jerusalem?

C. Use the maps in a Bible atlas to do these exercises.
1. The city of Bezer was located in the territory allotted to which tribe?
2. The city of Golan was located in the territory allotted to which tribe?
3. At its greatest extent, the Roman Empire stretched from the ——— Ocean in the west to the ——— Sea in the northeast and the ——— Sea in the southeast.
4. On which missionary journey did Paul land at Tyre on his return to Palestine?
5. Shechem is almost directly (north, south, east, west) of Jerusalem.

Review Exercises

A. Label each sentence according to its use (*dec., int., imp., exc.*) and its structure (*S, CD, CX, CD-CX*). End punctuation has been omitted. [22]
1. The Passover was approaching, and Jesus sent two disciples to prepare for its observance
2. Jesus directed them to a man who was carrying a pitcher of water
3. Did you know that carrying water was a woman's job in Bible times
4. How distinctive would be a man performing this task
5. The disciples found the man, and he led them to an upper room where they could make their preparations
6. Read this account in Mark 14:12–16

B. Label the word order of each sentence *N* (natural), *I* (inverted), or *M* (mixed). [22]
1. Rashness is not valor.
2. When it avenges injury with love, revenge is sweet.
3. Through obedience to the Bible comes true happiness.
4. People often do odd things to get even.

C. Label the style of each sentence *L* (loose), *P* (periodic), or *B* (balanced). [22]
1. Zacchaeus climbed up to see Jesus, but pride climbs up to see itself.
2. We are truly resigned when we put God between ourselves and our grief.

3. No matter how intelligent a man may be, if he is stubborn and refuses to learn, nobody can teach him.
4. Riches have made more men covetous than covetousness has made men rich.

---

32. Studying Bible Passages and Bible Doctrines

In preparing for a topic or in pursuing personal Bible study, a Bible student may benefit from reading a thorough, organized treatment of a specific Bible doctrine. Sometimes it is helpful to read how others understand a particular Bible passage. Various kinds of commentaries and doctrinal books can help to provide for interests of this kind.

Kinds of Commentaries

There are various kinds of commentaries. Bible handbooks contain much practical information, as well as general comments on each of the books of the Bible. *Halley's Bible Handbook,* for example, includes archaeological information, pictures, and maps. A history of the years between the Testaments fills several pages. At the end of the Scripture commentary are chapters on "How We Got the Bible" and "Church History."

Bible survey books seek to give a general overview of each book of the Bible. These kinds of commentaries often include outlines and detailed comments. These surveys can be helpful in understanding the overall messages of the various books of the Bible and how specific verses relate to that message. It would be foolish, however, to suppose that only one particular outline fits a particular book. So the serious Bible student must not allow such books to replace the hard work of honest Bible study.

Regular Bible commentaries give specific ideas and interpretations on every verse in the Bible. Any Bible commentary is helpful only if we use it with careful discernment. The writers of many such books do not uphold and practice all the Scriptures. Almost all deny that the doctrine of nonresistance applies to all New Testament believers at all times. Many agree that believers should be nonconformed to the world in heart, yet they deny that nonconformity applies to one's outward appearance and everyday life.

Many commentaries also explain away the plain teaching on the headship veiling. Unconditional eternal security and related Calvinistic ideas are other common errors. Some writers even suggest that the Creation might have taken place over thousands of years, or that certain parts of the Bible are not inspired. The reader must always be alert to such interpretations and reject them.

Even the best of commentaries should never replace personal Bible study. A good practice is to study a passage and seek to understand its meaning before turning to any commentary. Using the reference books discussed in the previous lessons to understand word meanings and to compare Scripture with Scripture is a much safer and more rewarding method of Bible study than reading commentaries can ever be. Checking what commentaries say about difficult passages may be profitable if the Bible student remembers that they represent only men's ideas.

Doctrinal Books

Sound doctrinal books can be valuable study aids. *Doctrines of the Bible* gives a well-organized treatment of Bible doctrines from a conservative Mennonite viewpoint. The table of contents shows the general outline of the entire book. At the beginning of each of the eight main parts, a detailed outline gives a clear survey of the contents of that section. As the editor states in the foreword, the book "is not intended as an exhaustive treatise on any subject"; its purpose is to make each point "clear and convincing."

Suppose you wish to know what the Bible teaches about angels. Chapter VIII of Part III is titled "Angels." The book groups Biblical teaching on angels under the following headings: "Their Origin," "Their Great Number," "Orders of Angels," "Attributes," "Office and Work," and "Some Things the Bible Does Not Teach." A topical Bible would provide much of the same information, but it would not give you the warnings against wrong ideas that are found under the last heading.

Ready Bible Answers (previously published as *Ready Scriptural Reasons*) gives clear, practical teaching on many Bible doctrines. The book contains thirty-two chapters, including "Flesh and Spirit," "Faith and Works," "The Christian's Associates," and "Peace and Nonresistance." Each chapter consists of a series of questions with clear, Biblical answers.

Are you studying the relationship of faith and works? Chapter 4, entitled "Faith and Works," gives a wide range of Biblical teaching by answering questions like this: "What is the relation of faith and works in the justification of a soul before God?" "How can salvation be by grace if it is dependent upon human works?" "Which should have the most emphasis in our teaching, faith or works?"

A wide array of books deals with specific areas of Bible doctrine. They may have titles such as *The Significance of the Christian Woman's Veiling, Studies in the Doctrine of Nonresistance,* or *Dying to Live With Christ.* As with Bible commentaries, doctrinal books represent the works of men. You must always use them with discretion, and you must be sure that you do not allow such books to take the place of Bible study. An important safeguard, especially for youth, is to use only reference books recommended by faithful Christian parents and church leaders.

Applying the Lesson

A. Answer these questions.
1. Why must a Bible commentary be used with great caution?
2. What danger could a commentary pose even if it contained no errors?
3. What are several doctrines that many commentaries do not uphold?
4. Name several examples of false teaching that commentaries may contain.

B. Use *Halley's Bible Handbook* to do these exercises.
1. What are two possible sites of the Tower of Babel (Genesis 11:1–9)?

2. How old was Methuselah when Adam died (Genesis 11:10–26)?
3. Hezekiah's tunnel carried water from where to where (2 Chronicles 29, 30, 31, 32)?
4. What false teaching is given concerning the Golden Rule (Luke 6:27–38)?
5. Scan the "Church History" section (pp. 757–804) to find answers to these questions.
   a. How many Christians are estimated to have been buried in the catacombs?
   b. What was the main theme of Augustine's book *The City of God*?
   c. What group that was a forerunner of the Reformation survives today?

C. Use *Doctrines of the Bible* to do these exercises.
1. List the seven Christian ordinances.
2. List five evidences of humility.
3. What four erroneous views of the atonement does this book refute?
4. Turn to the chapter titled "Faith," and answer these questions.
   a. What are three essential elements of faith?
   b. What are some ways in which people exercise faith even though they claim to have no faith?
   c. What are some ways in which the Spirit leads the saints into fuller faith?
   d. Name several Old Testament characters who illustrate how "faith worketh patience."
5. What is the difference between open communion and close communion?

D. Use *Ready Bible Answers* to do these exercises.
1. What two kinds of works might an unconverted soul perform?
2. How does the author use a surgeon's knife to illustrate Christian charity?
3. How can we know that God did not allow war in the Old Testament merely because of the hardness of the people's hearts?
4. Why must a new Christian break his association with former wicked companions?

Review Exercises
Write the six key words that help us remember the six basic listening skills. (Remember, these words start with the letters *A–F*.)

33. Chapter 4 Review

A. Copy this partial outline correctly.

The Science of Work

I. What is the meaning of work?
   A. defined as the act of moving something by applying a force
   B. It can be computed.
      1. By multiplying the force in pounds by the distance in feet
   C. Measured in unit called foot-pound
II. Resistances to be overcome
   A. Friction
   1. Is likely the greatest resistance to overcome
   2. results from two surfaces rubbing together
   3. Friction can be very harmful.
      a. By preventing machinery from moving
      b. by wearing parts down so that they are unusable
      c. Can produce too much heat
         (1) warps machinery
         (2) Ruins materials
         (3) Fires started
   4. can be reduced
      a. by smoothing the surfaces that rub together
      b. lubrication
         c. Use wheels and rollers rather than sliding surfaces on each other.
         d. By eliminating unnecessary rubbing
         e. reduce pressure between surfaces
   B. Overcoming gravity

B. Answer these questions about outlining.
   1. How does outlining a lesson force a student to analyze it thoroughly?
   2. What long-term benefits does outlining have?
   3. In preparing to outline a Bible passage, what must you determine first? What are the next two steps?
   4. What are some things to pay attention to in identifying the major divisions of thought in a passage?

C. Answer these questions about Bible reference books.
   1. Which kind of reference book described in this chapter requires the least caution, and why?
   2. Why is a modern dictionary not always a good source for discovering the meanings of Bible words?
   3. What danger could a commentary pose even if it contained no errors?
   4. What are several doctrines that many commentaries do not uphold?
   5. Name several examples of false teaching that many commentaries may contain.

D. Use a concordance to do these exercises.
   1. Write the reference for these verse portions.
      a. "With the lowly is wisdom."
      b. "Thou shalt rise up before the hoary head."
      c. "Lift ye up a banner upon the high mountain."
   2. Name the four books of the Bible in which the word *greedy* occurs, and tell how many times it occurs in each.

E. Use *Nave's Topical Bible* to do these exercises.
   1. List the first six subtopics into which the entry *children* is divided.
   2. At what three geographical locations does the Bible mention snow?
   3. Of what is snow figurative?
   4. What three places in the Bible bear the name *Rehoboth*?

F. Use a Bible dictionary to do these exercises.
   1. Find the entry *Kidron*.
      a. What does *Kidron* mean?
      b. What other spelling is used sometimes?
      c. How long is the valley through which this brook flows?
   2. Into what three main headings is the entry *Mount of Olives* divided?
   3. Name six uses of oil in Bible times.
   4. What does *hallelujah* mean?

G. Use *Strong's Exhaustive Concordance* to do these exercises.
   1. Look up *quarrel*.
      a. How many different Hebrew words are translated *quarrel*?
      b. What is the original meaning of the Hebrew word translated *quarrel* in Leviticus 26:25?
      c. List the various ways in which this word is translated in the King James Bible.
      d. What is the original meaning of the Hebrew root for this word?
   2. Look up *vex* and its various forms, and research their meanings in the "Greek Dictionary of the New Testament." Copy one of the following words or phrases to correctly complete the sentences below.

      tortured   mobbed
      injured   wore down

      a. Herod ——— the Christians (Acts 12:1).
      b. The wickedness of Sodom ——— Lot (2 Peter 2:7).
      c. Lot ——— his soul by living in Sodom (2 Peter 2:8).
      d. Jesus healed people who were ——— by unclean spirits (Luke 6:18).

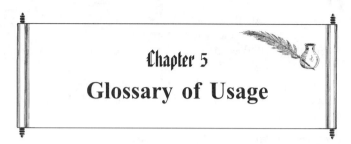

Chapter 5
Glossary of Usage

Book One Word List

Part 1 (Lesson 34)

ability, capacity
accompanied by, with
adverse, averse
affect, effect
agree to, with
all the farther, faster
allusion, illusion
already, all ready
altogether, all together
among, between

Part 2 (Lesson 35)

and etc.
anyways, nowheres,
   somewheres
as
at, to (*with* where)
awful, awfully
bad, badly
being as, that
beside, besides
better
but that, what

Part 3 (Lesson 37)

cannot help but
complement, compliment
contend against, for, with
correspond to, with
credible, credulous
different(ly) from, than
discover, invent
disregardless, irregardless
emigrate, immigrate
envelop, envelope

Part 4 (Lesson 38)

exalt, exult
farther, further
fewer, less
figure (out)
formally, formerly
get
had (hadn't) ought
hardly, scarcely
have got to
healthful, healthy

Part 5 (Lesson 39)

hear to
in, into
incredible, incredulous
inferior, superior
kind, kinds
later, latter
learn, teach
literally
lot, lots
mad

Part 6 (Lesson 40)

mighty
muchly
nohow
nowhere near
of
part from, with
piece
plus
pretend like
principal, principle

Part 7 (Lesson 42)

real, really
reckon
right
said, same
sight
so, such
sometime, some time
statue, stature, statute
suppose
suspect, suspicion

Part 8 (Lesson 43)

taunt, taut
their, there, they're
to, too, two
type
valuable, invaluable
wait for, on
want that
where
who's, whose
you all, you'ns, you's

Book Two Word List

Part 1

above
accept, except
adapt, adopt
advice, advise
ain't
all
all right
allude, elude, refer
almost, most
altar, alter

Part 2

always, all ways
amount, number
angry about, at, with
anymore, any more
as (if), like
awhile, a while
believe, feel
be sure and
burst, bursted, busted
can, may

Part 3

censor, censure
compare to, with
comprehensible, comprehensive
contemptible, contemptuous
continual, continuous
could (should, would) of
council, counsel
differ from, with
dilemma
disinterested, uninterested

Part 4

eminent, imminent, immanent
enormity
enthuse, enthused
everyday, every day
fabulous
flaunt, flout
good, well
haven't but, only
heap, heaps
hopefully

Part 5

how come
impact
imply, infer
in back of
ingenious, ingenuous
its, it's
kind (sort) of
lay, lie
let, leave
loose, lose

Part 6

maybe, may be
momentarily
nice
notable, noted, noteworthy, notorious
OK, okay
over with
persecute, prosecute
perspective, prospective
poorly
precede, proceed

Part 7

propose, purpose
quote
raise, rise
receipt, recipe
respectable, respectful, respective
right along
set, sit
some, somewhat
stationary, stationery
straight, strait

Part 8

than, then
them
this (these) here, that (those) there
transpire
try and
want in, off, out, through
way, ways
what for
worst kind, sort, way
your, you're

34. Correct Word Usage, Part 1

This chapter contains a listing of commonly misused or confused words. Book Two of this set contains a companion listing of other words. Each lesson includes ten items with brief explanations and illustrations to show how the words should be used.

Some example sentences are marked with labels that indicate levels of usage. *Standard* usage refers to what is proper for all speech and writing. Words and meanings in this category are shown in the dictionary without any special label. *Informal* usage is acceptable for everyday speech and for personal writing (such as friendly letters), but it is not recommended for public speaking or for compositions such as reports and explanations. Compare the following sentences.

Informal:
> We were <u>mighty</u> glad to see a service station just a <u>piece</u> down the road.

Standard:
> We were <u>very</u> glad to see a service station just a <u>short distance</u> down the road.

Many example sentences in this chapter are simply labeled *correct* if they represent standard usage, and *incorrect* if they do not. Study the illustrations below.

Incorrect:
> We appreciate <u>muchly</u> what <u>you'ns</u> have done for us.

Correct:
> We appreciate <u>very much</u> what <u>you</u> have done for us.

Ability, Capacity

Ability means "power to do."
Capacity means "power to receive (hold, absorb)." It also means "role; office; position."

> Study to the best of your <u>ability</u>. (not *capacity*)
> God has created man with the <u>capacity</u> for spiritual enlightenment.
> Brother Philip is serving in the <u>capacity</u> of treasurer.

Accompanied by, with

Accompanied by means "having as a companion" and refers to persons.
Accompanied with means "occurring with" and refers to things.

> Paul was <u>accompanied by</u> Barnabas on his first missionary journey.
> True success is always <u>accompanied with</u> diligence.

Note: In writing, change such passive voice constructions to the active voice if practical.

> Barnabas accompanied Paul on his first missionary journey.
> Diligence always accompanies true success.

Adverse, Averse

Adverse means "opposed; unfavorable." It usually refers to inanimate things.
Averse means "actively opposed (to something)." It involves an attitude of strong dislike or resistance.

> Because of <u>adverse</u> weather, we had to stay inside.
> The natural man is <u>averse</u> to self-denial.

Affect, Effect

Affect as a verb means "to influence" or "to give the appearance of."
Effect as a noun means "result." This is its most common use.
Effect as a verb means "to bring to pass" or "to cause."

> Your friends will <u>affect</u> the development of your character.
> Mrs. Hainly <u>affected</u> sympathy, but her voice revealed impatience.

> We can never fully measure the <u>effect</u> of our influence.
> The Holy Spirit <u>effects</u> a transformation in the believer's life.

Agree to, with

When two people or ideas are in harmony, they *agree with* each other. But when someone offers a suggestion that you approve, you *agree to* the suggestion.

> Did Leslie <u>agree with</u> you?
> This statement <u>agrees with</u> what the science book says.
> I can never <u>agree to</u> such a haphazard plan.

All the farther, faster

Avoid these and similar expressions. Instead, say "as far as," "as fast as," and so forth.

> This is <u>as far as</u> I have ever traveled west. (not *all the farther*)
> Fifty miles per hour is <u>as fast as</u> this old truck can go. (not *all the faster*)

Allusion, Illusion

An *allusion* is an indirect reference to something.
An *illusion* is a deceptive appearance or a false idea.

> The phrase "a behemoth of a machine" is an <u>allusion</u> to the huge animal described in Job 40.
> Luxury can easily give the <u>illusion</u> that all is well.

Already, All ready

Already means "earlier; previously."
All ready means "completely prepared." This phrase may also indicate that everyone in a group is prepared, and then the phrase can be separated.

> Kevin has <u>already</u> fed the heifers.
> Is Father <u>all ready</u> to begin milking?
> The boys are <u>all ready</u> to help him.
>> (Compare: All the boys are ready to help him.)

Altogether, All together

Altogether means "totally; thoroughly." It can also mean "in all."

All together means "in a group." A sentence with this phrase can always be reworded so that the words are separate.

> Man is <u>altogether</u> unable to provide his own salvation.
> There are twelve persons <u>altogether</u> in the Kimbal family.
> The Kimbal family was <u>all together</u> last Sunday.
> (Compare: All the Kimbal family was together last Sunday.)

Among, Between

Use *among* when referring to a group of more than two items.

Use *between* when referring to only two items. Also use *between* when referring to more than two items when each item is considered individually in relation to the others.

> Father divided the chores <u>among</u> the four boys. (divided *among* all the members in the group)
> Aunt Lucy must divide her time <u>between</u> caring for Grandmother and doing her other work. (divided *between* two things)
> Can you explain the difference <u>between</u> a cold front, a warm front, and an occluded front? (difference *between* each kind of front and each of the other two kinds)

Applying the Lesson

A. Choose the standard expressions in these sentences.

1. Following the Golden Rule will (affect, effect) an outlook that is (altogether, all together) different from that of a self-centered person.
2. God graciously gives us the (ability, capacity) to deal with every (adverse, averse) experience that we face.
3. God created man with the (ability, capacity) for spiritual understanding and the power to choose (among, between) right and wrong.
4. The words of God (affected, effected) the Israelites so strongly that the people (altogether, all together) declared, "All that the LORD hath said will we do."
5. Scoffers deny that God has (already, all ready) brought judgment once, and they cling to the (allusion, illusion) that God will never judge the world.
6. At first Mr. Lopez was (adverse, averse) to sending Pedro to Sunday school, but eventually he (agreed to, agreed with) his son's request.
7. The edge of the woods is (all the farther, as far as) the little children may go without being (accompanied by, accompanied with) an adult.
8. The neighbor's (allusion, illusion) to death was (accompanied by, accompanied with) a lighthearted remark.
9. Father (agreed to, agreed with) us that most of the proceeds from the watermelon sales could be divided (among, between) us four boys.
10. If this is (all the faster, as fast as) we can work, we will not be (already, all ready) to plant when Father returns.

B. Write the standard word or words for the underlined part of each sentence. If it needs no improvement, write *correct*.
1. People who do not believe the Bible sometimes make <u>illusions</u> to it unwittingly.
2. Only a person who is <u>all together</u> surrendered to God will obey Him completely.
3. We cannot fully measure the <u>effect</u> of our influence upon others.
4. God's questions to Job reveal that man has an extremely limited <u>ability</u> for a comprehension of the Almighty.
5. Every Christian should expect to face <u>averse</u> circumstances in life.
6. The testimony of true science always <u>agrees to</u> the testimony of the Scriptures.
7. We must never be deceived by the <u>illusion</u> that partial obedience is acceptable.
8. The class is <u>already</u> to go and sing for Brother Eli.
9. St. Louis, Missouri, is <u>all the farther</u> I have traveled from home.
10. <u>Between</u> the four of us, we had enough money to pay for the broken window.
11. Brother Fred has an amazing <u>capacity</u> to remember telephone numbers.
12. Aaron Johnson, <u>accompanied with</u> his two sons, came to borrow the tractor.
13. The cousins my age enjoyed the opportunity of being <u>all together</u> again.
14. This is <u>all the faster</u> I can walk with my lame knee.
15. We readily <u>agreed with</u> Juanita's plan for a walk to the creek.
16. Though I am <u>averse</u> to doing dangerous things, I do not want to avoid doing things just because they are difficult.
17. Darla and I divided the cleaning <u>among</u> ourselves.
18. Snow started falling two hours ago, and we <u>all ready</u> have four inches.
19. How does the North Atlantic Drift <u>effect</u> England's weather?
20. Severe thunderstorms, <u>accompanied by</u> hail and high winds, struck the area.

C. Write enough words to show how each sentence should be improved according to the rules you have studied. If a sentence needs no improvement, write *correct*.
1. Charles Kettering thought that early automobiles were all together too difficult and dangerous to start.
2. Turning a hand crank was all the faster that a person could crank the engine.
3. In addition, trying to start a car sometimes had averse results.
4. Many drivers had all ready suffered broken arms from engines that backfired.
5. People agreed with the idea that electricity was most likely the solution to the problem.
6. Mr. Kettering had no allusion about the kind of electric motor that was required.
7. Such a motor would need the capacity to put out a short but mighty burst of power.
8. An electric starter would need to be accompanied by a battery and a generator.
9. Kettering built a successful starter between the summers of 1910 and 1911.
10. The electric starter had a positive affect on people's interest in driving cars.

Review Exercises

A. Copy each underlined complement, and label it *PN, PA, DO, IO,* or *OC.* [17]
   1. A man found <u>traveling</u> <u>difficult</u> and lost his way in a snowstorm.
   2. Eventually a wagoner came by and rescued the stranded <u>man</u>.
   3. This kind benefactor was extremely <u>humble</u>.
   4. "Who are <u>you</u>?" asked the rescued traveler.
   5. "Tell <u>me</u> the <u>name</u> of the Good Samaritan," he responded.
   6. Thus he kept his <u>name</u> <u>secret</u>, refusing all honor and reward.

B. Label each underlined complement *DO ret., IO ret.,* or *OC ret.* [18]
   1. A man is made <u>heavenly</u> by a love of heaven.
   2. We are promised <u>grace</u> for every trial.
   3. A perfect example is given <u>man</u> by Christ's life on earth.
   4. The tomb was found <u>empty</u> by the women on Easter morning.
   5. Eternal praise is offered the <u>Lamb</u> by the heavenly multitudes.

---

35. Correct Word Usage, Part 2

And etc.

The abbreviation *etc.* stands for the Latin words *et cetera,* which mean "and the rest." Therefore, avoid using *and* with *etc.* Moreover, though *etc.* is correct for recipes, notes, and other informal uses, it should not be used in writing reports and business letters. Replace it with *and so on* or *and so forth.*

> People make bread from various grains: wheat, rye, barley, <u>and so on</u>.
> (not *etc.* or *and etc.*)

Even the phrase *and so on* should not be used very often. You can also use *such as* to show that a list is incomplete. Then you do not need *etc.* or *and so on.*

> People make bread from grains <u>such as</u> wheat, rye, and barley.

Anyways, Nowheres, Somewheres

Avoid the mistake of adding *s* to words like *anyway, anywhere, nowhere,* and *somewhere.*

> God did not want Balaam to go, but he went <u>anyway</u>. (not *anyways*)
> An angel rebuked Balaam <u>somewhere</u> along the way. (not *somewheres*)

As

Avoid the error of using *as* instead of *whether* or *that.*

> **Incorrect:** I'm not sure <u>as</u> we can finish this job today.
> **Correct:** I'm not sure <u>that</u> (or <u>whether</u>) we can finish this job today.

At, To

Do not use *at* or *to* after *where*.

Incorrect: Where are my boots <u>at</u>?
Where is Father going <u>to</u> this evening?
Correct: Where are my boots?
Where is Father going this evening?

Awful, Awfully

Use *awful* and *awfully* only to describe things that inspire awe, wonder, or terror. Do not use them to describe something merely unpleasant. Also avoid using them as intensives (words that add emphasis). If special emphasis is needed, use a word like *very, greatly, unusually,* or *extremely.*

Isaiah received a glimpse of the <u>awful</u> presence of God.
An <u>awful</u> flood ravaged the river town.

This sulfur water has a <u>disagreeable</u> taste. (not *awful*)
We were <u>greatly</u> surprised by the news. (not *awfully*)

Bad, Badly

Bad is an adjective meaning "not good." Do not use it as an adverb, especially to mean "very much." After the linking verb *feel,* the correct word is *bad,* not *badly.*

Badly is an adverb meaning "harmfully," "wickedly," or "poorly." It can also mean "very much."

In spite of David's faithfulness, Saul treated him <u>badly</u>. (not *bad*)
I felt <u>bad</u> about the broken dish. (not *badly*)
(Compare: I felt <u>happy</u> about the good results. [not *happily*])
Isaac needs new shoes <u>badly</u>. (not *bad*)

Being as, that

Do not use *being as* or *being that* to mean "because" or "since."

Incorrect:
<u>Being that</u> it rained, we could not work in the garden.
Correct:
<u>Because</u> it rained, we could not work in the garden.

Beside, Besides

Beside is a preposition meaning "by the side of."
Besides can be a preposition meaning "other than" or "in addition to." *Besides* can also be an adverb meaning "moreover."

Spotty was lying <u>beside</u> the front porch.
We have two other puppies <u>besides</u> Spotty.
We do not have room to keep three dogs; <u>besides</u>, it would cost too much.

Better

Avoid the error of using only *better* for the expression *had better.*

Incorrect: We <u>better</u> head for the house.
Correct: We <u>had better</u> head for the house.

But that, what

Do not use *but that* or *but what* after negative words. Use *whether* or *that,* or revise the sentence.

Incorrect: I do not know <u>but that</u> I shall go along too.
Correct: I do not know <u>whether</u> I shall go along too.
Revised: Perhaps I shall go along too.

Applying the Lesson

A. Choose the standard expressions in these sentences.

1. (Being that, Since) we are subject to falling, we (better, had better) avoid unnecessary temptations.
2. We need to follow Jesus (anywhere, anywheres), even though He does not always lead us (beside, besides) still waters.
3. We (better, had better) obey God's Word if we expect to dwell in heaven where the Lord (is, is at).
4. There is no question (but what, whether) God can accomplish His purposes, fulfill His promises, (and etc., and so on).
5. The poor widow probably felt (bad, badly) because she had nothing to give (beside, besides) two mites.
6. (Being as, Since) we had a late freeze, Father does not expect a large harvest of apples, peaches, (and etc., and so forth).
7. I am not sure (as, that) we can keep Tippy if he keeps on behaving so (bad, badly) when strangers come.
8. Frank was (awful, quite) sure he knew where he was (going, going to), but he lost his way.
9. Since it was not certain (as, whether) the county market would be open, we went (somewhere, somewheres) else.
10. I would not be (awfully, greatly) surprised (but that, that) we shall find Tabby sleeping beside Duke.

B. Write the standard word or words for the underlined part of each sentence. If it needs no improvement, write *correct.*

1. <u>Nowheres</u> in the Bible do we read of Jesus having long hair like a Nazarite.
2. Shortly after the ship left Phenice, an <u>awful</u> tempest arose.
3. We must guard our friendships, <u>being as</u> our friends influence our lives.
4. If your friends are tempting you to do wrong, <u>you better</u> take warning.
5. Where does Grandfather want us to <u>put these apples at</u>?
6. The students who behaved <u>bad</u> for the substitute will be punished.
7. <u>Besides</u> my regular assignments, I must write a report about our trip.
8. I am not sure <u>as</u> I can finish my report this evening.

9. Do you know where this bus is <u>going to</u>?
10. I do not know <u>but what</u> I should go along.
11. My uncle delivers gasoline, kerosene, diesel fuel, <u>and etc.</u>, which many farmers buy in bulk.
12. Father stacked the berry boxes <u>somewhere</u> in the garage.
13. We hardly <u>expected as</u> these plants would produce as well as they did.
14. <u>I better</u> spend some more time studying for that history test.
15. You never know <u>but what</u> a test may be harder than you expect.
16. The ketchup in this bottle has an <u>awful</u> taste.
17. Aunt Beatrice felt <u>badly</u> that her cake burned.
18. Do you know the older man who is sitting <u>besides</u> Father?
19. <u>Being that</u> it is raining, this is a good day to clean the basement.
20. We will need to sweep the cobwebs from the ceiling, carry out the trash, hose down the floor, <u>and etc.</u>

C. Write enough words to show how each sentence should be improved according to the rules you have studied. If a sentence needs no improvement, write *correct*.
1. In August 1904, St. Louis was the place where the Louisiana Purchase Exposition was held at.
2. Many people who lived anywheres near the city attended the exposition.
3. Vendors were selling sandwiches, cakes, candy, and etc.
4. An ice cream seller named Charles Menches had no idea as he would become the inventor of the ice cream cone.
5. On one awfully warm day, Menches ran out of ice cream dishes.
6. He needed more dishes bad.
7. Menches did not know but that he would have to start turning customers away.
8. He realized that he better do something quickly.
9. Besides his stand was the stand of a man who was selling a kind of waffle.
10. Being that nothing better was available, Menches placed a scoop of ice cream on a rolled-up waffle—and began selling the world's first ice cream cones.

Review Exercises

Write enough words to show how each sentence should be improved according to the rules you have studied. If a sentence needs no improvement, write *correct*. [34, 35]
1. Beside the Anabaptists of the 1500s, many Christians of earlier centuries suffered persecution for their faith.
2. A minister named Albert, who lived somewheres in France, taught against Catholic doctrines around A.D. 750.
3. This man declared that infant baptism, the worship of saints, and other Catholic practices were altogether unscriptural.
4. Albert had the capacity to express himself in writing as well as speaking.
5. A bishop named Boniface was averse to Albert's teachings.

6. Boniface accused Albert to the pope, bringing some awful charges against him.
7. The pope immediately condemned Albert as a heretic, even though he did not know but that the charges were true or false.
8. Being that Albert was excommunicated, he was shamefully deposed from the ministry.
9. He was cast into prison, where, it is thought, he died of hunger, thirst, and etc.
10. A monastery in France is where Albert was imprisoned at.

---

36. Improving Your Writing Style, Part 3: Active Voice

In the previous two writing style lessons, you learned that originality and the use of exact words characterize good writing style. That is, an effective writer looks for fresh, colorful ways of expressing himself, and he strives to use nouns, verbs, and modifiers that paint clear, vivid pictures.

Another element of good writing style is the deliberate use of verbs in the active voice. You should remember that transitive verbs can be active or passive. In the active voice, the subject *performs* the action of the verb. But in the passive voice, the subject merely *receives* the action.

Active voice:
> Jochebed <u>hid</u> the baby Moses in an ark of bulrushes.
> His sister <u>watched</u> the ark as it floated in the water.

Passive voice:
> The baby Moses <u>was hidden</u> in an ark of bulrushes by Jochebed.
> The ark <u>was watched</u> by Moses' sister as it floated in the water.

The active voice puts energy into writing because it makes the subject do something. Jochebed *hid* the baby; his sister *watched* the ark. In contrast, the passive voice introduces a passive subject that never gets into the action! The baby Moses did nothing; he simply *was hidden.* The ark did nothing; it merely *was watched.*

This difference between active voice and passive voice makes a great contrast in writing. While the passive voice is dull and sluggish, the active voice is lively and energetic. We can understand this; but unless we think carefully as we write, the passive voice will slip into our sentences and snuff out the action. See how that happens in the following example.

> Moses tended Jethro's sheep for many years. One day on the back side of the desert, Moses saw an unusual sight. A bush was engulfed in flames but was not consumed. Moses turned aside to see what was happening. As he

drew near to the bush, a voice was heard: "Moses, Moses."

"Here am I," he answered.

Did you catch it? *A voice was heard.* Why should we record this action with a passive verb? God Almighty called one of His servants. We want to capture that action: As he drew near to the bush, *God called to him,* "Moses, Moses." Or we could say that *he heard a voice.* Either way, we are using the active voice, and the action puts life into the writing style.

You see this, but did you see the other use of the passive voice in the example? *A bush was engulfed in flames but was not consumed.* Again we have a subject with no action; the bush is merely being acted upon. How can we write this in the active voice? To answer that question, consider *what action* was taking place and *who* or *what* was doing it. *Flames engulfed a bush but did not consume it.* Now we have action; now we have life.

Of course, the passive voice does exist for a good reason. Sometimes there is no clear doer of the action, and sometimes we deliberately avoid naming the doer. Also, the passive voice may fit well in a sentence that pictures someone as the victim of a tragedy or disaster: *Naboth was stoned to death.* However, the passive voice nearly always weakens writing style. It allows a person to write in vague generalities without saying exactly *who* does the things he describes. Therefore, in this lesson you will try to avoid the passive voice completely.

Your assignment in this lesson will be to write a Bible story. When some people write Bible stories, they tend to add details from their imagination. But such details can give wrong impressions that may actually hinder a proper understanding of the Bible. For example, in writing about the heavenly visitors coming to Abraham, a person may thoughtlessly write the following sentence.

> Abraham quickly prepared a meal <u>because he had just finished his own meal</u>.
> (This may actually be true, for the Bible says that the visitors came "in the heat of the day"—perhaps right after the noon meal. But the Bible does not specifically say that, so we should not write it.)

To stick with the facts, you might write something like this:

> Abraham quickly prepared a meal <u>while the visitors rested under the tree</u>.

A closely related trap that writers may fall into is misinterpreting Bible facts. Did Joseph relate his dreams *proudly*? The Bible gives no reason to think that he did. Did Jesus have long hair? No; He was a *Nazarene,* not a *Nazarite.*

This does not mean that a Bible story must be nothing more than a rewriting of a set of verses. Sometimes other Bible passages contain information about a Bible account. For example, the Bible account of the baby Moses does not give his mother's name, but we can find that detail in other Scripture passages. Further, as you write a Bible story, you might include details about the setting and customs. The story about Moses and the burning bush could include descriptive details about the desert land of Midian.

The Bible is the inspired Word of God and deserves to be treated with the highest reverence. Be creative but accurate in writing its stories, for they help to shape a reader's impressions of the Bible itself.

Applying the Lesson

A. Read the story below, and do the following exercises in class.

1. Find the one passive verb in each paragraph, and notice how it spoils the action. Suggest how to improve that sentence or clause with a verb in the active voice.

2. Tell whether each underlined expression has a *good* or *poor* effect on the story. If it is good, tell why. If it is poor, suggest how to improve it.

Isaac, the Peacemaker

1   While Isaac lived in the land of the Philistines, God [a]brought so many blessings upon him that he was envied by the Philistines. Finally the king said, "Get out of our land, for you are much mightier than we are." [b]Isaac did not use his might to prove that he could live wherever he pleased. Instead, he [c]peaceably moved his possessions and people to the valley of Gerar.

2   Here Isaac's servants reopened the wells that had been dug by Abraham many years before. Plenty of [d]water came gushing from a well in the valley. But the Philistines [e]quarreled with Isaac's herdsmen. They [f]said, "The water is ours"—even though [g]by custom, digging a well entitled a person to the land around it. But Isaac simply moved away and had his servants dig open another well. Again the Philistine herdsmen fought for the well, and again Isaac withdrew—[h]taking his wealth and his might with him.

3   This time Isaac [i]went farther away and had his servants dig yet another well. At last Isaac could live in peace, for no one came to quarrel about this well. The well was named Rehoboth, which means "broad places." Isaac [j]testified, "The Lord hath made room for us, and we shall be fruitful in the land."

4   Later Isaac moved to Beer-sheba, [k]the most important oasis in southern Canaan. Here Isaac was given this [l]reassuring message by God: "I am the God of Abraham thy father: fear not, for I am with thee, and will bless thee."

5   Soon visitors came to see Isaac—[m]the same Philistines who had earlier sent him away! Naturally, Isaac asked, "Why have you come to me? You [n]dislike me and sent me away from your land." They replied, "We have seen that the Lord is with you. Let a promise be made that we will be friends."

6   What a contrast! Instead of separating because of [o]bad feelings as before, this time they parted in peace. How this must have [p]thrilled Isaac's heart with joy! Surely he was blessed by God for his efforts to live in peace with his neighbors.

B. Write a story of 200–300 words about Naaman's healing from 2 Kings 5. *Use no passive voice* in your writing. Also put special effort into applying the other elements of writing style that you have studied: originality and exact words.

---

37. Correct Word Usage, Part 3

Cannot help but

Because both *not* and *but* are negative words, they make double negatives when used together. *But* should be omitted in expressions like *cannot help but* and *could not help but.*

> **Incorrect:** I could not help but feel sad when Shep was run over.
> **Correct:**   I could not help feeling sad when Shep was run over.

Complement, Compliment

A *complement* is something that completes or fits well with another thing. As a memory device, associate *complement* with *complete.*

A *compliment* is an expression of praise or commendation.

> Wholesome speech complements the Christian's profession.
> Brother Rudolph complimented Titus's neat work.

Contend against, for, with

To *contend against* is to struggle with something difficult or unpleasant.
To *contend for* is to put forth effort in support of something, such as a principle.
To *contend with* is to strive against an opposing person or thing.

> Many Christians have contended against the wrath of civil rulers.
> Jude wrote that we should "earnestly contend for the faith."
> It is common for carnal people to contend with each other.

Correspond to, with

Use *correspond to* when showing how two things relate.
Use *correspond with* when referring to communication between two persons.

> Our lives must correspond to the pattern upheld in God's Word.
> I regularly correspond with Delmar Landis, my cousin in Paraguay.

Credible, Credulous

Credible means "correct" or "believable" and refers to things.
Credulous means "gullible" or "too easily convinced" and refers to people.

> Harvey's account of the mishap seemed the most credible.
> Duane was too credulous when he believed Mr. Shawly's story.

Different(ly) from, than

Use the preposition *from* to introduce a prepositional phrase after *different* or *differently.*

Use the conjunction *than* to introduce an adverb clause after *different* or *differently.*

A Christian's goals are quite <u>different from</u> the world's goals.
(*From the world's goals* is a prepositional phrase.)
Therefore, a Christian lives <u>differently than</u> the world lives.
(*Than the world lives* is an adverb clause.)

Discover, Invent

Discover means "to find" and is used only in referring to things that already exist.

Invent means "to make for the first time."

After Benjamin Franklin <u>discovered</u> that lightning is a form of electricity, he <u>invented</u> the lightning rod.

Disregardless, Irregardless

Neither of these is a standard English word. The negative prefixes *dis-* and *ir-* are unnecessary with the suffix *-less.* Simply use *regardless.*

The remaining Jews fled to Egypt <u>regardless</u> of Jeremiah's warning.
(not *disregardless* or *irregardless*)

Emigrate, Immigrate

Emigrate and *emigration* speak of leaving one country and settling in another. As a memory device, associate <u>e</u>migrate with <u>e</u>xit.

Immigrate and *immigration* speak of entering a country and settling there. As a memory device, associate <u>i</u>mmigrate with <u>i</u>nto.

Abram and his family <u>emigrated</u> from the land of the Chaldees and <u>immigrated</u> to Canaan.

Envelop, Envelope

Envelop is accented on the second syllable. It is a verb that means "to cover or wrap."

Envelope is accented on the first syllable. It is a noun that means "a covering or wrapping."

Despair cannot <u>envelop</u> a person who trusts the Lord.
God created the earth with an <u>envelope</u> of life-sustaining air.

Applying the Lesson

A. Choose the standard expressions in these sentences.
1. One who truly knows the Lord cannot (help but love, help loving) Him.
2. The righteous remnant has always contended (against, for, with) the forces of evil and apostasy.
3. A simple life (complements, compliments) a meek spirit.

4. Saul insisted that he had kept the Lord's command (regardless, irregardless) of his obvious disobedience.
5. Unless our values are different (from, than) the world's, we will become like the world.
6. Many persecutors were so (credible, credulous) that they believed preposterous tales about the Christians.
7. Do not contend (against, for, with) others or insist on your own way.
8. We must reject any teaching that does not correspond (with, to) God's Word.
9. (Regardless, Disregardless) of Howard's penmanship last year, his handwriting is now a model of neatness.
10. Soon flames will (envelop, envelope) the old shack.
11. We students have been corresponding (with, to) students from the Oakdale Mennonite School.
12. My uncle Bernhard holds patents for several small gadgets that he (discovered, invented).
13. My ancestors came into America as (emigrants, immigrants) seeking religious freedom.
14. The whole family (complemented, complimented) Susan for her delicious meal.
15. After testing the tiller, we could not (help but admit, help admitting) that the salesman knew what he was talking about.
16. In 1968, Chili Fu (emigrated, immigrated) from North Korea at great risk.
17. At first we wondered whether his story was (credible, credulous).
18. This day has turned out quite differently (from, than) we had expected.
19. In 1898 Sir William Ramsay (discovered, invented) neon, a rare gas in the atmosphere.
20. A cornhusk is an example of an (envelop, envelope) in nature.

B. Write the standard word or words for the underlined part of each sentence. If it needs no improvement, write *correct.*

1. Because of their conformity to Christ, Christians cannot help but be a distinct people.
2. Therefore, they live differently than the world.
3. If we do not contend with the faith, we will drift with the tide.
4. Youth need spiritual conviction to do right irregardless of what others do.
5. A mature person does his best without looking for complements.
6. Joshua's and Norma's accounts of the mishap corresponded to Anita's.
7. A shroud of fog often envelopes the valley below our house.
8. We should finish weeding these beans disregardless of the heat.
9. Only an overly credible person would believe that story!
10. Mr. and Mrs. Mastiano immigrated from Italy as a young married couple.
11. Do you know who invented the law of universal gravitation?
12. We could not help but laugh at the monkey's antics.
13. The John Higgins family immigrated to the United States five years ago.

14. How many <u>envelops</u> do we have?
15. Our bishops have <u>corresponded with</u> government leaders on the draft issue.
16. The rescue team <u>contended with</u> cold rain and mud slides to reach the isolated hut.
17. Johannes Kepler <u>invented</u> important principles of planetary motion.
18. The story ending is <u>different than</u> I had expected.
19. This dark brown trim <u>compliments</u> the tan walls perfectly.
20. The plot in Kay's story seems more <u>credible</u> than the one in Jean's story.

C. Write enough words to show how each sentence should be improved according to the rules you have studied. If a sentence needs no improvement, write *correct.*
   1. In the 1890s, businesses were corresponding with many people just as they do today.
   2. Hundreds of workers were hired to address envelops by hand.
   3. Poor people who had emigrated into America sometimes did this kind of tedious work.
   4. It was a slow process irregardless of how fast a person could write.
   5. Joseph Duncan could not help but consider how inefficient the system was.
   6. It did not seem credulous that this was a good use of time and money.
   7. Duncan discovered a machine called an addressograph, which printed addresses automatically.
   8. If a man owned a business that involved much correspondence, this machine was an excellent compliment to his equipment.
   9. Years later, the addressograph had to contend with computers, and it became outmoded.
   10. But Joseph Duncan was the first man to devise a method different than the system of addressing mail by hand.

Review Exercises

Write enough words to show how each sentence should be improved according to the rules you have studied. If a sentence needs no improvement, write *correct.*
[34–37]
   1. Albert of France was accompanied with Clement of Scotland in his stand for the truth.
   2. Clement agreed to Albert in speaking against false doctrines.
   3. Among the two of them, these men influenced many people in France.
   4. Their preaching had a powerful affect on the multitudes, but it also stirred up opposition.
   5. Soon a judgment was pronounced upon Clement which was no different than the judgment upon Albert.
   6. Clement could not help but seek to clear himself before a church council; however, Boniface (the bishop) was able to keep that from happening.
   7. Boniface made the people believe that it was unlawful for Clement to speak before the council, being as he had been declared a heretic.
   8. Having discovered this fact, Clement wrote a book against Boniface, in which he explained the matter.

9. In the end, irregardless of the pope's disapproval, Clement was condemned to be burned at the stake.

10. The flames and smoke enveloped Clement, and soon he was in heaven with the Lord.

---

38. Correct Word Usage, Part 4

Exalt, Exult

Exalt means "to elevate" or "to glorify." It has the root *alt,* which means "high" as in *altitude.* The noun form of *exalt* is *exaltation.*

Exult means "to rejoice" and refers especially to triumphant rejoicing. The noun form of *exult* is *exultation.*

> "Exalt the LORD our God, and worship at his holy hill."
> David did not want the Philistines to exult over Saul's death.

Farther, Further

Farther is preferred in speaking of physical distance.

Further is preferred in speaking of degree. As a memory device, associate it with the verb *further,* which means "to advance to a greater degree."

> We drive farther to school than to church.
> The teacher explained the lesson further.
> He tried to further our understanding.

Fewer, Less

Fewer is plural and refers to quantity (things that are counted).

Less is singular and refers to mass (something that is not counted). It may also refer to the whole of something that is measured, even if the number of units is plural.

> The doctor said that Grandfather should eat less meat and fewer eggs.
>   (not *less eggs*)
> We had driven less than ten miles when a tire went flat.

Figure (out)

When *figure* is used as a verb, its standard meaning is "to calculate." *Figure* is informal when it is used to mean "to think; to suppose; to believe; to plan."

Figure out is an informal expression with meanings like "to understand," "to solve," or "to decide."

> **Informal:** What time do you figure the guests will arrive?
>   We will need to figure out where they all will sleep.
> **Standard:** You must figure carefully to solve a math problem correctly.
>   What time do you think the guests will arrive?
>   We will need to decide where they all will sleep.

Formally, Formerly
Formally means "according to an established form or rule."
Formerly means "previously."

> Mr. Gratz has <u>formally</u> become a United States citizen.
> He <u>formerly</u> lived in Saskatchewan, Canada.

Get
This overworked, general verb means "to come into possession of," with or without effort or initiative. More precise verbs often communicate more effectively. *Acquire* suggests adding to something already possessed.

> I must <u>acquire</u> some additional information for my report.

Earn suggests doing something to receive the thing possessed.

> Matilda certainly <u>earned</u> the five dollars she received.

Gain implies receiving possession of something valuable.

> Our labors have helped us to <u>gain</u> a bountiful harvest.

Obtain and *procure* imply receiving something by putting forth special effort.

> After several attempts, Father <u>obtained</u> the building permit.
> Brother Mack <u>procured</u> some used desks for our school.

Had (hadn't) ought
Avoid these nonstandard expressions. Use either *ought* and *ought not,* or *should* and *should not.*

> **Incorrect:**
> You <u>hadn't ought</u> to insist on your way; instead you <u>had ought</u> to practice the Golden Rule.
> **Correct:**
> You <u>ought not</u> to insist on your way; instead you <u>should</u> practice the Golden Rule.

Hardly, Scarcely
Either of these words conveys a negative meaning; do not use them with other negative words.

> **Incorrect:** We <u>won't hardly</u> arrive at Grandfather's before eight o'clock.
> **Correct:**   We <u>will hardly</u> arrive at Grandfather's before eight o'clock.

Have got to
Replace expressions like *have got to* and *has got to* with *must.*

> **Incorrect:**
> Dora <u>has got to</u> weed the flower beds, and <u>I've got to</u> prune the roses.
> **Correct:**
> Dora <u>must</u> weed the flower beds, and <u>I must</u> prune the roses.

Healthful, Healthy

Healthful means "promoting good health" and should be used to describe nonliving things.

Healthy means "having good health" and should be used to describe living things.

> Cleanliness, exercise, and proper rest are <u>healthful</u> practices that help to keep us <u>healthy</u>.

Applying the Lesson

A. Choose the standard expressions in these sentences.
1. In our daily lives, we should (exalt, exult) the Lord.
2. At first, Joshua sent (fewer, less) soldiers to Ai than he had taken to Jericho.
3. As Abraham walked with God, God revealed Himself (farther, further) to him.
4. Those who would please God (have got to, must) respect the authorities over them.
5. An orange makes a (healthful, healthy) addition to a breakfast.
6. Mr. Baldwin was (formally, formerly) from this neighborhood.
7. We are allowed to (borrow, get) no more than three books at a time from the school library.
8. The news of Mother's recovery filled us with (exaltation, exultation).
9. Aunt Louella's flowers are looking quite (healthful, healthy).
10. Benjamin hit the ball (farther, further) than he ever has before.
11. The judge (formally, formerly) opens the court session with a rap of his gavel.
12. I cannot (figure out, understand) what is wrong with the lawn mower.
13. One servant received only two talents, but he (gained, got) two more.
14. We too (had ought to, should) work with whatever talents the Lord gives us.
15. I see (fewer, less) weeds in your flower bed than in mine.
16. I am (planning, figuring) to weed my flowers today.
17. There is (hardly any, hardly no) reason for being ignorant of the Bible in America today.
18. You (have got to, must) be careful, or you will cause an accident.
19. People who live in glasshouses (hadn't ought, ought not) to throw stones.
20. We (had scarcely, hadn't scarcely) arrived when a blizzard struck.

B. Write the standard word or words for the underlined part of each sentence. If it needs no improvement, write *correct.*
1. Because of all that the Lord has done for us, we <u>had ought to</u> live for Him.
2. Our hearts <u>exalt</u> in answered prayer.
3. Often we should pray with <u>less words</u> and greater faith.
4. The Bible reveals all we need to know for salvation; we need no <u>farther</u> revelation.
5. By referring to Genesis 6:15 and a table of Bible measures, you can <u>figure</u> the approximate size of Noah's ark.

6. We <u>can't scarcely</u> imagine the terror of those who perished in the Flood.
7. We <u>ought not</u> fail to give thanks daily to our gracious heavenly Father.
8. The lost boy was found <u>further</u> away from his home than anyone had expected.
9. <u>You have got to see</u> the danger of thinking that little things do not matter.
10. Grandmother looks remarkably <u>healthful</u> again.
11. Mr. Roberts, our neighbor, <u>figures</u> that the Bible is a myth.
12. Did you <u>get</u> enough money to buy a bicycle by working for Brother Marcus?
13. We <u>didn't hardly expect</u> this much help to clean up the storm damage.
14. Antrim Gardener's Supply was <u>formerly</u> owned by Mr. Berkson.
15. Frances Worthington <u>exults</u> her opinion above everyone else's.
16. These expensive clocks usually have <u>fewer defects</u> than the cheaper ones.
17. The hungry refugees finally <u>got</u> some food from a kindhearted farmer.
18. A flower <u>has got to be pollinated</u> before it can produce seeds.
19. The tour guide addressed the group very <u>formerly</u>, allowing little opportunity for questions.
20. Apples are more <u>healthy</u> than cookies and candy.

C. Write enough words to show how each sentence should be improved according to the rules you have studied. If a sentence needs no improvement, write *correct.*
   1. Formerly in the United States, if a person wanted a drink of water in a public place, he had to use a public drinking cup.
   2. A man named Hugh Moore did not consider these tin cups very healthy.
   3. He thought a person hadn't ought to drink from contaminated utensils.
   4. If a more sanitary method were used, less diseases would be spread.
   5. "There has got to be something better," he thought.
   6. Moore figured out a way to make paper cups.
   7. He must have exalted over his solution to the problem.
   8. Moore got a patent for his "Health Cups" in 1908.
   9. Later they were called "Dixie Cups," and there wasn't hardly a railroad car in the nation without them.
   10. A farther development was the use of drinking fountains instead of paper cups.

Review Exercises

Write enough words to show how each sentence should be improved according to the rules you have studied. If a sentence needs no improvement, write *correct.*
[34–38]
   1. Two young maidens named Nunilo and Aloida, who lived in Spain, contended for the Christian faith in A.D. 851.
   2. Their mother professed Christianity; but she was not all together faithful, for she married a Muslim after her husband died.
   3. When their stepfather treated them bad, the two sisters went to live with their aunt, a sincere Christian.
   4. Soon the maidens were formally accused before a Muslim judge.

5. The judge promised that if they renounced Christianity, they would receive many gifts; and beside, he would obtain excellent husbands for them.
6. He said that they better embrace Mohammedanism, or they would be severely punished.
7. The sisters would not be persuaded, for they had all ready determined that they would never deny Christ.
8. The judge figured that his best choice was to commit Nunilo and Aloida to two different women, who would keep the maidens apart and instruct them in Mohammedanism.
9. But this made hardly no difference at all; both sisters remained as "stubborn" as ever.
10. Finally the Muslims got Nunilo and Aloida before the tribunal, made a public spectacle of them, and executed them with the sword.

---

39. Correct Word Usage, Part 5

Hear to

Do not use *hear to* for "listen to" or "consider."

Incorrect:
Joseph pleaded with his brothers, but they would not <u>hear to</u> him.
Mr. Narvon would not <u>hear to</u> letting Father pay for the bologna.
Correct:
Joseph pleaded with his brothers, but they would not <u>listen to</u> him.
Mr. Narvon would not <u>consider</u> letting Father pay for the bologna.

In, Into

In refers mainly to location.

Into refers to entrance or movement to a point of contact. With a verb like *put* or *take,* either preposition may be correct, depending on whether entrance or location is being emphasized.

Some lampshades are <u>in</u> this large box.
Put the box <u>in</u> the van. (location emphasized)

Put the box <u>into</u> the van. (entrance emphasized)
Be careful not to run <u>into</u> anyone.

Incredible, Incredulous

Incredible means "unbelievable" or "hard to believe" and refers to stories, experiences, and so forth.

Incredulous means "unbelieving" and refers to people.

Mrs. Zarger told an <u>incredible</u> story about surviving a tornado.
Noah could not convince the <u>incredulous</u> people that a flood was coming.

Inferior, Superior

The correct word after *inferior* and *superior* is *to,* not *than.*

Incorrect: This mower is <u>superior than</u> the one we had before.
Correct: This mower is <u>superior to</u> the one we had before.

Kind, Kinds

Use the singular words *this* and *that* with *kind,* and the plural words *these* and *those* with *kinds.* (Either singular or plural should be used throughout the construction.) The same applies to the words *sort* and *type* in expressions like this.

Incorrect: <u>These kind</u> of <u>books</u> can be rewarding.
Correct: <u>This kind</u> of <u>book</u> can be rewarding.
            <u>These kinds</u> of <u>books</u> can be rewarding.

Later, Latter

Later refers to time.
Latter refers to the second of two things mentioned. (If more than two things are named, use *last* to refer to the final one.)

We arrived <u>later</u> than we had expected.
Mother made a pie and a cake, and she served the <u>latter</u> for supper.

Learn, Teach

Learn means "to gain knowledge or skill."
Teach means "to impart knowledge" or "to instruct."

We can <u>learn</u> many things if we listen as others <u>teach</u> us.

Literally

The word *literally* means "actually; not figuratively." But by a strange twist of logic, some people use this word when they mean exactly the opposite.

Incorrect: My heart <u>literally</u> jumped into my throat when I heard the crash.
Correct: My heart <u>seemingly</u> jumped into my throat when I heard the crash.
            My heart jumped into my throat when I heard the crash.
            My heart <u>literally</u> pounded in my chest when I heard the crash.

Lot, Lots

Lot and *lots* are used informally in various expressions that mean "much" or "many." Replace them with standard expressions that are clear and precise.

Informal: We have <u>lots of</u> blessings for which we praise God.
Standard: We have <u>abundant</u> blessings for which we praise God.

Mad

The standard meaning of this word is "insane," "crazy," or "frenzied." Do not use it to mean "angry" when referring to people.

A <u>mad</u> dog terrorized the village for several hours.
The stranger was <u>angry</u> because his car wouldn't start. (not *mad*)

Applying the Lesson

A. Choose the standard expressions in these sentences.

1. God's grace (learns, teaches) us how to live in a wicked world.
2. Even though Bible miracles are humanly impossible, we must not read about them with (incredible, incredulous) minds.
3. Christ's blood is far superior (than, to) that of bulls and goats.
4. Hardships can (learn, teach) us to rely more fully on the Lord.
5. We need these (kind, kinds) of disciplines to help us grow.
6. When the Israelites shouted, the walls of Jericho (literally, seemingly) toppled to the ground.
7. The Israelite soldiers marched right (in, into) Jericho.
8. Both Elijah and Isaiah filled important roles, but only the (later, latter) prophet wrote a book of the Bible.
9. Jesus taught (in, into) Jerusalem until just a few days before His crucifixion.
10. As sources of fiber, cakes and cookies are far inferior (than, to) fruits and vegetables.
11. Sometimes the pioneers faced (incredible, incredulous) hardships and dangers.
12. Hundreds of animals, (angry, mad) with fear, fled from the raging fire.
13. Because of road construction, we came home (later, latter) than we had hoped.
14. We have helped Mr. Delp with his garden (lots of, many) times.
15. He especially likes (this, these) kind of tomato.
16. Eli rebuked his sons, but they would not (hear to, listen to) his words.
17. Their hearts were (literally, seemingly) as hard as stone.
18. The customer became (angry, mad) and stormed out of the shop.
19. What a (lot, great number) of stars are shining tonight!
20. A wise man will (hear to, consider) advice from other people.

B. Write the standard word or words for the underlined part of each sentence. If it needs no improvement, write *correct.*

1. Abishai wanted to kill King Saul, but David would not <u>hear to</u> it.
2. While David was fleeing from Saul, <u>lots of</u> discontented Israelites came to him.
3. Those who consider themselves <u>superior to</u> others are on a collision course with reality.
4. Do not live for wealth, or you <u>will literally drown</u> yourself in earthly cares.
5. Like the apostle Paul, we must <u>learn</u> ourselves to be content at all times.
6. After Noah and his family stepped <u>in the ark,</u> God shut the door.
7. Lot's sons-in-law were too <u>incredulous</u> to leave Sodom.
8. Both Judas and Peter failed their Lord, but the <u>latter</u> disciple repented.
9. Even though <u>a whole lot of people</u> reject truth, it remains unchangeable.
10. <u>Those kind</u> of wrong attitudes will produce a disastrous spiritual harvest.
11. The fall of the Roman Empire is an <u>incredulous</u> tale of corruption.
12. Many people were quite <u>mad</u> because of the traffic jam.

13. The ants can <u>learn</u> us important lessons if only we pay attention.
14. Mother declares that this soap is <u>inferior than</u> what she had been using.
15. I offered to do the dishes, but Grandmother would not <u>hear to</u> that.
16. My parents moved from Maryland to Ohio, and they have lived at the <u>later</u> place for twenty years now.
17. At more than seven feet tall, Alan Beachy <u>is literally</u> a giant of a man.
18. A policeman shot the <u>mad</u> dog before it <u>had bitten</u> anyone.
19. Do you know if Father has come <u>in the house</u> yet?
20. We have never planted <u>these kind</u> of beans before.

C. Write enough words to show how each sentence should be improved according to the rules you have studied. If a sentence needs no improvement, write *correct.*
   1. In 1890, an American named James Fargo went in a European bank and tried to cash a check.
   2. He was a rich man who had literally thousands of dollars.
   3. But the tellers would not hear to cashing his check, for Fargo was unknown to them.
   4. Fargo was incredible because of the situation.
   5. Instead of becoming mad, Fargo later asked an employee to see if he could solve the problem.
   6. Fargo learned that the solution was simple.
   7. These kind of problems could be eliminated with checks that the bearer signed twice: once when he obtained the checks and once when he cashed them.
   8. If the latter signature matched the first one, it would prove that the check was not stolen.
   9. Today lots of people use traveler's checks when traveling in foreign countries.
   10. Carrying these checks is superior than carrying large amounts of cash.

Review Exercises

Write enough words to show how each sentence should be improved according to the rules you have studied. If a sentence needs no improvement, write *correct.* [34–39]
   1. In A.D. 925, a thirteen-year-old boy named Pelagius fearlessly exulted the name of Christ before an Arabian king.
   2. The king would not hear to such a testimony; instead, he proposed some improper things to the youth.
   3. Pelagius would not agree with the evil suggestion.
   4. He said that he was all ready to die for Christ rather than pollute his soul and body with such abominations.
   5. The king promised that if Pelagius renounced his faith, he would be taken in the royal court and brought up in pomp and splendor.
   6. But the youth declared that he would obey only Christ's commands as long as he lived, irregardless of the consequences.

7. The king became so mad that he ordered the guards to torment Pelagius with tongs until he died or renounced Christ.
8. In the midst of incredulous suffering, the youth prayed that God would deliver him from his enemies.
9. The guards literally cut the boy limb from limb and threw the pieces into the river.
10. The glories of heaven await all who contend valiantly for the true Christian faith.

---

40. Correct Word Usage, Part 6

Mighty

The adjective *mighty* means "powerful," "great in size," or "extraordinary." In standard English, avoid using *mighty* as an intensive. Use words like *quite, deeply, highly,* or *greatly* instead.

> **Informal:** We were <u>mighty</u> surprised to see Aunt Gladys drive in.
> **Standard:** We were <u>quite</u> surprised to see Aunt Gladys drive in.
> We serve a <u>mighty</u> God.

Muchly

The form *muchly* is not a proper word. *Much* can be an adverb as well as an adjective.

> **Incorrect:** Your help is <u>muchly</u> appreciated.
> **Correct:**   Your help is <u>much</u> (or <u>greatly</u>) appreciated.

Nohow

Some people use *nohow* to mean "not at all" or "in no way." Avoid it in standard English.

> **Incorrect:**
> We were <u>nohow</u> ready for that first killing frost.
> **Correct:**
> We were <u>not at all</u> ready for that first killing frost.

Nowhere near

The informal expression *nowhere near* means "not nearly." Avoid it in standard English.

> **Informal:**
> Andrew thought the food was <u>nowhere near</u> enough to feed the multitude.
> **Standard:**
> Andrew thought the food was <u>not nearly</u> enough to feed the multitude.

Of

Do not use *of* after the prepositions *off, inside,* and *outside.* When *inside* and *outside* are used as nouns, the preposition *of* may follow.

The flowerpot fell <u>off</u> the windowsill. (not *off of*)
All the heifers are safely <u>inside</u> their pen. (not *inside of*)
The <u>inside of</u> this kettle is dirty.

Part from, with

Part from means "to leave; to go away from" and refers to people.
Part with means "to give up (a possession)" and refers to things.

After Jesus had blessed the disciples, He <u>parted from</u> them.
Many Christians have <u>parted with</u> their homes for Jesus' sake.

Piece

The word *piece* is used informally to mean "distance" and especially "short distance."

Informal:
Brother Leon lives only a <u>piece</u> down the road.
Standard:
Brother Leon lives only a <u>short distance</u> down the road.

Plus

The word *plus* is a preposition that means "added to," "increased by," or "along with." Do not use it as a conjunction meaning "and" to join two clauses.

Incorrect: We sang a few songs, <u>plus</u> we quoted some memory verses.
Correct: We sang a few songs, <u>and</u> we quoted some memory verses.
The salary <u>plus</u> commissions averaged $250 per week.

Pretend like

A noun clause after *pretend* must be introduced by the conjunction *that,* not the preposition *like.*

Incorrect: The killdeer <u>pretended like</u> it had a broken wing.
Correct: The killdeer <u>pretended that</u> it had a broken wing.

Principal, Principle

Principal is usually an adjective that means "most important." (It has the adjective suffix *-al.*) *Principal* can also be a noun that means "chief person" or "sum of money on which interest is paid."

Principle is always a noun meaning "law" or "truth." As a memory device, associate *princip<u>le</u>* with *ru<u>le</u>.*

"Wisdom is the <u>principal</u> thing; therefore get wisdom."
The <u>principal</u> borrowed for the building project was $25,000.
We desire to uphold the <u>principles</u> of God's Word in daily life.

Applying the Lesson

A. Choose the standard expressions in these sentences.
1. The fire consumed Elijah's sacrifice, (and, plus) it even burned up the stones of the altar and the water in the trench.
2. Only a fool is more ready to part (from, with) his honesty than his riches.
3. Gehazi pretended (like, that) he had gone nowhere.
4. Nominal Christianity often ignores the plain (principals, principles) of God's Word.
5. We should be (especially, mighty) thankful for parents and ministers who teach the whole Gospel.
6. Did Curtis only pretend (like, that) he was too sick to help?
7. The total of $55.00 includes the amount due (and, plus) a late charge.
8. The children should not be playing (inside, inside of) the van.
9. Corn is a (principal, principle) part of the Guatemalan diet.
10. It was (a mighty, an extremely) serious mistake for Saul to offer that sacrifice.
11. Still, Saul desired very (much, muchly) to be honored before the people.
12. With many tears, the Ephesian elders parted (from, with) Paul.
13. They were (nohow, not at all) sure that they would ever see his face again.
14. An oriental host usually accompanied his guests a (piece, short distance) down the road as they departed.
15. Travel in Bible times was (not nearly, nowhere near) as convenient as it is now.
16. Even today, many people never travel (outside, outside of) their home country.

B. Write the standard word or words for the underlined part of each sentence. If it needs no improvement, write *correct.*
1. Even the apostle Paul considered himself <u>nowhere near</u> perfect.
2. The worldly-wise become <u>muchly</u> confused by deceptive philosophies.
3. We are <u>mighty privileged</u> to have the Word of God freely.
4. Esau was <u>nohow</u> interested in spiritual things.
5. Only those who stayed <u>inside of</u> Rahab's house were spared in the overthrow of Jericho.
6. We should determine not to <u>part from</u> our faith at any price.
7. We dare not sacrifice <u>principal</u> for material gain or popularity.
8. A godly person does not merely <u>pretend like</u> he is working; he works to God's glory.
9. Mulch has improved the productivity of our garden <u>muchly</u> over the years.
10. Since the church is just a <u>piece</u> down the road, we sometimes walk to services.
11. Danny often <u>pretends that</u> he is driving a tractor.
12. Some people at sixteen years of age are <u>nowhere near</u> mature enough to have a driver's license.

13. We shelled five bushels of peas, <u>plus</u> we picked four bushels of green beans.
14. The <u>inside of</u> this birdhouse is quite dirty.
15. We visited Lloyd Stover, a young invalid who lives a <u>piece</u> down the road.
16. Is water the <u>principle</u> energy source for generating electricity in your area?
17. This is <u>nohow</u> what I had expected to see.
18. The normal travel expenses <u>plus</u> the large repair bill drained our budget.
19. As I <u>parted with</u> my new acquaintances, my heart overflowed with gratitude for wholesome friends.
20. Aunt Matilda always seems <u>mighty glad</u> for our visits.

C. Write enough words to show how each sentence should be improved according to the rules you have studied. If a sentence needs no improvement, write *correct.*

1. In 1936, a grocer named Sylvan Goldman noticed that it was a struggle for many customers to carry all their purchases, plus this kept happening day after day.
2. Sometimes a shopper could carry nowhere near as many items as he wanted to buy.
3. Goldman wanted very muchly to improve things for his customers.
4. He devised some shopping carts, but at first they were a mighty new idea.
5. Customers seemed nohow interested in using his carts.
6. So Goldman hired some people to pretend like they were customers.
7. They would push the carts a piece, stop to examine some merchandise, and then push the carts again.
8. Sometimes they took merchandise off of a shelf and put it into the carts.
9. Finally the principal caught on, and real customers began using the shopping carts.
10. Few grocers would be willing to part from shopping carts today.

Review Exercises

Write enough words to show how each sentence should be improved according to the rules you have studied. If a sentence needs no improvement, write *correct.* [35–40]

1. In A.D. 1161, while Henry II was king of England, about thirty German Christians moved in his country.
2. Their principle leader was a man named Gerard.
3. These people tried not to attract attention, but they were nohow able to escape notice.
4. Some natives made diligent inquiries about them and learned that they were "heretics."
5. Being as King Henry wanted to know about their doctrines, he brought them before a council in the city of Oxford.
6. These people had no regard for infant baptism, the mass, and lots of other Catholic institutions.
7. They also said that the pope must not be obeyed if he commanded something that did not correspond with the Word of God.

8. To keep their teaching from spreading further, these Christians were delivered to a Catholic prince to be punished.

9. They were branded on the forehead, stripped to the waist, and scourged until they were a piece away from the city.

10. Since no one was allowed to help these people and it was bitterly cold, they all perished outside of the city.

---

41. Improving Your Editing Skills, Part 5

The story is told of a famous sculptor who was putting the finishing touches on one of his statues. He worked for several hours, chipping off a fleck here and smoothing a tiny rough spot there, but making no significant change in the appearance of the sculpture. A visitor asked him, "Why do you spend so much time with all those details? They are so tiny that they make hardly any difference at all."

"Ah," said the sculptor, "but perfection is found in details."

That man expressed a great truth. Almost anyone can shape a piece of clay into a form that looks more or less like a horse. But the more finely detailed a work of art is, the more we are impressed with its excellence.

We must also pay careful attention to details in writing. Almost anyone can put words together in such a way that a reader can understand the main ideas. But if a writer is careless about details such as spelling, punctuation, and word usage, it will hinder the message he is trying to convey. That is why you are making a special study of word usage in this chapter.

In this lesson you will again practice the use of proofreading marks. See if you can find *every* mistake in the exercises.

Marks Used in Editing and Proofreading

∨ or ∧ insert (caret)	⌿ delete	.... stet (let it stand)	_____ use italics
¶ begin new paragraph	no ¶ no new paragraph	*lc* change to lowercase (small letter)	*uc* change to uppercase (capital letter)
# insert space	⌣ delete space	← move (arrow)	⊓⊔ transpose

Editing Practice

A. Use proofreading marks to correct the two capitalization or punctuation errors in each sentence.

1. "Ye are the light of the world." (Matthew 5:14.

2. one outstanding characteristic of light, is that light awakens.

3. How does God rouse all the cattle, birds and other creatures on a quiet Spring morning?

4. Does he shake them from their slumbers with a mighty earthquake or jar them with thunder from the heavens.

5. No, but from the East comes the light of the sun and ever so surely the wildlife of the world awakens.

6. Shining as a light to the world the christian wakens sinful men to an awareness of their lost condition.

7. I think, brother Thomas, that light also serves another important purpose, it reveals.

8. From the mighty Rocky Mountains to the delicate easter lily natural light reveals to us a world of natural details.

9. The light of a Christians life reveals the holiness of God it also reveals Bible requirements for getting to heaven.

10. Let's all sing "Ye are the Light of the World".

B. Use proofreading marks to correct the two usage errors in each sentence.

1. During the 1800s, thousands of people immigrated from England, France, Germany, and etc.

2. I do not know but that Katrina has all ready gone home.

3. All the boys felt badly about their carelessness, and they were mighty eager to apologize.

4. When Thomas Edison discovered the light bulb, he could not help but change the way people live.

5. If you're so awful eager to go, you better get busy and finish your work.

C. Use proofreading marks to correct the fifteen errors in the following paragraphs. No line has more than one error.

1. Angel Falls, located in Southeastern Venezuela, is the

2. highest waterfall in the world. At Angel Falls, the Churún

3. river plummets an amazing 3,212 feet (979 meters). This is

4. about is about 18 times farther than the distance the

5. water drops at Niagara Falls in North America !

6. The water seems to leap out ward as it plunges over the

7. cliff, barley touching the sheer rock face of the precipice

8. in its descent. At one point the water cascades in a direct,

9. uninterupted fall for 2,648 feet (807 meters). Can you

10. imagine water falling, falling, falling for half a mile

11. (0.8 kilometer). In contrast to its great height, the

12. falls is only 500 feet (150 meters) wide at it's base.

13. Angel Falls not discovered was until 1935. How could

14. such a wonder of creation elude discovery for somany years?

15. The falls lie in a remote part of Venezuela. Overland

16. access the to area is blocked by dense jungles and a great

17. escarpment so that the area was unknown even to the

18. natives until the early 1930s. The falls was discovered

19. when Venezuelans were surveying the region with aircraft.

20. To this day, over 65 years later the waterfall is best

21. observed from the air.

22. The falls were named for James Angel an American

23. pilot and explorer. In 1937 he crash-landed his airplane

24. on a mesa near the falls.

42. Correct Word Usage, Part 7

Real, Really

Real is an adjective meaning "actual" or "true"; *really* is an adverb meaning "actually" or "truly." Avoid using these words as intensives in standard English.

> **Informal:** We are <u>real</u> thankful for God's blessings.
> Japanese beetles are a <u>real</u> problem this year.
> **Standard:** We are <u>truly</u> thankful for God's blessings.
> Japanese beetles are a <u>serious</u> problem this year.
> Man is prone to reject the only source of <u>real</u> happiness.
> The Bible <u>really</u> is the eternal Word of God.

Reckon

Reckon means "to count or compute." It is used informally with the meaning "to think or suppose."

> **Informal:** I <u>reckon</u> you will be interested in the news.
> **Standard:** I <u>suppose</u> you will be interested in the news.
> We <u>reckoned</u> the cost of repairs, but it was too high.
> "For I <u>reckon</u> that the sufferings of this present time are not worthy to be compared with the glory which shall be revealed in us."

Right

Avoid using *right* as an intensive in standard English.

> **Informal:** This has been a <u>right</u> pleasant day.
> **Standard:** This has been an <u>especially</u> pleasant day.

Said, Same

In legal and business writing, it is proper to use *said* as an adjective meaning "aforementioned" and *same* as a pronoun meaning "aforementioned person or thing." The Bible also uses *same* in this way, but it sounds unnatural in general writing today.

> **Poor:** I had never visited <u>the said</u> place or even heard of <u>the same</u>.
> **Better:** I had never visited <u>that</u> place or even heard of <u>it</u>.
> **Bible:** "But he that shall endure unto the end, <u>the same</u> shall be saved."

Sight

Sight is used informally in expressions that mean "something strange or unpleasant to see" or "a large amount." You should generally use an expression that is more specific.

> **Informal:** After a week of rainy weather, the garden was <u>a sight</u>.
> All those weeds gave us <u>a sight of</u> work to do.
> **Standard:** After a week of rainy weather, the garden was <u>a weed patch</u>.
> All those weeds gave us <u>much</u> work to do.

So, Such

Do not use *so* and *such* as intensives in standard English. When used in that way, *so* and *such* have an emotional tone that is appropriate only for informal contexts. Study the following examples.

Informal:
   That road was <u>so</u> rough.
   It had <u>such</u> sharp curves.
Standard:
   That road was <u>quite</u> rough.
   It had <u>extremely</u> sharp curves.

So and *such* do have the standard function of telling *to what degree* about other modifiers. But in this use, they usually need a *that* clause to tell the exact degree intended. Such a clause may be omitted only if it is understood from the context. Compare the following sentences with the ones above.

Standard:
   That road was <u>so</u> rough <u>that we were constantly dodging potholes</u>.
   It had <u>such</u> sharp curves <u>that we traveled only seven miles in half an hour</u>.
   We had not realized that the road would be <u>so</u> poor.
   (The clause *as it was* is understood.)

Sometime, Some time

Use the word *sometime* when you mean "eventually" or "on some occasion." Use the phrase *some time* when you mean "a period of time."

   We should clean out the garage <u>sometime</u>.
   Cleaning out the garage will take <u>some time</u>.

Statue, Stature, Statute

A *statue* is a sculptured image.
Stature refers to height or to quality of development.
A *statute* is a law.

   The immigrants looked eagerly for the <u>Statue</u> of Liberty.
   Zacchaeus was a man of small physical <u>stature</u>.
   We must love and obey the <u>statutes</u> of God's Word.

Suppose

Always use the past tense of *suppose* in a phrase like *was supposed to*.

   Incorrect: Janice <u>is suppose to</u> go home with us.
   Correct: Janice <u>is supposed to</u> go home with us.

Suspect, Suspicion

Suspect is usually a verb that means "to distrust" or "to think possible." With the first syllable accented, *suspect* is a noun that means "a person under suspicion" or an adjective meaning "open to suspicion."

Suspicion is always a noun in standard English. Do not use it as a verb.

> We <u>suspected</u> that rats were raiding the feed bins. (not *suspicioned*)
> The police are questioning a <u>suspect</u> in the crime.
> The lawyer asked Jesus a good question, but his motive was <u>suspect</u>.
> Live above <u>suspicion</u> by avoiding questionable activities.

Applying the Lesson

A. Choose the standard expressions in these sentences.

1. Jesus has showed (a very great, such a great) love for humanity.
2. The (statues, statures, statutes) of the Lord are always just and holy.
3. Although life's trials may perplex us now, (sometime, some time) we shall understand them more perfectly.
4. (These, The said) trials can actually help to increase our faith.
5. It is better to (suspect, suspicion) that we might be wrong than to be over-confident of our own ideas.
6. Mr. Lawson (reckoned, supposed) that new shingles for his shed would cost $112.67.
7. Ira Brunk is a man of imposing (statue, stature, statute) and a soft voice.
8. The children have done their chores (especially, so) well this evening.
9. Feeding the calves can be done in a (real, really) short time.
10. It takes (sometime, some time), however, to bed down the heifers.
11. Christopher (reckons, supposes) that another cold front is approaching.
12. Angela did (right, especially) well with her embroidered quilt block.
13. When your parents tell you to do something, you are (suppose, supposed) to follow their instructions.
14. It is (much, a sight) easier to do as you are told than to explain why you did otherwise.
15. Philip Paul Bliss wrote many Gospel songs and composed music for (them, the same).
16. Our neighbor (suspects, suspicions) that someone has been prowling about his buildings.
17. We had a (right, very) pleasant visit with the Blain family.
18. Johnstown was a (sight, disaster area) after the dam broke.

B. Write the standard word or words for the underlined part of each sentence. If it needs no improvement, write *correct.*

1. A proud person finds it <u>real difficult</u> to accept advice.
2. Caleb and Joshua gave a good report of the land; <u>the same</u> were the only ones of their generation to enter Canaan.
3. Children and youth are <u>suppose</u> to respect older people.
4. The Bible teaches a six-day Creation <u>so</u> clearly that we know evolutionary theories are false.
5. Mr. Bartell expressed interest in coming to church <u>some time.</u>
6. Even a cripple can be robust in moral <u>statue.</u>
7. God has blessed us <u>right abundantly</u> in many ways.

8. They who constantly <u>suspicion</u> others often are harboring guilt themselves.
9. Truly we cannot <u>reckon</u> the value of the rewards in heaven.
10. Satan tries <u>real hard</u> to destroy every virtue he can in man.
11. We had <u>a sight of work</u> waiting for us when we returned.
12. You were <u>suppose</u> to have at least two incidents of conflict in the story.
13. Years ago many communities had <u>statues</u> against having businesses open on Sunday.
14. After quite <u>sometime</u>, Curvin finally arrived.
15. We studied those Scripture verses in devotions; <u>the same</u> have been a great encouragement to me.
16. After the storm, a <u>right</u> beautiful rainbow arched across the sky.
17. It is easy to <u>suspicion</u> people who act secretively.
18. I <u>reckon</u> you were right after all.
19. We had <u>so much corn</u> to put into the freezer.
20. By the time we finished, the kitchen looked a <u>sight</u>.

C. Write enough words to show how each sentence should be improved according to the rules you have studied. If a sentence needs no improvement, write *correct.*
1. Milk stored in glass bottles can cause some real problems.
2. A broken bottle of milk is quite a sight.
3. John Van Wormer reckoned that a better kind of milk container could be used.
4. He suspicioned that a paper milk carton might be the solution.
5. Van Wormer developed a carton that he called "Pure-Pak," for it was suppose to be thrown away after one use.
6. He did this in 1915, before there were many statures declaring that milk to be sold must be pure and fresh.
7. But it took Van Wormer sometime to perfect a machine that could produce milk cartons.
8. In addition, he found it right difficult to arouse much interest in paper cartons.
9. People were accustomed to buying milk in glass bottles, and they wanted to keep using the said containers.
10. But the cost of glass was rising so much that paper milk cartons eventually came into widespread use.

Review Exercises

Write enough words to show how each sentence should be improved according to the rules you have studied. If a sentence needs no improvement, write *correct.* [35–42]
1. In 1416, a real devout woman named Catharine Saube lived in Lorraine, France.
2. One day the said woman asked to be admitted into a Catholic convent.
3. She apparently had an honorable motive, even though such a request seems mighty strange to us.

4. About a year later, while living at the convent, Catharine was suspicioned of heresy and brought to trial.
5. One thing she said was that the church is suppose to include only men and women (not babies).
6. She also said that a person hadn't ought to confess his sins to a priest.
7. Since Catharine would not part from her faith, the death sentence was pronounced upon her.
8. The people begged the bailiff to show mercy, but he had Catharine burned anyways.
9. It appears that this Christian woman was so concerned about the nuns in the convent that she had become a nun to testify to the others.
10. As incredulous as it may seem, the whole convent and all the nuns in it were burned soon afterward—almost certainly because they had departed from the Catholic religion.

---

43. Correct Word Usage, Part 8

Taunt, Taut

Taunt is either a verb meaning "to mock or tease," or a noun meaning "a sarcastic or teasing remark."

Taut is an adjective meaning "stretched tight" or "tense."

He who <u>taunts</u> others despises the Creator, common to them all.
Pull the rope <u>taut</u> before tying your knot.

Their, There, They're

Their is a personal pronoun meaning "belonging to them."

There is an adverb meaning "at that place" or an expletive used to introduce a sentence.

They're is a contraction for *they are.* When you write this contraction, think of the words it stands for.

Brother Glen and Sister Hilda invited us to <u>their</u> home.
We always enjoy visiting <u>there</u>.
<u>They're</u> (They are) both over ninety years old.

To, Too, Two

To is a preposition or the sign of an infinitive.

Too is an adverb of degree or an adverb meaning "also."

Two is a number; it is related to words like *twice, twin,* and *twenty.*

The <u>two</u> horses were <u>too</u> tired <u>to</u> pull the load <u>to</u> the top of the hill.

Type

When using *type* to mean "sort" or "kind," use the phrase *type of.* Neither *type* alone nor the phrase *type of a* is correct.

Incorrect: This <u>type</u> book does not interest me.
    This <u>type of a</u> book does not interest me.
Correct: This <u>type of</u> book does not interest me.

Valuable, Invaluable

Valuable means "costly" or "worthy."
Invaluable means "having a value beyond measure; priceless."

Grandfather has a number of <u>valuable</u> books on his shelf.
A Christian education is an <u>invaluable</u> asset.

Wait for, on

Wait for means "to await" or "to remain in expectation."
Wait on means "to serve."

Please <u>wait for</u> me.
A polite clerk <u>waited on</u> me.

Want that

Do not use *want that* to express a desire for someone to do something. Rather, use an expression like *want him to.*

Incorrect: Father <u>wants that we</u> clean out the garage today.
Correct: Father <u>wants us to</u> clean out the garage today.

Where

A verb like *read, hear,* or *see* is often followed by a noun clause. Such a noun clause should begin with *that,* not *where.*

Incorrect: Father read <u>where</u> a new kind of spray is being developed.
Correct: Father read <u>that</u> a new kind of spray is being developed.

Who's, Whose

Who's means *who is* or *who has.* When you write this contraction, think of the words it stands for.
Whose is the possessive form of *who.*

<u>Who's</u> (Who is) responsible to find out <u>whose</u> books these are?

You All, You'ns, You's

The pronoun *you* is singular or plural. Do not use the expressions *you all, you'ns,* and *you's* as plural forms of *you.* If you want to clarify that more than one person is meant, use a plural or collective noun.

Incorrect: We want <u>you'ns</u> to come to our house for dinner.
Correct: We want <u>you</u> to come to our house for dinner.
    We want <u>your family</u> to come to our house for dinner.

Applying the Lesson

A. Choose the standard expressions in these sentences.
1. At every place of temptation or trial, God is (their, there, they're).
2. As Jesus' disciples, we should be ready to wait (for, on) those in need.
3. God's spiritual blessings to us are (valuable, invaluable).
4. We should never (taut, taunt) others for believing differently than we do.
5. Be not discouraged; these trials (to, too, two) will pass.
6. Later you may see (that, where) a hardship was a valuable experience.
7. We can always trust God, (who's, whose) grace is all-sufficient.
8. Too many people go astray because they value (their, there, they're) own pleasures above God's will.
9. The boys stood at the starting line, their muscles (taut, taunt).
10. Some of Great-aunt Elizabeth's dishes are quite (valuable, invaluable).
11. You may walk ahead to the bend in the trail and wait (for, on) the rest.
12. Everyone wants (to, too, two) get a good view from the lookout tower.
13. This (type, type of) fabric wrinkles more easily than that type.
14. (Who's, Whose) going to wash the dishes this evening?
15. Mother said that (you, you's) are all supposed to help with them.
16. She (wants that we, wants us to) have them finished by six o'clock.

B. Write the standard word or words for the underlined part of each sentence. If it needs no improvement, write *correct.*
1. Jesus sharply condemned the hypocrites; this type person lives in self-deception.
2. Jesus wants that His people follow Him consistently.
3. The Jewish leaders hated Jesus because He condemned they're hypocrisy.
4. Several times in the Gospels, we read where Jesus silenced His enemies.
5. Jesus Christ, whose the eternal Son of God, purchased man's redemption.
6. King Saul did not wait for Samuel as he should have.
7. He became to impatient and offered the sacrifice himself.
8. The gift of faith is a valuable possession indeed.
9. Where did you all go for your school trip?
10. You did not pull the yarn taunt enough in these stitches.
11. I saw where there was a misprint in our book.
12. This Friday we had a different type of a project in art class.
13. When others taunt us, we should either ignore them or answer graciously.
14. Have you's studied the three branches of American government?
15. Father wants that we have the chores done before he comes home.
16. We should not wait two long before we start.
17. A set of wrenches would be an invaluable wedding gift for my brother.
18. I cannot tell who's sweater is lying on the table.
19. We need to be patient enough to wait on those who are slower than we are.
20. I am not familiar with that church because we have not visited their often.

C. Write enough words to show how each sentence should be improved according to the rules you have studied. If a sentence needs no improvement, write *correct.*

1. I read where an American Indian named George Crum made the first potato chips.
2. This man, a valuable worker, was the chief cook at a hotel in Saratoga Springs, New York.
3. One day Crum helped to wait on a wealthy guest at the hotel.
4. The guest was a finicky type person.
5. He complained that the French-fried potatoes were to thick.
6. He wanted that the waiter bring him potatoes that were cut in thinner slices.
7. The cook, who's anger was stirred, cut some wafer-thin potato slices and fried them crisp.
8. He served them with the taut, "Are these thin enough?"
9. The guest sampled the potatoes and exclaimed, "Their delicious!"
10. As you'ns surely know, potato chips are a popular snack today.

Review Exercises

Write enough words to show how each sentence should be improved according to the rules you have studied. If a sentence needs no improvement, write *correct*. [34–43]

1. By 1545, the Waldenses had already been persecuted for over 350 years.
2. Waldensian teaching was practically identical to that of the Anabaptists on matters such as Communion, nonresistance, and etc.
3. The Waldenses rejected infant baptism, plus they refused to swear oaths.
4. They said the Catholic Church literally resembled the barren fig tree that Christ had cursed.
5. Statues were issued against them in France, Spain, Germany, and other places.
6. Waldenses were muchly despised throughout the land.
7. In one case, some martyrs were ridiculed with the taut that they were experiencing the baptism of fire, of which they had spoken.

Eighty Waldenses burned for their faith, *Martyrs Mirror,* page 313

8. In another case, a pope ordered that the bones of several noted Waldenses be dug up and burned—twenty years after they're deaths!
9. Many Waldenses faced death with great joy, no matter how awful they were treated.
10. Waldenses and Anabaptists still exist today, but most people of the later group are now known as Mennonites.

---

44.   Chapter 5 Review

A. Choose the standard expressions in these sentences.

1. We should be willing to serve others (irregardless, regardless) of whether we receive (complements, compliments).
2. The Golden Rule is a New Testament (principal, principle) that (affects, effects) every aspect of life.
3. One important way to contend (against, for, with) the faith is (to, too, two) make sure that our lives correspond (to, with) God's Word.
4. When circumstances become (adverse, averse), a casual person is likely to respond differently (from, than) he should.
5. There were (fewer, less) soldiers in Gideon's army than in the Midianite army, but that did not hinder God's (ability, capacity) to grant Israel a great victory.
6. As we cross this mountain, (a very, such a) thick fog sometimes (envelops, envelopes) us.
7. Because of Ellen's unusual (ability, capacity), she has (already, all ready) finished memorizing the passage; but I must study it (farther, further) today.
8. Loren demonstrates admirable spiritual (statue, stature, statute); I prize his (invaluable, valuable) friendship.
9. If Father agrees (to, with) our plan, we might move the old stuffed chair (in, into) the playhouse (sometime, some time) this evening.
10. A person (who's, whose) recovering from a heart attack should eat these (kind, kinds) of foods, for (their, there, they're) more (healthful, healthy) than fatty foods.
11. I was so (credible, credulous) that I did not even (suspect, suspicion) that the boy's story was (incredible, incredulous).
12. The salesman declared that Glidden paint is superior (than, to) Bruning, but we have had more success with the (later, latter) brand.
13. This accident (learned, taught) me that most pranks are (altogether, all together) wrong, for they may be accompanied (by, with) serious results.
14. I had the (allusion, illusion) that your motto was (much, muchly) different (from, than) mine until I saw them (beside, besides) each other.
15. Hold the rope (taunt, taut), and wait (for, on) Father.
16. Nevin pretended (like, that) he had divided the work equally (among, between) the four boys, but I (didn't, didn't hardly) think it was fair at all.

17. Daniel Estrada, who was (formally, formerly) from Mexico, says it was hard to part (from, with) his family when he (emigrated, immigrated) from his native country.
18. I feel (bad, badly) about breaking Mr. Horn's window, and I plan to pay for (it, the same) as soon as I can.
19. If we do not (exalt, exult) truth in our daily lives, God cannot (affect, effect) His will within us.
20. Alexander Fleming accidentally (discovered, invented) penicillin in 1928 when some *Penicillium notatum* spores fell (in, into) his cultures of bacteria.

B. Write enough words to show how each sentence should be improved according to the rules you have studied. Every sentence needs at least two improvements.
1. Being as we are totally dependent upon God, we hadn't ought to boast.
2. I reckon that we better get a fuller understanding of this Bible passage.
3. I can't hardly remember where that verse is at, but I'm real sure it is in the Book of Romans.
4. A Christian wants that his life be a good influence on his friends, plus he seeks to be a good witness to others.
5. We have got to exercise a lot of caution, for we are nohow immune to deception.
6. This type speech is nowhere near what it should be; you all are suppose to refrain from talking like that.
7. I had not heard but that Brother Leroy is in a right critical condition after falling off of the roof.
8. I figure that Danny could not help but get his shoes muddy, but you older children cannot hardly excuse your carelessness.
9. The neighbor boys seemed mighty surprised and even mad when they asked to swim in our pond and Father would not hear to it.
10. The boys were quite a piece from the house when the cloudburst hit, and they literally looked like drowned rats by the time they reached the porch.
11. I do not believe as this is all the faster that you all can work.
12. We heard an awful loud crash from somewheres in the house.
13. Father heard in town where some community people are upset about our efforts in passing out tracts, having street meetings, and etc.
14. The workshop looks a sight since Joseph and Kyle have been working on their bird feeders, and the said boys must clean it up after doing there chores.

C. Rewrite these sentences, using verbs in the active voice. If there is a good reason for the passive voice, write *acceptable*.
1. A rainbow was seen after the storm.
2. Joseph was sold as a slave.
3. All our corn has been harvested.

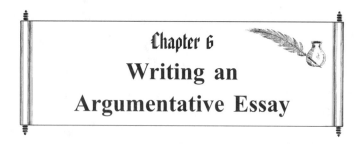

Chapter 6
Writing an
Argumentative Essay

45. Understanding an Argumentative Essay

We know that we must overcome the part of our nature that causes us to argue and fight to defend our rights and ideas. But a good argumentative essay uses a different kind of arguing—a profitable kind. It does not use nasty, biting words. It does not come from an angry, uncontrolled heart. Instead, it presents clear, logical evidence in support of a worthwhile proposition. It seeks to convince others by using facts, not with noise or angry outbursts. And sad to say, it has been mastered by relatively few people. This kind of arguing we must work to learn.

The writer of an argumentative essay tries to persuade the reader to accept a particular opinion or to take a particular action. While the purpose of an exposition is to have the reader say, "I understand," the purpose of an argument is to have the reader say, "I agree" or "I need to do something about that." This makes argumentative writing especially challenging—and rewarding. Are you ready for this challenge?

The Nature of an Argument

By definition, an argumentative essay must involve a controversy. Why try to persuade someone of an idea that he has already accepted? Why try to move him to action if he already is doing what you propose? Argumentative writing, therefore, always deals with a point that readers either disagree with or fail to act upon seriously.

Consider the following two statements. Which one would make a good subject for an argumentative essay?

> Times of personal devotions help to inspire a Christian to live faithfully.
> Every Christian should schedule a regular time and place for having personal devotions.

Few readers would disagree with the first statement. Devotions do inspire us, of course. There would be little point in trying to convince people of that. But the second statement may cause some readers to raise their eyebrows in question. Most would agree that daily personal devotions are important. But do we need to have a *regular time* and a *regular place*?

Even if a reader sees the value of a regular time and place, he likely falls short sometimes in his devotional life. So this makes an ideal subject for an argumentative essay. Some readers may be moved to conclude, "I agree." Those who already agree should be convinced even more strongly, and they may be moved to determine, "I must practice this more carefully."

In an effort to influence his readers, a writer needs to select the most convincing evidence he can find, and then arrange it so that his argument will be as logical and persuasive as he can make it. The writer's goal is not to show that he is right and the reader is wrong, nor to prove his point by a clever manipulation of words. Rather, he must present his argument in a spirit of humility, with a sincere desire that the reader accept truth for his own benefit.

The following argumentative essay discusses the subject of regular personal devotions. Read it carefully and thoughtfully. Can you sense an element of controversy? Does the writer develop the argument in a kind but convincing manner?

The Hazard of Haphazard Devotions

1   Every person needs a constant supply of oxygen to survive. If our breathing were to stop for only two or three minutes, permanent brain damage could result. Five or six minutes without breathing would likely prove fatal. Likewise, without regular fellowship with the Lord, our inner spiritual life will quickly suffer or even perish. Something as important as personal devotions, then, we dare not treat haphazardly. To sustain our spiritual life, we should schedule a regular time and place for personal devotions.

2   Some people will say that maintaining a consistent schedule is impractical or even impossible. This may be true in a few cases, such as when a mother must care for a sick baby. But our regular farm and business schedules belie this excuse. We do consistently those things that we consider important. Some may declare that following a schedule is actually undesirable because it takes away the spice of variety. According to them, too much regularity produces monotony and stifles spontaneous worship. But these people show that they do not comprehend the true character of worship or the weakness of human nature.

3   A definite schedule for personal devotions helps to put a person into a proper frame of mind for worship. As the approach of mealtime stirs the natural desire for food, so the approach of the regular devotional time arouses the spiritual appetite. We find it more difficult to enter the spirit of worship at other times of the day than at the time when we are accustomed to worship. Thus regularity proves an asset to concentration.

4   Moreover, maintaining a fixed schedule helps to impress on our minds the importance of our personal devotions. Having regular devotions writes in clear, bold letters upon our consciousness that this practice holds a place of priority. When we are tempted to let it slide, the force of habit speaks in a clear, firm voice, saying, "Do not neglect your devotions." Regularity is important, therefore, because of the way it affects our own thinking.

5   Having our devotions at a regular place avoids wasted moments. We need not consider each day what will be the best time for devotions. We need not decide where is the best place to go. And we can keep our Bible, prayer list, and commonly used reference books at a handy place.

6   With a regular time and place for our personal devotions, we have greater freedom from interruptions. Of course, we must first choose a time and a place generally free from disturbances. As other family members know when our scheduled devotional time is, they will be less likely to disturb us. This makes a strong contribution to the quality of our devotions.

7   Finally, a regular system probably does more than any other thing to prevent forgetfulness. If we fit devotions in whenever it suits each day, too many days will fly past with devotions forgotten because it fits in nowhere. But if having devotions is as habitual as washing our hands and combing our hair, we will seldom forget it. A regular schedule helps to assure that we do not miss this most important part of the day.

8   A definite schedule for our personal devotions is imperative. The regularity gives us the benefit of having our minds in gear for worship. It helps us use our time efficiently and frees us from distractions. It serves not only to impress us with the importance of our devotions but also to keep us from forgetting this vital practice. As long as we dwell in these bodies, we shall need this regular nurturing of our inner spiritual life.

[604 words]

The Structure of an Argument

1. *The introduction.* Like most compositions, an argumentative essay consists of three parts: introduction, body, and conclusion. The introduction of a shorter composition may be only a sentence or two. In an argumentative essay, it will be a complete paragraph. The introduction has several purposes. First, it must appeal to the reader's interest. If it fails to do this, no one will read the essay and it will not persuade anyone! Second, the introduction must prepare the reader for the *thesis—* the main idea that the argument is promoting.

Examine the introductory paragraph in the argument above. Notice first that it begins with a general statement: *Every person needs a constant supply of oxygen to survive.* This is followed by two details showing specifically how important oxygen is. These first three sentences are not directly related to the subject of scheduled personal devotions, but they form the basis of a comparison that will show its importance. In addition, they give information that should appeal to a reader's interest.

The fourth sentence finally introduces the general subject of the argument—personal devotions—by comparing it to the opening information about oxygen. The next sentence takes the reader a step closer to the actual thesis, giving him a fairly good idea of the point this argument will emphasize. Finally, the concluding sentence of the paragraph states precisely the thesis of the argument.

The introductory paragraph is like a funnel. It is wide at the beginning—with a general statement—and then it narrows down to the specific point of the argument.

2. *The body.* The introductory paragraph ends with a statement of the thesis, the main point of the essay. In the body, the writer sets out to prove his thesis. Here it is that his argument succeeds or fails. Therefore, he must be sure that he uses solid evidence and follows sound logic. If he uses flimsy evidence and faulty logic, the reader will feel justified in *disagreeing* with the writer.

The thesis having been clearly stated, the argument should first deal with several counter arguments that might be raised against the thesis. Doing this indicates that the writer has thought through his argument carefully and has tried to see the issue from other people's viewpoint. He is trying to be fair and considerate in dealing with the evidence.

If the writer wishes merely to concede that the counter arguments must be reckoned with, he should note them briefly in the first paragraph of the body and then move promptly to his first supporting point. If he wishes to explain more fully why the counter arguments are unsound, he might devote an entire paragraph to them.

Look back at the sample argument. Do you see the two counter arguments in the second paragraph? The writer devoted this entire paragraph to exposing the unsoundness of these two arguments, before moving on to his supporting points.

Some supporting points of an argument may directly contradict certain counter arguments. In such a case, it often proves effective to begin some paragraphs by stating a counter argument and following it with a well-developed supporting point of the thesis.

For example, the writer of the sample argument could have used the following counter arguments at the beginning of two paragraphs: *Some people may say that a consistent schedule is impractical or even impossible. Some may think a regular schedule stifles spontaneous worship.* He could have developed the first of those paragraphs with details to demonstrate that regular devotions is both practical and possible, and the second one with evidence to show why that objection is not valid.

The body of an argumentative essay consists primarily of convincing evidence that supports the thesis. Each paragraph (except the early paragraphs that deal with counter arguments) should consist of a well-rounded development of one supporting point or of one specific aspect of a supporting point.

Look at paragraphs 3–7 of the sample argument. Each of these paragraphs develops one supporting point. The first sentence of each paragraph states the point as a topic sentence. Each paragraph then continues with illustrations, examples, and reasons that develop its topic convincingly.

Generally the supporting points of an argument should be arranged in order of increasing importance. This allows you to put your best proofs into the last paragraphs of the body. Always save for last the evidence that will have the strongest appeal to your readers. By thus clinching the argument right at the end of the main part of the essay, you will be the most likely to convince readers of the point you are making.

The sample essay could also be effective with the five supporting points presented in a different order. Notice, however, that the first two arguments are more abstract and the last three are more concrete and practical. The final point definitely clinches the entire argument.

3. *The conclusion.* Having stated his point and supported it with his strongest evidence, the writer is ready to close his argument. He wants to conclude in a way that strongly impresses the reader with the truth of his message. How can he do this?

First, he should point the reader back to the thesis by restating it in different words. This brings the main point of the whole essay into clear focus one more time. Then the writer should briefly summarize the main points of his argument, again using different wording than he used previously. Finally, he should close his argument by making a general statement that clinches the importance of his thesis.

Look again at the conclusion in the sample argument. You will see that its pattern is reversed from that in the introduction. The first sentence of the conclusion is a rewording of the thesis (which is the last sentence of the introduction). The closing sentence makes a general statement (similar to the first sentence of the introduction). The conclusion is like an inverted funnel, narrow at the beginning and broadening to a general statement. The following illustration shows this pattern in the form of a diagram.

Introduction
  General ideas narrowing to thesis statement

Body
  Arguments presented and supported

Conclusion
  Thesis restated, followed by broadening to general ideas

Though your conclusion should repeat the ideas of the composition, it should not use the same words. Be fresh and creative. Try to repeat the ideas more briefly and pointedly. The following example shows how flat and unappealing a conclusion can be if the writer simply repeats the points of his argument.

> We certainly need to schedule a regular time and place for having personal devotions. Such a schedule puts a person into a proper frame of mind for worship, avoids wasted moments, provides greater freedom from interruptions, impresses on our minds the importance of having personal devotions, and probably does more than anything else to prevent forgetfulness. Having regular personal devotions is essential to our spiritual survival.

A profitable argument is carefully planned and well organized. It issues from a firm commitment to truth and a sincere interest in the welfare of the reader. Fix these principles firmly in your mind, and let them guide you in planning and writing your argumentative essay.

Applying the Lesson

A. Answer these questions.

1. How does the purpose of an argumentative essay differ from that of an exposition?
2. Why must an argumentative essay involve controversy?
3. What two things should be true of the first sentence of an argument?
4. What should the last sentence of the introductory paragraph do?
5. What does the illustration of a funnel tell about the introductory paragraph?
6. How can the inclusion of counter arguments actually strengthen an argumentative essay?
7. How might an argumentative essay affect a reader if it contains faulty logic?
8. Why is it important to save the strongest argument for last?
9. What three things should be found in the conclusion?
10. How can you keep the conclusion from being dull and repetitious?

B. Read this argumentative essay, and do the exercises that follow.

More Than a Produce Patch

Summer generally brings a welcome change of activities to families that have schoolchildren. Since there are no lunches to pack and no need to hurry children off to school, the morning schedule often is more relaxed. With schoolchildren at home during the day, much more work can be done than is possible during the school term. Therefore, a family garden makes a worthwhile summer project.

Not everyone has a special liking for work with soil and plants. But most people can enjoy the satisfaction that comes from having a family garden. The hard work itself produces a sense of fulfillment. "The sleep of a labouring man is sweet" (Ecclesiastes 5:12). Just the sight of a well-kept garden brings a sense of satisfaction. And what a joy it is to see canning shelves and freezers filled with vegetables from one's own garden.

Then, too, a careful shopper may be able to purchase vegetables in the store more cheaply than he can raise them himself. It takes less time and effort to buy a dozen ears of sweet corn than to raise them. But gardening has rewards that cannot be measured in dollars and cents. People who raise their own produce reap benefits that cannot be harvested in any grocery store or produce market.

Having a family garden assures that fresh, tasty vegetables reach the table. A family can harvest peas and corn before they are tough and starchy. In a matter of hours, the vegetables can be out of the garden and in the freezer or on the canning shelves. Thus the fullest flavor and the richest color are preserved.

A family garden provides opportunities to learn valuable lessons. As the gardener works closely with nature and the God who created it, he sees the law of sowing and reaping clearly illustrated. Occasionally the garden is a swamp at seeding time, and sometimes dry winds and a blazing sun wither the garden plants beyond hope. The gardener must simply accept the weather that God gives. He also learns that small things quickly grow into big things. If those small, innocent-looking weeds are not dealt with, they quickly become so big that they threaten the very existence of the cultivated plants.

Most important of all, a garden furnishes an ideal opportunity for a family to work together. Even young children can help with many gardening chores: planting seeds, pulling weeds, shelling peas, and husking corn. Grandparents often enjoy helping with the time-consuming shelling, canning, and freezing jobs. Children gain invaluable benefits as they spend hours working with their parents in raising and preserving garden produce.

If at all feasible, every family should plan a garden for the summer. The very sense of satisfaction brought by gardening makes it worthwhile, and so do the other benefits that cannot be measured with money. The gardening family can be confident of having high-quality vegetables to eat. Especially rewarding are the lessons that gardening teaches and the priceless benefits of working together as a family. The produce from your garden may last for a year, but the memories will endure for a lifetime.

[522 words]

1. Compare the introduction and the conclusion by following these directions.
   a. Copy the thesis statement and the restatement of the thesis.
   b. Copy the general introductory statement and the general closing statement.
2. List the five supporting points that the essay uses to support the thesis statement.
3. What two counter arguments does the essay mention?
4. Write the letter of the statement that tells how the essay deals with the counter arguments.
   a. The counter arguments are merely conceded.
   b. The counter arguments are addressed without reference to supporting arguments.
   c. Each counter argument is directly contradicted by a supporting argument.
5. Does the conclusion summarize all the main points of the argument?
6. Are the summarized points reworded from the way they are stated in the body?

Review Exercises

A. Label each sentence according to its use (*dec., int., imp., exc.*) and its structure (*S, CD, CX, CD-CX*). End punctuation has been omitted. [22]
   1. If you want my opinion, the boy has lied and he must be punished
   2. Where do we go from here
   3. Clean the floor with these mops, but do not use any detergent in your water
   4. No one could relax until the fire was under control
   5. What a beautiful picture she has drawn
B. Label the word order of each sentence *N* (natural), *I* (inverted), or *M* (mixed). [22]
   1. In the open hand is more power than in the clenched fist.
   2. The truly rich man carries his possessions within him.
   3. If you have received a kindness, pass it on.
   4. From sincere hearts come meaningful prayers.

C. Label the style of each sentence *L* (loose), *P* (periodic), or *B* (balanced). [22]
   1. Do not look at God through your circumstances; look at your circumstances through God.
   2. The key that opens to us the treasures of God's blessings each morning is prayer.
   3. Prayer is also the key that shuts us up under God's protection and care when we end our labors and go to sleep each evening.
   4. Sugared words, coated with sweetness to please the ears, often prove quite bitter.

---

46. Improving Your Editing Skills, Part 6

When you proofread a composition, you must give full attention to the work at hand. You will not detect errors very well if you have a preoccupied mind or you try to proofread in a distracting environment. This may be the reason that even professional proofreaders occasionally let errors get into print.

Overlooked errors can sometimes be humorous. Someone surely was not concentrating on his work when he allowed the following mistakes to slip through.

> **In a newspaper weather forecast:**
> "wisely scattered thunderstorms"
> **On some coupons printed for a car wash:**
> "Absolutely nothing touches your car except soup and water."

Just one letter is incorrect in each case. But what a difference those errors make!

In this lesson you will again proofread a number of sentences and paragraphs. Give full attention to your work so that you can find *every* mistake in these exercises.

Marks Used in Editing and Proofreading

∨ or ∧ insert (caret)	ꝶ delete	.... stet (let it stand)	_____ use italics
¶ begin new paragraph	no ¶ no new paragraph	*lc* change to lowercase (small letter)	*uc* change to uppercase (capital letter)
# insert space	⌣ delete space	← move (arrow)	⌐⌐⌐ transpose

Editing Practice

A. Use proofreading marks to correct the two errors of spelling or spacing in each sentence.

1. David, preparing selflesly to build the temple, inspires us to sacrifice our selves for the Lord's work.

2. In Moses's intercessory prayer, he asked that his own name be blotted out if God couldnot forgive the people's sin.

3. Each of Abraham's alters emphasizes the importance of worship.

4. The prophets who warned God's people of comming destruction were often persecuted.

5. Jeremaih, known as the "weeping prophet," was especially mistreated for his couragous preaching.

6. The Bible is entirelly reasonable; further more, it is absolutely essential for reaching heaven.

7. In Jesus' parabel of the prodigal son, two sons were actual ly lost.

8. The younger son, who took his be longings and left his father's house, represents sinners who wander awayfrom God.

9. The haughty, unforgivng elder son clearly represents the self righteous Pharisees.

10. Luke,the beloved phisycian, wrote two books of the Bible.

B. Use proofreading marks to correct the errors in word order in these sentences. Make punctuation changes as required by your corrections.

1. The Great Wall of China is one of the few objects man-made visible to the human eye from outer space.

2. This wall contains enough material around the earth to build a barrier 3 feet wide and 8 feet high.

3. Most the of present wall was built during the Ming dynasty, which lasted from the 1300s to the 1600s.

4. The wall was built to keep out barbarian invaders, who would sweep down and plunder the wealthy Chinese from the north.

5. Building the wall required untold amounts both of materials and labor.

6. One emperor ordered every third man in China to work on the wall it is said.

7. Soldiers were commanded to become masons, and prisoners were taken to mountaintops to pile bricks in fact.

8. With a height of 25 to 30 feet (8–9 meters) and a width of 15 to 25 feet (5–8 meters), the wall stretches over mountains, through valleys, and across plains nearly for 4,000 miles (6,400 kilometers).

9. The wall has been called "the world's longest graveyard" because thousands of workers were buried in the wall itself who died.

10. In spite of the wall, barbarians from the north found ways to get across this barrier at weakly guarded points frequently.

C. Use proofreading marks to correct all the errors in this essay. Your corrections should include one use of the stet symbol and one joining of two paragraphs. No line has more than one error.

1. Mount Everest is the highest mountian in the world.

2. Located in the Himalaya mountains between Tibet and

3. Nepal, it reaches an altitude of about 5.5 miles or 8.9

4. kilometers. Surveyors disagree on an exact figure, but

5. in 1954 the ~~Indian~~ government established its present

6. official height of 29,028 feet (8,848 meters).

7.   The British saw first Mount Everest in the middle

8. 1800s. They named it after Sir George Everest, a Brittish

9. surveyor-general of India who determined its location

10. and height approximate.

11.   The ~~rough~~ rugged terrain of Mount Everest, it's sudden

12. avalanches, fierce winds, extreme cold, and thin air all

13. combine tomake this mountain a formidable challenge to

14. climbers. From 1921 to 1952, eleven people lost there lives

15. as they took part in ten vain efforts to scale its heights.

16.   Though a few of these climbers came within 1,000 feet

17. (300 meters) of the top none managed to reach it.

18.   The first men known to conquer Mount Everest was Sir

19.   Edmund Hillary of New Zealand and Tenzing Norgay, a Tribes-

20.   man of Nepal. They reached the the summit on May 29, 1953.

---

47. Developing the Thesis Statement

When children argue, they usually begin with a single point of conflict. As the argument continues, they often bring in other issues until the original conflict is obscured. Sometimes no one can even remember how the argument started!

Good argumentative writing does not work that way. To write an effective argument, you must choose a single definite thesis. Then you must develop the argument with sound evidence that supports the one thesis you are defending.

In an argument, the thesis statement expresses the writer's position on a subject of controversy. That is, the writer takes a stand on some issue and tries to persuade others to take the same stand. Thus the thesis is the most important feature of the whole essay. Here are some pointers for developing a well-written thesis.

1. *The thesis should deal with a significant topic that is truly worth defending.* Do not write about petty subjects, such as the best place to live or the best kind of car. Worthwhile theses deal with topics like Bible truths, things you have studied in school, personal experiences, and proper ways of doing things.

Sometimes it takes careful thought to determine whether a thesis is worthwhile. Two statements may be closely related, yet only one of them makes a good thesis. Study the following examples.

Poor theses:
> The creature that swallowed Jonah was probably a fish rather than a whale.
> An automobile mechanic has one of the most important jobs in the community.

Good theses:
> The story of Jonah should be accepted as a true historical account.
> Every boy who expects to drive should learn to do simple mechanical work.

The first example makes a poor thesis because the Bible does not tell exactly what kind of creature swallowed Jonah. Neither does it really matter what species it was. But it does matter whether a reader accepts the story of Jonah as a true historical account. Jesus obviously considered it factual; and if a reader thinks otherwise, he is likely to disbelieve other parts of the Bible too.

The second example is poor because most other jobs are also important, and there is no point in trying to prove that one is more important than another. But it is wise for a boy to learn how to do basic car repairs. Otherwise, something as simple as a loose battery cable may someday leave him stranded along the highway.

As these examples show, one aspect of a topic may make a good thesis while another does not. You do not need to discard an entire subject just because one aspect of it makes a poor thesis. Sometimes you simply need to choose a different aspect.

2. *The thesis should deal with a topic that you can cover in one essay.* Some controversial subjects are so broad that it would take a whole book to present the argument effectively. You should choose a topic that is narrow enough to be covered in 500–600 words. Can you see why the following theses are too broad for one essay?

> Bible stories should be accepted as accounts of things that actually happened to real people.
> Creationism is more scientific than evolution.

Again, you do not need to completely discard a topic just because it is too broad. Perhaps you simply need to limit it to a narrower field. The first example above is a broad version of the first "good" example in the previous set. The second thesis could be narrowed so that it deals with just four or five reasons for believing in creation rather than evolution.

3. *The thesis should state the topic in clear, specific terms.* That is, the reader should not have to wonder what the point of the essay will be. Consider the following example.

> We need to drink the right kinds of liquids.

Exactly what kinds of liquids are the "right kinds"? Will the reader be expected to decide for himself? This thesis is poor because it does not indicate the specific topic that the essay will discuss. The following thesis is better.

> Water is a better thirst quencher than soft drinks.

A clear, specific thesis is helpful in two ways. It tells exactly what issue is being addressed, and it tells exactly what the writer intends to prove in relation to the issue.

4. *A positive statement usually makes a better thesis than a negative statement.* We do need to take a stand against wrong practices. But instead of arguing *against* something undesirable, it is usually better to argue *in favor of* something good. Compare the following theses with the previous examples. Do you see why they are not as effective?

> The story of Jonah should not be considered a legend or fable.
> We should avoid the habit of constantly using soft drinks.

In preparing to write an argumentative essay, take the time necessary to develop a clear, well-written thesis. Your thesis will help to determine the success or failure of your whole essay.

Applying the Lesson

A. Write the letter of the statement in each pair that would make a better thesis. Tell why it is better than the other choice by writing *more worthwhile, more clear and specific,* or *positive.*
1. a. The best time for having personal devotions is usually in the morning.
   b. We should try to have our personal devotions at the best time of the day.
2. a. A handwritten letter is better than a typewritten letter.
   b. Sending a personal letter is better than just sending a card.
3. a. To be truly obedient to our parents, we must obey them promptly and willingly.
   b. To be truly obedient to our parents, we must not be slow or reluctant in our response.
4. a. Both faith and works are necessary in the Christian life.
   b. Being a Christian means more than professing faith in Christ.
5. a. A successful writer must use his writing tools effectively.
   b. A broad vocabulary is one of the best tools of an effective writer.
6. a. As much as possible, we should try to avoid being late for church.
   b. As much as possible, we should try to be in church on time.

B. The following statements are poor theses for the reasons given in parentheses. Improve each one with a change that makes it refer to a different aspect of the same topic. (Hint: In most of the sentences, you need to change only the ending.)
1. We should begin each day in a proper way. (not clear)
2. To be a good witness, a Christian driver should not violate traffic laws. (negative)
3. Every student should learn to touch-type by using a manual typewriter instead of an electric model. (not worthwhile)
4. Working on a farm is a good way to learn many valuable lessons. (too broad)
5. The headship veiling was not only for women of Paul's day. (negative)
6. A person who professes Christianity must be nice in all situations. (too broad)
7. In relation to alcoholic drinks, we need to choose a safe course. (not clear)
8. Students should use pencil rather than ink to do most of their written work. (not worthwhile)
9. For help in understanding the Bible, we should not become too dependent on commentaries. (negative)
10. Geography is a more practical subject than history. (not worthwhile)

C. Write a thesis that you plan to use for writing an argumentative essay later in this chapter. You may choose one from Part A or B, or write one of your own.
   The score on your argumentative essay will make up a considerable part of your Chapter 6 test score.

Review Exercises

Label each underlined item *nominative absolute* or *participial phrase.* [21]
1. <u>Kneeling in Gethsemane to pray</u>, Jesus submitted to His Father's will.

2. A wicked bargain was agreed upon, <u>Judas having plotted with the chief priests</u>.
3. <u>Swinging a sword</u>, one of Jesus' disciples tried to defend Him.
4. Jesus gave His life on the cross, <u>His enemies thinking they had won a victory</u>.
5. <u>Our Saviour risen</u>, we have hope for the future.

---

48. Developing the Full Thesis

Writing an effective argument begins with writing an effective thesis statement. This sentence is the "center pole" of the entire essay. It provides the logic and unity for every detail.

But very few people could write effectively with no more preparation than having developed a good thesis statement. Although the work begins here, further preparation is needed to produce the finished essay. That preparation is the development of the full thesis.

Elements of the Full Thesis

The full thesis consists of three parts: the thesis statement, opposing points to the thesis, and supporting points for the thesis. It serves as the plan for writing the essay. Below is a full thesis for the sample argumentative essay in Lesson 45.

Thesis statement:
>   To sustain our spiritual life, we should schedule a regular time and place for personal devotions.

Opposing points:
>   hard to schedule consistently
>   spice of variety adds inspiration

Supporting points:
>   1. helps put us in proper frame of mind
>   2. impresses us with the importance of having devotions
>   3. avoids wasted moments
>   4. provides greater freedom from interruptions
>   5. helps prevent forgetting

Steps in Developing a Full Thesis

Developing the full thesis requires no complicated processes or polished writing skills. But it does demand careful, deliberate, and logical thought. You must think through your subject and organize your thinking. Unless you build this kind of solid framework, you can hardly build a strong argumentative essay.

Use the following steps to develop your full thesis.

1. *Write your thesis in one clear statement.* This is the first step because everything else revolves around your thesis statement. At first you may find it difficult to

summarize your ideas and state your point of argument in only one sentence. You will likely feel that what you want to say cannot be expressed so simply. This is normal, but it indicates that the exact point of your argument is not perfectly clear in your own mind.

Ask yourself some questions. "Exactly what opinion or idea do I plan to defend? Of what am I trying to convince others? What one point, above all others, do I want to make?" Forcing yourself to answer these questions in one simple statement crystallizes your thinking and prepares you for the remaining steps. Difficult though this may be, you must do it before you go any further.

You will possibly change the wording of your original thesis statement when you write your final essay. Change it if that improves it; the original statement will still have served the purpose of giving direction to your thinking and writing.

2. *Consider points of opposition to your thesis, and list those that you will mention in your essay.* If possible, include objections that you can directly counter with your supporting arguments.

Remember, the point of an argumentative essay is something that not everyone agrees upon. People as intelligent as you have considered it and have come to different conclusions. Evaluate their thinking. What has led them to their beliefs on the subject? What arguments might they give to refute your position? If you do not consider the subject as they see it, you will probably overlook some important aspects of it. Your argument will be unbalanced if you look only at one side.

Do the arguments used by your opposition follow sound logic? Do they hold any merit? Likely they do. It would be presumptuous to totally discredit every opinion that differs from yours. So take time to consider those arguments.

As you examine them, you may see two categories. Some arguments used by your opposition will seem so trite and meaningless that you can simply ignore them. They are not worth mentioning.

For example, someone in prison might argue that he cannot schedule personal devotions because all his schedules are made by others. A truck driver might say that he is seldom at the same place from one day to another. These arguments are obviously not worth considering, because those people are not in the audience for which the essay is intended. It is written for people who live at home in normal circumstances.

Other arguments may have the support of good logic; you will need to reckon with them. These are the ones you will include in your plan.

3. *List facts that support your thesis.* One of the most important skills for developing a profitable argument is the ability to discern between facts and opinions. A fact is a piece of information that can be known definitely. It is something true or real. A statement is a fact if it expresses a historical, scientific, mathematical, or statistical reality.

> King John signed the Magna Carta in June, 1215, at Runnymede.
> The square of the hypotenuse of a right triangle equals the sum of the squares of the other two sides.

A statement is also a fact, of course, if it expresses a truth revealed by God in His Word.

> God is omnipotent.
> The wages of sin is death.

In contrast, an opinion is a conclusion that a person forms or a belief that he holds about something. Expressions of likes and dislikes are opinions. Judgments about the relative values of nonmeasurable things (like beauty or contentment) are also opinions. Likewise, one's views of circumstances are opinions.

No one can personally verify every piece of information that he reads or hears. Then how can we know what is fact and what is opinion? In general, information is factual if it comes from reliable authorities. Christian parents, teachers, and ministers can help us discern what is reliable and what is not. Of course, the Bible is the final authority. We must accept Bible truth without question; and if something conflicts with the Bible, we must reject it without further consideration.

Look at the following statements. Can you determine which ones are facts and which are opinions?

a. Apples taste better than pears.
b. Apple trees cannot produce fruit in the far South, for they require a period of dormancy.
c. The apples from Luffton Orchard make better pies than the ones from Young's Orchard.
d. Most ripe apples are either red or yellow.

Statements *b* and *d* are facts. Although this may be information that you did not know previously, you could verify it by consulting reliable sources. But *a* and *c* are only opinions. Statement *a* expresses a like, and *c* expresses a value judgment.

The supporting points in your full thesis must be facts because facts are authoritative and convincing. Mere opinions carry little weight, for why should the reader think your opinion is better than his? Consider the audience for whom you are writing, and list facts that will be convincing to those people.

Where will you find convincing facts? Well, why are you convinced yourself about the thesis you plan to defend? Maybe it is because of statements that other people have made. Perhaps the Bible says something about the matter. The facts that are convincing to you will probably be convincing to others as well.

One of the best ways to clarify and broaden your thinking is to discuss your thesis with others. Express your ideas and ask what they think. "Iron sharpeneth iron; so a man sharpeneth the countenance of his friend" (Proverbs 27:17). Your parents in particular can probably give you some valuable insights.

Write down your supporting points as you gather them, without giving much attention to the number or order. When you are satisfied that you can give the subject a well-balanced treatment, choose four or five of the best points and discard the ones that carry less weight. Arrange the remaining points in the order of importance, with the most convincing argument coming last.

Developing the full thesis is a crucial part of writing an argumentative essay. Put into it the time and effort that it deserves, and you will be well rewarded when you do the actual writing.

Applying the Lesson

A. Write whether each statement expresses a fact or an opinion.
1. "If any would not work, neither should he eat."
2. Every Bible student should have a copy of *Strong's Concordance.*
3. "He that covereth his sins shall not prosper: but whoso confesseth and forsaketh them shall have mercy."
4. Since Jesus said, "Render to Caesar the things that are Caesar's," Christians should pay taxes willingly.
5. Iguaçú Falls is the most spectacular waterfall in South America.
6. Angel Falls is the highest waterfall in the world.
7. After a large meal, a boa constrictor can live for many months without food.
8. Meeting a thirty-foot anaconda in a rain forest would be one of the most terrifying things that could happen.
9. Being nearsighted is better than being farsighted.
10. In a nearsighted eye, the retina is too far back from the lens for a sharp image to be formed.

B. Develop a full thesis for the thesis statement that you wrote in Lesson 47. Your full thesis should include from three to five supporting points.

   You will use your full thesis to write an argumentative essay in Lesson 49. Also save it for use in Lesson 51.

---

49. Writing an Argumentative Essay

When you developed the full thesis, you built the framework of your argumentative essay. Now you are ready to finish the structure. As you write this first draft, use only every other line so that you can mark improvements later. The following steps will guide you through this process.

1. *Write an introductory paragraph that points to the thesis.* Remember that this paragraph should be like a funnel, opening with a broad, general statement and then narrowing down to the point of the argument. The first several sentences must catch the reader's attention and lead him to the idea you plan to emphasize. The last sentence should directly state the thesis.

Where can you find ideas for those first sentences? Sometimes they come easily. Other times you must work much harder to develop an opening that you like. You can begin your search for a meaningful opening by looking at the main words in your thesis. What general comment can you make in relation to those words, that will appeal to the reader and will lead naturally toward your thesis?

Below is the thesis of the sample argument in Lesson 45, with the key words in italics.

> To *sustain* our spiritual *life,* we should *schedule* a *regular* time and place for personal *devotions.*

Any of the following sentences could serve as the springboard of the introductory paragraph.

> Life must be sustained if it is to continue.
> A useful life is usually a scheduled life.
> Regularity promotes efficiency in many areas of life.
> Having regular devotions is like having frequent communication with one's supervisor.

Once you have a broad idea for your opening, you must find a way to move logically from that idea to your specific thesis. You may need to try several times before you develop a satisfactory introduction. Do not be surprised at that; rather, approach it as a puzzle to be solved. Enjoy the challenge of making unruly words fall into line. Try and try again until you succeed.

Developing a general statement from key words in the thesis is only one way to begin an introduction. You can use any opening statement that allows you to move logically toward the topic of your argument. The limit is your imagination.

Think of it this way. Your introduction is like bait. You are trying to attract your reader and draw him into your argument. If he does not take the bait, he fails to read your argument and it cannot have any effect on him. So you must make your introduction as appealing as possible!

2. *Deal promptly with the objections to your thesis.* Often the simplest way to do this is to devote the first paragraph of the body to the objections. If you choose this pattern, do more than mechanically listing the counter arguments. Give at least a brief explanation of why those objections are not valid. Notice how that is done in the argument in Lesson 45.

> Some people will say that maintaining a consistent schedule is impractical or even impossible. This may be true in a few cases, such as when a mother must care for a sick baby. But our regular farm and business schedules belie this excuse. We do consistently those things that we consider important. Some may declare that following a schedule is actually undesirable because it takes away the spice of variety. According to them, too much regularity produces monotony and stifles spontaneous worship. But these people show that they do not comprehend the true character of worship or the weakness of human nature.

Some of your supporting points may directly counter certain objections. When that is the case, begin each of the first several paragraphs of the body with an objection, followed by a supporting reason for your thesis. By using the development of your reasons to refute the objections, you can produce a very forceful argument. The following argument from Lesson 45 follows this pattern.

Not everyone has a special liking for work with soil and plants. But most people can enjoy the satisfaction that comes from having a family garden....

Then, too, a careful shopper may be able to purchase vegetables in the store more cheaply than he can raise them himself. It takes less time and effort to buy a dozen ears of sweet corn than to raise them. But gardening has rewards that cannot be measured in dollars and cents. People who raise their own produce reap benefits that cannot be harvested in any grocery store or produce market.

3. *In the main part of the body, develop each supporting reason thoroughly.* Use each main argument from the full thesis to write the topic sentence of one paragraph. Now ask yourself, "How can I convince someone that this point is valid? What details, definitions, reasons, or illustrations will drive the point home?" Remember, mere opinions carry no weight, but facts do.

Where can this supporting information be found? Cast about for it. Will statistics from an encyclopedia or another reference book support your point? Have you had any personal experience that would make a good illustration? Have you heard any stories that might serve as proof? What do others (classmates, teacher, parents, minister) say about the subject? These are all resources to draw from.

In developing your full thesis, you tried to list your arguments in the order of increasing importance. Be ready to change that order in the writing process. You may well discover as you develop a paragraph that its importance is greater (or less) than you had thought. Give careful consideration to this order, for the strength of your argument lies partly in its buildup to a climax.

4. *Write a conclusion that points back to the thesis.* In your introduction, you tried to catch the reader's attention. Assuming that you succeeded and that he followed through your complete argument, you now have one last opportunity to drive home your message. If you do this well, you will firmly clinch the point. But if you do it poorly, you will greatly weaken an argument that may otherwise be excellent. You should do three basic things in your concluding paragraph.

a. *Restate the thesis.* This brings the issue into clear focus once again, reminding the reader of exactly what point you are making. Remember to restate and not merely repeat the thesis. Vary the wording, but do not change the basic meaning. The following illustrations compare the theses of the sample arguments with the first sentence in each conclusion.

Theses:

To sustain our spiritual life, we should schedule a regular time and place for personal devotions.

A family garden makes a worthwhile summer project.

Conclusions:

A definite schedule for our personal devotions is imperative.

If at all feasible, every family should plan a garden for the summer.

b. *Briefly summarize your main arguments.* After reminding the reader of your basic point, quickly review the supporting reasons you have given. Do not merely repeat them in list fashion. Rather, take the ideas and a few key words, and reword the arguments. Combine closely related points into one sentence. Compare the following summary with the wording of the main points in the body of the first sample essay.

Body of essay:
> A definite schedule for personal devotions helps to put a person into a proper frame of mind for worship.
>
> Moreover, maintaining a fixed schedule helps to impress on our minds the importance of our personal devotions.
>
> Having our devotions at a regular place avoids wasted moments.
>
> With a regular time and place for our personal devotions, we have greater freedom from interruptions.
>
> Finally, a regular system probably does more than any other thing to prevent forgetfulness.

Concluding summary:
> The regularity gives us the benefit of having our minds in gear for worship. It helps us use our time efficiently and frees us from distractions. It serves not only to impress us with the importance of our devotions but also to keep us from forgetting this vital practice.

Note that the points in the summary come in a different order from that in the essay. One reason is the close relationship between "to impress us with the importance of our devotions" and "to keep us from forgetting this vital practice." But the summary does end with the last and strongest point, the same as the essay.

c. *Conclude with a general statement that strongly impresses the reader with the truth of your message.* How can you achieve this goal? The best closing sentence is a forceful statement that makes a direct appeal to the reader. Consider the following examples from two "persuasive parables" that Jesus gave.

"Go, and do thou likewise." (after the parable of the Good Samaritan)
"Watch therefore, for ye know neither the day nor the hour wherein the Son
    of man cometh." (after the parable of the ten virgins)

In addition, the closing sentence should portray the topic of the essay in a broad setting. That is, it should show how the topic fits into the "big picture," such as the whole of life, society in general, or the future. Notice how the final sentences of the two sample arguments do that.

As long as we dwell in these bodies, we shall need this regular nurturing of
    our inner spiritual life.
The produce from your garden may last for a year, but the memories will
    endure for a lifetime.

5. *Write an appealing title.* The title of your essay should be short—not more than five words if possible. It should relate directly to the thesis of your argument, and it should catch the reader's interest.

Writing a good title is often a challenge all its own. What is the secret of making it fresh and appealing? A good title often has rhyming words or an interesting word combination. Sometimes it is a question, and sometimes it uses alliteration (repetition of beginning consonant sounds). If the title is appealing enough that it causes a person to read the essay, it will have accomplished its purpose.

Look at the following titles. Can you tell why the second one in each pair is better than the first?

(1) a. **Fair:**   Scheduled Personal Devotions
    b. **Better:** The Hazard of Haphazard Devotions
(2) a. **Fair:**   Reasons for Family Gardening
    b. **Better:** More Than a Produce Patch
(3) a. **Fair:**   Are We Cultivating Neatness?
    b. **Better:** The Need for Neatness

In all the *b* titles, some of the appeal is due to alliteration. Title 3*b* also involves assonance, and title 1*b* contains word play on *hazard* and *haphazard.* In contrast, the *a* titles have no special literary appeal.

Consider again the three distinct parts of an argumentative essay. The introduction, like a funnel, leads the reader to the thesis. The body presents arguments to persuade the reader of the validity of the thesis. These arguments build to a climax, with the most convincing argument last. Finally the conclusion, like an inverted funnel, restates the thesis and brings the whole essay to a satisfying completion.

Applying the Lesson

Using the full thesis that you prepared in Lesson 48, write the first draft of an argumentative essay. It should contain 500–600 words.

---

50. Revising an Argumentative Essay

Almost without exception, producing a good finished essay requires proofreading and rewriting. Check the essay you wrote in Lesson 49, using the following questions to direct you.

Content and Organization

1. Does your essay include the three distinct parts: introduction, body, and conclusion?

2. Does the introduction, like a funnel, lead the reader from a broad opening sentence to the thesis? Is the thesis clearly stated?
3. Are the counter arguments clearly disposed of early in the argument?
4. Do the paragraphs of the body develop the main supporting arguments?
5. Is each argument well developed with convincing facts?
6. Is the most convincing argument placed at the end of the body?
7. Does the conclusion, like an inverted funnel, lead from the restated thesis to a forceful statement that appeals directly to the reader?
8. Does your essay have an appealing title?

Style

1. Do you see any sentences that you should write with more freshness and originality?
2. Do you see any vague, general terms that you could replace with exact, descriptive words?
3. Do you see any passive verbs that you could change to the active voice?

Mechanics

1. Have you used any unnecessary or repetitious words?
2. Have you omitted any words or phrases that are needed to make the meaning clear?
3. Have you transposed or misplaced any words, phrases, or clauses?
4. Have you misspelled any words? Especially check spellings like *ei* and *ie, ai* and *ia, ent* and *ant,* and so forth. Double-check your use of homonyms like *your—you're* and *their—there—they're.* Make sure that you have spelled technical terms and proper nouns correctly. Pay close attention to words that you have difficulty spelling correctly.
5. Have you used proper capitalization and punctuation?
6. Have you followed the rules of correct grammar and word usage?

Do not imagine that you can evaluate all these points at one time. Since the points under "Content and Organization" form a sequence, you should consider them in the order they occur. For "Style," you will probably need to evaluate your essay on each point separately. For the points under "Mechanics," it will take several readings to do a thorough job. Concentrate first on points 1–3, next on point 4, then on point 5, and finally on point 6.

Applying the Lesson

A. Proofread the essay that you wrote for Lesson 49, marking corrections on the first draft.

B. Recopy your essay in your best handwriting.

Your teacher may use the evaluation chart below to grade your argumentative essay. Remember, your score on this essay will make up a considerable part of your Chapter 6 test score.

Evaluation of an Argumentative Essay

Points   Points
possible   earned

Title

  _2_   ____ Appealing

  _2_   ____ Five words or less

  _2_   ____ Directly related to thesis

Introduction

  _4_   ____ Interesting; catches attention

  _4_   ____ Leads naturally to thesis

Body

  _4_   ____ Treats counter arguments promptly and effectively

  _4_   ____ Supports thesis with solid, convincing evidence

  _4_   ____ Consists of well-developed paragraphs

  _4_   ____ Gives points in logical order, with strongest one last

Conclusion

  _4_   ____ Restates thesis in different words

  _4_   ____ Summarizes main points briefly and in different words

  _4_   ____ Ends with effective concluding sentence

Style

  _2_   ____ Freshness and originality

  _2_   ____ Exact, descriptive words

  _2_   ____ Active voice

Mechanics

  _3_   ____ Correct spelling

  _3_   ____ Correct capitalization and punctuation

  _3_   ____ Correct grammar

  _3_   ____ Avoids careless repetition, omitted words, transpositions

  _60_   ____ **Total points**

---

51. Improving Your Speaking Style, Part 1: Eye Contact

Over the past few years, you have had several assignments in which you went to the front of the classroom and addressed your classmates as an audience. In those assignments, you worked mainly to develop a speech with good content and organization. After all, the most important part of an effective speech is having something meaningful to say.

But having something meaningful to say is not enough. You must also say it in a meaningful way. Your *speaking style* contributes greatly to the effectiveness of what you say. How well do you communicate with an audience if you speak in a mumble? Can you capture the listeners' attention if your eyes are glued to your notes? Will a dead monotone stir an audience to action? Of course not. Interesting and meaningful content requires appealing presentation to make an effective speech. This is the first of three lessons that give pointers on improving your speaking style.

The things you have learned in the three writing style lessons this year also apply to speaking. Originality adds spark whether your communication is written or oral. Exact words always paint clear images, and the active voice always helps to make sentences lively and energetic. By all means try to have these ingredients in your speaking as well as your writing. However, these speaking style lessons will emphasize skills relating not to the words you say but to your manner in saying them. This first lesson is on *eye contact,* which occurs when your eyes directly meet those of another person.

Eye contact with the audience is a vital part of effective public speaking. Because many people feel self-conscious before a group, they tend to look somewhere else—at their notes, the floor, or the back wall. But eye contact is so important that you dare not neglect it. Eye contact establishes an unspoken link with your listeners. It arrests their attention and shows that you are talking directly to them. It helps you to know whether you are communicating clearly. The listeners' reactions and facial expressions reveal whether you are talking loudly enough, whether your points are clear to them, and whether they enjoy what you are saying. Moreover, eye contact actually helps you to emphasize important points.

This means that you must look directly at your listeners. You are speaking to *people,* not to your notes or the walls. You are speaking to *individuals,* not to an abstract mass called an audience. Merely glancing at the group or running your eyes unseeingly over the audience is not eye contact. Look directly at individual listeners. You will know which person's eyes you meet, but that person will not know whether you are looking at him or at the person beside him. If you meet the eyes of persons in every part of the audience—in the front, in the back, to the left, and to the right—it will help each listener to feel that you have spoken directly to him.

Plan to establish eye contact with your listeners from the very beginning, with your introduction. This immediately communicates that you have something you want to tell them, something you consider worthwhile. Throughout the speech, maintain regular eye contact with your audience. However, you should not act like a programmed machine, raising your head at scheduled intervals. Rather, look at your audience naturally as you look at your friends when you talk to them.

Eye contact is especially important when you want to emphasize a certain point. Suppose in a discussion of honesty, you want to warn against exaggeration. You look down at your notes and carefully read this sentence: "We always weaken what we exaggerate." But imagine how much more effective that statement will be if you look directly at an individual in the group and say, "We always weaken what we exaggerate." Eye contact is an unobtrusive but forceful way of telling your audience, "Now, listen to this."

Finally, you should look at your audience as you conclude your speech. Though it is almost finished and you may be eager to return to your seat, your work is not quite done. Give it your best to the end. Have a well-planned conclusion, give it with fervor, look directly at your listeners—and you will end your speech on a solid, positive note.

You may think, "But I'm too nervous to look up while I'm talking. I'll get all mixed up if I do that." Those feelings are normal. But take your mind off yourself and concentrate on your subject. Think about your listeners and how they will benefit from what you have to tell them. Also remember that they are kind, sympathetic friends, who understand the difficulty you face and who want you to succeed. Like most hard tasks, this one becomes easier once you begin and also as you gain experience.

Your teacher will likely use the chart below to evaluate your speaking style assignments. This lesson introduces eye contact, so this assignment will be evaluated only for that one point of emphasis. In the next speaking style lesson, you will be evaluated on eye contact and the point of emphasis in that lesson. The third lesson will introduce a final point of emphasis, thus giving three items that your teacher will evaluate in your speaking.

Evaluation of Speaking Style

Part	Points of Emphasis		
	Eye Contact	Voice Control	Enthusiasm
1.	————	....	....
2.	————	————	....
3.	————	————	....

G = Good   F = Fair   P = Poor

Applying the Lesson

Prepare to give orally the argumentative essay that you wrote in Lesson 50. Practice good eye contact as you speak.

---

52. Chapter 6 Review

A. Write the correct word or phrase for each blank.

1. Every argumentative essay deals with a ————.
2. The main idea promoted in an argument is the ————.
3. The introduction and conclusion of an argumentative essay should resemble a ————.
4. The plan for writing an argumentative essay is called a ————.
5. Directly meeting the eyes of another person is called ————.

6. By looking at your listeners, you send the message that you have something ——— to tell them.
7. You should look at your audience naturally as you look at your ———.
8. Meeting your listeners' eyes is especially important when you ——— a certain point.

B. Answer these questions.
1. Why should an argumentative essay deal with counter arguments?
2. In what order should the supporting points be arranged?
3. If a thesis statement is poor, what are four possible ways of improving it?
4. What is a good way to determine whether a statement expresses a fact or an opinion?
5. What are four things that help to make titles appealing?
6. If a title is truly effective, what purpose will it accomplish?

———————————

That the
communication of thy faith
may become effectual
by the acknowledging of every
good thing which
is in you in Christ Jesus.

Philemon 1:6

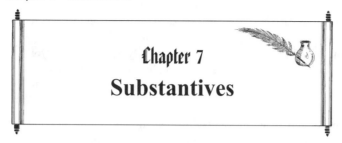

Chapter 7
Substantives

53. Identifying Nouns

As you have known for years, a noun is the name of a person, place, thing, or idea. Nouns constitute the backbone of language. To a large extent, we use nouns to express the main ideas in our communication.

Concrete and Abstract Nouns

A noun names a person, place, thing, or idea. Nouns are either concrete or abstract. A concrete noun names a person, place, or thing, usually with physical substance that we can perceive through the senses. An abstract noun names an idea that does not have physical substance and that we cannot perceive through the senses.

Concrete:

mechanic	school	thread
Robert	Lewis County	potatoes

Abstract:

thought	grace	opinion
habit	holiness	pride
purpose		

Names referring to God, spiritual beings (like *angel*), and spiritual places (like *heaven*) are also concrete nouns. Although they do not have physical substance that we can perceive through our senses, they are real persons, places, and things.

Common and Proper Nouns

Nouns are either common or proper. A common noun is the general name of a person, place, or thing. It is the name *common* to a group of items, and it is not capitalized. A proper noun is the particular name of a person, place, or thing. It is the name *proper* for one specific item, and it is capitalized. In Lesson 1 you studied ten groupings of proper nouns.

Gender of Nouns

All nouns have gender. Masculine gender refers to persons or animals that are male (*boy, father, rooster*). Feminine gender refers to persons or animals that are female (*girl, mother, hen*). Common gender refers to persons or animals that are either male or female, or to a group that may include any combination of genders (*child, parent, chickens*). Neuter gender refers to nonliving objects or to abstract nouns, which can be neither male nor female (*house, ocean, faithfulness*).

Noun-forming Suffixes

Many nouns, especially abstract nouns, end with noun-forming suffixes. The following are common noun-forming suffixes: *-ment, -ity, -ness, -ion, -ation, -dom, -ance, -ence, -ude, -al, -ship, -hood, -er, -or,* and *-ar.* The pairs of words below illustrate how these suffixes are used to form nouns from other parts of speech or from other nouns.

fulfill—fulfillment	similar—similarity, similitude
decide—decision	survive—survival, survivor
martyr—martyrdom	neighbor—neighborhood

Other Words Used as Nouns

A word is classified as a certain part of speech not only because of its basic meaning but also because of how it is used in a sentence. When used with their normal meanings, some words are always nouns, some are never nouns, and some may be either nouns or other parts of speech. Can you place each of the following words into one of those three categories?

good	map	from	quietude
pleasantly	permanence	find	sustain

Quietude and *permanence* are always nouns. *From, pleasantly,* and *sustain* are never nouns. *Good, map,* and *find* are sometimes nouns and sometimes other parts of speech.

Perhaps you notice that *map* can actually serve as an adjective sometimes, as in *map skills.* But dictionaries generally do not label *map* as an adjective. This is an example of an attributive noun—a noun that precedes another noun and functions as an adjective. In its basic essence, however, such a word is a noun.

Applying the Lesson

A. Copy each noun, and label it *C* (concrete) or *A* (abstract).
1. Trials and temptations test our faithfulness to the Lord.
2. The cultivation of godly fear prepares a person for usefulness.
3. The Bible assures the care of angels for the believers.
4. In the New Testament we find the principles that will guide us to heaven.
5. The car was not working properly, so Father took it to the garage.
6. Before supper Susan should water the flowers bordering the garden.
7. A sense of restfulness pervaded the secluded spot along the creek.
8. The reassurance of the guide relieved our anxiety.

B. Copy each noun, and write *M* (masculine), *F* (feminine), *N* (neuter), or *C* (common) to label its gender.
1. David, a godly king, influenced the people toward righteousness.
2. Solomon began his reign well, but his wives turned his heart to idolatry.
3. The women showed their loyalty to Jesus by bringing spices to His tomb.
4. By faith the parents of Moses hid their son to spare his life.
5. The ewe bravely protected her lambs from the danger posed by the dogs.
6. While Mother was sick, Susan Detweiler worked as a maid for our family.

7. Dorcas was a kind seamstress who sewed garments for the needy.
8. My uncle raises goats on Rocky Acres Farm.

C. Add a noun-forming suffix to each word in parentheses so that it fits in the sentence.
1. In the (solitary) of Gethsemane, Jesus conquered (tempt) through (persevere) in (pray).
2. If Jesus felt any (hesitate) to do the Father's will, He found (fulfill) in (submit) and (obey).
3. He endured the (intense) of the conflict so that He might offer man the (forgive) of sins and provide spiritual (vital) to overcome sin.
4. Our (confide) rests in the (Father) of God and the (Lord) of Jesus Christ.
5. The Holy Spirit is a (reveal) to those who would receive (enlighten) and flee (dark).
6. Being a (partake) of God's (king) requires the (refuse) of all (err).
7. (Heathen) binds men through the (dominate) of (superstitious).
8. In (real), (free) can be the (possess) of only those with a (commit) to the truth.

D. Write whether each word is *always, never,* or *sometimes* a noun.

1. attitude	4. apply	7. beautify	10. commonly
2. content	5. redemption	8. teacher	11. book
3. stream	6. fire	9. written	12. brotherhood

Review Exercises

A. Identify the structure of each sentence as *S* (simple), *CD* (compound), *CX* (complex), or *CD-CX* (compound-complex). [22]
1. The oil industry took on new importance when Edwin L. Drake drilled an oil well near Titusville, Pennsylvania, in 1859.
2. William A. Smith had experience with drilling salt wells, and Drake hired him to direct his oil drilling operations.
3. The drill was powered by a six-horsepower steam engine.
4. On Saturday afternoon, August 27, the workmen stopped drilling and went home.
5. Smith looked into the well the next afternoon, and he found a dark fluid that proved to be oil.

B. Identify the word order of each sentence as *N* (natural), *I* (inverted), or *M* (mixed). [22]
1. Into the Titusville area flocked many other prospectors.
2. Soon many wells were producing much oil.
3. The price for a barrel of oil dropped from twenty dollars to ten cents.
4. To transport the oil, men used wagons, barges, and railroads.
5. A pipeline was built to a railroad station five miles away as early as 1865.

C. Identify the style of each sentence as *L* (loose), *P* (periodic), or *B* (balanced). [22]
1. At the site of Drake's original well in Drake Well Park, visitors today can see a replica of his engine house and derrick.
2. In other states around Pennsylvania, even larger oil deposits were soon found.

3. Texas produced the first North American gusher, a well that spewed out over 800,000 barrels of oil before it could be brought under control.
4. A tremendous demand for gasoline developed with the advent of the automobile in the early 1900s.
5. The more oil that the oil fields produced, the more oil the world seemed to need.

---

54. Verbals and Clauses as Nouns

Most nouns are single words or compound words whose normal, basic meanings make them nouns. Sometimes, however, other words and word groups serve to name persons, places, things, or ideas. The most common of these are verbals, verbal phrases, and clauses. Study the following sentences. In each one, the subject is underlined.

Grace has been defined as "God's riches at Christ's expense."
(simple single word)
To believe is man's part in salvation. (infinitive)
Doing good works will follow true faith. (gerund phrase)
How faith has been defined is "Forsaking all, I take Him." (noun clause)

Verbals as Nouns

Verbals hold two jobs. On the one hand, they are verb forms that have many characteristics of verbs. On the other hand, they function in a sentence as some other part of speech. Two kinds of verbals can function as nouns: the gerund and the infinitive. When the gerund or the infinitive has adverb modifiers or complements, the word group is a verbal phrase. The entire verbal phrase then functions as a noun.

1. *Gerunds and gerund phrases.* A gerund is the present participle (the *-ing* form) of a verb used as a noun. It functions as the subject of a sentence, as a verb complement, or as the object of a preposition. Rather than expressing action, as a verb does, the gerund *names* an action.

Reading is an important skill.
(The subject *Reading* names an action; it is a gerund.)
Carolyn enjoys reading missionary stories. (The direct object reading missionary stories names an action; it is a gerund phrase.)
Grandmother's hobby is quilting.
(The predicate nominative *quilting* names an action; it is a gerund.)
Grandfather built a chest for storing her quilts.
(The object of the preposition, *storing her quilts,* names an action; it is a gerund phrase.)

Sentence diagrams can help you to evaluate the place that a verbal or verbal phrase fills in a sentence. Remember that a verbal used as a noun is diagramed on a pedestal. Observe specifically the noun position filled by each gerund.

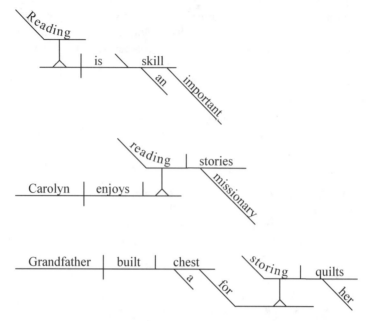

Be especially careful that you do not confuse a gerund functioning as a predicate nominative with the present participle form of a true verb. In both cases the *-ing* form may follow a form of *be*. If the word is a gerund, however, it must name an action and rename the subject. If the word is part of the verb phrase, it will express the action that the subject is performing. Examining the meaning of the sentence and reading the skeleton should help you decide which it is.

Brenda's present responsibility is <u>helping at the new school</u>.
> (*Helping at the new school* renames the subject *responsibility;* it is a gerund phrase.)

She is <u>helping</u> several of the teachers.
> (*Helping* does not rename the subject *She;* it expresses the action that the subject is performing; it is part of the verb phrase.)

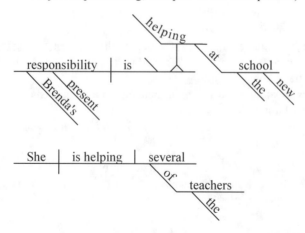

2. *Infinitives and infinitive phrases.* An infinitive is the basic form of a verb preceded by *to.* An infinitive is a noun when it names an action and fills a noun function in the sentence.

<u>To fly</u> was man's dream for centuries.
    (The subject *To fly* names an action; it is an infinitive.)
Brother Charles is planning <u>to fly to Mexico</u>.
    (The direct object *to fly to Mexico* names an action; it is an infinitive phrase.)
The Christian's desire is <u>to use modern inventions for God's glory</u>.
    (The predicate nominative *to use modern inventions for God's glory* names an action; it is an infinitive phrase.)

Notice on each diagram how the infinitive fills the place of a regular noun in each sentence.

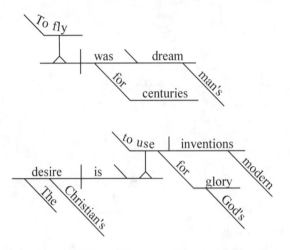

Do not confuse infinitives with prepositional phrases that begin with *to. To* plus the basic form of a verb makes an infinitive. *To* plus a noun or pronoun makes a prepositional phrase.

Jonah tried <u>to flee</u>, but finally he went <u>to Nineveh</u>.
    (*To flee* is *to* plus a basic verb form; it is an infinitive. *To Nineveh* is *to* plus a noun; it is a prepositional phrase.)

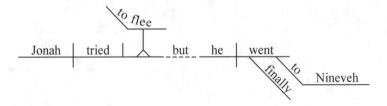

Noun Clauses

A noun clause is a dependent clause with a noun function in a complex sentence. Unlike an adjective or an adverb clause, a noun clause is a basic part of the independent clause except when it serves as the object of a preposition. In a complex sentence containing a noun clause, therefore, the two clauses are sometimes hard to identify.

When a sentence contains a noun clause used as a verb complement, the two clauses are usually quite easy to identify. Especially obvious are the clauses that function as direct and indirect quotations. Almost always they are noun clauses used as direct objects. In the following sentences, the noun clauses are in brackets and the skeletons of both clauses are underlined.

Father said [that you should return promptly].
(The clause in brackets is the direct object of *said.*)

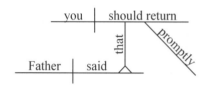

The salesman offered [whoever was present] a free sample.
(The clause in brackets is the indirect object of *offered.*)

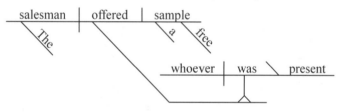

Firewood is [what we use for heat].
(The clause in brackets is a predicate nominative renaming *Firewood.*)

When a sentence contains a noun clause used as a subject, the two clauses may be difficult to identify. The entire noun clause serves as the subject of the independent clause; therefore, the skeleton of that independent clause may be difficult to detect. In the following sentences, the noun clauses are again in brackets. The skeletons of the noun clauses are underlined, and the verbs of the independent clauses are underlined.

[Whoever entered the ark] survived the Flood.
(The clause in brackets is the subject of the independent clause.)

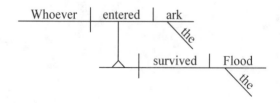

[Whose book <u>this</u> <u>is</u>] <u>should be</u> easy to tell.
(The clause in brackets is the subject of the independent clause.)

A noun clause functioning as the object of a preposition is not a basic part of the independent clause. Therefore, the two clauses should be easy to identify. The following sentences show the noun clauses in brackets, with the skeletons of both clauses underlined.

<u>Christopher Columbus</u> <u>was</u> greatly <u>interested</u> in [<u>what</u> <u>lay</u> across the Atlantic].

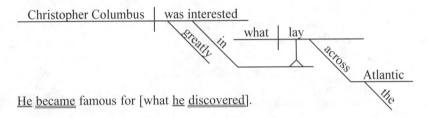

<u>He</u> <u>became</u> famous for [what <u>he</u> <u>discovered</u>].

Applying the Lesson

A. If the underlined item is a noun phrase, identify its function by writing *subject, direct object, predicate nominative,* or *object of a preposition.* If it is not a noun phrase, write *none.*

1. A good exercise for a discouraged person can be <u>reading the Book of Psalms</u>.
2. We can avoid many pitfalls by <u>applying the principles in the Book of Proverbs</u>.
3. <u>Reading the accounts of Old Testament saints</u> should inspire us to faithfulness today.
4. God's faithful people always will be <u>finding encouragement in God's Word</u>.
5. Faithfulness to the Lord includes <u>keeping Jesus on the throne of one's heart</u>.
6. <u>To keep self on the cross</u> demands a complete surrender to the lordship of Jesus Christ.
7. The Christian's safety lies partly in <u>submitting to a Scriptural brotherhood</u>.
8. A young person should seek <u>to establish noble goals for life</u>.
9. The path <u>to true happiness in this life</u> lies not in material wealth but in spiritual health.
10. One of Satan's effective strategies is <u>to choke spiritual interests through the cares of life</u>.

B. Copy each verbal or verbal phrase, and write whether it is a gerund (*G*), a gerund phrase (*GP*), an infinitive (*I*), or an infinitive phrase (*IP*).

1. Crocheting is one thing that keeps Grandmother Stoltzfus busy.
2. To concentrate requires blocking out distractions.
3. Others will seldom need to discipline us if we practice disciplining ourselves.
4. Sanding can require much effort before a piece of wood is ready for staining.
5. To copyedit is to make a manuscript as free from mistakes as possible.
6. The first stand of corn will soon be ready for harvesting.
7. Budgeting your time wisely is important if you have many assignments due.
8. Our first major project for this summer will be to build a small chicken house.

9. Grandfather Wenger is scheduled to preach.
10. Finding these old coins was quite a pleasant surprise.

C. If the underlined word group is a noun clause, identify its function by writing *subject, direct object, indirect object, predicate nominative,* or *object of a preposition.* If it is not a noun clause, write *none.*
1. The Book of Nehemiah clearly demonstrates <u>why God's people must work together</u>.
2. <u>Whoever will build God's kingdom</u> must depend on God and zealously labor in the cause.
3. Nehemiah's faithfulness was <u>what inspired the people to rise up and build</u>.
4. Nehemiah recognized <u>where compromise with the enemy would lead</u>.
5. The pioneers built sturdy houses with <u>whatever hand tools they possessed</u>.
6. <u>When power tools became commonplace</u>, many jobs became much easier to accomplish.
7. The beauty and comfort of these old chairs tells <u>whoever examines them</u> a story of skill.
8. The workmanship of these delicate carvings is <u>what Father admires most</u>.
9. <u>How much patience those craftsmen exercised</u> is hard to imagine.
10. We should give <u>whichever sheep are coughing</u> a shot of an antibiotic.
11. These lively goats will go <u>wherever they can climb in these rocky pastures</u>.
12. The little kids will show affection to <u>whoever gives them attention</u>.

D. Copy each noun clause.
1. Why these rows of corn have wilted remains a mystery to Father.
2. We are pleased with how well the rest of the corn is growing.
3. Have you decided whose suggestion you will follow?
4. The person to clean up this mess should be whoever left the door open.
5. Grandfather gives whoever pays him a visit much cheer and encouragement.
6. Whoever appreciates church history will certainly enjoy this new book.
7. We had a panoramic view of the valley from where we stood on the mountainside.
8. Please give whoever is tending the market stand this message.
9. The best place to fish is wherever the fish are biting.
10. We could hardly decide if the shed was worth another paint job.

Review Exercises

A. Identify each underlined word as a direct object (*DO*), an indirect object (*IO*), a predicate nominative (*PN*), a predicate adjective (*PA*), or an objective complement (*OC*). [17, 18]
1. Arriving at the scene of the explosion, firemen found the building completely <u>destroyed</u>.
2. George Washington Carver was a great American <u>scientist</u>.
3. If you will give <u>me</u> your coat, I will hang it in the closet.
4. Such <u>behavior</u> we cannot tolerate here.
5. We considered his illness a valid <u>reason</u> for absence from school.
6. The cause of the accident remains <u>mysterious</u>.

B. Identify each underlined word as a retained direct object (*DO ret.*), a retained indirect object (*IO ret.*), or a retained objective complement (*OC ret.*). [18]

1. A place of comfort was given <u>Lazarus</u> after he died.
2. David was told a <u>parable</u> to show him his sin.
3. During Solomon's reign, the people were made <u>weary</u> by heavy taxes.
4. Jesus' crucifixion was considered a <u>defeat</u> by His enemies.
5. Moses was shown God's <u>glory</u> while he was on the mount.
6. Many difficult questions were asked <u>Jesus</u> by His enemies.

---

55. Plural and Possessive Nouns

Plural Forms

Most one-word nouns show number; that is, their form shows whether they are singular or plural. The following rules will help you to write the plural forms of nouns correctly.

1. *General rules.*

   a. To form the plurals of most nouns, add -*s*.

book—books	nation—nations
river—rivers	decision—decisions

   b. To form the plural of a noun ending with *s, sh, ch, x,* or *z,* add -*es*. You may need to double a final *s* or *z*.

bus—buses *or* busses	box—boxes
crutch—crutches	quiz—quizzes

2. *Nouns ending with* y.

   a. To form the plural of a noun ending with *y* after a vowel, add -*s*.

quay—quays	valley—valleys	alloy—alloys

   b. To form the plural of a noun ending with *y* after a consonant, change the *y* to *i* and add -*es*.

liberty—liberties	blueberry—blueberries

3. *Nouns ending with* f *or* fe.

   a. For many nouns, change the *f* to *v* and add -*s* or -*es*.

leaf—leaves	knife—knives

   b. For other nouns, simply add -*s*.

belief—beliefs	roof—roofs	waif—waifs

   c. For most nouns ending with *ff,* simply add -*s*.

tariff—tariffs	puff—puffs

    d. Sometimes either ending is correct for a word.

        scarf—scarves *or* scarfs   staff—staffs *or* staves

4. *Nouns ending with* o.
    a. To form the plural of a noun ending with *o* after a vowel, add -*s*.

        vireo—vireos   ratio—ratios   igloo—igloos

    b. To form the plural of a noun ending with *o* after a consonant, add -*s* or -*es*. Sometimes either ending is correct.

        potato—potatoes   silo—silos   motto—mottoes *or* mottos

    c. For most musical terms ending with *o,* simply add -*s*.

        solo—solos   soprano—sopranos

5. *Compound nouns.*
    a. In general, change the most important word to the plural form.

        son-in-law—sons-in-law
        passerby—passersby
        post office—post offices

    b. Simply add -*s* to nouns ending with -*ful.*

        spoonful—spoonfuls   pailful—pailfuls

    c. For a few nouns, each part of the compound word is made plural.

        manservant—menservants   womanservant—womenservants

6. *Nouns with irregular plural forms.*
    a. In only seven nouns, the internal vowels are changed for the plural forms. Of course, if a compound word contains one of these roots, the plural is formed in the same way.

        foot—feet; goose—geese; tooth—teeth
          (forefoot—forefeet *but* mongoose—mongooses)
        louse—lice; mouse—mice (titmouse—titmice)
        man—men; woman—women (kinsman—kinsmen)

    b. Four plural nouns have an archaic -*en* ending.

        child—children, ox—oxen (still used today)
        brother—brethren (used within the church, but archaic otherwise)
        hose—hosen (archaic; found once in the King James Bible)

    c. Some nouns have the same form whether singular or plural.

        bison—bison   series—series
        deer—deer   species—species
        sheep—sheep

7. *Nouns with foreign plural forms.*
    A number of nouns borrowed from foreign languages have retained their foreign plural forms. In addition, the regular English pattern is often acceptable.

Singular Ending	Plural Ending	Example
-is	-es	thesis—theses
-ex *or* -ix	-ices	vertex—vertices *or* vertexes
-a	-ae	nebula—nebulae
-us	-i	gladiolus—gladioli *or* gladioluses
-um *or* -on	-a	bacterium—bacteria

Possessive Forms

Possessive nouns show possession or ownership. The following rules will help you to write possessive forms correctly.

1. *Singular nouns.*
    a. Make the possessive form of most singular nouns by adding 's. This includes nouns that end with a single *s* sound.

        the apostle's journey   Lois's faith

    b. If a singular noun contains two *s* or *z* sounds in the last syllable, add only an apostrophe. Adding a third *s* or *z* sound makes the word awkward to pronounce.

        Jesus' disciples   Xerxes' rule

2. *Plural nouns.*
    a. If a plural noun does not end with -*s,* add 's.

        the firemen's courage   the larvae's appetite

    b. If a plural noun ends with -*s,* add only an apostrophe.

        the students' assignments   the puppies' barks

3. *Compound nouns and noun phrases.*
    Make the last word in the compound possessive.

        my sister-in-law's flowers   the man of God's warning

Usage of Possessive Nouns

1. Normally, only nouns naming persons or animals are written in possessive forms. For inanimate objects, you should generally use a prepositional phrase. Exceptions include poetic or figurative language and various common expressions, such as those used for measures of time or money.

    a fawn's spots
    the corners of the box (*not* the box's corners)
    an hour's delay; a moment's notice; a dollar's worth

2. Show joint ownership of several nouns by making only the last noun possessive. Show separate ownership by making each noun possessive.

>**Joint ownership:**
>Have you seen Cheryl and Linda's books?
>(one set of books owned by two girls together)
>**Separate ownership:**
>Have you seen Cheryl's and Linda's books?
>(two sets of books owned by two girls separately)

3. A noun coming before a gerund should usually be possessive. To see why, replace the gerund with a regular noun form. It is clear that the preceding noun should be possessive.

>Paul's preaching stirred varied responses.
>>(*Preaching* was what stirred responses. *Paul's* modifies *preaching* by telling whose. Compare: Paul's admonition, *not* Paul admonition.)
>
>We appreciated Joshua's painting the fence.
>>(*Painting* was what we appreciated. *Joshua's* modifies *painting* by telling whose. Compare: Joshua's work, *not* Joshua work)

Do not confuse this with a noun followed by a participle.

>The children watched Joshua painting the fence.
>>(The sentence does not mean that they watched *Joshua's painting,* but that they watched *Joshua* in the action of *painting.* The participle *painting* modifies the direct object *Joshua.*)

Applying the Lesson

A. For each noun, write the singular possessive, the plural, and the plural possessive forms. Use the foreign plural spellings for numbers 31–40. If possessive forms should generally not be used, write *none.*

1. giraffe	15. soprano	28. turkey
2. enemy	16. postman	29. louse
3. major general	17. calf	30. ox
4. wolf	18. Eskimo	31. phenomenon
5. child	19. sheep	32. antithesis
6. mosquito	20. webfoot	33. paramecium
7. brother (church)	21. bondwoman	34. vertebra
8. seamstress	22. dormouse	35. neurosis
9. pony	23. son-in-law	36. helix
10. air mass	24. secretary-general	37. pupa
11. hero	25. goose	38. narcissus
12. trout	26. chief	39. apex
13. donkey	27. finch	40. cerebellum
14. mouthful		

B. Write correctly each phrase that has an error. If it is correct, write *correct.*
 1. Demas' love for this world
 2. Peter's and Paul's epistles
 3. David and Jonathan's backgrounds
 4. the vineyard's site
 5. the two thiefs' reactions
 6. his father's-in-law's advice
 7. surprised by Peter's knocking
 8. for a day's wages
 9. the two king's alliance
 10. leaving handfuls of grain
 11. Mary's and Martha's brother Lazarus
 12. commended Mary choosing the better part
 13. answered Nicodemus's question
 14. the upper room's furnishings
 15. found Jesus talking with the teachers
 16. ironed several handkerchieves
 17. three bucketsful of beans
 18. amused by the monkey's chattering
 19. after a weeks delay
 20. with my three brother's help

Review Exercises

A. Identify each underlined word or word group as a gerund (*G*), a gerund phrase
 (*GP*), an infinitive (*I*), or an infinitive phrase (*IP*). Then tell whether it functions
 as a subject (*S*), a direct object (*DO*), a predicate nominative (*PN*), or the object
 of a preposition (*OP*). [54]
 1. Answering the telephone is an important part of this job.
 2. With amazing patience, Brother James began to explain the solution to the
 algebra problem.
 3. In addition to grumbling, the children of Israel failed to respect their leader
 Moses.
 4. A most important rule in any game is to play fairly.
 5. To lose is no disgrace if you do your best.

B. Tell whether each noun clause functions as a subject (*S*), a direct object (*DO*), an
 indirect object (*IO*), a predicate nominative (*PN*), or the object of a preposition
 (*OP*). [54]
 1. I cannot forget what he told me yesterday.
 2. The question now is how to remedy the problem.
 3. From where I was sitting, I could not see the speaker.
 4. He told whoever would listen the story of his accident.
 5. Why the car drifted off the road could not be explained.

56. Personal and Compound Personal Pronouns

A *pronoun* is a word that takes the place of a noun. The noun to which a pronoun refers is its *antecedent*. This lesson reviews two of the six classes of pronouns, and the next lesson deals with the other four classes.

Personal Pronouns

Personal pronouns are words like *he, you,* and *them,* which often refer to persons. The pronouns in this class are probably the first ones that come to your mind when you think of pronouns. Personal pronouns have different forms to show person, number, case, and gender.

1. *Person.* The person of a pronoun shows the relationship between the pronoun and the speaker. First person pronouns (*I, me, my, mine, we, us, our, ours*) refer to the speaker himself. Second person pronouns (*you, your, yours*) refer to the person that the speaker is talking to. Third person pronouns (*he, him, his, she, her, hers, it, its, they, them, their, theirs*) refer to the person or thing that the speaker is talking about.

2. *Number.* The number of a pronoun shows whether it is singular or plural. First and third person pronouns have different forms according to number, but second person pronouns do not.

3. *Case.* The case of a pronoun relates to its use in the sentence. The three cases in the English language are nominative, objective, and possessive.

The *nominative case* pronouns are as follows: *I, you, he, she, it, we, they.* These pronouns function as subjects, predicate nominatives, or appositives to one of these. Be especially careful to use the nominative case in compound structures of these sentence parts.

> Delmar and <u>I</u> have been helping Brother Andrew with his chores. (subject)
> The van drivers, Marcus and <u>he</u>, are ready to leave. (appositive to subject)
> <u>We</u> students enjoyed Brother Frank's talk about Guatemala.
> (subject followed by appositive)
> The ones to ask first would be <u>they</u>. (predicate nominative)

The King James Bible uses the archaic forms *thou* (singular) and *ye* (plural) as second person pronouns in the nominative case.

> "<u>Ye</u> have heard that it was said by them of old time, <u>Thou</u> shalt not kill."

The *objective case* pronouns are as follows: *me, you, him, her, it, us, them.* They function as object complements, objects of prepositions, or appositives to any of these. Be careful to use the objective case in compound structures of these sentence parts and with appositives.

> Father questioned Fred and <u>me</u> about the missing hammer. (direct object)
> Aunt Thelma sent <u>you</u> and <u>her</u> an interesting letter. (indirect objects)
> Mother gave several small jobs to <u>us</u> girls. (object of preposition followed by an appositive)

The objective case is also used as the *subject of an infinitive.* This is a new grammatical construction for you, but since you are familiar with infinitives, you should find it easy to understand. Begin by considering this sentence with a simple infinitive phrase.

Mother wants <u>to clean the basement</u>.

Mother wants what? *To clean the basement.* The infinitive phrase is the direct object in the sentence. Look at the diagram of this sentence.

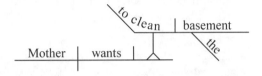

To this same sentence, we will add one more word.

Mother wants *me* to clean the basement.

Now find the direct object. Mother wants what? *To clean the basement?* No, she wants *me* to clean it! *Me to clean the basement* is clearly the thing that Mother wants—the direct object. *Me* is the subject that will perform the action of the infinitive. A diagram may help to show this more clearly.

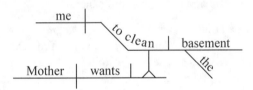

The direct object in each of the following sentences is an infinitive phrase with a subject. Notice that each of these subjects is in the objective case, not nominative.

Brother James asked <u>them to sweep the floor</u>.
Aunt Laura was helping <u>us to bake cookies</u>.
Father let <u>me mow the hay</u>.

In the last sentence above, the main verb is *let* and the word *to* is understood: *let me (to) mow the hay.* (Compare "allowed me to mow the hay.") In former years you learned that *let* is always used with another verb form that tells what action is permitted. This verb form is always an infinitive with a subject and with *to* understood.

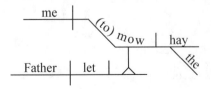

The King James Bible uses the archaic forms *thee* (singular) and *you* (plural) as the second person pronouns in the objective case.

> "But I say unto <u>you</u>, That ye resist not evil: but whosoever shall smite <u>thee</u> on thy right cheek, turn to him the other also."

The *possessive case* pronouns are as follows: *my, mine, your, yours, his, her, hers, its, our, ours, their, theirs.* These pronouns show ownership. Most possessive case pronouns function as adjectives, modifying the nouns they precede. Absolute possessive pronouns function as substantives, representing both the possessor (the antecedent) and the thing possessed (the understood noun that could be stated).

> <u>Your</u> poem sounds better than <u>mine</u>.
>> (*Your* functions as an adjective modifying *poem. Mine* is an absolute possessive pronoun that stands for *my poem,* thus representing both the speaker and the speaker's poem.)

The King James Bible uses the archaic forms *thy* and *thine* as second person singular pronouns in the possessive case. *Thy* precedes consonant sounds, and *thine* precedes vowel sounds. In archaic usage, *my* also precedes consonant sounds, and *mine* precedes vowel sounds.

> "Take now <u>thy</u> son, <u>thine</u> only son Isaac."
> "Ye shall do <u>my</u> judgments, and keep <u>mine</u> ordinances."

4. *Gender.* The gender of a pronoun is *masculine, feminine, neuter,* or *common.* This is the same as for nouns, as you studied in Lesson 53. Only third person singular pronouns have specific forms for gender. They are as follows: *he, him, his* (masculine); *she, her, hers* (feminine); *it, its* (neuter). All other personal pronouns are of common gender.

5. *Agreement of pronouns and antecedents.* A pronoun must agree with its antecedent in person, number, and gender. In the following sentence, the pronouns are underlined and the antecedents are italicized.

> *Father* prayed that <u>his</u> witness would help *people* to yield <u>their</u> lives to the Lord.
>> *(His* is third person singular, masculine gender, to agree with *Father. Their* is third person plural, common gender, to agree with *people.)*

Compound Personal Pronouns

The compound personal pronouns end with *-self* or *-selves.* Below is a table showing the nine compound personal pronouns (including one archaic form).

	Singular	Plural
First person:	myself	ourselves
Second person:	yourself (thyself)	yourselves
Third person:	himself, herself, itself	themselves

Be sure to use the correct forms of compound personal pronouns. The following forms should be avoided: *ourself, themself, hisself, theirselves.*

A compound personal pronoun can serve in two ways. If it is *intensive,* it serves to add intensity or emphasis to another noun or pronoun. Such a pronoun serves as an appositive, emphasizing a person or thing by referring to it a second time.

If a compound personal pronoun is *reflexive,* it shows an action done by the subject to itself. In this use, the pronoun functions as the direct object, the indirect object, or the object of a preposition and shows an action *reflected* back to the subject.

Intensive:
We *ourselves* must decide how to handle this emergency.
The boys *themselves* built this shop.
The boys built this shop *themselves.*

Reflexive:
Conrad made *himself* a sturdy workbench. (indirect object)
You girls may each choose a vase for *yourselves.* (object of preposition)

Usage of Personal and Compound Personal Pronouns

1. *Use the proper case when a pronoun follows* than *or* as. Such a pronoun is either a subject or an object in an elliptical clause. Therefore, you must consider what the completed construction of the clause would be, and choose the correct pronoun case to fit that construction. Sometimes either case is correct, depending on the meaning.

Charles is taller than <u>I</u>.
(Completed construction: than *I am tall. Me* does not fit.)
We do not see Uncle Mark's family as often as <u>them</u>.
(Completed construction: as often as *we see them.*)
We do not see Uncle Mark's family as often as <u>they</u>.
(Completed construction: as often as *they see Uncle Mark's family.*)

2. *Never use apostrophes with personal pronouns in the possessive case.* The possessive forms of some other classes of pronouns require apostrophes. With personal pronouns, however, use apostrophes only to form contractions.

<u>He's</u> keeping his garden clean, but <u>ours</u> and <u>theirs</u> are becoming weedy.

3. *When you speak about another person and yourself, refer to the other person first and yourself last.* This not only represents correct grammar but also complements the Bible principle, "In honour preferring one another."

Lauren helped <u>Curtis and me</u> for a while today.

4. *Do not use compound personal pronouns to replace personal pronouns.* Use them only as intensive or reflexive pronouns, as illustrated above.

Incorrect: Mother told no one but <u>ourselves</u> about the surprise.
Jesse and <u>myself</u> volunteered to help.

Correct: Mother told no one but <u>us</u> about the surprise.
Jesse and <u>I</u> volunteered to help.

Applying the Lesson

A. Copy each personal pronoun, including any possessive form used as an adjective. Label its person (*1, 2, 3*), number (*S, P*), case (*N, O, P*), and gender (*M, F, N, C*).
   1. When Mary sat at Jesus' feet, she had chosen the good part, and Jesus declared that it would not be taken from her.
   2. Martha's service lacked joy because it became more important than devotion to her.
   3. Our daily prayers should not be self-centered; we should include intercessions for others.
   4. Multitudes can take their petitions to the Lord at the same time without straining His abilities in the least.
   5. My friend, God will surely provide all that you need from His infinite store of grace.
   6. O young person, if you would enjoy the fullness of God's blessing, submit your will to Him.
   7. They who walk with the Lord do not run with the world or pursue its pleasures.
   8. We can never repay the Lord for the great love He has shown to us.

B. Write a personal pronoun to fit each description.
   1. first person, plural, objective case
   2. third person, plural, nominative case
   3. second person, possessive case (2 forms)
   4. first person, singular, possessive case (2 forms)
   5. third person, singular, objective case, feminine gender
   6. third person, singular, possessive case, neuter gender

C. Copy each compound personal pronoun, and write whether it is intensive (*I*) or reflexive (*R*).
   1. We surprised ourselves with the amount of work we were able to do.
   2. Father said himself that he was pleased with our progress.
   3. Anita cut herself on a piece of broken glass.
   4. The boys made large sandwiches for themselves.
   5. The Law of Moses came from God Himself.
   6. Sinai itself was moved at the presence of God.
   7. If you prove yourself trustworthy, others will be likely to trust you.
   8. We must forgive others, for we need forgiveness ourselves.

D. Diagram these sentences, which contain infinitives with subjects.
   1. Mother told Susan to bake a cake.
   2. The children watched her mix the batter.
   3. She let them lick the bowl.
   4. Then they helped her to wash the dishes.

E. Find the errors in pronoun usage, and write the correct words or phrases. If a sentence has no error, write *correct*.
   1. The man of faith must commit hisself wholly to the Lord.
   2. Slanderers never hurt others as much as they hurt theirselves.
   3. God will faithfully guide ourselves if we follow Him.

4. God rightly expects we to obey His Word fully.
5. We must never endanger ourself by taking foolish chances.
6. When people truly seek the Lord, He will bless them Himself.
7. The greatest blessings of time and eternity are our's as we follow Christ.
8. Although the rich man had not realized it, Lazarus was richer than him in the things that really matter.
9. In family worship this morning, Father called on Clara and I to recite the memory passage.
10. Have you seen the books that Grandfather gave to me and Peter?
11. The hot weather does not seem to affect Calvin as much as I.
12. The boys helped themself to large servings of ice cream.
13. Me and Darlene plan to wash the dishes.
14. Us girls have planned the menu for the picnic.
15. Brother Leroy wants John and me to help him in the garden this evening.
16. The best artists in our room are Elizabeth and her.
17. Before us students are ready for that test, we must study more.
18. Mr. Ulrich says that the stray dog must be your's.
19. The bass singers are Adrian and him.
20. Leon poured hisself a large glass of lemonade.

Review Exercises

A. Write the letters of the correct plural forms in each sentence. [55]

1. Fools will not hearken to the (^{a}reproofs, ^{b}reproves) of their (^{a}superiors, ^{b}superiores).
2. Many (^{a}man-hours, ^{b}men-hours) will be required to harvest all these (^{a}tomatos, ^{b}tomatoes).
3. As we neared the kitchen, we caught several (^{a}whiffs, ^{b}whives) that told us Mother was preparing some tasty (^{a}dishs, ^{b}dishes).
4. We threw several (^{a}handsful, ^{b}handfuls) of bread into the water to feed the (^{a}trout, ^{b}trouts).
5. At most (^{a}zoos, ^{b}zooes), the (^{a}monkies, ^{b}monkeys) are a favorite attraction.
6. When the (^{a}altos, ^{b}altoes) faltered, Brother Howard asked if some of the (^{a}sopranos, ^{b}sopranoes) could help them with their part.
7. We checked the price of (^{a}truss's, ^{b}trusses) from several different (^{a}companys, ^{b}companies).
8. One of Sister Sandra's standard (^{a}policys, ^{b}policies) is to give numerous (^{a}quizzs, ^{b}quizzes) in her history classes.

B. Write the letter for the correct foreign plural form of each singular noun. [55]

1. apex   a. apa   b. apices
2. emphasis   a. emphasae   b. emphases
3. bacterium   a. bacteria   b. bacterii
4. esophagus   a. esophaga   b. esophagi
5. criterion   a. criteria   b. criterii
6. curriculum   a. curricula   b. curriculae

57.   Other Pronoun Classes

Demonstrative Pronouns

The four demonstrative pronouns (*this, that, these, those*) point out specific persons or things. A demonstrative pronoun is a pronoun only when it functions as a substantive. If it precedes and modifies a noun, it is an adjective telling *which* rather than a pronoun.

> We must return good for evil because *that* is the right thing to do.
> (subject of clause: pronoun)
> I read *those* verses this morning in my devotions.
> (precedes and modifies a noun: adjective)

Two rules for correct usage of demonstrative pronouns deserve special mention.
1. Never use *them* as a demonstrative pronoun.
2. Do not say *this (these) here* or *that (those) there.*

> **Incorrect:** <u>Them</u> are precious verses for the tempted.
> We memorized <u>these here</u> verses last year.
> **Correct:** <u>Those</u> are precious verses for the tempted.
> We memorized <u>these</u> verses last year.

Relative Pronouns

There are six relative pronouns: *who, whom, whose, which, what, that.* You learned in previous years that a relative pronoun introduces an adjective clause which modifies the antecedent of the relative pronoun.

> Every person <u>*who* desires noble character</u> must determine to do right.
> (The relative pronoun *who* introduces an adjective clause that modifies *person,* the antecedent of *who.*)

You have learned that the same pronouns may introduce noun clauses. They are also classed as relative pronouns when they function in that way. A relative pronoun has no antecedent when it introduces a noun clause.

> Every person should determine to do <u>*what* is right.</u>
> (The relative pronoun *what* introduces a noun clause that is the direct object of the infinitive *to do.* There is no antecedent for *what.*)

That is a relative pronoun only when it has a substantive function. If it simply introduces a clause, it is a conjunction.

> The story <u>that</u> we read is true.
> (direct object in adjective clause: relative pronoun)
> We know <u>that</u> the story is true.
> (no substantive function; simply introduces noun clause: conjunction)
> We know <u>that</u> is true. (subject in noun clause: relative pronoun)

Correct usage of the relative pronouns requires that *who* and *whom* refer only to people, *which* refer only to things, and *that, what,* and *whose* refer to either people or things. In the King James Bible, however, *which* often refers to people.

> A person <u>whom</u> God blesses is rich indeed. (not *person which*)
> These two pups, <u>which</u> survived the tornado, have become special pets. (not *pups who*)
> The students <u>that</u> did not study well had trouble with the history test <u>that</u> Brother Allen gave.
> "And as Jesus passed by, he saw a man <u>which</u> was blind from his birth" (John 9:1).

Three of the relative pronouns actually are different forms of the same word, used to show different cases. *Who* is nominative, *whom* is objective, and *whose* is possessive.

> Curtis Miller, <u>who</u> works for my father, enjoys repairing machinery.
> (nominative *who* for subject of clause)
> Mr. Lance, for <u>whom</u> we have often prayed, has come to church today.
> (objective *whom* for object of preposition)
> We do not know <u>whose</u> papers these are.
> (possessive *whose* for adjective)

Compound relative pronouns are formed by adding *-ever* or *-soever* to simple relative pronouns. They introduce only noun clauses.

> <u>Whoever</u> follows the Lord walks safely in <u>whatever</u> path He directs.

Interrogative Pronouns

The interrogative pronouns (*who, whom, whose, which, what*) introduce questions. Each of these pronouns also serves a specific function in the sentence, such as a subject or a direct object. When *who, whom, whose,* and *which* are interrogative pronouns, the same usage rules apply as when they are relative pronouns. The only exception is that the interrogative pronoun *which* can refer to persons as well as things.

> <u>Who</u> is ready to recite the memory verse?
> (*Who* acts as a subject and refers to a person.)
> <u>Whom</u> shall we ask to help us?
> (*Whom* acts as a direct object and refers to a person.)
> <u>Whose</u> did you find? (*Whose* acts as a direct object and refers to a person.)
> <u>Which</u> is the oldest student? (*Which* acts as a subject and refers to a person.)
> <u>What</u> are you looking for?
> (*What* acts as the object of a preposition and refers to a thing.)

Indefinite Pronouns

The indefinite pronouns, as their name suggests, do not refer to definite persons, places, or things. Unlike most other pronouns, they often have no specific antecedents. Many indefinite pronouns are always singular: *each, either, neither, one, another, anybody, anyone, anything, everybody, everyone, everything, somebody, someone, something, nobody, no one, nothing.* Most of the pronouns in this group contain the singular word element *other, one, thing,* or *body.*

When one of these singular pronouns functions as a subject, a prepositional phrase with a plural object often comes between the subject and the verb. Be careful to make the verb agree with the subject, not with the object of the preposition. If any other pronoun refers to the singular subject, it must also be singular.

> Each of the four Gospels presents *its* own picture of Jesus Christ.
> Everyone among God's children needs a time of daily communion with *his* Lord.

A few indefinite pronouns are always plural: *both, few, many, others, several.* Use plural verbs with these pronouns, and use plural pronouns in referring to them.

> Few in Noah's day were convinced of *their* accountability to God.

A few indefinite pronouns may be either singular or plural: *some, any, none, all, most.* The number of the pronoun depends on the number of its antecedent. When one of these pronouns is used as a subject, that antecedent often occurs in a prepositional phrase between the subject and the verb. If the antecedent is singular, the indefinite pronoun is singular because it refers to a certain portion of that one thing. If the antecedent is plural, the indefinite pronoun is plural because it refers to certain individual items in that set of things.

> None of this *room* has been swept.
> (No portion of this one thing has been swept.)
> None of these *rooms* have been swept.
> (No items in this set of things have been swept.)

> All of this *loaf* was sliced extra thick.
> (The whole of this one thing was sliced.)
> All of these *loaves* were sliced extra thick.
> (All items in this set of things were sliced.)

Make the possessive forms of indefinite pronouns by adding *'s*. This is different from the possessive forms of personal pronouns, which do not have apostrophes.

> Somebody's blue coat was hanging there, but Arlene could not find hers.

The words listed as indefinite pronouns are pronouns only if they have a substantive function in a sentence. Many of these words also function as modifiers, and then they are adjectives.

> We could find only several of the answers. (pronoun used as direct object)
> We could find only several answers. (adjective modifying direct object)

Applying the Lesson

A. Copy each pronoun, and write whether it is personal (*P*), compound personal (*CP*), demonstrative (*D*), indefinite (*ID*), interrogative (*IR*), or relative (*R*). Include the possessive pronouns used as adjectives.

1. We can limit many of our temptations by feeding ourselves on God's Word.
2. A second key to limiting temptation is to view it as Satan's attempt to destroy us; this produces an urgency which motivates one to overcome.

3. Anything that helps us avoid wrong influence also limits temptation, for Satan often works through the influence of others.
4. Who can expect to resist temptation if he allows himself to feed on unwholesome thoughts?
5. What are the principles to which you will commit yourself in dangerous times like these?
6. All whose hearts are set on the Lord seek to free themselves from everything that displeases Him.

B. Choose the correct words in parentheses.
   1. Both of the messages (was, were) inspirational.
   2. Each of these songs (call, calls) us to worship the Lord.
   3. One of the stanzas (refer, refers) to the glorious worship scene in heaven.
   4. Most of us (have, has) never visited the mission in Mexico.
   5. Everyone (need, needs) the advice of others at times.
   6. Anybody who gives (himself, themselves) to truth will find true satisfaction.
   7. Some of the compositions (deal, deals) with similar themes.
   8. Several of these customers (want, wants) one hundred ears of sweet corn.
   9. (Is, Are) any of this sweet corn already ordered?
   10. (Have, Has) all of these sweet corn ears filled out nicely?
   11. Either of these recipes (make, makes) delicious cupcakes.
   12. Another of the boards (have, has) split.

C. Write one or two words to show how to correct each error. If the sentence is correct, write *correct.*
   1. Are you the kind of person who others can trust?
   2. These here Scripture verses emphasize the importance of right attitudes.
   3. We trust in the eternal King, which made heaven and earth.
   4. Everybody's highest desire should be to praise God by his daily life.
   5. These apples tend to be tart, but them are sweet and juicy.
   6. At first we did not recognize whom the visitors were.
   7. Most of our nearby friends and neighbors was here to help.
   8. The friendly dog who appeared on our porch last week is still here.
   9. Surely this must have been somebodys prized collie.
   10. Them are the best peaches we have picked this year.
   11. Have you heard whom the substitute teacher will be?
   12. The first person who we should ask is Father.

Review Exercises

Write the letters of the correct forms in each sentence. [55]
   1. ([a]Moses's, [b]Moses') submission stands in sharp contrast to ([a]Korah's, Dathan's, and Abiram's; [b]Korah, Dathan, and Abiram's) rebellion.
   2. It was ([a]Barnabas's, [b]Barnabas') confidence in Saul that led to the early ([a]church, [b]church's) accepting him.
   3. Many taunts came from the ([a]Jew's, [b]Jews') lips as they watched ([a]Christ, [b]Christ's) dying on the cross.

4. The birth of (ᵃMary's, ᵇMarys') newborn Son was heralded by the (ᵃangels', ᵇangels's) message to humble shepherds.

5. Mr. Turner lost (ᵃtwo days' wages, ᵇthe wages of two days) when he failed to heed his (ᵃfather's-in-law, ᵇfather-in-law's) advice.

6. The (ᵃmen's, ᵇmens') hats were on the (ᵃcloset's top shelf, ᵇtop shelf of the closet).

7. (ᵃFather's, ᵇFather) and Mother's coats were lying on the table, but baby (ᵃSeth's, ᵇSeths') blanket had been thrown across a chair.

8. (ᵃTitus's, ᵇTitus') report outlined a typical American (ᵃfarmer's, ᵇfarmers') problems over the last one hundred years.

---

58. Improving Your Writing Style, Part 4: Figurative Language

The first lesson on writing style challenged you to make your writing fresh and imaginative, to not be satisfied with the first thing you write. Maybe a paragraph is clear; maybe everyone can understand it; maybe you even think it reads well. But can you state your point in a more interesting and original way? Is it as effective as you can make it?

In exploring various ways to express yourself, you will probably gain new ideas and begin to enjoy working them into your writing. You may even discover that some of your ideas go beyond literal expressions and become figurative. This is excellent! Figurative statements, used with skill and prudence, will help to make your writing even more forceful and appealing. This lesson describes four kinds of figurative language that can add sparkle to your style.

Simile

A *simile* makes a figurative comparison by using *like* or *as*. Not all descriptions that use these words are similes; some are simple comparisons between things that actually are alike. In the following sentence from the sample essay, the underlined part is a simple comparison, not a simile.

> But if having devotions is as habitual as washing our hands and combing our hair, we will seldom forget it.

By contrast, a simile makes an imaginative comparison between things that are not alike in a literal sense.

> "How long shall the words of thy mouth be like a strong wind?" (Job 8:2). Shep looked as humiliated as a peacock that had lost its tail feathers.

The same general ideas could be conveyed by the sentences "How long will you talk so much?" and "Shep looked greatly humiliated." How much more colorful the pictures become with the use of figurative language!

Metaphor

A *metaphor* makes a figurative comparison without using *like* or *as*. Some metaphors contain a form of *be* and say that one thing *is* another thing. Others use literal terms to describe something that happens only in a figurative sense.

> "I am the voice of one crying in the wilderness, Make straight the way of the Lord" (John 1:23).
> John's message had been a living exclamation point in the wilderness, but in prison it turned into a question mark.

Personification

Personification is a special kind of metaphor in which something inanimate is represented as having the characteristics of a living creature. Often a quality is said to speak or act as only humans can do.

> Anger casts reason outside and bolts the door.
> Having regular devotions writes in clear, bold letters upon our consciousness that this practice holds a place of priority. When we are tempted to let it slide, the force of habit speaks in a clear, firm voice, "Do not neglect your devotions."

Hyperbole

A *hyperbole* is what might be called an artistic exaggeration—something that everyone knows is not literally true but which makes a vivid picture in the mind.

> When we face a problem, we sometimes try a hundred different solutions before we remember to pray.
> Tyndale's New Testament was in great demand even before the ink was dry.

Try to be fresh and original in your use of figurative language. If you write the first figure of speech that comes to your mind, you will usually write a cliché—an expression so overused that it has lost its effectiveness. Some of the clichés that you saw in Lesson 3 are figures of speech. Here are a few more examples.

as green as grass   like lightning
as strong as a horse   like pulling teeth

Be sure to keep your figurative language consistent. If you begin with one figure and then shift to another, you may produce an illogical comparison called a ***mixed metaphor***. Study the following examples.

> As the young man faced the audience, a great wave of self-consciousness suddenly washed away his courage and completely dried up his inspiration.
> These saints were brave soldiers in the vineyard of the Lord.

The careful use of figurative language will greatly improve your writing style. Although you will not use this element of effective style as often as some of the others you have studied, a sprinkling of figurative language adds a spice that greatly improves the flavor of your writing.

Applying the Lesson

Rewrite the argumentative essay below in a livelier, more effective style by following the steps listed here. You may also need to change other words in the sentences.

1. Improve the single-underlined expressions to make them more specific.
2. Change the five passive verbs to the active voice.
3. Replace the double-underlined forms of *be* with specific action verbs.
4. Use figurative language as indicated by the words in brackets.

The Need for Neatness

Our world <u>has</u> much evidence of man's untidiness. The countryside along many roads is marred with trash. In almost every community, we find some places where <u>things are untidy</u>. Even worse, some of us would probably need to admit that our own rooms look like [hyperbole]. Therefore, the virtue of neatness should be cultivated by every one of us.

It is true, of course, that not all of us <u>are</u> naturally interested in neatness. Personalities and training <u>are</u> varied. However, neatness is well worth every effort required to learn it. We need not be hopelessly enslaved by present habits. For we can say with the apostle Paul, "I can do all things through Christ which strengtheneth me." Indeed, many people have learned to be neat without the benefit of childhood training.

Some people <u>say</u> that being neat takes too much time away from more important things. But neatness <u>is</u> actually a saver of time. If we <u>are</u> neat, we will rarely waste time looking for papers that [personification]. We will not need to rewash <u>things</u> because of dirty spots that are seen by Mother. And with a little practice, we can learn to do neat work just as efficiently as sloppy work.

Neatness <u>is</u> a characteristic of godliness. "God is not the author of confusion." He created an orderly world, and He commands, "Let all things be done decently and in order." It is only fitting, then, that habits of neatness are developed by us.

Neatness certainly deserves a high priority in our lives. The trash along the roadsides should not bear testimony against us. Our <u>things</u> should exemplify order. We can be neat if we <u>put</u> our minds to it. And when our determination <u>is</u> fruitful, we shall find it a <u>real</u> help to our schedules and a glory to our heavenly Father. What a privilege we have to make our parts of this world <u>nice places</u> of order!

---

59. Identifying Substantives

Nouns and pronouns have specific functions in sentences: subjects, direct and indirect objects, predicate nominatives, and so forth. Words, phrases, or clauses that you would not necessarily identify as nouns or pronouns can also function in these ways. The term *substantive* is used for any word or word group that names something and serves as a noun or pronoun.

1. *Single-word nouns and compound nouns are substantives.* This includes all the words that obviously name persons, places, or things. You would recognize them as nouns without knowing how they were used in a sentence.

> God Almighty controls the affairs of men.

2. *Pronouns are substantives.* This includes the words in all six classes of pronouns that you reviewed in Lessons 56 and 57. However, a possessive pronoun that modifies a noun is not considered a substantive, for it functions as an adjective.

> I shall lift my voice in praise to Him who does everything well.
> (*My* is an adjective, not a substantive.)

3. *Infinitives and infinitive phrases may be substantives.* An infinitive is the basic form of a verb preceded by *to.* When an infinitive has a subject, the subject is part of the substantive. Infinitives and infinitive phrases used as adjectives or adverbs are not substantives.

> To write can be one way to serve the Lord.
> (*To write* is an infinitive used as a subject. *To serve the Lord* is an infinitive phrase used as an adjective.)
> The teacher asked me to give my report tomorrow.
> (*Me to give my report tomorrow* is an infinitive phrase with a subject; it is used as a direct object.)

4. *Gerunds and gerund phrases are substantives.* A gerund is the present participle of a verb (the *-ing* form) used as a noun. But remember that the present participle can also be used as a main verb or as an adjective.

> I learned butchering when I was a growing boy.
> (*Butchering* is a gerund used as a direct object. *Growing* is an adjective.)
> Leann's job, washing the kitchen windows, is taking too long.
> (*Washing the kitchen windows* is a gerund phrase used as an appositive to the subject. *Taking* is the main verb.)
> The faultfinding Pharisees criticized Jesus for eating with sinners.
> (*Eating with sinners* is a gerund phrase used as the object of a preposition. *Faultfinding* is an adjective.)

5. *Prepositional phrases may be substantives.* Such a phrase names a place or a thing and usually functions as the subject of a sentence with a linking verb.

> Before the wood stove is a good place to warm up.
> (prepositional phrase used as a subject)

6. *Noun clauses are substantives.* A noun clause is a dependent clause that functions as a substantive in a complex sentence.

> Whoever plays with temptation cannot sincerely pray the Lord's Prayer.
> (clause used as a subject)
> We should never long for what displeases the Lord.
> (clause used as the object of a preposition)

We cannot fully understand <u>why the Lord loves us</u>.
(clause used as a direct object)

7. *Any item used as a subject of discussion is a substantive.* Such an item is not being used in its normal sense; it is referred to as a symbol, a letter, a word, or a word group. Remember that a word or a letter used as a subject of discussion should be italicized (underlined).

You should pronounce <u>*shew*</u>, the archaic spelling, and <u>*show*</u>, the modern spelling, in the same way.
(The underlined words are direct objects.)
The <u>*m*</u> in your answer should be <u>*cm*</u>.
(The first underlined item is the subject, and the second is the predicate nominative.)

8. *Any title is a substantive.* Such a substantive may also be called a noun phrase.

<u>"Where Are the Doughnuts?"</u> is a short story about the entangling web of dishonesty. (title used as a subject)
The book <u>*Echoes From My Heart*</u> contains many inspirational poems.
(title used as an appositive to the subject)

The term *substantive* is a convenient label that includes nouns, pronouns, and any other expressions that serve as nouns. When you look for substantives in a sentence, first find the largest elements (the clauses) and then look for verbals and other kinds of noun phrases. Last of all, find the nouns, pronouns, and other small elements that serve as substantives.

Applying the Lesson

A. Copy all the words (including noun phrases) that function as substantives in these sentences.
1. In the person of the Holy Spirit, God indwells all who truly obey Him.
2. Believers know true peace and joy through faith in Jesus Christ.
3. You must double both the *c* and the *m* in the word *accommodate*.
4. What are the sounds of the *ch* and the *d* in *schedule*?
5. Which of the poems makes effective use of figurative language?
6. Bradley, one of my close friends, recently broke a leg.

B. Copy the phrases and verbals that function as substantives in these sentences.
1. By standing firmly for the right, we can learn to avoid evil.
2. To do the Father's will is the only way to have eternal life.
3. Below zero is very unusual for southern Maryland.
4. Abundant rainfall has made farming more profitable this year.
5. Most people want to learn, but some dislike studying very long.
6. Under your bed is not a place for trash!

C. Copy the clauses and titles that function as substantives in these sentences.
1. Men have learned much about how different weather systems work.
2. What produces tornadoes is not well understood.

3. The short story "Oh, How I Wish" teaches forcefully that covetousness can be a subtle snare.

4. "On Rocky Paths" is a good story for whoever feels burdened by hardships.

D. Copy all the substantives in these sentences. Do not list separately a substantive within another substantive phrase or clause.

1. I can overcome every difficulty by exercising faith in God.

2. Who of us can stand against the devil by ourselves?

3. Anyone can become what the Lord wants him to be.

4. To be a consistent Christian requires constant vigilance and prayerfulness.

5. Those who grow careless will inevitably begin to yield to the devil.

6. How one views God will affect every area of life.

7. After lunch sounds like a good time to read *Pioneer Minnie*.

8. The blue jays are preventing other birds from eating.

9. We must try to hurry, for the timetable indicates that our flight will soon leave.

10. After supper Father wants me to wash the car.

11. Father wants to rest, but soon he will begin mowing the hay.

12. *For Their Faith* depicts how some Christians have been persecuted.

Review Exercises

A. Choose the correct words in these sentences. [56]

1. The congregation appointed Brother Mark and (he, him) to serve as ushers for the meetings.

2. We want Brenda and (she, her) to clean the kitchen windows this afternoon.

3. The last ones to arrive at school this morning were (me and Harvey, Harvey and I, Harvey and me).

4. I understand that you and (I, me) will be responsible to burn this trash.

5. (We, Us) girls need clearer instructions from Mother and (she, her).

6. You may have finished your work sooner than (he, him), but his paper is neater than (yours, your's).

B. Choose the correct words in these sentences. [57]

1. Here is a letter from your friend (who, which) moved to Paraguay.

2. Mopsy was a kitten (who, which) was always getting into trouble.

3. You will find that (this, this here) prescription will take care of your cough.

4. Brother Gary is a speaker to (who, whom) most people enjoy listening.

5. None of the workers really (enjoy, enjoys) this cold, damp weather.

6. In my opinion, each of the boys (deserve, deserves) credit for his effort.

7. Wesley was growing so rapidly that all of his shoes (was, were) becoming too small.

8. (Everyones, Everyone's) story will be read to the class tomorrow.

60. Chapter 7 Review

A. Copy each noun, and write whether it is concrete (*C*) or abstract (*A*). Also label its gender (*M, F, N, C*).
1. Youth should zealously pursue growth in godliness.
2. When people devote themselves to truth, they will receive a blessing.
3. The song of Deborah and Barak describes a great victory won by divine aid.
4. Abraham and Sarah sojourned in Canaan with their servants and possessions.
5. The children enjoy the stories that Grandmother tells about her life as a girl.
6. Every day one of the older students helps Sister Ann to drill her pupils in multiplication.

B. Write the plural form of each noun. Use the foreign plural spellings for numbers 15–24.

1. belief	9. journey	17. paralysis
2. bison	10. brother (two forms)	18. bacillus
3. editor in chief	11. solo	19. codex
4. motto	12. wharf	20. prognosis
5. eyetooth	13. species	21. nova
6. footman	14. worry	22. latex
7. child	15. perihelion	23. rhombus
8. sister-in-law	16. alga	24. compendium

C. Write the possessive form of each noun.

1. Rameses	5. albatross	8. Zenas
2. goose	6. father-in-law	9. mouse
3. horses	7. babies	10. prince
4. board of directors		

D. Copy each pronoun, and write whether it is personal (*P*), compound personal (*CP*), demonstrative (*D*), indefinite (*ID*), interrogative (*IR*), or relative (*R*). Include the possessive pronouns used as adjectives.
1. One can never better himself by running others down.
2. What can those who pursue selfish interests expect in life?
3. The youth whom God can bless must set his goals high and stick to them.
4. Each of our goals should complement an appreciation for God and His Word.
5. Who is this whose books have fallen to the floor?
6. Both of the boys have proven themselves capable of that.

E. Copy each substantive in these sentences, and label it *N* (one-word or compound noun), *pron.* (pronoun), *G* (gerund or gerund phrase), *I* (infinitive or infinitive phrase), *prep.* (prepositional phrase), *C* (clause), *T* (title), or *S* (subject of discussion). If a substantive is within a substantive phrase or clause or within a title, do not list it separately.
1. The Bible indicates that the human mind is a battlefield.
2. To keep our minds free from evil requires faith and commitment.
3. *Chronicles of Mansoul* describes allegorically the battle for man's soul.

4. By filling our minds with right thoughts, we can avoid whatever would defile our minds.
5. The word *amusement* implies preventing serious thought.
6. The theme of "Think About It," which Aunt Alice wrote, is to think through issues.
7. On the porch will be fine; Father wants us to sort these peaches right away.
8. In the dictionary is the place to look for the meaning of the word *plenary*.

F. Write the underlined items correctly. If an item has no error, write *correct*.
   1. The night was disturbed by our ten <u>heifers bawling</u>, but neither of the dogs <u>were</u> barking.
   2. <u>Clyde and me</u> checked to see what was wrong, but the bull that was loose was not <u>our's</u>.
   3. The Tostens, <u>which</u> bought the adjacent farm, are friendly neighbors; but some of their ideas <u>seem</u> impractical.
   4. The girls <u>who</u> Sister Twila named began peeling peaches while the other girls busied <u>theirselves</u> with washing jars.
   5. <u>Me and Elaine</u> could not work as fast as <u>them</u>.
   6. <u>This here</u> is the recipe I used, yet none of the pies <u>tastes</u> like Mother's.
   7. This is <u>Clyde's and Dale's puppy</u>, but <u>them</u> belong to the Eberlys.
   8. Shirley and <u>myself</u> are a few months older than <u>her</u>.
   9. <u>These here</u> baskets are for <u>Stanley and I</u>.
   10. Although <u>Keith's and Kaylene's car</u> disappeared last week, the police still do not know <u>whom</u> the thief was.
   11. Everyone except Noah and <u>himself</u> knows Mr. Gable, <u>who</u> we often sing for.
   12. Since the <u>floor's shine</u> is mostly worn off, <u>me and Yvonne</u> plan to wax it today.
   13. We picked our apples by <u>ourself</u> and then helped them with <u>their's</u>.
   14. Although most of the herd <u>have</u> been fed, <u>them</u> in the corner have not been.
   15. <u>This book's cover</u> is badly torn, and we cannot tell <u>whom</u> the owner is.
   16. We listened to the <u>frogs' croaking</u> and the barking of the neighbor's dog, <u>who</u> often prowls around our farm.

G. Choose the correct words for the descriptions below. You will not use all the answers.

cliché	narrative	figurative comparison
hyperbole	simile	mixed metaphor
metaphor	personification	simple comparison

   1. Four specific kinds of figurative language.
   2. Figurative language with an illogical combination of ideas.
   3. A figure of speech or other colorful expression that is worn out from overuse.
   4. A comparison with *like* or *as* that is not a figure of speech.

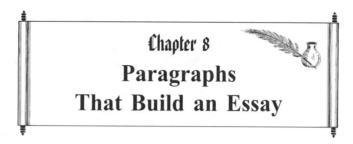

Chapter 8
Paragraphs
That Build an Essay

61. What a Paragraph Is

In Chapter 6 you worked with the argumentative essay. You studied the structure of the whole essay and the method for putting it together. In this chapter you will study paragraphs—the smaller units that make up an essay. Paragraphs are blocks of thought that build one upon another until the essay is complete.

The Paragraph—a Unit of Thought

A paragraph is an organized unit of thought that develops one main idea. The topic sentence of the paragraph clearly states that main idea. In argumentative writing, the topic sentence usually comes at or near the beginning of a paragraph.

Very few paragraphs consist of only a topic sentence. In an argumentative essay, each paragraph includes several other sentences that support and develop the topic sentence. Each sentence must serve clearly to build the main idea of the paragraph. This gives the paragraph unity and helps it to communicate clearly.

Two things can mar the unity of a paragraph. First, a writer may allow one thought to lead him to a related thought, somewhat like a sheep wandering from one tuft of grass to another. Though each sentence may fit logically enough with the previous one, it fails to develop the topic of the whole paragraph. In an extreme case, the resulting group of sentences may ramble so aimlessly that it hardly deserves to be called a paragraph.

The second threat to paragraph unity is the failure to divide paragraphs at the proper places. Since a paragraph should be one organized unit of thought, we must begin a new paragraph whenever we begin discussing a new thought. A clear understanding of the structure of a paragraph, as discussed in the next section, will help you to discern where one paragraph should end and another should begin.

How long should your paragraphs be? How many sentences should they have? The answer varies, of course. Primarily, a paragraph must be long enough to develop the topic sentence fully and convincingly. Sometimes you may accomplish that with fewer words; sometimes it will require more. As a general guide, paragraphs in the body of your argumentative essays should average five or six sentences, with a total of seventy to one hundred words. To write this many words, you will need to find substantial material to build worthwhile paragraphs.

The Paragraph—a Miniature Essay

Each paragraph in the body of an argumentative essay resembles a miniature essay. It has an introduction, a body, and a conclusion. As the essay begins by stating its main point in the thesis, so the paragraph begins by stating its main point in the topic sentence. As the body of an essay substantiates the thesis statement with several supporting paragraphs, so the body of a paragraph substantiates the topic sentence with several supporting sentences. An essay ends with a summarizing paragraph, and a paragraph ends with a summarizing sentence. The following chart shows these comparisons.

Essay:
Thesis statement introduces main idea.
Body gives support to thesis statement.
Concluding paragraph summarizes thoughts given.

Paragraph:
Topic sentence introduces main idea.
Body gives support to topic sentence.
Concluding sentence summarizes thoughts given.

Consider the following paragraph, which comes from one of the arguments in Chapter 6. Its introduction (topic sentence) is in boldface, its body in regular type, and its conclusion in italics.

> **Having a family garden assures that fresh, tasty vegetables reach the table.** A family can harvest peas and corn before they are tough and starchy. In a matter of hours, the vegetables can be out of the garden and in the freezer or on the canning shelves. *Thus the fullest flavor and the richest color are preserved.*

Seeing the similarity between a paragraph and an essay should help you in two ways. First, it should help you construct paragraphs that make their point effectively. Second, it should help you realize that you must give the same careful thought to developing a paragraph that you give to developing an essay.

The Paragraph and the Full Thesis

In Chapter 6 you worked with the full thesis. You learned that it includes the main point (thesis) of the argument, several objections to the thesis, and a number of points supporting the thesis. How is the full thesis related to the individual paragraphs in the finished essay?

The paragraph divisions in the body of your essay should relate directly to the supporting points in the full thesis. Each main point in the full thesis requires at least one paragraph for full development. But sometimes you have three or four ideas that support a main point, and each of these ideas needs more explanation than you can give in one paragraph. Then it is good to develop each supporting idea into a separate paragraph with its own illustrations, examples, or other details.

Suppose we were writing an argument to develop the thesis that most likely the pre-Flood world was quite different from the world we know today. One of our main points to support this thesis might be "The pre-Flood world apparently never experienced rainfall." Read the following paragraph, which develops this main point.

Supporting point developed with one paragraph:
> Furthermore, the pre-Flood world apparently never experienced rainfall. According to Genesis 2:5, 6, a mist rose from the earth to water the ground.

Evidently moist air did not rise high into the atmosphere as it does today. Also, the rainbow that appeared to Noah after the Flood seems to have been a new thing (Genesis 9:12–17). These facts strongly imply that rainfall was unknown before the Flood.

The paragraph clearly represents one unit of thought. It begins with a topic sentence, follows with several sentences of development, and concludes with a summarizing sentence. But does it make its point effectively? Most readers will not be satisfied with the brief statements of the supporting facts. They will want a more thorough explanation of each point before they are willing to accept the argument of the paragraph.

To accomplish this, we will need to break the paragraph apart, treating each separate idea in a paragraph of its own. Thus we will have a set of paragraphs all developing one major point of the full thesis. See how this is done in the following paragraphs.

Supporting point developed with several paragraphs:

Furthermore, the pre-Flood world apparently never experienced rainfall. According to Genesis 2:5, 6, a mist rose from the earth to water the ground. This was probably similar to the morning mists that rise from lakes or from the night-cooled ground. In some climates, morning dews and mists still provide a significant amount of moisture. "The dew of Hermon" (Psalm 133:3) keeps vegetation there green long after the surrounding countryside has become parched and barren. Heavy mists, therefore, do provide one explanation of how lush plant life could grow without rainfall.

With the ground being watered only by mists, the water cycle before the Flood must have operated in a different way than it does now. The atmosphere would have received and released water, but the moist air apparently stayed close to the ground instead of rising high as it does today. If that is true, the water cycle as we know it was nonexistent and rainfall was impossible.

The strongest indication that rainfall was unknown before the Flood is the rainbow that appeared to Noah. It takes rain to make a rainbow, and the rainbow was a token of God's promise to never again send a worldwide flood. Thus it seems obvious that it had not rained before. These facts—the watering of the earth by mists that stayed close to the ground, and the appearance of the rainbow after the Flood—strongly support the conclusion that rain never fell until the time of the Flood.

At this point, you may be wondering how you know when one paragraph is sufficient to give supporting information for a main point, and when you should write several paragraphs. To answer that question, you must consider whether the information you can give in one paragraph will be completely clear and convincing. If the details of your paragraph are readily understood without further explanation, one paragraph is sufficient. But if they include broad statements that readers may question, like those in the example above, you must write more to make your points clear and to remove the questions from your readers' minds.

You must also consider how extensively you plan to treat your subject. For an essay of five hundred to six hundred words, you will not go into as much detail as you would in a longer article, like one for a church periodical or a book. Match the degree of thoroughness to the occasion of your writing.

Applying the Lesson

A. Read the following excerpt from an argument, and do the exercises that follow.

¹Another excuse that people sometimes give for poor penmanship is that neat penmanship takes too much time. ²But careful penmanship actually saves time. ³If you hand in neat assignment papers, you will never need to take time to recopy them. ⁴Time lost in this way can always be put to better use. ⁵When your notes to yourself are easily readable, you will not waste time trying to decipher them. ⁶And if you send in a neatly written order, business personnel can fill it promptly without needing to contact you for a clarification. ⁷Careful penmanship also contributes a great deal to accuracy. ⁸If you form your *a*'s and *o*'s carefully, no one will mistake your *boot* for a *boat*. ⁹If you set up your arithmetic computations in neat columns, you will make fewer mistakes than if they are in disarray. ¹⁰Neither will the teacher reduce your score because of an illegible paper. ¹¹If you fill in orders by writing the item numbers neatly and clearly, you will most likely receive what you expect. ¹²Accuracy is so important that every person should strive to develop neat penmanship.

1. This paragraph treats two different subjects and should be divided in two. Write the number of the sentence that should begin the second paragraph.

2. One sentence in each paragraph should be deleted because it mars the unity of the paragraph. Write the numbers of those sentences.

3. Write a good concluding sentence for the first paragraph.

B. The following paragraph contains three subpoints that support a main point in an argumentative essay. They need further development to make them more clear and convincing. Choose one of the subpoints, and expand it into a well-developed paragraph.

Modern technology has brought a number of disadvantages. One is a loss of quiet meditation time. Another is the loss of a close working together with other family members. A third is that many business dealings have become more impersonal. Though we appreciate many things about modern inventions, they have not been a blessing in every way.

Review Exercises

Tell whether each description refers to the introduction (*I*), body (*B*), or conclusion (*C*) of an argumentative essay. If it applies to none of them, write *none*. [45]

1. Contains the thesis statement telling exactly what the argument is about.
2. Begins broadly and then narrows to the point of the argument.
3. Begins by stating the point of the essay, and ends by broadening to general ideas.
4. Contains the reasons and logic that support the writer's point.
5. Summarizes the main points of the essay.
6. Usually presents the strongest point first.
7. Seeks to attract the reader's attention.
8. Refutes the counter arguments of opponents.

---

62. How to Develop Paragraphs

A paragraph that resembles a miniature essay must include a substantial amount of material. This substance makes up the middle part of the paragraph. To a large extent, the strength of an argument depends on the strength of this paragraph development.

Writers sometimes struggle to find meaningful material to develop their paragraphs. Actually, this matter of paragraph development is not as complicated and mysterious as it might seem. Developing a paragraph follows essentially the same pattern that you often follow in everyday life.

"That was quite a thunderstorm we had last evening!" you say to your friend one morning.

"Oh?" he answers. "I didn't hear anything unusual."

What happens next? You raise your eyebrows and look at your friend in amazement. He is ignorant of some important facts, and you are anxious to give him the details!

"We heard it rumbling up the valley for over an hour before it hit us. And when it finally struck, a blast of wind shook the whole house. It blew so hard that it tore several big limbs right off the maple tree out front. One bolt of lightning after another was striking close by. And rain! It poured for over an hour. In fact, we had more than four inches of rain in less than two hours. I don't think I've ever seen such a thunderstorm before in my life!"

Give the details. This is how you establish the truth of what you have said. If your friend is not convinced by your description of the blasting wind, the bolts of lightning, and the pouring rain, you will give him further evidence. You will be glad to take him to your front yard and show him the broken tree branches lying beside the walk; to show him the huge puddles in the garden where your mother's cabbage is half submerged; to point out the barn roof where two sheets of tin are now missing. You will find all the evidence you can to confirm what you say.

You must do the same thing when you develop a paragraph. Give plenty of details to prove your point. Think. Look around. Remember. Research. Pull together all the concrete, specific details that you can find, and then present them clearly and logically.

Kinds of Details

1. *Specific facts.* The details in the example above are specific facts: wind was blowing, lightning was flashing, and rain was pouring. Specific facts tell exactly *what* the topic sentence is talking about. But too many writers use vague generalities. They may write about "unpleasant weather" or "frightening happenings" without giving the specific facts of the storm they experienced.

Be specific, and at the same time be sure your facts are accurate. Suppose we want to write against the use of tobacco. As one of our supporting details, we could write this:

Every year many people in the United States die from smoking cigarettes.

This is undoubtedly true, but it is not specific. How many people die each year? The statement becomes more meaningful if we make it more specific. Does the following statement sound better than the first one?

Every year thousands of people in the United States die from smoking cigarettes.

We are probably safe in making that statement. But we still have not shown more than a general understanding of our subject. For a topic like this, we must do some extra study and find definite figures. Then and only then can we write with the kind of specific accuracy that shows readers we know what we are writing about.

Every year an estimated 400,000 people in the United States die from smoking cigarettes. Another 50,000 die from breathing someone else's smoke.

We also need other information that we can use as supporting evidence. An encyclopedia may give the following facts about smoking. They could be used as material to further develop some paragraphs on this subject.

Smokers have an average life expectancy three to four years less than that of nonsmokers. The life expectancy of a heavy smoker—one who smokes two or more packs of cigarettes a day—may be as much as eight years less than that of a nonsmoker.

One test showed that cigarette smokers died from heart attacks at a rate 70 per cent higher than did men who had never smoked. Lung cancer death rates are up to thirty times higher in cigarette smokers than in nonsmokers.

Many smokers develop emphysema, a disease that destroys the walls of the air sacs in the lungs.

Specific facts add to our writing a force that is difficult to oppose.

2. *Sound reasons.* Sometimes a paragraph develops a main point with reasons rather than simple facts. Instead of merely emphasizing facts that tell *what,* it presents reasons that tell *why* something is true. Such a paragraph calls the reader to evaluate, to think through, to understand why he should accept the writer's argument.

When we give reasons in a paragraph, we must be sure that they do give solid support to our main point. As you read the following paragraph, consider whether it gives sound reasons.

> Alcoholic beverages should be completely avoided. First, these drinks are very expensive. People actually spend millions of dollars on strong drink every year. Also, thousands of people are hurt and killed through the use of alcohol. It is not wise to do things that endanger our health and safety. Finally, a person can get along well without using strong drink. We should not spend our money for things we could live without. Therefore, total abstinence from alcoholic drinks is the best policy.

This paragraph uses faulty reasoning to prove its point. It is true that strong drink is expensive, but so are cheese, winter coats, and automobiles. It is also true that alcohol causes many deaths, but it is not true that we should avoid doing anything that endangers our safety. If we did, we would not even walk across a city street! And although we can live without alcohol, it is not true that we should avoid buying anything we could live without. If we say that, we will need to avoid buying things like candy and ball gloves.

There is nothing wrong with the point that the paragraph makes. Total abstinence from alcoholic drinks certainly is the best policy, but you will never convince a reader with reasons like the ones given. Such reasons confuse the issue rather than making a strong argument. Therefore, you must always make sure your reasons are sound.

3. *Pertinent illustrations.* People cannot argue against real life. The things that happen must be true. For this reason, few methods of paragraph development carry more force than a pertinent illustration. Sentences that illustrate the main point show exactly *how* it applies in practical experience.

When we use this method, we might give a single detailed example to illustrate our point, or we might give several examples more briefly. Whichever we do, we must be sure our illustration fits the point well. An unsuitable illustration will fail to make our point just as surely as unsound reasons will fail.

Notice the clear illustration in the following paragraph. It validates the topic sentence quite effectively.

> Alcoholic beverages should be completely avoided. Even if one person can drink in moderation, his influence may lead to the ruin of a person who cannot handle alcohol. One man kept a bottle of liquor in his closet for an occasional drink. He never became drunk, but his son developed a serious drinking problem while he was still in his teens. When someone asked the young man how his problem had started, he told about a time years before when he had become

drunk on his father's liquor. "I became an instant alcoholic through that one experience," he said. "Ever since then, alcohol has always seemed like an easy escape from reality, especially when I face a problem." The testimony of this young man and many others makes it clear that total abstinence from alcoholic drinks is the best policy.

Order of Increasing Importance

A basic principle of argumentative writing is that you should save your strongest argument for last. The same principle holds true for the development of individual paragraphs within the argument. This buildup in importance adds to the force of the paragraph and thus to the strength of the whole essay. Sometimes no specific buildup is evident for the entire set of reasons. But even then, one reason often stands out as the strongest of all. Save it for last. Use it to clinch the point you are making.

Read the following paragraphs. Do you agree that the order of the sentences affects the strength of the argument?

Weak: Points given in random order

Young people should sense a definite responsibility to honor their parents. For one thing, God is well pleased when youth honor their elders. What could any godly person value above the smile of God's approval? Then too, this honor contributes greatly to a smooth, peaceable homelife. When children conscientiously do what they know their parents want, tension and conflict cannot grow. A youth's level of honor for his parents also tells much about his own character. Not many disrespectful youth grow up to become strong Christians or loyal church members. Therefore, honoring our parents is not optional but mandatory.

Forceful: Points arranged in order of importance

Young people should sense a definite responsibility to honor their parents. For one thing, this honor contributes greatly to a smooth, peaceable homelife. When children conscientiously do what they know their parents want, tension and conflict cannot grow. A youth's level of honor for his parents also tells much about his own character. Not many disrespectful youth grow up to become strong Christians or loyal church members. Above all, God is well pleased when youth honor their elders. What could any godly person value above the smile of God's approval? Therefore, honoring our parents is not optional but is an indispensable part of upright character.

By now it should be clear that you can choose among several kinds of details to develop your argumentative paragraphs. You can use specific facts that tell *what,* sound reasons that tell *why,* or pertinent illustrations that show *how.* If you choose the method best suited to each main point, and arrange the details so that the strongest one comes last, your paragraphs will help to make your argument truly convincing.

Applying the Lesson

A. The following paragraphs show how a given topic sentence can sometimes be developed by *facts, reasons,* or *illustrations*. Write which method is used in each paragraph.

    1.   Mental arithmetic is an excellent skill to develop. For one thing, paper and pencil may not always be available when you need to solve a problem. Mental math is also a good way to develop mental discipline. And you may miss some valuable opportunities if you cannot compute mentally. Therefore, put forth diligent effort toward gaining skill in solving problems mentally.

    2.   Mental arithmetic is an excellent skill to develop. Suppose you make a purchase and receive too much change. If you have mentally calculated what the change should be, you can correct the error on the spot instead of having to go back later. Or suppose someday you want to haul fifty-pound bags of feed with a truck whose load limit is one and one-half tons. Could you calculate mentally the greatest number of bags you should haul at one time? In these and similar situations, you will have a definite advantage if you can solve math problems mentally.

    3.   Mental arithmetic is an excellent skill to develop. It is an ability that almost anyone can learn if he really wants to. First you must have a thorough mastery of the number facts in all four operations—addition, subtraction, multiplication, and division. Then you need to learn specific shortcuts that allow mental calculation, such as the regrouping method in addition and the double-and-divide method in multiplication. Finally, you must practice and practice until you use the shortcuts almost automatically. It takes patience and perseverance to learn mental arithmetic, but the benefits are well worth the effort.

B. Arrange the numbers of the sentences in this paragraph so that the reasons come in the order of importance. The details should begin with the physical aspect and end with the spiritual aspect.

    [1]Youth who wish to be productive should purpose to get plenty of sleep. [2]When the body is well rested, one's mental powers can function at their best. [3]A person's ability to study, to recall information, and to reason through problems is directly related to the amount of rest he has had. [4]Furthermore, a well-rested body contributes positively to one's spiritual well-being. [5]A tired body and a dull mind tend to weaken a person's defenses, making him vulnerable to temptation. [6]The amount of rest one receives certainly affects his physical fitness. [7]Those who consistently receive sufficient rest will generally be healthier than those who frequently drain the battery of their energy supply. [8]Truly, as Benjamin Franklin said, "Early to bed and early to rise, makes a man healthy, wealthy, and wise."

C. Write an argumentative paragraph for one of these topic sentences.

    1. Every upper grade student should learn the basics of song leading.

2. The youth of the congregation should generally remain in the auditorium after church to do their visiting.
3. Keeping a personal prayer list enhances one's private prayer life.
4. For their own benefit, young people should relate regularly to elderly folks.
5. "When pride cometh, then cometh shame."
6. We must not allow superstitions to control our actions.
7. A person's character is much more important than his physical features.
8. Humor must always be kept under proper control.

---

63. Building Coherence Into Paragraphs and Essays

If the structure of your essay will prove substantial, you must write its paragraphs carefully. Each of them must have unity, developing one main idea. Each should have a definite beginning, middle, and ending. And each must be developed with specific details.

Another essential quality of effective paragraphs is coherence. A paragraph must be more than a group of disconnected sentences about one topic. The sentences must be written in such a way that the thoughts flow smoothly and logically from one sentence to another. A writer can use several methods to give his paragraphs this quality.

Not only the individual paragraphs but also the whole essay needs coherence. The same methods used for linking sentences within a paragraph can also link paragraphs within an essay. In this lesson you will study three general methods for building coherence into your paragraphs and essays.

Transitional Words

Transitional words help to produce coherence by showing relationships between ideas. These words are road signs that tell the reader where the essay is taking him next. Therefore, you must choose your signs discerningly so that they direct your reader effectively.

In writing an argument, you will primarily use the following categories of transitional words.

Conceding a counter argument:

admittedly	it is true that	no one denies
granted	no doubt	to be sure

Giving a contrasting thought:

although	nevertheless	otherwise
but	of course	still
even so	on the contrary	the fact remains
however	on the other hand	yet

Adding another thought:

again	besides	likewise
also	furthermore	moreover
and	in addition	too

Giving an example or illustration:

for example	in fact	specifically
for instance	in other words	to illustrate

Adding emphasis:

assuredly	in fact	of course
certainly	indeed	undoubtedly
clearly	obviously	unquestionably

Concluding a point or an essay:

as a result	in conclusion	therefore
consequently	in summary	thus

Read the following sample essay. Its thesis is supported by three main points: the first one in paragraph 2, the second one in paragraphs 3 and 4, and the third one in paragraph 5. Transitional words are underlined.

In Church on Time

1   Just as the congregation broke into the strains, "We now have met to worship Thee," Simon slid into his seat and reached for a hymnal. <u>But</u> his thoughts did not focus on the song; instead, he was trying to remember if he had combed his hair. As unobtrusively as possible, he ran his hand over the top of his head. <u>Then</u> Simon thought of his shoes—were they clean? He had not had time to look them over until now. His thoughts ran on as he reviewed his personal appearance. Only as the song leader announced the second hymn did his thoughts return to present reality. Though we have probably all found ourselves in Simon's place, being seated in the auditorium in good time should be one of our highest priorities.

2   <u>First</u>, we need to be in church well before the service begins so that we have time to prepare for worship. It is difficult to enter into a worshipful spirit if we come into the auditorium tense and frustrated from hurrying to church or giddy and lighthearted from visiting beforehand. <u>But</u> if we sit and meditate reverently for ten minutes before the service begins, worship will more readily flow from our souls during the service. True worship involves disciplining ourselves physically, emotionally, and spiritually to concentrate upon God and His Word. <u>Therefore</u>, worship finds its richest expression when it comes from those who have truly prepared their hearts.

3   <u>Furthermore</u>, being seated on time is important for the subtle messages it sends to others. To those who will be leading out in the service, punctuality says that here are people who enjoy worship, who love the Lord, who hunger for His Word. This inspires them in turn, and it <u>also</u> encourages them to serve to the best of their abilities. Any such encouragement will help to make the worship experience more meaningful.

4   By our promptness, <u>moreover,</u> we send a subtle message to our peers. <u>For one thing,</u> this message announces that we have come to church for the right reasons: not primarily to visit but to worship. We <u>also</u> demonstrate our desire to develop spiritual maturity and holy reverence. <u>And</u> if some of them are less punctual, our example may well encourage them to be more diligent themselves.

5   <u>Finally,</u> taking our seats promptly is important because a worship service is to be a personal meeting with the God we love. Can you imagine a person so careless that he arrives late for an appointment with a king or president? If one person loves another, does he wait as long as possible to come to an appointed meeting with that person? Of course not! Neither should one who truly loves the Lord find it difficult to meditate quietly for several minutes before a worship service begins.

6   Being seated in good time for a worship service is a noble goal. Most likely, the excuses for being late will never disappear, nor will the temptations to linger in social visiting. <u>But</u> we can and should rise above those things and exercise as much diligence in being punctual as we do in other areas that we consider important.

You need to use transitional words carefully for the best effect. You may tend to place them only at the beginning of sentences, but they are sometimes more effective elsewhere. Note the underlined transitional expressions in the sample argument above. While the majority are at the beginning of sentences, a few are in the middle.

There is no specific rule for the placing of transitional words; you must simply put them where they sound best. This suggests that you should do a bit of experimenting. Try the expression in several different positions to see where it serves the most effectively. In the following examples, note the differences caused by moving the transitional words.

> True worship involves disciplining ourselves physically, emotionally, and spiritually to concentrate upon God and His Word. <u>Therefore,</u> worship finds its richest expression when it comes from those who have truly prepared their hearts.
>
> True worship involves disciplining ourselves physically, emotionally, and spiritually to concentrate upon God and His Word. Worship finds its richest expression, <u>therefore,</u> when it comes from those who have truly prepared their hearts.

We <u>also</u> demonstrate our desire to develop spiritual maturity and holy reverence.

<u>Also,</u> we demonstrate our desire to develop spiritual maturity and holy reverence.

Now look at the transitional words that link one paragraph to the previous one. Most of them are at the beginning, but one (*moreover*) is in the middle. Try changing the positions of these words. Do any of them provide smooth links in other positions? You should readily observe that some of them could be positioned elsewhere, but some cannot.

In particular, *First* in paragraph 2 cannot be moved because a different position would make it modify a different word. In paragraphs 3 and 4, the position of *Furthermore* and *moreover* could perhaps be changed. But in paragraph 5, *Finally* should not be moved because again it would change the word modified.

Use transitional words only when they definitely add to the smooth flow of the sentences. You cannot use these mechanical devices to substitute for a lack of logical relationships between ideas. If you try to do that, or if you use too many transitional words, your paragraphs will sound stilted and unnatural.

Repetition of Key Ideas

The repetition of a key idea produces coherence in a subtle but highly effective way. This technique serves especially well because it not only produces coherence but also emphasizes the main idea.

Give special attention to the phrase *key ideas*. First, the repeated items are *key* ideas because they are the main ones being emphasized. Minor ideas do not deserve this kind of repetition. Second, the repeated items are key *ideas* because you do not need to always repeat the same word. You can use synonyms and pronouns as well.

If a key word (or a synonym or pronoun for it) is repeated throughout an entire paragraph, that paragraph is strongly tied together from beginning to end. Read paragraph 3 from the essay again, noting the repeated ideas of the underlined words.

> Furthermore, being seated <u>on time</u> is important for the subtle messages it sends to others. To those who will be leading out in the service, <u>punctuality</u> says that here are people who enjoy worship, who love the Lord, who hunger for His Word. <u>This</u> inspires them in turn, and <u>it</u> also encourages them to serve to the best of their abilities. Any such encouragement will help to make the worship experience more meaningful.

Repetition is especially effective when the same subject occurs in a series of sentences. Since the subject is the most important noun in the sentences, this provides a particularly strong link. Paragraph 2 from the sample essay is shown below. The underlined words all refer to worship; and in the last three sentences, the subject of every main clause is *worship*. All these repeated ideas strongly link the sentences into a coherent paragraph.

> First, we need to be in church well before the service begins so that we have time to prepare for <u>worship</u>. It is difficult to enter into a <u>worshipful</u> spirit if we come into the auditorium tense and frustrated from hurrying to church or giddy and lighthearted from visiting beforehand. But if we sit and meditate <u>reverently</u> for ten minutes before the service begins, <u>worship</u> will more readily flow from our souls during the service. True <u>worship</u> involves disciplining ourselves physically, emotionally, and spiritually to concentrate upon God and His Word. Therefore,

<u>worship</u> finds its richest expression when <u>it</u> comes from those who have truly prepared their hearts.

Another effective use of repetition is to place a word (or a form of it) from the latter part of one sentence at the beginning of the second. This provides a strong link between two sentences. Paragraphs 2 and 4 illustrate this technique.

> First, we need to be in church well before the service begins so that we have time to prepare for <u>worship</u>. It is difficult to enter into a <u>worshipful</u> spirit if we come into the auditorium tense and frustrated from hurrying to church or giddy and lighthearted from visiting beforehand.

> By our promptness, moreover, we send a subtle <u>message</u> to our peers. For one thing, this <u>message</u> announces that we have come to church for the right reasons: not primarily to visit but to worship.

Reference to Previous Ideas

Referring to an idea in a previous paragraph provides a strong link between paragraphs. This works in the same way as repeating key ideas within a paragraph. Reference to a previous idea is especially effective when a paragraph adds to or contrasts with the previously stated idea.

In the sample essay, only paragraph 4 builds directly on the main idea of the previous paragraph. Note that both paragraphs 3 and 4 begin by referring to a subtle message, and the idea of sending messages provides a common thread for those paragraphs.

> Furthermore, being seated on time is important for the <u>subtle messages</u> it sends to others. To those who will be leading out in the service, <u>punctuality says</u> that here are people who enjoy worship, who love the Lord, who hunger for His Word....

> By our promptness, moreover, we send a <u>subtle message</u> to our peers. For one thing, this <u>message announces</u> that we have come to church for the right reasons: not primarily to visit but to worship....

Note also the mention of loving God in paragraph 3 and the more extended discussion of that idea in paragraph 5. This repetition helps to link those separated paragraphs, and thus it contributes to the coherence of the entire essay.

Applying the Lesson

Read this argumentative essay, and do the exercises below.

Exercise With Fringe Benefits

1   [1]People of industrialized nations face a dilemma today. [2]They spend money for modern inventions that reduce the drudgery of manual labor. [3]They realize how important it is to get enough physical exercise. [4]So the people spend more money for exercise equipment to keep themselves physically fit. [5]It is much better to get one's exercise by natural physical activities than by using exercise equipment.

2   ⁶Exercise equipment is appropriate in special cases, such as for therapy after an accident. ⁷But the purchase of exercise equipment is usually a waste of money. ⁸A fitness bench with barbells may cost several hundred dollars. ⁹The price of a treadmill may be as high as one thousand dollars. ¹⁰Surely this would be better spent to help needy people or to support mission work.

3   ¹¹The use of exercise equipment is generally a waste of time. ¹²It takes hours of use, week after week, to gain the benefits that exercise machines are designed for. ¹³Why not spend them in weeding a busy mother's garden or mowing the lawn for someone who is physically unable? ¹⁴We might go for a walk with an elderly person who would greatly enjoy our company. ¹⁵Or we could go romping with some younger children—they will probably love it! ¹⁶We will find plenty of physical activities to fill our exercise time if we only look for them.

4   ¹⁷The use of exercise equipment generally goes along with an improper emphasis on the physical body. ¹⁸Advertisements promoting the use of such equipment often show people with large, strong muscles. ¹⁹These pictures are used to inspire a zeal for a strong, attractive body. ²⁰The Bible says, "Bodily exercise profiteth little: but godliness is profitable unto all things" (1 Timothy 4:8). ²¹If all the zeal used for physical fitness were directed into godliness, what a blessing it would be!

5   ²²In conclusion, exercising with machines is no match for exercising by natural physical activities. ²³First of all, the money spent for exercise equipment could generally be put to better use. ²⁴In the second place, the time spent at using the equipment would be better used in helping someone. ²⁵As a third point, the zeal involved in using exercise machines is inappropriate for someone professing godliness. ²⁶On the one hand, using exercise equipment will gain us a few physical benefits. ²⁷But on the other hand, engaging in physical activities that help others will gain physical, social, and spiritual benefits for ourselves, our families, and our friends.

1. Show how to improve the coherence of the essay by following the directions below. For each improvement, write the number of the sentence involved, and write enough words to show the change you are making. Be sure to include the first word of a sentence, with correct capitalization, if you change a sentence beginning.

   a. A dilemma is a situation in which a person must deal with two undesirable choices. Insert *on the one hand* and *on the other hand* to introduce the two choices in paragraph 1.

   b. Place a transitional expression in sentence 5 to show a contrast of thought.

   c. Introduce paragraph 2 with a transitional expression suitable for conceding a counter argument.

   d. Repeat the key word *money* in sentence 10.

e. The first supporting statement, in paragraph 2, begins with *But*. Use suitable transitional words to introduce the other two supporting statements in the essay.

f. A key idea in paragraph 3 is "time." Emphasize that idea more strongly by replacing a pronoun in sentence 13 with *that time*. Also place a transitional word in sentence 14 to show the addition of a thought.

g. In paragraph 4, forms of *use* occur in almost every sentence even though that word does not refer to a key idea. Remove two of these forms, along with other words as needed to make the sentences read correctly.

h. In paragraph 5, every sentence begins with a transitional expression. Delete all those expressions except for the word *But* in sentence 27.

2. Write the answers.

a. What key word occurs at least twice in every paragraph of the essay?

b. Paragraph 2 illustrates the technique of referring to an idea in a previous paragraph. How does it do that?

c. A key word in paragraph 3 is *time*. Copy two different words that refer to the same idea.

d. From paragraph 4, copy a repeated word that means "strong interest and enthusiasm."

e. One element of good writing style is alliteration (the repetition of beginning consonant sounds). From sentence 27, copy two pairs of words that illustrate alliteration.

---

64. Improving Your Editing Skills, Part 7

As the title of this lesson indicates, editing involves a number of skills—things that you must practice in order to do them well. One important skill is to see what is actually written on the page, rather than what you expect to see. Consider the following example.

```
The children of Israel, serving as slaves in the land

of Eygpt, cried out for deliverance.
```

Is everything in order? The word *Israel* is capitalized and has the *ae* in the right order. The modifying phrase is properly set off by commas, and *deliverance* is spelled correctly. But there is one mistake! If you did not catch it, you saw the misspelled word *Eygpt* as *Egypt*. It is because proofreaders see what they expect to see that they sometimes overlook mistakes—even if they think they are fully concentrating on their work.

When you proofread, you need to inspect each word and punctuation mark separately. Put special effort into seeing what is actually written so that you can correct *every* mistake.

Marks Used in Editing and Proofreading

$\vee$ or $\wedge$ insert (caret)	$\mathscr{L}$ delete	. . . . stet (let it stand)	use italics
¶ begin new paragraph	no ¶ no new paragraph	*lc* change to lowercase (small letter)	*uc* change to uppercase (capital letter)
# insert space	‿ delete space	← move (arrow)	⎍ transpose

Editing Practice

A. Use proofreading marks to correct the two capitalization or punctuation errors in each sentence.

1. Many christians were living in the city of rome by the end of the first century.

2. Their worship and their teachings stood in sharp contrast, to the Paganism of the Romans.

3. Several waves of intense persecution swept across the church, driving many of the saints to the Catacombs for refuge

4. The catacombs, underground tunnels beneath the city of Rome covered about 600 acres (240 hectares.)

5. The passageways were lined with holes used for burial, therefore superstitious Romans avoided the catacombs.

6. Furthermore anyone pursuing the Christians could easily lose his way—and his life in the five hundred miles of unmarked tunnels.

7. One point of interest especially to us today, is the pictures that the early Believers drew on the walls.

8. Most of the artwork shows Biblical scenes, especially gospel scenes from the Life of Christ.

9. `In addition to the pictures left by the Christians`

   `several thousand inscriptions give much information,`

   `about the beliefs of the early church.`

10. `When persecution subsided the catacombs were abandoned`

    `and completely forgotten, they were rediscovered in`

    `1578.`

B. Use proofreading marks to correct the one or two usage errors in each exercise.

1. I cannot help but tell you some mighty interesting details about the personal lives of a few United States presidents.

2. James Buchanan, as you may all ready know, was different from all the others because he was unmarried.

3. Incredible as it sounds, James A. Garfield had the capacity to write Greek with one hand and Latin with the other—at the same time!

4. Being as George Washington did not have strong, healthful teeth, he wore false teeth carved from rhinoceros ivory.

5. Thomas Jefferson was one of the first people in this country to grow a tomato; before that, lots of people had the allusion that tomatoes were poisonous.

6. Regardless of the cold and rain, William Henry Harrison stood outside and made the longest inaugural speech of any American president. It proved to be to long, for he caught a severe cold and died one month later.

7. John Quincy Adams and Abraham Lincoln are remembered for there height; the former was 5 feet 4 inches tall, and the later was 6 feet 4 inches tall.

8. Gerald Ford, accompanied with his dog, once returned from an evening stroll to find himself literally locked out of the White House.

9. Dwight D. Eisenhower liked to paint but couldn't hardly draw; therefore, others would sketch the outlines of pictures for him. As a result, the paint-by-number method became right popular.

10. Edith Galt married Woodrow Wilson some time during his first term as president, plus she learned to ride a bicycle in the halls of the White House.

C. Use proofreading marks to correct all the errors in this essay. No line has more than one error.

1. Towering above it's surroundings in the rugged Alaska

2. Range is Mount McKinley. the highest peak in North America.

3. McKinley soars to 20,320 feet (6,194 meters) above sea level.

4. Although many mountains rank higher above sea level then

5. McKinley, few dominate the surrounding ter rain more impres-

6. sively. From base to peak, McKinley rises a stupendeous

7. 18,000 feet (5,500 meters)! By contrast Mount Everest soars

8. more than 29,000 feet (8,800 meters) above sea level but it

9. rises a mere 12,000 feet (3,700 meters) above its base.

10. As moist air blows inland from the gulf of Alaska, the

11. Alaska Range forces the air to rise, therefore, significant

12. amounts of snowfall on these mountains. Heavy snowfall on

13. high mountains often produce glaciers, and Mount McKinley

14. is no exception. Seventeen major glaciers, four of which

15. are over twenty five miles long (40 kilometers), grace the

16. sides of this massive mountian. Because of the conditions

17. that produce this snowfall, however, clouds often conceal

18. the summit. Indeed, many of the 400,000 or more visiters

19. from around the world have had to home return without

20. out enjoying a clear view of the majestic Mount McKinley.

---

65. Chapter 8 Review

Read the following short argumentative essay, and revise it according to the directions below.

Should Christians Bother Themselves With a Study of Church History?

The history of the Christian church spans two millennia and touches every continent on the earth. In a wide range of circumstances, Christians either have succeeded in preserving the faith or have drifted into apostasy. Although new and unique issues will continue to face the church, very few of them are totally different from what Christians have faced before.

Some people may say that they simply have no interest in church history. But these people are ignoring the fact that God's Word directs us to know our history. This Scriptural call is one important reason for us to study church history.

A few people will even say that studying church history since the New Testament age is a waste of time. According to such reasoning, Christians should simply study the Scriptures without considering more recent happenings in the church. God calls us to learn not only about the past but also from the past. Romans 15:4 and 1 Corinthians 10:11 clearly state that Bible history is written "for our learning" and "for our admonition." Seeing how God's people overcame spiritual threats in more recent times will help us to deal with similar issues. Likewise, observing what brought failure to the church in the past will help us to avoid similar mistakes.

1. Write a better title for the essay.
2. Write a thesis statement to end paragraph 1.
3. Develop paragraph 2 more fully by referring to Deuteronomy 6:20–25 and Psalm 78.
4. In paragraph 3, add a transitional expression to sentence 3 and sentence 4.
5. Add a concluding sentence to paragraph 3.
6. Write a conclusion for this essay.

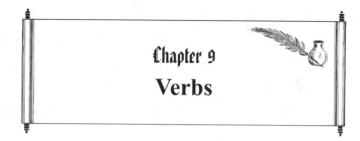

Chapter 9
Verbs

66. Verbs and the Principal Parts of Verbs

Nouns and verbs make up the core of language. Nouns give substance to language by naming persons, places, things, and ideas. Verbs are the engines of language, making the nouns act or exist in specific ways.

Basic Facts About Verbs

1. *A verb expresses action or being to tell what the subject does or is.* The verb joins with the subject to make the basic framework, or skeleton, of a sentence.

> <u>God</u> <u>blesses</u> His people.   <u>God</u> <u>is</u> the giver of every good gift.

2. *Every clause has a verb, which is the simple predicate of the clause.*

> We <u>have read</u> the Bible many times.

In an elliptical clause, the verb may be understood. Elliptical sentences are found mainly in dialogue.

> Which books of the New Testament <u>were written</u> by a Gentile?
> Luke and Acts. (Luke and Acts <u>were written</u> by a Gentile.)

3. *Many simple predicates are verb phrases, consisting of the main verb and one or more helping verbs.* The main verb always comes last in a verb phrase.

Other words often interrupt a verb phrase. Many of these are adverbs like *not, never, hardly, always, ever,* and *surely.* In a contraction like *don't,* the *n't* is also an adverb. In a question, the subject often comes between the helping verb and the main verb.

> My parents <u>have</u> always <u>lived</u> in this community.
> We <u>haven't</u> <u>found</u> the missing wrenches yet.
> <u>Does</u> this calf still <u>need</u> a bottle?

4. *Sometimes the simple predicate is a compound verb, in which two or more verbs are joined by a conjunction.* The parts of a compound verb share the same subject. They may also share the same helping verb, which may appear only before the first main verb.

> I <u>found</u> some interesting information and <u>jotted</u> down several notes about the history of Swiss cheese.
> In every music class, we <u>have been drilling</u> the scale, <u>singing</u> the notes of several songs, or <u>reviewing</u> the rudiments of music.

Principal Parts of Verbs

5. *Verbs have three principal parts, which are used to form the different tenses: the first principal part (present form), the second principal part (past form), and the third principal part (past participle).*

Present	Past	Past Participle
talk	talked	(have) talked
sing	sang	(have) sung

6. *The first principal part is the basic form of a verb—the form you would use with* to.

talk	eat	sing	work	play

7. *The second and third principal parts of most verbs are formed by adding* -ed *to the first principal part.* Other spelling changes may also be necessary. If the verb ends with *e,* drop the *e* before adding *-ed.* If the verb ends with *y* after a consonant, change the *y* to *i.* If a one-syllable verb ends with a single consonant after a short vowel, double the final consonant.

Present	Past	Past Participle
wash	washed	(have) washed
rake	raked	(have) raked
study	studied	(have) studied
drop	dropped	(have) dropped

8. *The second and third principal parts of some verbs have irregular forms.* The correct forms of a few of the commonly misused ones follow. Use an English handbook or a dictionary to find the correct forms whenever you are in doubt.

First (Present)	Second (Past)	Third (Past Participle)	First (Present)	Second (Past)	Third (Past Participle)
awake	awoke	(have) awoke	know	knew	(have) known
	or awaked	(have) awaked	lay	laid	(have) laid
bid	bade	(have) bidden	leave	left	(have) left
	or bid	(have) bid	let	let	(have) let
blow	blew	(have) blown	lie	lay	(have) lain
bring	brought	(have) brought	raise	raised	(have) raised
burst	burst	(have) burst	rise	rose	(have) risen
come	came	(have) come	see	saw	(have) seen
creep	crept	(have) crept	set	set	(have) set
dig	dug	(have) dug	shrink	shrank	(have) shrunk
do	did	(have) done		*or* shrunk	(have) shrunken
drag	dragged	(have) dragged	sit	sat	(have) sat
drink	drank	(have) drunk	swim	swam	(have) swum
drown	drowned	(have) drowned	swing	swung	(have) swung
forbid	forbade	(have) forbidden	tag	tagged	(have) tagged
	or forbad	(have) forbid	take	took	(have) taken
go	went	(have) gone			

9. *In addition to the three principal parts, most verbs have two other forms—the present participle and the -s form.* The present participle, which ends with *-ing,* is used in progressive verb forms. The *-s* form is used with third person singular subjects in the present tense.

> The Lord is <u>reigning</u> from His heavenly throne. He <u>reigns</u> over all.

Applying the Lesson

A. List all the verbs and verb phrases. Underline the main verb in each verb phrase.
  1. "The fear of the LORD is the beginning of knowledge: but fools despise wisdom and instruction."
  2. "My son, hear the instruction of thy father, and forsake not the law of thy mother."
  3. "My son, if sinners entice thee, consent thou not."
  4. "Where no counsel is, the people fall."
  5. A godly youth will be seeking good friendships and providing good friend-ship for others.
  6. A good student listens well in class, prepares his lessons thoroughly, and does his work neatly.
  7. Has Justin been cleaning the milk house all morning?
  8. Will the lunches be packed in time?

B. Write the correct form of each underlined verb; do not change the tense. If it is correct, write *correct.*
  1. Aunt Lena has <u>chose</u> to buy a pair of Siamese fighting fish for her aquarium.
  2. God <u>gave</u> these fish a strange way of spawning and caring for their eggs.
  3. By the time the female is ready to spawn, the male has <u>took</u> many gulps of air and spit out air bubbles to make a nest.
  4. Often this nest of air bubbles has <u>rose</u> a half inch above the water surface by the time it is complete.
  5. When the nest is ready, the male chases the female until she <u>swim</u> near the nest.
  6. There the female lays her eggs, and the male catches them before they have <u>sank</u> to the bottom.
  7. Soon the male has collected a mouthful of eggs and <u>brung</u> them to the nest.
  8. Before the two-day incubation is over, several eggs will have <u>fell</u> from the nest; but the male promptly puts them back.
  9. The male is also busy replacing air bubbles that have <u>bursted</u>.
  10. By the time all the eggs hatch, the male has <u>become</u> very busy, for now he must return squirming little fish to the nest.
  11. Soon the male can no longer keep up, but by then the little fish have <u>growed</u> enough to fend for themselves.
  12. The strangest part of the story is that before all the little fish can swim to safety, the male has <u>ate</u> many of them.

C. Write the correct past form of each verb in parentheses. Use the past participle only if there is a helping verb in the sentence.
  1. Our noisy dog has (awake) me too often.

2. The powerful elephants (drag) the trees out of the forest.
3. Have you ever (swing) a bucket of water over your head to demonstrate centrifugal force?
4. Have you (do) the chores you were expected to do this morning?
5. The squirrel (dig) up a nut it had buried in the fall.
6. Have you (drink) any of Aunt Betsy's mint tea?
7. Father (forbid) the younger children to go to the creek alone.
8. Yesterday my jacket (lie) out in the rain all day.
9. Have you (speak) as kindly as you should have?
10. The hot peppers have usually (cost) more than this.

Review Exercises

A. Identify each underlined item as a gerund (*G*), a gerund phrase (*GP*), an infinitive (*I*), an infinitive phrase (*IP*), or a noun clause (*NC*). If the underlined word group is not a noun, write *none*. [54]
   1. Attending a public auction can be quite interesting.
   2. If you expect to find a bargain, you may be disappointed.
   3. On the other hand, what you purchase there can be extremely useful.
   4. Do you want to bid?
   5. Hurry! The auctioneer is raising his gavel.

B. Tell whether each underlined item functions as a subject (*S*), a direct object (*DO*), an indirect object (*IO*), the object of a preposition (*OP*), or a predicate nominative (*PN*). [54]
   1. From where our house is located, we hear lots of traffic.
   2. Tonight we are planning to visit Brother Lamar and his family.
   3. Praying for government leaders is a Bible command.
   4. One sure way to learn is to listen.
   5. Eighty-year-old Susan gives whomever she meets a cheerful greeting.

---

67. Simple and Perfect Tenses

Verbs have different forms to indicate action or existence in the past, present, or future. English verbs have three simple tenses and three perfect tenses.

Simple Tenses

1. *The present tense shows action or existence in the present.* It also records a statement of general truth, even if the context of the sentence is past. Present tense uses the first principal part (present form). The third person singular form ends with -*s*.

> John Kramer, who works for Father, is my cousin.
> In 1543, Copernicus wrote that the earth revolves around the sun.

2. *The past tense shows action or existence in the past.* It uses the second principal part (past form).

> Johannes Kepler <u>formulated</u> the three laws of planetary motion.

3. *The future tense shows action or existence in the future.* The future tense uses the first principal part (present form) with the helping verb *shall* or *will.* In formal writing, use *shall* for first person subjects and *will* for second and third person subjects. In general usage, *will* is acceptable for all three persons.

> Since I <u>shall</u> be absent tomorrow, you <u>will</u> need to pass out the books.

To show determination, strong desire, or promise, reverse the normal pattern of *shall* and *will* in formal English.

> We <u>shall</u> go along, and you <u>will</u> stay at home. (simple future tense statement)
> We <u>will</u> go along, and you <u>shall</u> stay at home. (statement of determination)

The King James Bible uses formal English. Understanding the distinctions between *shall* and *will* contributes to a clear understanding of many Bible verses. Study the following examples.

> "Hold thou me up, and I shall [simple future] be safe: and I will [determination] have respect unto thy statutes continually" (Psalm 119:117).
> "But [Thomas] said unto them, Except I shall [simple future] see in his hands the print of the nails, and put my finger into the print of the nails, and thrust my hand into his side, I will [determination] not believe" (John 20:25).

Perfect Tenses

4. *The present perfect tense shows an action or a condition that began in the past and is completed as of the present or continues into the present.* This tense uses the third principal part (past participle) with the helping verb *have* or *has.*

Both the simple past and the present perfect tenses refer to things that happened before the present. The simple past, however, merely indicates that an action or existence occurred at some past time. The present perfect indicates that what began in the past is now completed or is still continuing.

> **Simple past:**   I <u>fed</u> the calves earlier.
> **Present perfect:** We <u>have fed</u> all the livestock.
> **Simple past:**   We <u>received</u> ten inches of snow.
> **Present perfect:** Since eight o'clock we <u>have received</u> ten inches of snow.

5. *The past perfect tense shows an action or a condition that was completed by a certain time in the past.* This tense uses the third principal part (past participle) with the helping verb *had.*

The past perfect tense requires that two past actions or conditions be expressed or implied. That which was completed first must be expressed in the past perfect tense.

Incomplete: Only one past action
We <u>had traveled</u> for several hours.
Complete: Two past actions stated
We <u>had traveled</u> for several hours before dawn <u>broke</u>.
Complete: One past action stated and one implied
We <u>had traveled</u> for several hours before dawn.

Use the past perfect tense either to clarify which of two past actions or conditions occurred first or to emphasize that one action or condition was completed at the time of the other. Compare the differences in meaning and emphasis in the following sentences.

Unclear: Sounds as if the two actions occurred at the same time
Menno Simons <u>regretted</u> how he <u>lived</u> as a Catholic priest.
Clear: Clarifies that the regretting came later
Menno Simons <u>regretted</u> how he <u>had lived</u> as a Catholic priest.
Completed action not emphasized: Both verbs in simple past tense
Menno Simons <u>gained</u> a number of his convictions before he <u>left</u> the Catholic Church.
Completed action emphasized: First action in past perfect tense
Menno Simons <u>had gained</u> a number of his convictions before he <u>left</u> the Catholic Church.

6. *The future perfect tense shows an action or a condition that will be completed by a certain time in the future.* This tense uses the third principal part (past participle) with either *shall have* or *will have* as helping verbs.

The future perfect tense requires that two future actions or conditions be expressed or implied. That which will occur first or whose completion is to be emphasized must be expressed in the future perfect tense; the other may be expressed in the simple future or simple present tense.

Incomplete: Only one future action
My parents <u>will have lived</u> on this farm for thirty years.
Complete: One future condition implied and one future action stated
By the end of next month, my parents <u>will have lived</u> on this farm for thirty years.

The future perfect tense serves a function similar to that of the past perfect tense. Use it either to clarify which of two future actions or conditions will occur first, or to emphasize that one action or condition will be completed at the time of the other. Compare the differences in meaning and emphasis in the following sentences.

Unclear: Sounds as if Cousin Laura will serve five years *after* the stated time
At the end of June, Cousin Laura <u>will serve</u> in the rest home for five years.
Clear: Clarifies that her serving will be completed at the stated time
At the end of June, Cousin Laura <u>will have served</u> in the rest home for five years.

Completion of action not emphasized: Both verbs in simple tenses
Before this harvest <u>ends</u>, you <u>will pick</u> many tomatoes.
Completion of action emphasized: Completed action in future perfect tense
Before this harvest <u>ends</u>, you <u>will have picked</u> many tomatoes.

A *conjugation* is a listing of certain forms of a verb. Here is a conjugation of *copy* in the simple and perfect tenses.

Copy

Person	*Singular*	*Plural*
	Present Tense	
First:	I copy.	We copy.
Second:	You copy.	You copy.
Third:	He copies.	They copy.
	Past Tense	
First:	I copied.	We copied.
Second:	You copied.	You copied.
Third:	He copied.	They copied.
	Future Tense	
First:	I shall copy.	We shall copy.
Second:	You will copy.	You will copy.
Third:	He will copy.	They will copy.
	Present Perfect Tense	
First:	I have copied.	We have copied.
Second:	You have copied.	You have copied.
Third:	He has copied.	They have copied.
	Past Perfect Tense	
First:	I had copied.	We had copied.
Second:	You had copied.	You had copied.
Third:	He had copied.	They had copied.
	Future Perfect Tense	
First:	I shall have copied.	We shall have copied.
Second:	You will have copied.	You will have copied.
Third:	He will have copied.	They will have copied.

Applying the Lesson

A. Copy each verb or verb phrase, and write which tense it is.
1. God has promised His grace to all who put their trust in Him.
2. God's holy angel camps around those who fear God.
3. Even though Christ had not yet come, God provided a way of atonement for Old Testament saints.
4. Though they fully expected opposition, the saints of the past followed God's way.
5. By the time we shall share in Christ's glory, we shall have shared in His reproach.

6. Before God will bring the consummation of all things, He will have destroyed all His enemies.
7. Satan rebelled against God and drew a host of other angels after him.
8. Long before Jesus came, Satan had tried several times to exterminate the Hebrews.

B. Write the correct verb form for the tense shown in italics.
1. If this wind continues, the snow (drift) across the roads by morning. *future perfect*
2. This stove always (keep) the house warm before. *present perfect*
3. Before we completely (recover) from the first storm, a second one came. *past perfect*
4. By the end of the week, Sarah (go) to Mexico. *future perfect*
5. Rachel (take) great care to keep Grandmother warm. *present perfect*
6. We read the note that Father (write). *past perfect*

C. In each sentence, changing one verb to a perfect tense would make the meaning clearer or would put more emphasis on the completion of one action. Write that verb in the correct perfect tense.
1. The girls finished their cleaning before the boys completed their hoeing.
2. We could not recognize the object that the small boy drew.
3. The rain will chase us out of the garden before we finish picking the peas.
4. When Mother finishes this book, she will write five books.
5. I shall catch ten large trout if I can land this one.
6. Aunt Marlene arrived before Mother came home from the hospital.
7. Brother Sheldon graded the essays that we wrote.
8. Many people will influence you before you reach maturity.

D. Write short sentences for these descriptions, using pronouns and the correct verb forms.
1. First person singular, present tense of *learn.*
2. Second person, present perfect tense of *write.*
3. Second person, future tense of *speak.*
4. Third person plural, past tense of *kneel.*
5. Third person singular, feminine, past perfect tense of *run.*
6. First person plural, present tense of *forgive.*
7. First person plural, future perfect tense of *go.*
8. First person singular, past perfect tense of *come.*
9. Third person plural, past tense of *begin.*
10. Third person singular, masculine, future perfect tense of *choose.*

Review Exercises

Write the letters of the correct forms in each sentence. [55]
1. The children returned from picking (ªmulberrys, ᵇmulberries) with bright smiles and even brighter (ªstains, ᵇstaines) on their hands and faces.
2. Mr. (ªJones's, ᵇJones') decision to repair the (ªroofs, ᵇrooves) on his buildings is long overdue.

3. Samuel warned Israel that a king would take their ([a]manservants, [b]menservants) and their ([a]maidservants, [b]maidsservants) and put them to his work.
4. When ([a]Artaxerxes', [b]Artaxerxes's) letter arrived, the Jews' ([a]enemy's, [b]enemies) made them stop rebuilding the temple.
5. I appreciate the ([a]basises, [b]bases) upon which my ([a]brethrens', [b]brethren's) convictions are built.
6. According to ([a]God's, [b]Gods') Word, man has inhabited the earth for approximately six ([a]millennia, [b]millennae).
7. My ([a]sister's-in-law, [b]sister-in-law's) frequent ([a]posts card, [b]post cards) keep me informed about her activities.
8. Wash these breakfast ([a]dishs, [b]dishes), and then peel those ([a]potatos, [b]potatoes) for lunch.
9. ([a]Henry's, [b]Henry) singing often brightens ([a]our home's atmosphere, [b]the atmosphere of our home).
10. ([a]Samuel, [b]Samuel's) and Jonathan's spirits rose when they saw ([a]Mother, [b]Mother's) approaching with some hot chocolate.

---

68. Moods of Verbs

A *mode* is a manner of doing something. When people want to go somewhere, they can choose among several different modes of travel. They can walk, ride a bicycle, drive a car, or travel by plane—to name a few possibilities. They choose the mode that best fits their purpose.

Just as there are different modes of travel, there are different modes of verbs. However, we generally use the term ***mood*** instead of *mode* when referring to verbs. The mood of a verb is its manner of communicating, as determined by the intention of the speaker or writer. For example, a preacher during his sermon communicates in several different ways. The following sentences are some of the things he might say; each underlined verb is in a different mood.

> Stephen <u>demonstrated</u> outstanding boldness in witnessing for Jesus.
> <u>Open</u> your Bibles to Acts 6.
> If I <u>were</u> Stephen, could I face such a mob so courageously?

In the first sentence, the speaker intends simply to state a fact. So he uses a declarative sentence, which declares that something is true. The mood of this verb is indicative (in·dik′·ə·tiv) because it indicates a fact about Stephen.

In the second sentence, the speaker intends that his listeners do something. He expresses his intention by using an imperative sentence. Since the sentence is imperative, the verb is in the imperative mood.

What is the speaker's intention in the third sentence? He is making no request, neither is he indicating that something is true. In fact, he is expressing an idea that could *not* be true: "If I were Stephen" (when obviously he is not Stephen). The verb in this clause is in the subjunctive mood.

These examples illustrate the three moods of English verbs: indicative, imperative, and subjunctive.

The Indicative Mood

The *indicative mood* states a fact or asks a question. Since we generally use language to *indicate* real actions or conditions, we use the indicative mood far more often than any other mood. The verbs in most declarative and interrogative sentences are indicative.

The Roman Empire <u>became</u> the greatest government power of its time.
What peoples <u>invaded</u> this empire and <u>caused</u> its fall?

The Imperative Mood

The *imperative mood* gives a command or makes a request. The verbs in all imperative sentences are imperative.

<u>Find</u> more information about these invaders.
Please <u>write</u> a report about what you discover.

A verb in the imperative mood may appear to ask a question even though it actually makes a request. A sentence with such a verb ends with a period rather than a question mark because the verb is imperative.

<u>Will</u> the ushers please <u>pass</u> the offering baskets.
<u>Shall</u> we <u>stand</u> and sing this song.

The Subjunctive Mood

You have probably used the *subjunctive mood* even if you have never heard of it before. Have you ever made a statement like this one?

If I were you, I would mow the front lawn first.

Why do you say "I were"? Have you not learned that the correct expression is "I was"? Yet here it is—"if I were you"—and it sounds quite natural. You use the form *were* because this verb is in the subjunctive mood.

The subjunctive mood does not tell or ask about something that actually happens. Rather, it often expresses a condition contrary to fact, as in the example above. I am not you, and I can never be you. I will always be me! The subjunctive mood may also express a doubt, a wish, or a recommendation.

The subjunctive mood is much less common today than it was long ago. It is still required in a few expressions like "if I were you," and it may be used in certain other phrases. But today we often use helping verbs like *would* and *should* for ideas that formerly were expressed with the subjunctive mood.

You have studied verbs in the indicative and imperative moods ever since you studied declarative and imperative sentences. So these moods generally pose no problem for you. But the subjunctive mood requires more careful attention because a few of its forms are less familiar to you.

Subjunctive Verb Forms

Actually, almost all the subjunctive verb forms are identical to those of the indicative mood. There are only three places where they differ. Learning the correct subjunctive verb forms for these three exceptions will help you to use the subjunctive mood properly. The following paragraphs describe these three situations.

1. *The verb* be *in the present tense.* In the indicative mood, we must use three different forms for the verb *be* in the present tense. In the subjunctive mood, however, we use only the form *be.* Notice this difference on the chart below. (The conjunction *if* is included with the subjunctive forms because subjunctive verbs are common in *if* clauses.)

Present Tense *(Indicative Mood)*		Present Tense *(Subjunctive Mood)*	
I am	we are	(if) I <u>be</u>	(if) we <u>be</u>
you are	you are	(if) you <u>be</u>	(if) you <u>be</u>
he is	they are	(if) he <u>be</u>	(if) they <u>be</u>

Again, note that the subjunctive mood uses the word *be* no matter what the subject. Here are some examples of this usage.

"If I <u>be</u> a master, where is my fear? saith the Lord of hosts."
(subjunctive *I be* rather than indicative *I am*)
"If thine enemy <u>be</u> hungry, give him bread to eat."
(subjunctive *enemy be* rather than indicative *enemy is*)

2. *The verb* be *in the past tense.* Here the indicative mood uses *was* and *were.* As with the present tense, the subjunctive mood again uses a single form, this time *were.* Study the difference between the two forms in the chart below.

Past Tense *(Indicative Mood)*		Past Tense *(Subjunctive Mood)*	
I was	we were	(if) I <u>were</u>	(if) we were
you were	you were	(if) you were	(if) you were
he was	they were	(if) he <u>were</u>	(if) they were

Here the subjunctive mood is the same as the indicative mood except for two places: *I were* and *he were.* These may sound strange; but in examples such as the following, you will probably recognize that you have heard and even used them yourself.

If I <u>were</u> taller, I could reach that box.
(subjunctive *I were* rather than indicative *I was*)
"If my kingdom <u>were</u> of this world, then would my servants fight."
(subjunctive *kingdom were* rather than indicative *kingdom was*)

3. *Third person singular verbs in the present tense.* In the present tense, indicative mood, verbs always add -*s* for the third person singular. He *eats.* He *sees.* He *thinks.* The subjunctive mood, however, does not add this -*s.* The following chart shows the forms for the verb *go.*

Present Tense		**Present Tense**	
(Indicative Mood)		*(Subjunctive Mood)*	
I go	we go	(if) I go	(if) we go
you go	you go	(if) you go	(if) you go
he goes	they go	(if) he go	(if) they go

He go is the only place the subjunctive mood is different. Following this pattern with other verbs, we would have *he eat, he see, he think,* and so forth. Such usage is not as common as the subjunctive uses of *be,* yet these examples should have a familiar ring to them.

"If any man speak, let him speak as the oracles of God."
   (subjunctive *man speak* rather than indicative *man speaks*)
If another tire go flat, we will be in trouble!
   (subjunctive *tire go* rather than indicative *tire goes*)

For the second example, we may be more likely to say, "If another tire were to go flat." Even then we would be using the subjunctive mood, *tire were,* rather than the indicative mood, *tire was.*

The English of the King James Bible follows the rules of formal usage. Also, the subjunctive mood was used much more in the 1600s than it is today. For these reasons, the King James Bible contains many examples of subjunctive verbs. Understanding the subjunctive verb forms described above will help you to understand some of the "unusual" verb forms in the King James Version, and thus it will make the Bible clearer to you.

Using the Subjunctive Mood

1. *Use the subjunctive mood in the following situations.* The subjunctive mood occurs most often in a clause introduced by *if, whether, as if, as though,* or *that.* In the example sentences below, the underlined verbs are in the subjunctive mood.

   a. Expressing doubt or uncertainty.

   "And Pilate marvelled if [Jesus] were already dead."
   "For which of you, intending to build a tower, sitteth not down first, and counteth the cost, whether he have sufficient to finish it?"

   b. Expressing a wish or desire.

   "Grace be unto you."   I wish it were not so late.

   c. Expressing a supposition, a condition contrary to fact, or something unlikely.

   How would you feel if your own life were in danger?
   "If righteousness come by the law, then Christ is dead in vain."

   d. Expressing recommendation, request, command, or necessity in a *that* clause.

   I move that a committee be appointed to investigate the matter.
   Daniel asked that Melzar prove the four young men for ten days.

2. *In a* that *clause expressing recommendation, request, command, or necessity, use the present subjunctive form even if other verbs in the sentence are in a different tense.*

Father will ask that the judge <u>consider</u> his religious convictions.

(*Consider* is present tense even though *will ask* is future tense.)

God has commanded that children <u>obey</u> their parents.

(*Obey* is present tense even though *has commanded* is present perfect tense.)

Jesus directed that His disciples <u>wait</u> at Jerusalem.

(*Wait* is present tense even though *directed* is past tense.)

3. *Use the subjunctive mood to avoid unnecessary* would *phrases.* When a sentence has a dependent *if* or *that* clause, the main clause often uses *would* as a helping verb. *Would* may seem to fit in the dependent clause too, but that is not a standard usage. You will avoid repeating *would,* and you will express your idea more concisely, if you use the subjunctive mood in the *if* or *that* clause. Study these examples and explanations.

Two *would* phrases:

If I <u>would be</u> you, I *would* use a different recipe.

Improved with subjunctive:

If I <u>were</u> you, I *would* use a different recipe.

(Subjunctive form *I were* fits in a statement that is contrary to fact.)

Two *would* phrases:

I *would* like to propose that these old curtains <u>would be replaced</u>.

Improved with subjunctive:

I *would* like to propose that these old curtains <u>be replaced</u>.

(Subjunctive form *be replaced* is used in a recommendation. Also note that the recommendation is given in the present tense.)

Two *would* phrases:

If you <u>would have started</u> sooner, you *would* have arrived on time.

Improved with subjunctive:

If you <u>had started</u> sooner, you *would* have arrived on time.

(*If you had started sooner* is a statement contrary to fact. This requires using the subjunctive mood. Is *had started* a subjunctive form? Yes, because the subjunctive and the indicative forms are exactly the same. Remember, subjunctive mood differs from indicative mood only in the three situations listed earlier in this lesson.)

The verbs in most sentences are in the indicative mood—the mood that tells or asks about things as they really are. But a verb in the imperative mood is necessary for telling someone to do something, and a verb in the subjunctive mood is useful for speaking of something that is doubted, wished, or supposed.

Applying the Lesson

A. Copy each underlined verb, and write whether its mood is indicative (*ind.*), imperative (*imp.*), or subjunctive (*sub.*).

1. If the Gospel <u>were lived</u> as much as it is professed, this world <u>would be</u> a better place.
2. The Gospel standard <u>requires</u> that the Christian <u>practice</u> nonresistance in his daily life.
3. "<u>Marvel</u> not, my brethren, if the world <u>hate</u> you."
4. <u>Trust</u> in the Lord with all your heart.
5. The hypocrite <u>acts</u> as if God <u>were</u> a man whom he might deceive.
6. Never <u>act</u> as if the world <u>were</u> a friend to grace.
7. <u>Will</u> you please <u>talk</u> more quietly.
8. The Lord <u>strengthen</u> you in these trials.
9. I <u>move</u> that the treasurer <u>purchase</u> a fan for each classroom.
10. If I <u>be</u> in the wrong, I <u>expect</u> you to tell me frankly and graciously.
11. The serviceman <u>recommends</u> that the belts <u>be replaced</u> now.
12. This tree <u>looks</u> as if it <u>were</u> ready to die.
13. If the title deed <u>be</u> clear, Father <u>will buy</u> the property.
14. I <u>wish</u> this weather <u>were</u> more seasonable.

B. Choose the words that are correct for the subjunctive mood.

1. David would not have enjoyed God's blessing if he (would have killed, had killed) King Saul.
2. If the Christian (pray, prays) in faith, God promises to hear and answer.
3. I wonder if this verse (be, is) the one Mr. Caldwell referred to.
4. If the Christian soldier (fail, fails) to take God's armor, he will surely suffer defeat.
5. The blessing of the Lord (be, is) upon you as you face life's daily challenges.
6. God commands that prayer (be, is) offered in Jesus' Name.
7. The stranger spoke as if he (was, were) well versed in local history.
8. Suppose this (was, were) our last public worship service.
9. If the passerby (would not have noticed, had not noticed) the smoke, the house may have burned completely.
10. Even if the temperature (would have dropped, had dropped) below freezing, the breeze would have kept the frost from forming.
11. I wish this garden (was, were) more productive.
12. Brother Harold requested that each student (choose, chose) a verse or saying for a motto.
13. If this assignment (prove, proves) as easy as Larry says, I shall be surprised.
14. The fire chief gave orders that all traffic (be, was) routed off the main road.
15. If that bull (was, were) to charge, we would be in trouble!
16. That cat acts as if she (was, were) the queen of the farm.

C. Write a subjunctive verb or verb phrase to replace each underlined *would* phrase.
  1. We would go to church this morning if the snowplow <u>would have opened</u> our road.
  2. I would appreciate if this cocoa <u>would be</u> a little sweeter.
  3. I move that the treasurer <u>would make</u> copies of the financial report before each meeting.
  4. Our elderly neighbors have requested that the church <u>would hold</u> a service in their home.
  5. If that storm <u>would have been</u> much worse, we would have suffered severe damage.
  6. If we children <u>would have worked</u> harder, we would easily have been finished on time.

Review Exercises

A. Choose the correct words in these sentences. [56]
  1. Grandfather was telling my brothers and (I, me) about life during the Great Depression.
  2. How much his boyhood life differed from (ours, our's) today!
  3. His family and (he, himself) ground wheat in a hand mill, cooked it, and ate it for cereal.
  4. He told how (they, them) and other families roasted corn from their corncrib and ground it to make mush.
  5. "For dessert," he said, "(we, us) children would take turns licking a three-cent postage stamp!"
  6. I fear that I am not as thankful as (he, him) for the blessings we enjoy today.

B. Choose the correct words in these sentences. [57]
  1. During (that, that there) depression, many people lost their jobs and went out to the country to work for farmers.
  2. Most of the food prices (seem, seems) unbelievably low to us today.
  3. A loaf of bread sold for four to six cents and a fat hog for five dollars; either (seem, seems) extremely cheap today.
  4. Some of Grandfather's time (was, were) spent in catching pigeons, which he sold for twelve cents apiece.
  5. A man (who, which) was selling magazines traded a subscription for a fat hen.
  6. On one occasion when the family desperately needed money, God sent a man to (who, whom) they sold all the old rags they could find.
  7. One day they walked to town; and the grocer, (who, which) wanted to make a sale, agreed to drive them home if they would buy a basket of sweet potatoes.
  8. "For meal after meal, we ate beans and potatoes," Grandfather said. "But sometimes, for (everyone's, everyones) relief, we varied the menu and ate potatoes and beans!"

69. Transitive and Intransitive Verbs

Verbs are classified according to their tense, their form, and their mood. They are also classified as either transitive or intransitive.

Transitive Verbs

The word *transitive* comes from a Latin word that means "passing over." A transitive verb passes its action to a substantive in the sentence. Transitive verbs are in the *active voice* or the *passive voice,* depending on the receiver of their action.

1. *A transitive verb in the active voice passes its action to the direct object.* The subject performs the action, and the direct object receives the action. A verb with a direct object may also have an indirect object or an objective complement.

> God strengthened Stephen for his trials.
> (*Stephen* is the direct object of *strengthened.*)
> God gave Stephen strength for his trials.
> (*Strength* is the direct object of *gave,* and *Stephen* is the indirect object.)
> God made Stephen strong to face his trials.
> (*Stephen* is the direct object of *made,* and *strong* is the objective complement.)

The direct object may be a verbal, a verbal phrase, or a noun clause.

> A selfless person wants to serve. (verbal)
> A thoughtful person enjoys making others happy. (verbal phrase)
> A meek person recognizes that he is small in God's eyes. (noun clause)

2. *A transitive verb in the passive voice passes its action to the subject.* In the passive voice, the subject receives the action rather than performing it. Often the doer of the action is named later in the sentence, by a substantive in a phrase beginning with *by.* A verb in the passive voice consists of the past participle with a form of *be* as a helping verb.

> Stephen was strengthened for his trials by God.
> (*Stephen* receives the action of *was strengthened.*)
> Strength and wisdom were given to this faithful martyr by God.
> (*Strength* and *wisdom* receive the action of *were given.*)

Intransitive Verbs

Just as *transitive* means "passing over," so *intransitive* means "not passing over." An intransitive verb does not pass its action to a substantive in the sentence. Intransitive verbs divide into two groups: intransitive complete and intransitive linking.

1. *An intransitive complete verb expresses action but does not pass the action to a receiver.* The meaning of the skeleton is complete without a complement.

> For a long time, the exhausted man slept.
> The lambs romped playfully in the pasture.

Some intransitive complete verbs may seem to pass their action to the subject. However, both the meaning of the sentence and the form of the verb show that the subject actually is performing the action.

> A coherent paragraph <u>reads</u> smoothly.
> (intransitive complete; *reads smoothly* means the paragraph flows smoothly; subject performs this action; verb is simple present form)
> The paragraph <u>was read</u> smoothly by Rachel
> (transitive verb in the passive voice; subject receives the action performed by *Rachel;* verb consists of a past participle with a form of *be* as a helping verb)

Some verbs may be either transitive or intransitive complete, depending on their use in a sentence. Most dictionaries give specific definitions for both transitive and intransitive uses of such verbs.

> We <u>hoed</u> the entire bean patch this morning.
> (transitive; *bean patch* receives the action)
> We <u>hoed</u> in the garden all morning.
> (intransitive complete; no receiver of the action)

2. *An intransitive linking verb expresses a condition or a state of being.* Such a verb often has little meaning of its own; it serves mainly to link the subject to the subjective complement. The subjective complement may be either a predicate nominative, which renames the subject, or a predicate adjective, which modifies the subject.

The most common linking verbs are the forms of *be: am, is, are, was, were, be, been, being.* Linking verbs also include verbs of sense (*taste, feel, smell, sound, look, appear*) and some other verbs (*grow, seem, stay, become, remain, turn, prove*).

> Anton van Leeuwenhoek <u>was</u> a Dutch naturalist.
> (*Naturalist* is a predicate nominative renaming *Anton van Leeuwenhoek.*)
> His efforts at making a simple microscope <u>proved</u> effective.
> (*Effective* is a predicate adjective modifying *efforts.*)

Do not confuse a linking verb followed by an adjective with an intransitive complete verb followed by an adverb or with a transitive verb in the active or passive voice. Except for the forms of *be,* most of the linking verbs can also function as transitive verbs or as intransitive complete verbs. A verb is intransitive linking only when it expresses a condition or a state of being rather than an action.

> Diane <u>felt</u> quite contented with the decision. (*Felt* expresses a condition; it links *Diane* and *contented. Felt* is intransitive linking.)
> Diane <u>felt</u> carefully for the light switch. (*Felt* expresses action; there is no receiver of the action. *Felt* is intransitive complete.)
> Diane <u>felt</u> the smoothness of the sanded board. (*Felt* expresses action; *smoothness* receives the action. *Felt* is transitive active.)
> A friendly attitude usually is <u>felt</u> easily. (*Felt* expresses action; *attitude* receives the action. *Felt* is transitive passive.)

A sentence diagram can help you to quickly tell whether a verb is transitive or intransitive. If a direct object follows the verb, it is a transitive verb in the active voice. If the verb is a past participle with a form of *be* as a helping verb, it is a transitive verb in the passive voice. If the verb is not passive and it has no complement, it is an intransitive complete verb. And if a predicate nominative or predicate adjective follows the verb, it is an intransitive linking verb.

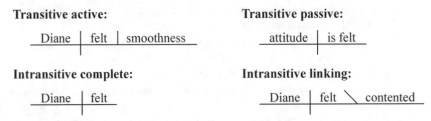

Transitive active:

Diane | felt | smoothness

Transitive passive:

attitude | is felt

Intransitive complete:

Diane | felt

Intransitive linking:

Diane | felt \ contented

Applying the Lesson

A. Copy each verb and the substantive that receives its action. Label the verb *active* or *passive.*
1. About 1440, Johannes Gutenberg invented a printing press with movable type.
2. Gutenberg's interest in such a printing press was motivated by his desire to print Bibles.
3. Until that time, Bibles were copied laboriously by hand.
4. This process made the cost of Bibles prohibitively high.
5. Few common people could own a personal copy of the Bible.
6. Within a few decades of this invention, Europe was shaken by the Protestant Reformation and the Anabaptist movement.
7. The fires of these revivals could be spread rapidly through the printed page.
8. Certainly God was accomplishing His purpose through Gutenberg's work.

B. Write whether each underlined verb is transitive (*T*) or intransitive complete (*IC*).
1. The Norwegian Sea, part of the Atlantic Ocean, <u>lies</u> north of Great Britain.
2. It <u>extends</u> fingers called fjords deep into the coast of Norway.
3. Although it is in the far north, ice rarely <u>covers</u> the Norwegian Sea.
4. The North Atlantic Current <u>brings</u> a warming influence.
5. The North Sea <u>borders</u> Great Britain on the east.
6. The North Sea <u>served</u> as an important buffer zone for Great Britain.
7. Large numbers of fish <u>live</u> in the waters of the North Sea.
8. Great reserves of oil and natural gas <u>do lie</u> beneath its waters.

C. Copy each linking verb and the words that it links.
1. The Bible is the inspired revelation of God to man.
2. It will always be the fountain of true wisdom.
3. Its promises have been a source of encouragement to saints of all ages.
4. Even before the New Testament era, its truth had been the anchor to every saint.
5. Its prophecies prove accurate every time.
6. Its counsels should taste sweet to our spiritual senses.

D. Copy each verb, and label it *TA* (transitive, active voice), *TP* (transitive, passive voice), *IC* (intransitive complete), or *IL* (intransitive linking).

1. The Pharos at Alexandria is listed as one of the seven wonders of the ancient world.
2. The Pharos was the tallest lighthouse ever built.
3. This lighthouse stood on an island two hundred yards from the mainland.
4. The lighthouse was built at the entrance of the harbor at Alexandria.
5. The Pharos was a magnificent marble structure.
6. This great structure endured for sixteen hundred years.
7. Either wood or oil fueled the lamp of the lighthouse.
8. The huge lamp cast a powerful beam far out across the waters.
9. Every day donkeys carried supplies of fuel up broad ramps to the top of the lighthouse.
10. The base of the Pharos became the home of a military barracks.
11. The structure of this lighthouse proved amazingly solid.
12. However, an earthquake destroyed the Pharos in the fourteenth century.

Review Exercises

Name the tense of the underlined verb in each sentence. [67]

1. Ever since childhood, most of us <u>had</u> the privilege of reading daily from the Bible.
2. The sincere reader <u>will find</u> that this is like drawing water from a living well.
3. Archaeologists <u>have found</u> two ancient wells in the area of Beer-sheba.
4. The larger one <u>is</u> 12½ feet in diameter and about 66 feet deep.
5. Through centuries of time, the ropes of the water buckets <u>had worn</u> deep grooves in the old stone curb of the well.
6. When I am old, <u>will</u> I <u>have made</u> "grooves" in my mind by drawing daily from the well of living water?

---

70. Forms of Verbs

All verbs have six tenses—three simple and three perfect. Within these tenses, verbs also have three different forms that give them slightly different shades of meaning. The three forms are *simple, progressive,* and *emphatic.* We use these different verb forms to give precise expression to the ideas we want to convey.

Verb Forms in the Active Voice

1. *The simple form of a verb expresses an action or a condition as simply as possible.* The only helping verbs used with the simple form are *shall* and *will* (for the simple future tense) and forms of *have* (for the perfect tenses). The simple form is the one you immediately think of when you are asked to give a particular verb in any tense. In all the previous lessons of this chapter, the focus has been on the simple form of verbs.

Simple form:
    Present: I <u>help</u> my mother.
    Past: I <u>helped</u> my mother.
    Future: I <u>shall help</u> my mother.
    Present perfect: I <u>have helped</u> my mother.
    Past perfect: I <u>had helped</u> my mother.
    Future perfect: I <u>shall have helped</u> my mother.

2. *The progressive form uses the present participle with a form of* be *as a helping verb.* In contrast to the simple form, the progressive form emphasizes that an action or a condition is in progress. Each of the six tenses has a progressive form.

Progressive form:
    Present: I <u>am helping</u> my mother.
    Past: I <u>was helping</u> my mother.
    Future: I <u>shall be helping</u> my mother.
    Present perfect: I <u>have been helping</u> my mother.
    Past perfect: I <u>had been helping</u> my mother.
    Future perfect: I <u>shall have been helping</u> my mother.

3. *The emphatic form uses the first principal part with a form of* do *as a helping verb.* As its name suggests, this form gives added emphasis, perhaps in response to a question or a doubt. Only the present and past tenses have emphatic forms, because sentences like "I do will help" and "I did had helped" would be extremely awkward.

Emphatic form:
    Present: I <u>do help</u> my mother.
    Past: I <u>did help</u> my mother.

The helping verbs *do* and *did* are also used in questions and negative statements. The verb form in such a sentence is simple rather than emphatic.

    <u>Do</u> you <u>help</u> your mother? (present tense, simple form)
    I <u>did</u> not <u>help</u> my mother. (past tense, simple form)

Verb Forms in the Passive Voice

4. *The simple form of a verb in the passive voice is the past participle with a form of* be *as a helping verb.* This is the simplest verb form that will pass an action to the subject of a sentence.

Simple form:
    Present: I <u>am helped</u> by my sister.
    Past: I <u>was helped</u> by my sister.
    Future: I <u>shall be helped</u> by my sister.
    Present perfect: I <u>have been helped</u> by my sister.
    Past perfect: I <u>had been helped</u> by my sister.
    Future perfect: I <u>shall have been helped</u> by my sister.

5. *The progressive form of a verb in the passive voice is made with the addition of* being *as a helping verb.* As in the active voice, the verb phrase contains a present participle—but the *-ing* is added to *be* rather than the main verb. Such a verb phrase contains two forms of *be:* a form like *am, is,* or *was* for the passive voice, and *being* for the progressive form. In the passive voice, however, the progressive form commonly occurs only in the present and past tenses. The other forms are too awkward because of the many helping verbs required.

Progressive form:
Present: I am being helped by my sister.
Past: I was being helped by my sister.

(Forms seldom used because of their awkwardness)
Future: I shall be being helped by my sister.
Present perfect: I have been being helped by my sister.
Past perfect: I had been being helped by my sister.
Future perfect: I shall have been being helped by my sister.

6. *The emphatic form never occurs in the passive voice, because it is too awkward and illogical.* The emphatic form would require constructions like *I do am helped* and *I did was helped.*

Study the following chart, which compares the three forms of verbs in both the active voice and the passive voice.

Comparison of Verb Forms
Active Voice

	Simple Form	*Progressive Form* Made with a form of *be* and *-ing*	*Emphatic Form* Made with a form of *do*
Present:	I help.	I am helping.	I do help.
Past:	I helped.	I was helping.	I did help.
Future:	I shall help.	I shall be helping.	(too awkward)
Pr. perf.:	I have helped.	I have been helping.	
Past perf.:	I had helped.	I had been helping.	
Fut. perf.:	I shall have helped.	I shall have been helping.	

Passive Voice

	Simple Form Made with a form of *be* and a past participle	*Progressive Form* Made with two forms of *be* and a past participle	*Emphatic Form* (not used at all)
Present:	I am helped.	I am being helped.	
Past:	I was helped.	I was being helped.	
Future:	I shall be helped.	(too awkward; seldom used)	
Pr. perf.:	I have been helped.		
Past perf.:	I had been helped.		
Fut. perf.:	I shall have been helped.		

Applying the Lesson

A. Identify the form of each underlined verb as *simple, progressive,* or *emphatic.*
   1. As the nineteenth century <u>dawned</u>, large herds of bison <u>were roaming</u> the Great Plains.
   2. White men, as well as Indians, <u>hunted</u> bison extensively, for the flesh of bison <u>does resemble</u> that of cattle.
   3. Although we <u>do plan</u> to travel through the Great Plains, we likely <u>will look</u> in vain for vast herds of bison.
   4. Some farmers <u>have been crossing</u> bison successfully with beef cattle; this cross <u>combines</u> the good qualities of both animals.
   5. The past decades <u>do show</u> a definite growth in the bison population, and these trends <u>are indicating</u> a significant increase over the next fifty years.
   6. Concerned people <u>have been trying</u> to protect the bison, and these efforts <u>did help</u> to bring them back from the brink of extinction.

B. Copy the chart below, and fill in the blanks with all the forms for the following two skeletons.
   1. She seeks.   2. You tap.

Verb Forms
Active Voice

	Simple Form	*Progressive Form*	*Emphatic Form*
Present:	_____	_____	_____
Past:	_____	_____	_____
Future:	_____	_____	
Pr. perf.:	_____	_____	
Past perf.:	_____	_____	
Fut. perf.:	_____	_____	

Passive Voice

	Simple Form	*Progressive Form*	*Emphatic Form*
Present:	_____	_____	
Past:	_____	_____	
Future:	_____		
Pr. perf.:	_____		
Past perf.:	_____		
Fut. perf.:	_____		

C. Write the progressive form and the emphatic form of each underlined verb. If such a form is awkward or nonexistent, write *none.* Do not change the tense of the verb.
   1. Father <u>expects</u> to plant corn this afternoon.

2. Grandmother Ebersole <u>needs</u> someone to help her clean this Saturday.
3. Gospel literature <u>was distributed</u> by our congregation in the nearby villages.
4. Next week a group <u>will hold</u> a street meeting in the city.
5. Brethren from our congregation <u>have placed</u> tract racks at various local businesses.
6. Before our little mission was started on Stone Ridge Mountain, no church had held regular services in that area.

D. Identify the tense, voice, and form of each underlined verb.
1. Because the birds <u>were being fed</u> regularly, they became quite tame.
2. The squirrels certainly <u>do enjoy</u> the ear corn we put out for them.
3. Even before winter set in, we <u>had been filling</u> the bird feeders.
4. Our family <u>keeps</u> a record of the kinds of birds that come to our feeders.

Review Exercises

A. Write whether the underlined sentence part is a nominative absolute (*NA*) or a participial phrase (*PP*). [21]
1. <u>Jesus Christ having died</u>, the Old Testament system has been done away.
2. <u>The New Testament being in force</u>, believers worship on the Lord's Day.
3. <u>Seated at the Father's right hand</u>, Jesus intercedes for believers.
4. <u>Trusting in the Father's grace</u>, believers find strength to overcome.

B. Rewrite each sentence, changing the underlined subordinate clause to a nominative absolute. [21]
1. <u>Since the electricity had gone off</u>, we ate a cold supper in a cold kitchen.
2. We could not wash the dishes <u>because electricity is needed to pump and heat the water</u>.
3. <u>After the repair crews had worked many hours</u>, electricity was restored to the area.
4. <u>Because electricity is so important in our lives</u>, we hardly know what to do without it.

---

71. Subject–Verb Agreement

For the vast majority of sentences, you have very little problem with subject–verb agreement. Some situations, however, do deserve special attention. The following rules give you specific direction in these problem areas.

1. *When the verb precedes the subject, think ahead to the subject and make the verb agree with it.* In many questions and in most sentences beginning with *there* or *here,* the verb or a part of the verb phrase precedes the subject.

<u>Do</u> <u>temptations</u> <u>threaten</u> to overwhelm you?
There <u>are</u> abundant <u>blessings</u> <u>promised</u> to the overcomer.

2. *Make the verb agree with the subject, not with some other substantive in the sentence.* Be especially careful when a prepositional phrase comes between the subject and the verb, and when a subject and its predicate nominative differ in number.

A <u>book</u> of poems <u>makes</u> a worthwhile gift.
A <u>goose</u>, in addition to several ducks, <u>was swimming</u> on our pond.
The <u>vegetable</u> for our lunch <u>is</u> peas.
<u>Peas</u> <u>are</u> my favorite vegetable.

3. *Use a contraction as you would use the words it represents.* Be especially alert to the contractions *here's, there's, how's, what's,* and *don't.*

Incorrect: <u>Here's</u> (Here is) the books that you wanted.
          This book <u>don't</u> (do not) help me much.
Correct: <u>Here are</u> the books that you wanted.
          This book <u>doesn't</u> help me much.

4. *Use a plural verb with a compound subject joined by* and. The conjunction *and* means that the verb expresses action or condition for all parts of the subject.

<u>Hydrogen</u> and <u>oxygen</u> <u>combine</u> to form water. (Two <u>elements</u> <u>combine</u>.)
<u>James</u> and <u>John</u> <u>were</u> sons of Zebedee. (<u>Both</u> <u>were</u> sons.)

Sometimes a compound subject names only one person or thing, as when one person holds two positions or one dish is composed of two foods. In this case, the verb is singular and an article or a possessive pronoun is used only before the first noun. In contrast, if the compound subject names two different persons or objects, the verb is plural and an article or a possessive pronoun is used before each of the nouns.

The <u>missionary</u> and <u>tentmaker</u> <u>was</u> zealous for the Lord.
     (One <u>man</u> <u>was</u> zealous.)
The <u>physician</u> and the <u>tentmaker</u> <u>were</u> fellow laborers.
     (Two <u>men</u> <u>were</u> fellow laborers.)
<u>Ham</u> and <u>eggs</u> <u>is</u> a favorite breakfast dish at our house.
     (One <u>dish</u> <u>is</u> favorite.)

5. *Follow these rules for compound subjects joined by* or *or* nor.
   a. If both subjects are singular, use a singular verb.

      Neither <u>Luther</u> nor <u>Zwingli</u> <u>was</u> willing to break with the state church.

   b. If both subjects are plural, use a plural verb.

      <u>Traitors</u> or <u>spies</u> <u>were</u> sometimes able to have large groups of Anabaptists arrested.

   c. If one subject is singular and one is plural, make the verb agree with the subject that is nearer to the verb.

      Neither the <u>minister</u> nor the <u>worshipers</u> <u>were expecting</u> the soldiers.
      Neither the <u>worshipers</u> nor the <u>minister</u> <u>was expecting</u> the soldiers.

6. *Use a singular verb with a singular indefinite pronoun.* These pronouns are as follows: *each, either, neither, one, another, anybody, anyone, anything, everybody, everyone, everything, somebody, someone, something, nobody, no one, nothing.*

> <u>Either</u> of these Scripture verses <u>is</u> suitable for this scrapbook page.
> <u>Nobody</u> <u>has offered</u> to wash the dishes.

7. *Use the correct verb with indefinite pronouns that may be either singular or plural.* These include *some, any, none, all,* and *most.* Such a pronoun is singular if its antecedent is singular. (The antecedent is usually stated in a prepositional phrase after the pronoun.) The indefinite pronoun then means a certain portion of that one thing and takes a singular verb. But the pronoun is plural if the antecedent is plural. Then the indefinite pronoun means certain individual items in that set of things, and it takes a plural verb.

> <u>Some</u> of the hamburger <u>has gotten</u> too dark.
> <u>Some</u> of the hamburgers <u>have gotten</u> too dark.

8. *Use a singular verb with a noun that is plural in form but singular in meaning.* This includes nouns like *news* and *gallows,* names of diseases like *measles* and *mumps,* and words ending with *-ics* like *civics* and *ethics.*

> Untreated <u>rabies</u> <u>is</u> generally fatal.
> <u>Physics</u> <u>includes</u> a study of matter and energy.

9. *Usually a plural verb is used with a noun that names an item made of paired parts.* This includes words like *shears, trousers, pliers, glasses, tweezers,* and *tongs.* If the subject is *pair* followed by one of these nouns in a prepositional phrase, the verb must agree with the singular *pair.*

> Mother's new <u>shears</u> <u>were left</u> on the floor.
> Mother's new <u>pair</u> of shears <u>was left</u> on the floor.

10. *If a collective noun refers to a group acting as a unit, use a singular verb. If a collective noun refers to individual members of the group acting separately, use a plural verb.* A collective noun names a collection of individuals. Some common collective nouns are *group, family, congregation, herd, flock,* and *swarm.* In many sentences, a word like *its* or *our* helps to show whether the group is acting unitedly or separately.

> The <u>family</u> <u>is enjoying</u> a quiet evening at home.
>   (Family acting as a unit, doing the same thing.)
> The <u>family</u> <u>are preparing</u> their different gifts for Grandfather's birthday.
>   (Family members acting individually, doing different things; note the plural *their.*)

11. *Use a singular verb with a title or a word that is a subject of discussion.*

> <u>*Lights in Dark Places*</u> <u>recounts</u> stories of Christian witness under test.
> <u>*Crises*</u> <u>is</u> the plural of *crisis.*

12. *Use a singular verb with a subject that is plural in form but which indicates a quantity or is regarded as a unit.*

Two tons was our order. (This quantity was our order.)
Fifty miles is too far to drive tonight. (This distance is too far to drive tonight.)

13. *Make the verb after a relative pronoun agree with the antecedent of the relative pronoun.*

Some of the *work* that was assigned required much patience.
Some of the *jobs* that were assigned required much patience.

Sometimes a relative pronoun follows a phrase like *the only one.* Then the antecedent is singular, and the verb in the relative clause should be singular.

She was *the only one* of the students who was ready.
   (*Who was ready* modifies *one;* the antecedent of *who* is the singular *one.* The sentence indicates that only one student was ready.)
She was *one* of the students who were ready.
   (*Who were ready* modifies *students;* the antecedent of *who* is the plural *students.* The sentence indicates that several students were ready.)

14. *For words like* plenty, abundance, *and* rest *and for fractions followed by a phrase beginning with* of, *the object of the preposition following the subject determines the number of the subject.*

The rest of the cake was eaten.
The rest of the cookies were eaten.

One-third of the class is absent.
One-third of the students are absent.

Applying the Lesson
A. Choose the correct word or phrase.
   1. (What's, What are) some Bible promises for the tempted?
   2. One of the verses that (have, has) encouraged me is 1 Corinthians 10:13.
   3. Neither carelessness nor indifference (mark, marks) the sincere Christian.
   4. None of our sincere prayers (fail, fails) to touch God's heart.
   5. An important aid to our own consistency (is, are) friends who are consistent.
   6. The congregation (is, are) contributing their various abilities to the life and work of the church.
   7. An abundance of crops (have, has) already been harvested.
   8. I have memorized some of the Scripture verses that (was, were) read.
   9. Christian ethics (include, includes) treating others as we would have them treat us.
   10. The writer and artist (is, are) working on a new book.
   11. "Jesus' Disciples" (describe, describes) in poetic form the lives of the Twelve.
   12. Over one-half of the earth's population (live, lives) in Asia.
   13. Here (is, are) some interesting stories from long ago.

14. Either the employer or the employees (was, were) mistaken.
15. Some of God's creatures (use, uses) tools.
16. Brown capuchin monkeys and thread-waisted wasps (hammer, hammers) with stones.
17. A troop of these monkeys (is, are) using stones to crack nuts for their meal.
18. Now a feast of nuts (satisfy, satisfies) their hunger.
19. The wasp's pliers—its mandibles—(hold, holds) a pebble.
20. The wasp (don't, doesn't) have great strength, but with its pebble hammer it soon packs shut a nest that will protect its young.
21. The weaver ant appears to be the only one of God's creatures that (use, uses) its own young as tools.
22. One of the unique characteristics of weaver ant larvae (is, are) their ability to make silk, which the adult ant uses in making its nest.
23. The larva and silk producer (release, releases) silk on a branch or leaf when the adult ant squeezes it.
24. The branches or leaves (is, are) then held together with this silk.
25. The meat or the potatoes (smell, smells) burnt.
26. My trousers (is, are) neatly pressed and hanging in the closet.
27. Put the bread that (was, were) buttered on the plate.
28. The only one of the calves that (is, are) weaned should be moved today.
29. One hundred pounds (is, are) more than Mrs. Haddock can lift into her car.
30. The news of the fire (was, were) quite a shock.
31. Neither the teacher nor the students (was, were) expecting the fire drill.
32. *Larvae* (rhyme, rhymes) with *Harvey.*
33. Either of these books (give, gives) useful information for your report.
34. Fifty years (is, are) a long time to be confined to a wheelchair.
35. The kittens and the little rabbits (play, plays) together.
36. An ice cream cone or a Popsicle (refresh, refreshes) a hot, tired worker.

B. Rewrite each sentence, following the directions in parentheses and changing the verb as needed to agree with the subject. Do not change the tense of the verb.

1. The sermons today were preached with conviction. (Insert *Each of* before *sermons.*)
2. Mrs. Keller is one of our customers who have ordered garlic bread. (Insert *the only* before *one.*)
3. Neither evil powers nor our carnal nature is able to force us away from God. (Reverse the order of the subjects.)
4. There's a great blessing in store for those who love the Lord. (Change *a great blessing* to *many blessings.*)
5. Most of these poems emphasize the beauty of nature. (Change *these poems* to *this poem.*)
6. The herd of elk are seeking to protect themselves from the storm. (Change the ending to *migrating across the plain.*)
7. This pair of scissors is dull and nicked. (Change *This pair of* to *These.*)
8. These library books don't belong here. (Insert *One of* before *These.*)

9. Mother and Helen bake bread each week. (Change *and* to *or.*)
10. I want all of the material that blends well with this green. (Change *material* to *scraps.*)
11. One-fourth of the soybeans have been harvested. (Change *soybeans* to *soybean field.*)
12. This pair of glasses needs to be replaced. (Change *This pair of* to *These.*)
13. Neil is one of the boys who have muddy shoes. (Insert *the only* before *one.*)
14. All of this hay was moved from our other farm. (Change *this hay* to *these bales.*)
15. My fingers that were burned might have permanent scars. (Change *fingers* to *hand.*)
16. Joseph and Lloyd feed the cows. (Change *and* to *or.*)
17. There's quite a collection of pictures here from previous generations. (Change *collection of* to *few.*)
18. Either the applesauce or the pears have a sour smell. (Reverse the order of the subjects.)
19. These pies don't look very good. (Insert *One of* before *These.*)
20. Plenty of food has been provided for the crew. (Change *food* to *refreshments.*)
21. The group of girls are finding various jobs to do. (Change the ending to *singing for Sister Lucille.*)
22. These answers make good sense. (Insert *Either of* before *These.*)

Review Exercises

Choose the words that are correct for the subjunctive mood. [68]

1. If the man (was, were) trustworthy, we could believe his story more easily.
2. It is a shame indeed if a man (refuse, refuses) to do his duty.
3. If I (would have known, had known) you were here, I would have come sooner.
4. He lifted the sack of feed as if it (was, were) a bag of cotton.
5. The doctor ordered that Aunt Amy (rest, rests, rested) for the next two weeks.
6. Brother Edgar moved that the question (be, is, was) referred to a committee.
7. On any committee it is important that each member (do, does, did) his part of the work.
8. If Thomas (would have seen, had seen) the pothole, he would have swerved to miss it.
9. The Christian must always live in peace with his neighbors if it (be, is) possible.
10. If everyone (was, were) to respect and esteem others, how pleasant our relationships would be!

72. Improving Your Editing Skills, Part 8

Usually we observe the things that we have trained ourselves to notice. For example, one person walks along a woodland trail and laments the lack of wildlife. Another, walking the same trail, enjoys seeing numerous squirrels and chipmunks and birds—and hearing others. Where were those creatures the first time? They were there, but our friend failed to see them because he had not trained himself to catch the movements and sounds around him.

Editing written material works much the same way. One person reads through a paragraph and assures himself that it contains no mistakes. Another, reading the same paragraph, spots several misspellings and grammatical errors. Why the difference? One has trained his eyes to look for these errors; the other has not.

How do you train yourself to catch mistakes in writing? The more careful you are to use correct English in everyday speech and writing, the sharper you become in detecting errors. But if you excuse your errors and say or write things you know are incorrect, you will grow less sensitive. Do you allow yourself to use expressions like "It don't matter" or "He done it again" or "Them apples sure are good"? If so, you will find it hard to catch all the mistakes when you are editing—especially those that involve a fine detail of English grammar.

Whenever you become aware of an error in your use of English, you need to consciously raise yourself to a proper use of the language. This is the only way to develop a high degree of skill in editing.

Marks Used in Editing and Proofreading

$\vee$ or $\wedge$ insert (caret)	_____ꟼ delete	. . . . stet (let it stand)	_____ use italics
¶ begin new paragraph	no ¶ no new paragraph	*lc* change to lowercase (small letter)	*uc* change to uppercase (capital letter)
# insert space	⌒ delete space	← move (arrow)	⊓⊔ transpose

Editing Practice

A. Use proofreading marks to correct the ten spelling or spacing errors in these paragraphs. A line may have more than one error or none at all.

1. Matthew Henry, the well known Bible commentater, was once

2. robbed. Instead of weeping or fretting, he wrote the follow

3. ing entry in his dairy: "Let me be thankful. First, because

4. I was never robbed before. Second, because although they

5. took my wallet, they didnot take my life. Third, because

6. although they took my all, it was not much. Forth, because

7. it was I who was robbed, not I who robed."

8.   How well this ilustrates the Bible command to give

9. thanks in every thing (1 Thessalonians 5:18)! In all the

10. circumstances off life, God is good to His children.

B. Use proofreading marks to make these corrections in the selection below.
   a. Divide the first paragraph into two paragraphs.
   b. Correct two errors in sentence division.
   c. Improve the word order in two places.

1.   A prominent agnostic was scheduled in a certain city

2. to speak. Knowing about this, the local Christians began

3. praying that God would hinder the meeting fervently. They

4. feared that the speaker's persuasive arguments could

5. destroy the faith of their youth. When the evening arrived,

6. the agnostic took his place on the platform. "Ladies and

7. gentlemen," he began; then he paused and raised his hand

8. to his forehead. He tried several more times. But finally

9. turned to the chairman. "For some reason, my mind seems

10. clouded," he said, "and I am unable to continue."

11.   The agnostic left the city. Never to return.

C. Use proofreading marks to correct all the errors in this essay. No line has more than one error.

1.   Mont Blanc (pronounced *mông bläng'* or *mônt blangk*) is a

2. famous mountain in south eastern France. Reaching an alti-

3. tude of 15,771 feet (4,807 meters), this is the most highest

4. peak in the Alps. Its name in French means "white mountain."

5. And a white mountain it is, for above 8,000 feet (2,400

6. meters) a thick blanket of snow all ways covers its slopes.

7.   The French side of Mont Blanc slopes moderately and

8. has numerous glaciers. The most famous being Mer de Glace

9. (Sea of Ice). Two laboratories have built on the mountain

10. for the study of glaciers.

11. Climbers first reached thesummit of Mont Blanc over two

12. centuries ago, today the mountain is a resort center. Many

13. visitors climb its slopes, and a cog railway runs almost half

14. way up the mountain to Mer de Glace.

15. Interestingly, the base of Mont Blanc extends into three

16. different countries, France, Italy, and Switzerland. To

17. overcome its hinderances to travel, the French and Italians

18. have drilled through this mountain! In 1965 they opened a

19. tunnel with a length of 7 miles (11.7 kilometers) to connect

20. there countries. This tunnel is used for automobile traffic.

---

73.   Chapter 9 Review

A. Copy each verb or verb phrase, and write which tense it is. Also write whether it is *simple, progressive,* or *emphatic* in form.
1. Abraham's faith has earned him the name "The Father of the Faithful."
2. Lot finally did enter Sodom, but he had been making poor choices before.
3. The saints of all ages will be joining in worship before God's throne.
4. By the end of this month, I shall have read through the Bible twice.
5. Reading the Bible every day does not guarantee meaningful devotions.

B. Most of these sentences have mistakes in the use of verb principal parts. Write the correct verb, or write *correct.*
1. The new mango grove has growed quite well this year.
2. Have the boys went to pick oranges yet?
3. The wounded alligator drug itself out of the stream.
4. The three boys have drunk all the iced tea.
5. Have the girls did their baking?

C. Rewrite each sentence, changing one verb to a perfect tense so that the meaning is clearer or a completed action is emphasized.
1. Before we realized what was happening, the creek flooded our lane.
2. By the time Justin goes to school, we shall live here for ten years.
3. When Father called the fire department, he ran toward the burning car.

D. Copy each underlined verb, and write whether its mood is indicative (*ind.*), imperative (*imp.*), or subjunctive (*sub.*).
1. Absalom <u>allowed</u> pride to saturate his being.

2. He declared, "Oh that I <u>were made</u> judge in the land."
3. Please <u>turn</u> to 2 Samuel 15 and read this account.
4. <u>Did</u> you <u>notice</u> how subtly Absalom stole the hearts of the people?
5. He acted as though he <u>were</u> totally devoid of love and respect for his father.

E. Choose the words that are correct for the subjunctive mood.
   1. If God (delight, delights) in us, we need not fear man's scorn or wrath.
   2. The Bible commands that we (be, are) careful to avoid the appearance of evil.
   3. Father insisted that the unkind teasing (stop, stopped).
   4. If we (were, would be) ignorant of the Gospel, we would surely want to hear it.
   5. Suppose our freedom of religion (was, were) to be taken from us tomorrow!

F. Copy each verb, and label it *TA* (transitive, active voice), *TP* (transitive, passive voice), *IC* (intransitive complete), or *IL* (intransitive linking).
   1. Wintergreen grows well in densely to lightly shaded areas.
   2. This evergreen makes a good ground cover.
   3. A single plant can spread out to an area of one square yard.
   4. Wintergreen produces delicate bell-shaped flowers.
   5. The flowers are often hidden under the leaves.
   6. The plant bears scarlet, aromatic berries.
   7. These berries are eaten in cold weather by wild animals and birds.
   8. Oil of wintergreen is a familiar flavoring in candy, toothpaste, and medicine.

G. If the underlined verb or contraction does not agree with the subject, write the correct form. If it does agree, write *correct.*
   1. Clifford or Eugene <u>help</u> Mr. Dargon with his chores every day.
   2. He and his wife <u>was</u> injured in separate accidents last month.
   3. The news of these accidents <u>were</u> quite a shock to us.
   4. Six weeks <u>is</u> a long time to be laid up with injuries.
   5. Nearly one-fourth of our plants <u>seems</u> to be damaged.
   6. Nothing in these paragraphs <u>tell</u> us what we want to know.
   7. "Heroes of Faith" <u>is</u> a good title for Hebrews 11.
   8. <u>Does</u> the lives of these faithful saints inspire your faith?
   9. Marie is the only one of my cousins who <u>are</u> close to my age.
   10. My favorite snack <u>is</u> hard pretzels.
   11. The class <u>was</u> divided in their opinions on the best answer.
   12. We finally concluded that it <u>don't</u> matter which way you solve the problem.
   13. Most of the pudding <u>has</u> a scorched taste.
   14. Neither the broccoli nor the peppers <u>is</u> selling as well as we had hoped.
   15. All of the lawn that <u>was</u> mowed should be raked.
   16. The church and school <u>have</u> been built on a plot donated by Brother Leslie.
   17. The tweezers <u>are</u> not in the drawer.
   18. Sweaters or jackets <u>offers</u> little protection in this bitter cold.
   19. Our family <u>has</u> enjoyed the visit with Brother Eli.
   20. <u>There's</u> always small jobs around the farm that Grandfather can help with.

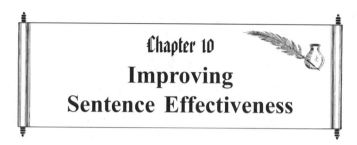

Chapter 10

Improving
Sentence Effectiveness

74. Achieving Unity and Coherence

The sentence represents the basic unit of communication. Therefore, any sincere effort to improve our writing must include a critical look at the effectiveness of the sentences that make up our writing. Unity and coherence rank as two of the most important qualities of every effective sentence.

Unity

To have unity, a sentence must communicate only one main idea clearly and logically. The following rules will help you to write unified sentences.

1. *Avoid writing run-on sentences.* A run-on sentence consists of two or more sentences written together as one, with no punctuation or with only a comma between them. Correct the problem by dividing the clauses into separate sentences, by using proper coordination, or by making one of the clauses a dependent clause.

> **Lacks unity:** Run-on sentence
> The Bible has answers to all moral questions, we must find them.
> **Unified sentences:**
> The Bible has answers to all moral questions. We must find them.
> The Bible has answers to all moral questions, but we must find them.
> The Bible has answers to all moral questions; however, we must find them.
> Although the Bible has answers to all moral questions, we must find them.

2. *Avoid writing sentence fragments.* The thought of a sentence fragment is incomplete because a sentence part is missing, or because the fragment belongs with another sentence.

> **Lacks unity:** Sentence fragment
> Congregational singing has filled a vital role in Christian worship. <u>For hundreds of years.</u>
> **Unified sentence:**
> Congregational singing has filled a vital role in Christian worship for hundreds of years.

Remember that a sentence fragment is different from an elliptical sentence, in which words are omitted because they are understood.

3. *Avoid cluttering a sentence with unnecessary details.* All the words in a sentence should work together to clearly express one main idea. Any modifying details should serve to clarify and strengthen that one idea. If a detail fails to do this, it mars the unity because it detracts from the main idea. Such a detail merely adds clutter to the sentence and should be removed.

Some details do not directly contribute to the main idea, but they do help to make the sentence understandable to the reader. You can use dashes or parentheses to set off such a detail, thus indicating its secondary importance. You can also put the detail into a separate sentence, and it can be the main idea there.

> **Lacks unity:** Cluttered with distracting details
> The son of the godly king Hezekiah, Manasseh, who became one of the most wicked kings to take the throne, had the longest reign of all the kings of Judah.
>
> **Unified sentences:**
> Manasseh had the longest reign of all the kings of Judah.
> (unnecessary details removed)
> Manasseh (the son of Hezekiah) had the longest reign of all the kings of Judah. (less important detail set off with parentheses)
> Manasseh had the longest reign of all the kings of Judah. Though the son of the godly king Hezekiah, he became one of the most wicked kings to take the throne. (less important detail put into a separate sentence)

Coherence

In a sentence with coherence, all the different parts stick together and communicate smoothly and clearly. The following rules will help you to write coherent sentences.

1. *Avoid unclear pronoun reference.* Sometimes a pronoun follows two nouns in a sentence, and either noun could logically be the antecedent. Rewrite such a sentence to make the antecedent clear.

> **Lacks coherence:** Two possible antecedents
> Sister Carol spent a day with Aunt Julia soon after <u>she</u> moved into this area.
> **Coherent:**
> Soon after Sister Carol moved into this area, she spent a day with Aunt Julia.
> Soon after Aunt Julia moved into this area, Sister Carol spent a day with her.

Another type of unclear pronoun reference occurs when a pronoun (especially *it* or *they*) is used in an abstract way, with no clear antecedent.

> **Lacks coherence:** Abstract pronoun
> We should obey our parents because <u>it</u> is important.
> At this bank <u>they</u> pay interest on some checking accounts.
> **Coherent:**
> We should obey our parents because obedience is important.
> We should practice obedience to our parents because it is important.
> This bank pays interest on some checking accounts.

2. *Avoid misplaced modifiers.* The position of modifiers like *almost, even, nearly,* and *only* can make a considerable difference in the meaning of a sentence. Compare the meanings of the following sentences. Can you also hear how you would emphasize different words in reading these sentences?

> Only George picked a bushel of lima beans. (Nobody except George picked lima beans.)
> George only picked a bushel of lima beans. (George did nothing other than picking lima beans.)
> George picked only a bushel of lima beans this morning. (George picked no more than one bushel of lima beans.)

Also position adjective phrases and clauses carefully so that they modify the right words.

> **Lacks coherence:** Misplaced modifier
> Finding many unclear sentences, my essay needed revision.
> (Did my essay find the unclear sentences?)
> Brother Galen read a poem from the teacher's guide that contained ten stanzas. (Did the teacher's guide contain ten stanzas?)
> **Coherent:**
> Finding many unclear sentences, I decided to revise my essay.
> From the teacher's guide, Brother Galen read a poem that contained ten stanzas.

3. *Avoid the careless separation of sentence skeletons, verb phrases, and infinitives.* When a long modifier or a long parenthetical element divides a skeleton or a verb phrase, the reader often has a hard time following the flow of the main thought.

> **Lacks coherence:**
> David, although he was facing great trials, behaved himself wisely. (divided skeleton)
> The creek has, ever since yesterday's heavy rain, flooded this road. (divided verb phrase)
> Father wants us to quickly finish our chores. (split infinitive)
> **Coherent:**
> Although he was facing great trials, David behaved himself wisely.
> Ever since yesterday's heavy rain, the creek has flooded this road.
> Father wants us to finish our chores quickly.

Many split infinitives not only disrupt the coherence but also weaken the emphasis of a sentence. Occasionally, however, a split infinitive provides the smoothest, clearest way to express an idea.

> **Acceptable split infinitive:**
> To always plan ahead is a mark of wisdom. (Placing *always* in any other position either changes the meaning of the sentence or makes the sentence awkward.)

Applying the Lesson

A. Rewrite these sentences, improving the unity.
1. Jesus asked the woman of Samaria for a drink. Even though Jews normally would not speak to Samaritans.
2. Zacchaeus opened his heart to Jesus' gracious words he renounced his dishonest ways.
3. As soon as Peter heard the report of the women, who had gone early in the morning to anoint Jesus' body, he ran to Jesus' tomb, which was in a garden.
4. The Israelites often fell into sin, the Lord kept calling them to repentance.
5. Uncle Paul gave some rabbits to Joel. For helping him on the farm.
6. Grandmother served a delicious apple pie that she had made with the large red apples we had picked.
7. A brisk breeze has been blowing all afternoon, the temperature has already dropped below freezing.
8. We received a good price for the black walnuts. Which the children picked up on our farm.

B. Rewrite these sentences, improving the coherence.
1. Mary anointed Jesus' head with ointment at Simon's house that cost three hundred pence.
2. In this verse it warns us against making a joke of evil things.
3. God promises to safely lead His people.
4. Saul honored David because he had bravely fought the Philistine giant.
5. When Paul preached to the Christians at Troas, it lasted all night.
6. Mary Magdalene saw a man near the sepulcher that she thought was the gardener.
7. It was too cold almost to work outside.
8. Darlene had, before morning was over, baked twelve loaves of bread.
9. Ananias came to Saul because he was now willing to learn the way of truth.
10. We only walked as far as the hickory grove in our woods.
11. Gray stratus clouds have been, ever since late morning, thickening to a heavy overcast.
12. They say that too many sweets are harmful to the body.
13. With my broken arm, I could only write with my left hand.
14. The neighbor's dog interrupted the class that was looking in the window.
15. In the mountains of Guatemala, they make terraces in steeply sloped fields.
16. Some Guatemalan farmers have fallen even out of their fields.
17. Eleanor sent her friend a letter that lives in Alabama.
18. I try to every evening before bedtime write a few sentences in my diary.

C. Rewrite these paragraphs, improving the unity and coherence of the sentences.

The leopard is the third largest member of the cat family, which lives in Africa and Asia. The lion and the tiger are only larger than the leopard. The male leopard has an average length of five feet. A weight of 150 to 200 pounds. Its tail helps to balance the leopard as it leaps through the air, which ranges from two to four feet long. The female, which is often occupied with caring for her young, is very similar in appearance to the male, she is slightly smaller.

Leopards can be more dangerous than lions or tigers even. Being agile tree climbers, their prey is often startled by an ambush from above. They may, since they are very much at home in the trees, carry their prey high into a tree to eat it. In fact, they may carry carcasses into trees weighing 80 to 150 pounds. They say that once a leopard learns that humans are easy prey, it becomes a deadly threat to man. A nocturnal prowler, a leopard may, without provocation or warning, attack a village, which is usually quite different from a North American town.

Review Exercises

A. Write the six key words that help us remember the six basic listening skills. (Remember, these words start with the letters *A–F.*) [10]

B. Tell whether each statement about outlining is true or false. [25–27]
1. An outline should contain all paragraphs, all sentences, or all topics.
2. We should never put just one subordinate point under an item.
3. The main headings of an outline should overlap in thought.
4. When forming an outline of a lesson, our first step is to read the lesson carefully, noting the major divisions.
5. Outlining a Bible passage is a good way to study the passage.
6. There may be several different ways to outline the same Bible passage.
7. Before we are ready to outline a Bible passage, we must answer this question: What is the primary truth these verses are teaching?
8. Before finalizing the main divisions of an outline, we should fill in the details.

---

75. Adding Emphasis

When we talk, we use various methods to emphasize our most important ideas. We raise our voices in volume and in pitch; we gesture with our hands; and we may look directly into the eyes of our listeners. Since we cannot use these methods to emphasize written ideas, we must find some other means to show emphasis. This lesson discusses methods that writers can use to give the desired emphasis to their ideas.

Repetition

1. *Repeat key words.* You have learned that a good way to gain paragraph coherence is to repeat key words and synonyms for them. Something similar applies to gaining emphasis in a sentence. By repeating certain key words, you will strongly emphasize the ideas represented by those words.

This repetition must be done carefully so that it does not become tiresome and meaningless. First, you must repeat words not thoughtlessly but deliberately for the purpose of gaining a certain effect. Second, the words must have the same meaning each time they are repeated. Many English words have several meanings that vary widely from each other. Using the same word several times with different meanings can make a sentence hard to follow.

Unemphatic:
I warned Charles not to be so careless, but he did not seem to care. (thoughtless repetition)
As we looked into the clear water, we could clearly see some fish clear at the bottom of the pool. (repeated words with different meanings)

Emphatic:
Elaine seemed carefree, and yet she was careful about everything; she cared especially about always doing her best.
Clear minds produce clear thinking, clear speaking, and clear writing.

2. *Write a series of similar questions, commands, or short statements.* When a number of short, pointed sentences come in quick succession, they are strongly emphatic.

Indeed, God's Word must hold a prominent place in your life. Read it. Study it. Memorize it. Live it.

Position

1. *Place the main idea of a sentence in the main clause.* The mistake of putting the main idea in a subordinate clause is called upside-down subordination, and it may result in an absurd statement. Compare the following sentences.

Wrong emphasis: Upside-down subordination
When a great fish swallowed Jonah, he had been cast into the sea.

Proper emphasis:
When Jonah was cast into the sea, a great fish swallowed him.

2. *Place similar phrases or clauses at the same position in a series of sentences.* If the similar phrases or clauses are at sentence beginnings or endings, you will gain emphasis by repetition as well as position.

God's Word does have the answer to every man's need. To the wayward, it shines as a beacon light. To the sin-sick, it offers the healing balm of Gilead. To the discouraged, it holds a ray of hope. To the tempted, it is the sword that puts the foe to flight. To the persecuted, its promises inspire courage and faith.

3. *When you list items in a series, be sure to arrange them in the order of importance.* Remember, the most important item should always come last.

Unemphatic:
The flood caused the death of many people, the destruction of many homes, and the desolation of much cropland.

Emphatic:
The flood caused the desolation of much cropland, the destruction of many homes, and the death of many people.

4. *Emphasize a point by writing a single short sentence after several longer ones.* The sudden change sharply emphasizes the short sentence, especially if it comes at the end of a paragraph.

> Haman wanted to get rid of Mordecai even before the date specified in the decree. He built a gallows fifty cubits high to hang the man he despised. <u>But Haman's plan failed.</u>

Sentence Style

Use different sentence styles according to the emphasis you want. You can give varying degrees of emphasis by writing loose, periodic, and balanced sentences. A loose sentence gives the main idea first and the details later. A periodic sentence saves the main idea until last, where it receives the greatest emphasis. You must read all the way to the *period* in order to get the main idea. A balanced sentence contains two well-matched clauses. One kind of balanced sentence has clauses beginning with words like "the more... the more" or "the sooner... the better." Another kind uses a slight change of wording to produce a notable or unexpected contrast.

Loose:
> Rhoda was greatly surprised to hear Peter's voice because he had been chained in prison, and sixteen soldiers had been appointed to guard him. (The sentence could end after *voice* or *prison.*)

Periodic:
> Since Peter had been chained in prison and sixteen soldiers had been appointed to guard him, Rhoda was greatly surprised to hear his voice.

Balanced:
> The more time we spend thinking right, the less time we will have to think wrong.
> Success is not achieving what we pursue; it is pursuing what we ought to achieve.

Your paragraphs should consist mostly of loose sentences because these are the most natural and easy to read. But when you want to make a point stand out, you can emphasize it by using a periodic or balanced sentence.

Read the following paragraph, in which most of the sentences are loose. The one periodic sentence is underlined. Notice how that sentence is more emphatic than the loose sentences.

> Animals deserve the same rights that humans have, according to one popular idea today. Some people say that animals are mistreated and deprived of a decent life when farmers confine them in small pens. "Why should we take advantage of animals for our own benefit simply because we are smarter?" they ask. We do need to avoid cruelty to animals, for the Bible says that a righteous man regards the life of his beast. But the Bible also says that man is to have dominion "over the fish of the sea, and over the fowl of the air, and over every living thing that moveth upon the earth." The ironic thing is that many people have no qualms about confining old people in nursing homes, even against their

wishes. Yet some of these people are the very ones who clamor loudly for animal rights. <u>As the values of the world become more perverted and some animals receive more rights than people, let us continue to uphold the principles clearly taught in the Bible.</u>

Unusual Word Order

Place an important idea in a sentence with unusual word order. For example, if you want to emphasize a word that would normally come in the latter part of a sentence, you can make it stand out more by moving it to the beginning. The very unusualness of the sentence draws attention to the idea and emphasizes it.

Normal emphasis:
   The Bible is God's eternal Word. It can never be destroyed!
More emphatic:
   The Bible is God's eternal Word. Destroyed it can never be!
   (Main verb *destroyed* moved to sentence beginning.)

Normal emphasis:
   We should never consider giving up.
More emphatic:
   Never should we consider giving up.
   (Adverb *never* moved to sentence beginning.)

Normal emphasis:
   We have not yet seen his best efforts.
More emphatic:
   His best efforts we have not yet seen.
   (Direct object *his best efforts* moved to sentence beginning.)

Remember, though, that *unusual* word order and *awkward* word order are two different things. An awkward sentence also draws attention to itself, but for the wrong reason! Whenever you try to improve a sentence, be sure the final product is smooth and readable.

Awkward:
   God's eternal Word the Bible is. (Predicate nominative *God's eternal Word* sounds awkward at sentence beginning.)

Direct Quotations

Use more direct quotations than indirect quotations. Even an argumentative essay will have an occasional quotation. Do you see the indirect quotations in the first paragraph below? The argument is more forceful if they are changed to direct quotations.

Lacks emphasis: Indirect quotations
   Young people should be sober-minded rather than silly and lighthearted. A youth may ask if this means he must always go around with a long face. Of course it does not; the Bible also tells us to rejoice evermore. But there is a great difference between spiritual rejoicing and carnal merrymaking.

Emphatic: Direct quotations

Young people should be sober-minded rather than silly and lighthearted. A youth may ask, "Does this mean I must always go around with a long face?" Of course it does not; the Bible also says, "Rejoice evermore." But there is a great difference between spiritual rejoicing and carnal merry-making.

As you seek to add emphasis to your sentences, remember two important principles. First, it takes more than the devices in this lesson to produce effective emphasis. Just as speaking forcefully and making dramatic gestures cannot make a poor speech truly emphatic, so these methods cannot make poor sentences truly emphatic. The main emphasis must result from worthwhile sentence content. Second, overusing specific methods for emphasis will actually destroy emphasis. If a speaker shouts and gestures with every sentence, how can a listener know what is truly emphatic? Therefore, do not try to emphasize every sentence, but only those sentences whose ideas truly deserve emphasis.

Applying the Lesson

A. Rewrite these sentences with more emphasis, following the directions in parentheses.

1. Though David faced Goliath fearlessly, the giant threatened him. (Write with the main idea in the main clause.)
2. We greatly admire this hero of faith. (Write with unusual word order.)
3. As a person's faith in God is greater, he has less confidence in his own abilities. (Write a balanced sentence.)
4. If we allow the unfounded theories of men to shake our confidence in the Bible, our trust in God Himself cannot stand firm. (Use repetition of the key word *shake* in three forms.)
5. Some people say that if the heart is right, nothing else matters. (Use a direct quotation.)
6. The truth is that everything matters if the heart is right. (Write a periodic sentence.)
7. When Daniel went to his house and prayed as usual, he knew about the king's decree. (Write with the main idea in the main clause.)
8. We dare not feed such disrespectful attitudes. (Write with unusual word order.)
9. The wash dried quickly with a gentle breeze blowing and the sun shining brightly. (Write a periodic sentence.)
10. When the wind diminished, dust lay everywhere—on the floor, on the furniture, on the windowsills, and even on the dishes inside the cupboard. (Use repetition of a key word.)
11. The gale tore the roof off the house, flattened the sweet corn, and littered the yard with tree branches. (Arrange the series in effective order.)
12. The slothful worker watches the hours he works; the diligent worker makes his hours count. (Write a balanced sentence.)

B. Rewrite this paragraph with greater emphasis. Not every sentence needs improvement.

> Do you know the meaning of the expression "crossing the Rubicon"? The Rubicon was a stream that marked the boundary between Italy and Gaul. Julius Caesar, who was governor of Gaul, proved himself a brilliant general. He brought a vast area of Europe under Roman rule. The common people acclaimed him a great hero as news of his conquests reached Rome. But as the people honored him more, the Senate feared him more. The Senate ordered the military hero to lay down the command of his armies and become a private citizen, finally. But Julius Caesar defied the order and started toward Rome with an army. He knew full well that taking his army into Italy would mark him as a revolutionary who intended to overthrow the Roman government. So it meant there was no turning back when Caesar's army crossed the Rubicon. "Crossing the Rubicon" means making a dangerous and irreversible decision to this day.

Review Exercises

Here is a list of pointers for writing an argumentative essay, including several that are incorrect. Write the numbers of the incorrect sentences. [45–49]

1. Choose a limited subject about which not everyone agrees.
2. Begin with an introduction that will attract the attention of readers.
3. State the point of your argument in clear, positive, and specific terms.
4. Avoid any mention of arguments that your opponents might make against your thesis.
5. Support each point in your argument with details, reasons, illustrations, or opinions.
6. Give your strongest supporting point last.
7. In the conclusion, restate the thesis in different words.
8. Briefly summarize your main points before ending the essay.

---

76. Improving Your Speaking Style, Part 2: Voice Control

In Lesson 51 you learned that eye contact is one important element of an effective speaking style. Look directly at individuals in your audience. Establish eye contact early in your speech, use eye contact to emphasize major points throughout the speech, and close the speech on a solid note with eye contact.

Your *voice control* also affects your speaking style. Actually, your voice reveals many things about you. It shows whether you are careless or careful, tense or relaxed, timid or confident. This becomes especially important when you speak to a group. The listeners should sense that you are eager to communicate something worthwhile to them. If your voice suggests that you are bored with your subject, the listeners will be bored too!

The following paragraphs discuss four important elements of proper voice control.

1. *Articulation.* You need to open your mouth well and pronounce each word distinctly, for your talk will lose its effect if the listeners cannot understand you. They may be able to miss a considerable number of sounds and still understand what you mean; but the greater the number of sounds missed, the greater the chance of misunderstanding.

Of course, you must also avoid the extreme of exaggerated articulation. Your voice sounds best when it is clear, natural, and relaxed.

2. *Volume.* This is probably the first thing you think of when you consider voice control. Be sure to speak loudly enough so that your listeners need not strain to hear you. No matter how many other good qualities your voice may have, your talk will not be effective if the audience cannot hear what you say.

On the other hand, speaking too loudly is just as ineffective as speaking too softly. Your voice must not be so loud that your listeners feel uncomfortable. Rather, you should have a pleasant variety, using the greatest volume for your most important points. This variety will help you to avoid a boring manner of speech.

Look at the following sentences. What pattern of volume would be appropriate for each one?

Shall we then decide that our work is vain? Never!

Never must we consider our efforts useless just because we do not see immediate results.

It may appear that our work is vain. But that is only the opinion of certain people.

The first example should begin with moderate volume and build up to strong volume for the word *Never.* The reverse pattern should be used in the second example—beginning loud and gradually becoming softer. In the third example, the volume should increase through the word *vain* and then decrease. These differences in volume help to put proper emphasis where it belongs.

3. *Pitch.* This aspect of the voice is directly affected by emotions. When you are calm and confident, your voice pitch is generally lower than when you are excited or anxious. Therefore, make a deliberate effort to relax and use the lower tones in your voice range.

You must modulate your pitch according to what you are saying. In everyday speech, do you state a fact, ask a question, and make an exclamation with every word at the same pitch? Of course not—and neither should you do that in speaking to a group. Raise and lower the pitch of your voice to communicate as you would in a normal conversation. Few things deaden a talk more than a voice droning on and on in a monotone.

Pitch and volume generally go together, with high pitch accompanying strong volume and lower pitch accompanying lower volume. Notice how this is true as you again read the sample sentences above. When you do use falling pitch and volume (especially at the end of a sentence), be careful not to reduce them too much. Otherwise, your listeners will fail to catch the last words.

4. *Speed.* Regulating your flow of speech is another aspect of voice control. Try to speak at the same comfortable speed that you use in conversation. You should not have long, awkward pauses, but neither should you try to fill in pauses by using *uh*'s and *ah*'s. Try to use a natural variety, speaking faster to express excitement or enthusiasm and slowing down to emphasize major points.

Which of the following sentences should be spoken slowly? Which should be spoken more rapidly? The answers should be obvious.

> To sustain our spiritual life, we should schedule a regular time and place for personal devotions. (thesis statement)
> If we fit devotions in whenever it suits each day, too many days will fly past with devotions forgotten because it fits in nowhere. (supporting detail)

Some voices just naturally sound more pleasant than others; there is little we can do about that. But regardless of the natural sound of your voice, you will communicate at your best if you speak clearly and use a variety of volume, pitch, and speed. A well-modulated voice is constantly changing to express the meanings known and *felt* by the speaker. If you follow these guidelines and put your heart into your message, you will communicate well with your audience.

Applying the Lesson

Prepare a talk of three to six minutes on one of the following topics or on another idea approved by your teacher. It should be something with a specific lesson for the listeners. Concentrate especially on effective voice control. Remember also to maintain eye contact with your listeners.

1. A sickness or hospital experience in the family
2. A personal experience that made a strong impression on you
3. Memories of Grandfather (or another person)

Review Exercises

Tell whether each of these statements is true or false about eye contact with an audience to whom you are speaking. [51]

1. Eye contact should be established soon after you begin speaking.
2. You do well to center your attention on one general area of the audience.
3. Eye contact helps you to know whether you are communicating clearly.
4. Eye contact gives individuals in the audience the feeling that you are talking directly to them.
5. Throughout your speech, you should raise your head at scheduled intervals.
6. You add emphasis to a point when you look at the audience as you are saying it.

77. Writing to the Point

Every sentence expresses a complete thought. Its purpose is to communicate a specific point. But sometimes a sentence presents a point in an obscure manner, rather than stating it as clearly and directly as possible. Conciseness and parallelism are two broad categories that relate to writing clear, direct sentences.

Conciseness

Concise sentences communicate without wasting words. The following guidelines should help you write concise sentences.

1. *Avoid deadwood—words that add no meaning to a sentence.* Most often, deadwood consists of modifiers whose meanings are implied in the words they modify.

> **Full of deadwood:**
> The round, brilliant sun arched in a high vault across the clear daytime sky.
> (The sun is always round; "to arch" and "move in a high vault" have the same idea; the sun is visible only in the daytime.)
> **Concise:**
> The brilliant sun arched across the clear sky.

2. *Avoid redundancy—the careless repetition of words or ideas.* You learned in Lesson 75 that repetition of key words can give emphasis to sentences. Thoughtless repetition, however, results in clutter. One kind of thoughtless repetition occurs when pairs of synonymous expressions are used together.

> **Redundant:**
> In deep thanksgiving and gratitude, we acknowledge God's daily blessings showered upon us day after day.
> **Concise:**
> In deep gratitude, we acknowledge God's daily blessings showered upon us.

Another kind of redundancy occurs when a word is repeated for no good reason. Again, the repetition adds clutter rather than emphasis and meaning.

> **Redundant:**
> We have a large, thick book for our history book.
> The story that the visitor told was an interesting story about his childhood.
> **Concise:**
> We have a large, thick history book.
> The visitor told an interesting story about his childhood.

3. *Avoid wordy expressions.* A wordy expression uses more words than necessary to express an idea. Why write "the person who drove the car" when "the driver" is just as clear? Why use "at a future time" when "later" means exactly the same thing? A reader finds it annoying to sift through a peck of words in order to gain a few ounces of thought.

Wordy:
> As a general rule, the truck that hauls our milk is here by this point in time.
> On days when it is cloudy, the panel of solar cells cannot recharge very well.

Concise:
> Generally, the milk truck is here by now.
> On cloudy days, the solar panel cannot recharge very well.

Here is a list of wordy expressions. Notice how the thought of each can be expressed just as clearly in one or two words.

Wordy:	**Concise:**
continue on	continue
similar to	like
meet up with	meet; encounter
green in color	green
be aware of the fact	know
before the season of spring	before spring

4. *Avoid pretentious writing.* A writer falls into the trap of pretentiousness when he has the notion that flowery words and unusual expressions produce a fine, distinctive writing style. Both in everyday life and in writing, simplicity and directness are best.

Pretentious:
> Time glided by on gilded wings as our skates etched intricate designs on the lustrous surface of the ice. Above our heads, the moon reigned serenely as the queen of the night, flooding us with a rich profusion of silvery rays.

Concise:
> Time flew by as we skated on the smooth, shiny ice. From high overhead, the bright full moon shone upon us with a flood of silvery light.

5. *Avoid padded writing.* Students are most likely to fall prey to this temptation when they strive to reach a minimum word count for an assignment. Instead of adding significant ideas, however, they merely add extra details. The result may be one of the previously noted problems or simply a padded writing style—sentences stuffed with unnecessary modifiers and compound parts.

Padded:
> The two little boys in blue jackets and caps ran and jumped with the large, long-haired, light brown dog in the lush green grass of the back yard.

Concise:
> The two little boys played with the large dog in the back yard.

Parallelism

A sentence has parallelism when matching parts fit together well. This helps to make a sentence smooth to read and easy to understand. The following guidelines will help you to write sentences with parallelism.

1. *Write compound parts in similarly patterned constructions.* When you use compound parts, look for ways to make those parts as parallel as practical. For example, if one part of a compound subject includes a prepositional phrase, also include a phrase in the other part. If a preposition has a compound object, try to make the two parts similar in length and structure.

Unparallel:
> The throaty roar of the old vacuum pump, the contented cows, and the mixture of the smells in the barn flooded Uncle Lloyd with memories.

Parallel:
> The throaty roar of the old vacuum pump, the long rows of contented cows, and the mixed smells of the barn flooded Uncle Lloyd with memories.

2. *Use coordinating conjunctions to join only matching sentence parts.* The parts joined must have the same structure (words, phrases, or clauses of the same kind) and the same function in the sentence (subject, modifier, and so forth). If you cannot easily make the joined parts parallel, you may need to restructure the sentence as illustrated by the second example below.

Unparallel:
> Swans look majestic whether in the water or flying overhead.
> Slowly and with great effort, the injured deer dragged itself to the creek.

Parallel:
> Swans look majestic whether floating in the water or flying through the air.
> With great effort, the injured deer slowly dragged itself to the creek.

3. *Avoid illogical shifts in areas such as tense, person, and voice.*

Unparallel:
> As my foot slipped off the rock, a sudden pain shoots through my ankle.
> When one sprains an ankle, they sometimes cannot walk for a while.
> Uncle Stanley had emergency first-aid training, and now his skill was put to use.

Parallel:
> As my foot slipped off the rock, a sudden pain shot through my ankle.
> When one sprains an ankle, he sometimes cannot walk for a while.
> Uncle Stanley had emergency first-aid training, and now he put his skill to use.

4. *Be consistent in the use of articles before nouns in a series.* Either use an article before each noun, or use one only before the first noun.

Unparallel:
> The duck family, the pair of swans, and geese come regularly to our pond.
> Water is a useful substance, whether it is a solid, liquid, or a gas.

Parallel:
> The duck family, the pair of swans, and the geese come regularly to our pond.
> Water is a useful substance, whether it is a solid, liquid, or gas.

5. *Repeat introductory words before long phrases or clauses in a series.* Although not strictly required by rules of grammar, repeating such words strengthens the parallelism of the sentence.

Weak parallelism:
> If the Christian soldier goes forth <u>with</u> the whole armor of God, the energy of the Holy Spirit, and the encouragement of faithful brethren, he will surely overcome.

Strong parallelism:
> If the Christian soldier goes forth <u>with</u> the whole armor of God, <u>with</u> the energy of the Holy Spirit, and <u>with</u> the encouragement of faithful brethren, he will surely overcome.

6. *In a compound part, you may omit one of the words only if the other word would correctly fill its place.* If one main verb in a compound is omitted, all the helping verbs must match the main verb that remains. If just *a* or *an* precedes two or more nouns, the article must match all the nouns. Otherwise, both words in the compound must be stated.

Unparallel:
> We <u>have</u> and <u>will be</u> <u>praying</u> for you. (*Have* does not match *praying.*)
> He <u>lives</u> in Maryland, and <u>I</u> in Virginia. (*Lives* does not match *I.*)
> A Christian education is <u>an</u> <u>opportunity</u> and <u>privilege</u>.
> > (*An* does not match *privilege.*)

Parallel:
> We <u>have</u> <u>prayed</u> and <u>will be</u> <u>praying</u> for you.
> We <u>are</u> and <u>will be</u> <u>praying</u> for you.
>
> He <u>lives</u> in Maryland, and <u>I</u> <u>live</u> in Virginia.
> They <u>live</u> in Maryland, and <u>we</u> in Virginia.
>
> A Christian education is <u>an</u> <u>opportunity</u> and <u>a</u> <u>privilege</u>.
> A Christian education is <u>a</u> <u>blessing</u> and <u>privilege</u>.

7. *In defining a word, use another word of the same part of speech.* Define a noun with a noun, an adjective with an adjective, and so on. Use an infinitive to define a verb. A clause beginning with *when* or *where* seldom makes a good definition.

Unparallel:
> A <u>paradox</u> is <u>when</u> a true statement expresses two ideas that seem to contradict each other.

Parallel:
> A <u>paradox</u> is a true <u>statement</u> expressing two ideas that seem to contradict each other.

Applying the Lesson

A. Rewrite these sentences, making them more concise.

1. It is necessary that we believe that God divinely inspired the Bible.

2. Each and every Christian should order his daily affairs of life so that the inhabitants of his surrounding community can recognize the fact that he has been with Jesus.

3. When told to wash in the muddy, winding, rushing Jordan River, Naaman angrily, proudly, and abruptly declared that he certainly never would ever do that.

4. The turtle slowly inched its way along the muddy mire beside the creek.

5. The rich millionaire found that his new, expensive limousine did not bring the satisfaction or gratification that he expected.

6. The season of winter, as a general rule, is a cold, wet, rainy season in the land of Palestine.

7. One proof of the idea that the earth is spherical in shape is the fact that the earth casts a round shadow on the moon during the time of a lunar eclipse.

8. As thousands of immigrant newcomers poured into the eastern United States, pioneer settlers in America continually moved west toward the setting sun.

B. Rewrite these sentences, improving the parallelism of each one in two ways.

1. God has not and will not cease to bless His people, warn the sinners, and to rule in the kingdoms of men.

2. God reigns wisely and in perfect justice, and His promises will always be kept.

3. If someone believes the Bible, they know that God created the world in six days, He destroyed the world with a great flood, and He will again destroy the world by fire.

4. As we study the Bible, we sometimes understood a truth more clearly or in a fuller way.

5. To honor is when a person respects the wishes as well as the commands of a parent, teacher, or a church leader.

6. When you want to discern God's will, a person should consider the Word of God, the Spirit's leading, and the counsel of spiritual brethren.

7. If a coastline has many quiet bays or other inlets that are sheltered, it was more favorable for shipping than a straight coastline.

8. A fjord is where a long, narrow arm of the sea extends inland between steep cliffs, especially along coasts like those of Norway, Maine, or of Alaska.

C. Rewrite these paragraphs, improving the conciseness and parallelism.

The Dead Sea is one of the most unique, unusual bodies of water to be found anywhere upon this entire planet earth. This sea, a body of water 48 miles long and spanning 10 miles wide, covers the deepest inland depression on the earth. In fact, the surface on the top of the sea averages nearly 1,300 feet below sea level, and a maximum depth of about 1,300 feet is reached in the northern part.

The Dead Sea has within its watery depths a higher, more maximum amount of mineral content than any other body of water. Its extreme salinity occurs as a result of a spectacular combination of circumstances that characterize this sea. For one thing, several streams and rivers disgorge and empty their watery, liquid tribute into the mighty depths of the sea, but no streams remove any of that tribute away. Thus, the one and only solitary means by which water naturally leaves the Dead Sea is by the process of evaporation. The intense heat and having low humidity cause a high, rapid rate of evaporation. Water, of course, is evaporated, but minerals not. Therefore, the waters have and are becoming more concentrated with minerals.

Review Exercises

Identify the tense (*present, past,* etc.) and form (*simple, progressive, emphatic*) of each underlined verb in these verses from the Psalms. [67–70]

1. "I <u>have set</u> the LORD always before me" (16:8).
2. "My heart <u>is inditing</u> a good matter" (45:1).
3. "I <u>had fainted</u>, unless I had believed to see the goodness of the LORD in the land of the living" (27:13).
4. "My heart was hot within me, while I <u>was musing</u> the fire burned: then spake I with my tongue" (39:3).
5. "I will praise thee with uprightness of heart, when I <u>shall have learned</u> thy righteous judgments" (119:7).
6. "Man <u>did eat</u> angels' food: he sent them meat to the full" (78:25).
7. "Good and upright is the LORD: therefore <u>will</u> he <u>teach</u> sinners in the way" (25:8).
8. "Thou makest darkness, and it is night: wherein all the beasts of the forest <u>do creep</u> forth" (104:20).

---

78. Providing Variety

Monotony is rarely a virtue. In writing paragraphs, it certainly is not. Variety adds appeal and interest to sentences. But variety can serve an even deeper purpose: it can help you emphasize the main points of a paragraph.

In this lesson you will study six methods for producing sentence variety. Not every paragraph will have every one of these kinds of variety, but nearly every paragraph should have at least one or two of them.

1. *Vary the lengths of sentences.* Avoid both extremes: too many short, choppy sentences and too many long, tiresome sentences. A short sentence after several longer ones can be especially effective because it provides variety as well as emphasis. Compare the following paragraphs. Do you agree that the third one is much better than the other two?

Poor: Too short and choppy

> Do you want strong, healthy muscles? Give your body a proper diet. Muscle tissue consists primarily of protein. So your diet should include protein-rich foods....

Poor: Too long and stringy

Do you know that if you want strong, healthy muscles, you must give your body a proper diet? Since muscle tissue consists primarily of protein, your diet should include protein-rich foods such as meat, fish, eggs, and dairy products....

Good: Varying sentence lengths

Do you want strong, healthy muscles? Give your body a proper diet. Since muscle tissue consists primarily of protein, your diet should include protein-rich foods such as meat, fish, eggs, and dairy products. Muscle contraction requires large amounts of energy. Foods rich in carbohydrates—fruits, vegetables, grains, and sugars—supply your body with this energy. Muscle contractions also occur only in the presence of calcium, so your diet must include calcium-rich foods like milk, milk products, and leafy green vegetables. Do not lightly esteem a wholesome diet; rather make sure that you give your body the nutrients it needs. On that diet depends your muscular health.

2. *Vary the word order in sentences.* Sentences have three kinds of word order. In normal or natural word order, the complete subject comes before the complete predicate. In inverted word order, the complete predicate comes before the complete subject. In mixed word order, part of the predicate comes before the subject and part of it comes after.

Normal: An eagle soared over the valley.
Inverted: Over the valley soared an eagle.
Mixed: Over the valley an eagle soared.

Use natural word order the most frequently because it is the most simple and direct. In almost every paragraph, though, several sentences should have mixed word order. And once in a while, write a sentence with inverted word order. Writing good sentences with inverted word order may take special effort, but this may add just the sparkle needed to transform a humdrum paragraph to an emphatic one.

Read again the last example paragraph above. The third sentence has mixed word order, and the last sentence has inverted word order. Do you see how these sentences contribute to the interest and effectiveness of the paragraph?

3. *Vary the beginnings of sentences.* Of course, if you vary the word order, you will automatically vary sentence beginnings. Below are five specific pointers for providing this kind of variety.

a. Begin with a single-word adverb, an adverb phrase, or an adverb clause. This naturally will produce a sentence with mixed word order.

Normal:
The tree fell to the ground with a great crash.
Begins with an adverb phrase:
With a great crash, the tree fell to the ground.

b. Begin with a participial phrase that modifies the subject. Since the participial phrase is part of the complete subject, such a sentence still has normal word order.

Normal:
Ella, engrossed in her book, did not hear Mother call.
Begins with a participial phrase:
Engrossed in her book, Ella did not hear Mother call.

c. Begin with a transitional expression. This includes a word like *and, but,* or *therefore.* Refer to Lesson 63 for a list of transitional expressions.

Normal:
The archaic meaning of *mansion* has nothing to do with a luxurious dwelling.
Begins with a transitional expression:
However, the archaic meaning of *mansion* has nothing to do with a luxurious dwelling.

d. Begin with an appositive to the subject. An appositive normally follows the noun that it explains. For variety, you can reverse this order and have the appositive come first.

Normal:
A thesaurus, a handy reference for any writer, lists many synonyms.
Begins with an appositive:
A handy reference for any writer, a thesaurus lists many synonyms.

e. Begin with a nominative absolute. In Lesson 21 you learned that a nominative absolute is a phrase consisting of a substantive and a participle. To add variety and a special appeal, you can occasionally change an introductory adverb clause to a nominative absolute. Compare the following sentences.

Begins with an adverb clause:
When supper had ended, Jesus washed the disciples' feet.
Begins with a nominative absolute:
Supper having ended, Jesus washed the disciples' feet.

4. *Vary the sentence types according to use.* An occasional interrogative, imperative, or exclamatory sentence breaks the monotony of all declarative sentences. Notice how this is true in the following paragraph, which includes both an interrogative and an exclamatory sentence.

Many kinds of birds consume great quantities of insects. One person watched a yellow-throated warbler devour over seven thousand aphids in about forty minutes. A scarlet tanager can eat over six hundred gypsy-moth caterpillars in less than twenty minutes. How many mosquitoes do you suppose one nighthawk can consume in one feeding? Biologists estimate the answer to be five hundred. What vast numbers of insects these voracious eaters destroy every summer day!

5. *Vary the sentence types according to structure.* These four types are simple, compound, complex, and compound-complex. A sprinkling of compound and complex sentences does more than provide variety. It also shows precise relationships among ideas because the conjunctions used to join clauses have specific meanings.

Can you find at least one of each of these sentence types in the last paragraph under point 1 above? Most of them, of course, are simple. Sentence 3 is complex, sentence 6 compound, and sentence 7 compound-complex.

6. *Vary the sentences according to style.* As with variety of sentence structure, a sprinkling of periodic sentences and an occasional balanced sentence do more than provide variety. These sentence styles also strengthen emphasis in a paragraph.

Read the following paragraph, in which the first sentence is periodic, the last sentence is balanced, and the others are loose. Observe the added force that this variety gives. What other kinds of variety does the paragraph have?

"Put thou my tears into thy bottle," found in Psalm 56:8, is an intriguing request. These words apparently refer to the ancient custom of using tear bottles. Such a bottle was frequently made of glass, beautifully decorated, with a long, slender neck and a funnel-shaped mouth. At a funeral, a priest would go from one mourner to another, wiping away tears with a piece of cotton and squeezing them into a tear bottle. This reminds us of a beautiful promise that appears two times in the last book of the Bible. "And God shall wipe away all tears from their eyes" (Revelation 7:17; 21:4). The more we find comfort in God on earth, the more we can look forward to God's eternal comfort in heaven.

Applying the Lesson

Read the following paragraphs, and improve the sentences according to the directions below. If an exercise is marked with a star, write only enough words to show what the improvement is.

A Test of Three R's

[1]"You should prepare for a test tomorrow." [2]These words may have brought you a touch of anxiety or a note of challenge sometimes. [3]You perhaps know the embarrassment of a low test score. [4]You probably know the pleasure of a good score. [5]The thought of school life without tests is strange.

[6]The school of life includes tests too. [7]These real-life tests are far more important than school tests. [8]We may hardly notice them. [9]Our developing character indicates how we are scoring. [10]Our heavenly Father, watching our lives from His all-wise perspective, is recording our performance. [11]We should ask ourselves how we are faring on these tests.

[12]One test measures how well we relate to others. [13]We face this test every day because we are not hermits. [14]As others relate to us imperfectly, we must try harder to relate properly to them. [15]We fail this test whenever we lose our temper, nurse a grudge, or harbor jealousy. [16]We make passing grades when we exercise Christlike courtesy even toward the exasperating, when we extend sincere sympathy to the hurting, and when we exhibit a friendly interest in the concerns of others.

[17]We must occasionally take a test on our response to criticism. [18]This test becomes especially difficult when the criticism comes in a crude or an unkind way. [19]Yet the test is valid even in such circumstances. [20]Resenting the person who brings criticism or refusing to consider any value in it marks a definite failure. [21]We certainly cannot accept every bit of criticism at face value. [22]Neither should we label criticism worthless until we have given careful thought to it. [23]We pass this test, whether the criticism comes as a friendly remark or as a stern rebuke, as we learn to benefit from criticism.

[24]Still another test we face frequently is how well we respect authority. [25]This focuses on our attitudes and responses toward those in authority at home, at school, in the church, in the workplace, and in civil government. [26]Disrespectful nicknames for those in authority and careless disregard for their direction constitute failure. [27]The apostle Paul, a man of authority himself, passed this test with high honors when he apologized for unknowingly speaking against the high priest. [28]The level of our respect for any authority both reflects and affects the level of our respect for God's authority. [29]This test, therefore, counts heavily in the total score of our character.

1. Rewrite sentence 1 as an imperative sentence, number 2 as an interrogative sentence, and number 5 as an exclamatory sentence.
*2. Begin sentences 3 and 4 with single-word adverbs.
3. Rewrite sentences 6 and 11 as interrogative sentences.
4. Change sentence 7 to inverted word order.
*5. Combine numbers 8 and 9 into a compound-complex sentence.
6. Begin sentence 10 with a participial phrase modifying the subject.
7. Change sentence 13 to the periodic style.
8. Change sentence 14 to the balanced style.
*9. Begin sentence 16 with a transitional expression.
*10. Begin sentence 17 with a single-word adverb.
*11. Combine sentences 21 and 22 into a compound-complex sentence.
12. Begin sentence 23 with an adverb clause.
*13. Begin sentence 27 with an appositive to the subject.

Review Exercises

Label each underlined verb *TA* (transitive, active voice), *TP* (transitive, passive voice), *IC* (intransitive complete), or *IL* (intransitive linking). [69]

1. The beginning of anxiety <u>is</u> the end of faith.
2. Faith and fear <u>can</u> never <u>exist</u> together.
3. Faith in God <u>makes</u> the uplook good, the outlook bright, and the future glorious.
4. By faith a bridge <u>is built</u> from this world to the next.
5. Faith's hand never <u>knocks</u> in vain at mercy's door.

79. Chapter 10 Review

A. Rewrite these sentences, improving the unity and coherence.
  1. Falling on His face, Jesus' prayer was that the cup might pass from Him, however, He also prayed that God's will be done.
  2. He longed to, in this dark hour, feel some support from His disciples.
  3. While the disciples should have been praying. They slept.
  4. If the disciples had prayed, it might have, when they faced the temptations of the coming hours, helped them to be loyal to their Lord.
  5. In the midst of His intense suffering, even Jesus considered the needs of His disciples.

B. Rewrite these sentences, improving the emphasis by the methods indicated in parentheses.
  1. Mother does not want a cat in the house. (unusual word order)
  2. If you do not overcome temptations, they will master you. (balanced sentence)
  3. Grandfather's visits always bring joy. With his cheerful ways, he brightens the atmosphere. He lightens the workload with his helpful hands. His practical knowledge enlightens our inquisitive minds. (similar phrases in similar positions)
  4. The electricity suddenly went off as storm clouds rolled in from the west and streaks of lightning split the dark sky. (periodic sentence)
  5. Smoking causes heart disease, death, stomach maladies, and respiratory ailments. (order of importance)

C. Rewrite these sentences, improving the conciseness and parallelism.
  1. We should be aware of the fact that people who follow Jesus do not fight and war against those who speak evil of them, mistreat them, or who even kill them.
  2. Justification is when someone is declared righteous.
  3. All day the wind blew stiffly and out of the north, and by evening several heavy snow squalls were produced by the moisture from the lake.
  4. At this point in time the family of which I am a part is cleaning and looking after Aunt Marge.
  5. When we are harvesting the beans, corn, and the tomatoes at one and the same time, you have little time for extras.

D. Rewrite each sentence or set of sentences, varying them in one of the six ways described in Lesson 78.
  1. The boys raced in from the garden.
  2. Brindle, a very friendly Jersey, has become a family pet.
  3. The goat that Father bought milks well. Her curious ways have quickly endeared her to the children.
  4. We were surprised to see Brother Chester back in church this morning.
  5. As the barometric pressure drops lower, the weather is likely to become stormier.

6. The snowy white lambs frisking in the meadow make a beautiful picture.
7. The sheep are acting restless. The cattle are coming in to the barn. A major storm is coming directly toward our region.
8. The wind picked up considerably. We were locked into our little dell by morning.

E. Name the element of voice control that each description refers to.
  1. The rate of speaking.
  2. The highness of the voice.
  3. The distinctness of speaking.
  4. The loudness of the voice.

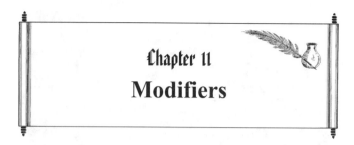

Chapter 11

Modifiers

80. Recognizing Adjectives

To modify something is to change it. Teachers modify their lesson plans to fit the needs of different classes. Weather forecasters modify their reports as weather patterns change. Hog farmers modify their feeding program in an effort to make their hogs grow faster. Students modify their reports to make them clearer and more interesting.

In grammar, too, we are familiar with modifiers. Adjectives and adverbs modify the meanings of other words to make them more descriptive and more precise. Adjectives modify substantives by telling *which, whose, how many,* or *what kind of.* These modifiers include two main classes: limiting and descriptive.

Limiting Adjectives

A *limiting adjective* limits a substantive by telling *which, whose,* or *how many.* The following six groups of words may function as limiting adjectives.

1. *The articles are always limiting adjectives.* A and an are indefinite articles because they indicate no specific nouns. *The* is a definite article because it indicates a specific noun.

> <u>a</u> prophet of God (any prophet)
> <u>the</u> prophet of God (a certain one)

2. *Number words are often used as limiting adjectives.*
   a. Cardinal numbers (*one, two, three,* and so forth) tell *how many.*

> <u>one</u> Mediator   <u>five</u> books of the Law

   b. Ordinal numbers (*first, second, third,* and so forth) tell *which.*

> <u>first</u> time   <u>sixth</u> day of the week

3. *Indefinite pronouns are sometimes used as limiting adjectives.* These words are adjectives only when they precede substantives to tell *which* or *how many.* When they stand alone and function as substantives, they are pronouns.

> <u>each</u> student   <u>another</u> assignment

4. *Demonstrative pronouns are sometimes used as limiting adjectives that tell* which.

> <u>this</u> test   <u>those</u> desks

5. *The interrogative pronouns* whose, which, *and* what *are sometimes used as limiting adjectives.*

<u>whose</u> pens   <u>what</u> lessons

6. *Possessive nouns and pronouns are often used as limiting adjectives that tell* whose. Remember to use apostrophes with nouns and indefinite pronouns, but not with personal pronouns.

<u>Lucinda's</u> sweater   <u>anybody's</u> guess
the <u>teachers'</u> plans   ideas that are <u>theirs</u>

Descriptive Adjectives

Descriptive adjectives describe substantives by telling *what kind of.* These are the words that shade and shape our language. Descriptive adjectives can be classified according to their structure.

1. *Some words in their simplest form are descriptive adjectives.*

<u>small</u> pictures   <u>easy</u> work

2. *Some descriptive adjectives can be identified by adjective-forming suffixes.* The following list includes some of the most common of these suffixes.

-ish: ticklish, yellowish   **-ary:** momentary, solitary
-like: businesslike, ladylike   **-al:** seasonal, commercial
-ic: frantic, static   **-some:** burdensome, awesome
-an, -en: republican, silken   **-ant, -ent:** vacant, excellent
-y: tasty, healthy   **-able, -ible:** changeable, permissible
-ful: wonderful, colorful   **-ive:** constructive, decisive
-less: fruitless, timeless   **-ous:** humorous, vigorous

3. *Some descriptive adjectives are formed by changing the spellings of nouns.* In general, adjectives of this kind are proper nouns.

Greece—Greek   France—French

4. *Nouns are often used as descriptive adjectives without any spelling change.* These are known as attributive nouns.

<u>brick</u> wall   <u>chicken</u> barbecue   <u>dirt</u> road   <u>English</u> class

5. *Present and past participles may be used as descriptive adjectives.*

<u>cooling</u> breeze   <u>broken</u> glass

6. *Infinitives may be used as descriptive adjectives.* Such an infinitive immediately follows the substantive it modifies.

a crown <u>to win</u>   a test <u>to take</u>

Remember to separate with commas two or more descriptive adjectives used in a series and having equal rank. If necessary, review the specific details of this rule in Lesson 2.

Many <u>tall</u>, <u>graceful</u> coconut palms grew near the seashore.

Positions of Adjectives

An adjective may occur in three positions relative to the substantive it modifies. An *attributive adjective* precedes the substantive it modifies. The adjective *attributes* (assigns) a quality to the substantive that follows. Most adjectives appear in this position.

A narrow, winding road leads to the pleasant cottage.

An *appositive adjective* follows the substantive it modifies. This places special emphasis on the adjectives. Appositive adjectives often come in pairs, in which case they are set off by commas.

This cottage, small but tidy, makes a good home for Grandfather Weaver's.

A single adjective may also follow the substantive, especially when it refers to position or when it is modified by an adverb phrase.

The bedroom upstairs is kept ready for guests.

Their root cellar, dug out of solid rock, keeps vegetables very well.

In the first example above, *upstairs* is an adjective because it tells which bedroom. (Compare "the upstairs bedroom.") Since *upstairs* tells which, it is a limiting adjective.

A *predicate adjective* follows a linking verb and modifies the subject. You can usually tell that it is a predicate adjective because the word would also fit in the attributive position, before the subject.

Grandmother's flower beds are trim and colorful.
(Compare: trim and colorful flower beds)

Applying the Lesson

A. Copy each underlined adjective. First label it *L* (limiting) or *D* (descriptive); then label it *AT* (attributive), *AP* (appositive), or *PR* (predicate).
1. Our God, eternal in the heavens, is also a loving heavenly Father.
2. Angelic hosts, serving God faithfully, minister to God's people.
3. Christlike attitudes are pleasant and honorable.
4. Every loyal Christian, walking according to Gospel standards, has spiritual enemies to resist.
5. Several books to review are stacked in this box for the committee members present.
6. Whose farm is the first place across that twisting river in the valley below?

B. Copy each adjective and the word that it modifies.
1. Faithful people have preserved an accurate understanding of the Gospel for many centuries.
2. A proper understanding is essential for godly living.
3. This evil world, darkened by sin, should be brighter because of our presence.
4. Things above should be the constant focus of the believer's attention.
5. God's eternal Word is the answer to man's every need.
6. The sure promises of God remain a solid anchor for the tempted soul.

C. Copy these sentences, replacing each *L* or *D* with a limiting or descriptive adjective other than an article. Add commas as needed.

1. *L* puppies *D* and *D* romped on the *D* grass.
2. *L* antelope, *D* across the *D* plains, appears *D*.
3. Dale is throwing *D D* bales into the *D* pen *L*.
4. Susan dropped the *D D* rug that she was shaking from the window *L* to the *D* ground.
5. The *D* kittens, *D* on the *D* porch, seem *D*.
6. Although *L D* dog looks *D,* he really is quite *D*.

D. For each word in parentheses, write an adjective form that fits in the sentence.

1. The (Scripture) command to be (forgive) toward others includes a very (importance) warning.
2. Even in the midst of (storm) trials, those who have a (child) trust in God can remain (peace).
3. Brother Krahn has suggested a (sense) solution to the (complicate), (distress) problem.
4. Many years ago, buffalo with (mass) heads and (shag) fur roamed the (tree) plains of the (America) West.
5. In this (mountain) country, we would become (lone) if we had no (faith), (sympathy) neighbors.
6. Mr. Langley is a (vigor), (dedicate) worker with (Spain) ancestry.

Review Exercises

For each number, write the letter of the selection that has better unity or coherence. [74]

1. a. Surely you have heard of Seeing Eye dogs, they help blind people.
   b. Surely you have heard of Seeing Eye dogs. They help blind people.
2. a. But do you know about Hearing Ear dogs, which help deaf or hearing-impaired people?
   b. But do you know about Hearing Ear dogs? Which help deaf or hearing-impaired people.
3. a. When an alarm clock rings, a baby cries, or a visitor knocks at the door, the dog must alert his owner.
   b. When an alarm clock rings, a baby cries, or a visitor knocks at the door, he must alert his owner.
4. a. A dog does best for this work that is friendly, alert, and curious.
   b. A dog that is friendly, alert, and curious does best for this work.
5. a. Trainers choose dogs, which must pass a strict medical examination and have especially good hearing, between six months and two years old.
   b. Trainers choose dogs between six months and two years old. They must pass a strict medical examination and have especially good hearing.
6. a. It takes about four months to train a dog completely.
   b. It takes about four months to completely train a dog.

81. Adjective Phrases and Clauses

Not only single words but also phrases and clauses can function as adjectives in a sentence. Adjective phrases come in a variety of forms: prepositional, participial, and infinitive.

Prepositional Phrases

A prepositional phrase consists of a preposition and its object, along with any modifiers of the object. When a prepositional phrase serves as an adjective, it usually comes right after the substantive it modifies.

> The buckets under this shelf and the barrels behind that door contain grain for the calves.

Participial Phrases

The present and past participles of most verbs end with -*ing* or -*ed*. (A few past participles end with -*t* or -*en*, such as *lost* and *stolen*.) These verb forms are called participles when they serve as adjectives. If a participle has modifiers or complements, it is a participial phrase. A participial phrase may come before or after the word it modifies.

> The students, studying the lesson carefully, tried to understand the subjunctive mood.
>
> Dedicated to his task, their teacher tried to help them.

Participles can show three different tenses. Use the present participle to express action or being that occurs at the same time as that of the main verb in the sentence.

> The girls, pushing themselves to their limit, thoroughly cleaned their bedroom.
> (The girls pushed themselves at the same time they cleaned.)

The past participle can also express an action that occurs at the same time as that of the main verb. In addition, it may express a completed action.

> The girls, pushed by a specific deadline, thoroughly cleaned their bedroom.
> (The girls were pushed by the deadline at the same time they cleaned.)
> The deadline, set by Mother, spurred them to work hard.
> (Mother set the deadline before the deadline spurred them to work.)

The present perfect form indicates that the action or being occurs before that of the main verb in the sentence. The present perfect form consists of the past participle preceded by *having*.

> Having been pushed by a specific deadline, the girls finished in record time.
> (Indicates that the girls were pushed by the deadline before they finished.)
> Having set the deadline, Mother left the girls to their work.
> (Indicates that Mother set the deadline before she left the girls.)

Infinitive Phrases

An infinitive phrase, consisting of an infinitive and its modifiers and complements, can be used as an adjective. (Infinitives can also be used as substantives or adverbs.)

An infinitive used as an adjective immediately follows the substantive it modifies, and it usually tells *which* or *what kind of.*

Brother Conrad gave us several maps to label for our next class.
(The infinitive phrase tells *what kind of* maps.)
The colored pencils to use on the maps are on the table.
(The infinitive phrase tells *which* pencils.)

Adjective Clauses

An adjective clause is a dependent clause that modifies a substantive. Either a relative pronoun or a relative adverb introduces an adjective clause. The relative pronouns are *who, whom, whose, which,* and *that;* the relative adverbs are *when, where,* and *why.* These words are called relative pronouns and relative adverbs because they *relate* the adjective clause to the substantive that the clause modifies. Therefore, adjective clauses are sometimes called relative clauses.

The friends that we choose strongly influence our lives.
The years when Grandfather Steckle lived with us hold many precious memories.

Sometimes the relative pronoun or the relative adverb is omitted, making the clause harder to identify.

The book I brought describes the regions the first pioneers settled.
(Compare: book that I brought; regions where the first pioneers settled)

The words listed as relative pronouns and relative adverbs do not always introduce adjective clauses. Relative pronouns may also introduce noun clauses, and *when* and *where* may introduce noun or adverb clauses.

When Father comes in, we shall discover who the visitor was.
(*When Father comes in* is an adverb clause telling *when* about *shall discover. Who the visitor was* is a noun clause serving as the direct object of *shall discover.*)

Restrictive and Nonrestrictive Modifiers

Participial phrases and adjective clauses may be restrictive or nonrestrictive. If the phrase or clause restricts the meaning of a substantive by identifying *which one,* it is restrictive. A restrictive phrase or clause is essential to the meaning of the sentence and is not set off with commas.

The students having spare time may read the books that are on this table.

In the example above, the participial phrase restricts the meaning of *students* by telling *which ones.* Not all the students may read the books—only the ones having spare time. The adjective clause restricts the meaning of *books* by telling *which ones.* The sentence is not referring to all the books—only the ones on this table. The underlined modifiers are not set off with commas, for they are necessary to the meaning of the sentence.

If the modifying phrase or clause simply gives additional information about the substantive, it is nonrestrictive. A nonrestrictive phrase or clause does not identify a substantive by telling *which one*. Since it is not essential to the meaning of the sentence, it is set off with commas.

> <u>Gasping in alarm</u>, Mother rushed to pick up little Philip, <u>who was toddling toward the road</u>.

In this example, the participial phrase does not identify *Mother* by saying "the mother gasping in alarm." It simply gives additional information about *Mother*. The adjective clause does not identify *Philip* by saying "the Philip who was toddling toward the road." It simply gives additional information about *Philip*. The underlined modifiers are set off with commas, for they are not necessary to the meaning of the sentence.

Modifiers Within Other Modifiers

One adjective phrase or clause may contain other adjective phrases or clauses. The object of a preposition, the complement of a participle or an infinitive, and any substantive in an adjective clause may have a phrase or clause modifier. Study the following sentences, in which arrows point from the underlined modifiers to the words modified.

> Uncle George, <u>who owns the orchard across the road</u>, gave us the apples <u>in the crate on the porch</u>.
>
> <u>Studying the examples in the book</u>, I finally understood the concept <u>that the teacher, undisturbed at my ignorance, had carefully explained</u>.

The ability to understand adjective phrases and clauses will help you to construct sentences that express your thoughts clearly and precisely. Learn to recognize and use them well.

Applying the Lesson

A. Copy each adjective phrase. If a phrase is part of a longer phrase, include it with the longer phrase and also copy it separately. Label each phrase *prep.* (prepositional), *part.* (participial), or *inf.* (infinitive).

1. Having rejected the Lord, Jehoiakim burned the scroll containing Jeremiah's prophecies.
2. The king's decision to burn the scroll did not change God's word, forever settled in heaven.
3. The principles revealed in the Bible teach us the only way to know God.
4. The joy found in obedience to the Lord far outweighs any pleasures offered by this world.
5. The time to transplant the tomatoes in these flats may also be the time to pick the first crop of peas.
6. Harvey's words of quiet reassurance calmed the trapped people, but he did not have the ability to rescue them.
7. The geese swimming on the lake stirred the woodsman's desire to have some fresh meat.

8. Having weeded the flower beds around the house, the girls affirmed their resolve to keep them neat and made a schedule to accomplish their goal.

B. Copy the correct participles in parentheses.
1. The cows, (drinking, having drunk) from the water trough, slowly walked toward the meadow.
2. The old grandfather clock, (standing, having stood) in that corner for years, was damaged in the fire.
3. (Opening, Opened) just yesterday morning, the new store is already crowded with customers.
4. We should go out right now and fasten down that piece of tin (blowing, blown) in the wind.
5. (Being, Having been) washed, Skip promptly rolled in the dirt.
6. (Watching, Having watched) closely for the road sign, Father almost ran into the stopped car.

C. Copy each adjective clause.
1. Those whose faith rests in God have a security the world cannot know.
2. The young person who sets noble goals for himself develops discipline that will be a lifelong blessing.
3. Any place where God leads us is a good place to be.
4. The God we serve knows that we are frail creatures of the dust.
5. In times when God seems distant, we know who must be at fault.
6. He extends to every faithful Christian His grace, which is all-sufficient.

D. Write whether each underlined phrase or clause is restrictive (*R*) or nonrestrictive (*N*). Also copy each word that should be followed by a comma, and add the comma.
1. For a long time the people of Samaria were "bewitched" (amazed) by the deeds of Simon the sorcerer <u>who is also known as Simon Magus</u>.
2. The wonders <u>that Simon performed</u> were supposed to have been wrought by the power of God.
3. One day Philip <u>having arrived from Jerusalem</u> began to preach the Gospel in Samaria.
4. This was the Philip <u>who had been chosen as one of the seven deacons</u>.
5. Many Samaritans <u>including Simon himself</u> believed the Gospel and were baptized.
6. Simon stayed with Philip for a time, marveling at the signs and wonders <u>that Philip performed</u>.
7. Later the Samaritans <u>who had received Christ</u> also received the Holy Spirit when Peter and John laid hands on them.
8. <u>Having seen this</u> Simon offered the apostles money so that he too might be able to bestow the Holy Spirit upon others.
9. Peter soundly rebuked Simon, saying the money <u>that he offered</u> would perish with him and urging him to repent of his wicked idea.
10. The word *simony* <u>which today refers to the sale of church offices</u> is derived from the name of Simon the sorcerer.

Review Exercises

Write the letter of the method used to produce emphasis in each selection. You will not use all the letters. [75]

a. direct quotations
b. unusual word order
c. periodic sentence
d. balanced sentence

e. repetition of key words
f. short sentence after several longer ones
g. series of similar questions, commands, or short statements

1. A disobedient dog is worthless. Therefore, training of a Hearing Ear dog begins with lessons in obedience. A dog must learn to obey when called, to obey when walking on a leash, and to obey when told to sit, stay, or lie down.
2. A number of these dogs have performed in ways that surpassed their training. Some have learned to tell the difference between a baby's normal cry and a cry of distress. Others have saved their owners from death by warning them of gas leaks and fires. These dogs are amazing.
3. Since some deaf people have trouble speaking and can therefore not tell a dog what they want him to do, Hearing Ear dogs learn to recognize hand signals.
4. A ringing alarm clock the dog must not ignore.
5. Teaching the right response to an alarm clock takes several steps. The trainer begins by lying down. He sets off an alarm clock by a remote switch. He calls the dog to his side. He praises the dog and gives him a small treat.
6. Later the trainer pretends to be sleeping when the dog comes. The longer he pretends to be sleeping, the harder the dog must work to get his treat.

---

82. Improving Your Writing Style, Part 5: Triplets

Originality
Exact Words
Active Voice
Figurative Lang.
Triplets

The word *triplets* usually refers to a set of three children. In writing, a triplet is a set of three expressions with similar construction. Such a set provides a way to add special force and appeal to a sentence. Below are some Bible verses that contain triplets.

> "Jesus saith unto him, I am <u>the way</u>, <u>the truth</u>, and <u>the life</u>: no man cometh unto the Father, but by me" (John 14:6).
>
> "He answered for himself, Neither <u>against the law of the Jews</u>, neither <u>against the temple</u>, nor yet <u>against Caesar</u>, have I offended any thing at all" (Acts 25:8).
>
> "He is Lord of lords, and King of kings: and they that are with him are <u>called</u>, and <u>chosen</u>, and <u>faithful</u>" (Revelation 17:14).

A number of Bible verses repeat a word three times, such as "Holy, holy, holy" (Isaiah 6:3) and "O earth, earth, earth" (Jeremiah 22:29). These repeated words add emphasis, but they are not triplets of the kind we are considering here. Triplets contain expressions with different words but similar structure.

The expressions in a triplet may be words, phrases, or clauses; and they may serve as a group of subjects, verbs, objects, or modifiers. Some of the poetic lines in the Bible come in groups of three; such a group is also a kind of triplet. In the following example, note that each underlined expression consists of a verb followed by a prepositional phrase.

> "Blessed is the man that <u>walketh not in the counsel of the ungodly</u>, nor <u>standeth in the way of sinners</u>, nor <u>sitteth in the seat of the scornful</u>" (Psalm 1:1).

The structure of the triplet provides a sense of completeness. Having a set of three ideas enables you to present a thought without being overly burdensome with details. A triplet is especially effective if the three expressions use rhyme or alliteration, or if they show a distinct progression of thought. The following sentences illustrate the effective use of triplets.

> Some people's exercise consists of <u>jumping to conclusions, running others down</u>, and <u>dodging responsibility</u>.
> The Bible—<u>pure, powerful</u>, and <u>permanent</u>—meets the needs of mankind. (alliteration)
> Faith <u>perceives the invisible, believes the incredible</u>, and <u>receives the impossible</u>. (rhyme)
> "Jesus Christ the same <u>yesterday</u>, and <u>to day</u>, and <u>for ever</u>." (progression of thought)

Forcing yourself to look for ways to employ triplets may also help you to think through your sentences thoroughly. However, you must avoid the tendency of using empty repetition. Also be sure that the three ideas fit well together as a unit of thought.

Of all the elements presented in these writing style lessons, the triplet is the one least frequently used. You simply cannot always write a set of three similarly constructed expressions. But if you specifically look for sentences that could include triplets, you will find some places where they definitely improve the appeal of your writing style.

Applying the Lesson

A. Rewrite each sentence, using a triplet to replace the underlined expression. For numbers 1–3, add two expressions that are parallel to the underlined item, using the words in parentheses for ideas. For numbers 4–6, replace the underlined expression with words of your own. Use rhyme or alliteration in your triplets if you can.

> **Examples:** The three Hebrews would not <u>bow to the image</u>. (budge, burn)
> A person of integrity cannot be <u>persuaded</u> to do wrong.
>
> **Answers:** The three Hebrews would not bow to the image, budge from their faith, or burn in the furnace.
> A person of integrity cannot be bribed, flattered, or frightened into doing wrong.

1. A Christian can experience <u>pardon for the past</u>. (peace, paradise)
2. If you make a mistake, do not <u>refuse to correct it</u>. (accuse, excuse)
3. To show true charity, we must <u>help people with our hands</u>. (hearts, voices)
4. Jesus showed kindness <u>to everyone</u>.

5. A person of integrity refuses <u>to become guilty of wrong</u>.
6. Money cannot buy <u>everything</u>.

B. Write a composition on the topic "Rewards of Sharing." Use at least one triplet in your composition, and also put special effort into using the other elements of effective writing style that you have studied.

---

83. Recognizing Adverbs

Though adjectives modify the substantives in sentences, adverbs modify—or change the meanings of—other words to make them more descriptive and more precise. The points in this lesson and the next will help you to recognize adverbs.

1. *Adverbs modify verbs.* Most adverbs modify verbs by telling *how, when,* or *where* something happened or existed.

God has <u>richly</u> blessed us, and we should <u>daily</u> thank Him and turn our thoughts <u>Godward</u>.

The words *not, never, ever, almost, always, hardly, scarcely,* and *seldom* are always adverbs. Often they qualify verbs by limiting or altering their meanings. Even if the word *not* is compounded with *can* in *cannot* or joined with a verb in a contraction ending with *n't,* it is an adverb.

Finite man can<u>not</u> attain true wisdom if he does<u>n't</u> believe God's Word.

2. *Adverbs modify adjectives and other adverbs.* Adverbs of this kind are often called adverbs of degree because they tell *to what degree.* Almost without exception, they come immediately before the words they modify. The following words are commonly used as adverbs of degree.

almost	especially	quite	thoroughly
completely	extraordinarily	rather	too
dangerously	extremely	so	unusually
definitely	greatly	somewhat	very
entirely	partly	surprisingly	

Study the following sentences. Note especially how the underlined words are diagramed.

You must not judge people <u>too</u> soon, or you may reach <u>completely</u> wrong conclusions.

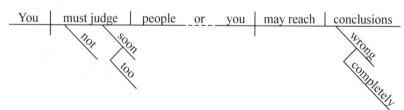

The prophets warned Israel quite clearly, yet the nation remained almost entirely idolatrous.

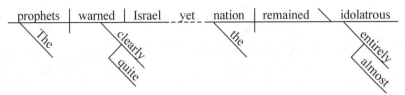

3. *Adverbs modify verbals.* These adverbs tell *how, when, where,* or *to what degree* about the action or existence indicated by the verbal. Remember that verbals include gerunds, infinitives, and participles. In the following examples, the verbals are italicized and the adverbs modifying the verbals are underlined.

Standing firmly for the truth will bless our lives.

(*Firmly* tells *how* about the gerund *Standing.*)

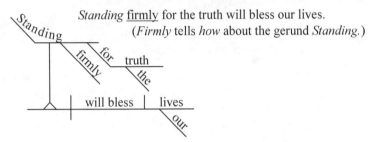

A fully *dedicated* person is determined *to stand* daily for the truth.

(*Fully* tells *to what degree* about the participle *dedicated. Daily* tells *when* about the infinitive *to stand.*)

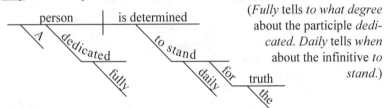

Forms of Adverbs

Many adverbs are adjectives to which the suffix *-ly* has been added. However, an *-ly* ending is not a sure indicator of an adverb, because some words ending with *-ly* are other parts of speech. And some words *not* ending with *-ly* are adverbs—especially those that tell *when* or *where.* You must observe how a word is used in a sentence before you can decide what part of speech it is.

If we trust calmly in the Lord, we shall surely know that He is lovingly guiding us.

We should always look up when troubles threaten us.

(In both examples above, all the underlined words are adverbs.)

The godly person must live a holy life. (The underlined words are adjectives.)

Many adverbs can also function as adjectives or prepositions, without any change in form.

We took a fast train to the city. (*Fast* is an adjective modifying *train.*)

The train traveled <u>fast,</u> and we did not fall <u>behind</u> schedule.
(*Fast* is an adverb modifying *traveled; behind* is a preposition.)
We boys went with Father, but Mother and the girls stayed <u>behind</u>.
(*Behind* is an adverb modifying *stayed.*)

When there are two adverb forms like *slow* and *slowly,* the *-ly* form is usually better in standard English.

Informal: Grandfather worked <u>slow,</u> but he kept at it.
Standard: Grandfather worked <u>slowly,</u> but he kept at it.

Infinitives can be used as adverbs. An infinitive that modifies a verb almost always tells *why.*

You come to school <u>to study,</u> not <u>to play.</u>
(*To study* and *to play* tell *why* about *come.*)
<u>To learn,</u> you must apply yourself diligently.
(*To learn* tells *why* about *must apply.*)

An infinitive that modifies an adjective usually follows the adjective and tells *to what degree* or *how* (that is, *in what way*). Sometimes it may not answer any specific question, but it definitely modifies the adjective by telling *to do what* about it.

These lessons are not easy <u>to understand.</u>
(*To understand* modifies the predicate adjective *easy* by telling *how.*)
The horses, eager <u>to work,</u> are champing at their bits.
(*To work* modifies the adjective *eager* by telling *in what way.*)
Too excited <u>to think,</u> the boys dashed for the house.
(*To think* tells *to what degree* about the adjective unit *Too excited.*)

In the last example, note that the infinitive modifies the unit *Too excited.* These words are considered a unit because it is not logical to say that the infinitive modifies either word separately ("Too *to think*" or "excited *to think*"). Below is the diagram of this sentence.

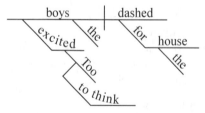

An infinitive that modifies an adverb usually follows the adverb and tells *to what degree* or *how.* Again, the infinitive may merely qualify the adverb by telling *to do what* about it. And the infinitive almost always modifies an adverb unit similar to that in the last example above.

Tornado winds may blow too swiftly <u>to measure.</u>
(*To measure* tells *to what degree* about the adverb unit *too swiftly. Too* is also an adverb modifying *swiftly.*)

These plates were not cleaned well enough <u>to use</u>.
(*To use* qualifies the adverb unit *well enough*. *Enough* is also an adverb modifying *well*.)

Applying the Lesson

A. Copy each underlined adverb, and write whether it modifies a verb (*v.*), an adjective (*adj.*), an adverb (*adv.*), or a verbal (*vbl.*).
   1. Our earthly lives, passing <u>swiftly by</u>, <u>definitely</u> represent an investment too important <u>to waste</u>.
   2. We should <u>always</u> give our <u>very</u> best efforts in serving the Lord <u>faithfully</u>.
   3. We came <u>to help</u>; therefore, tell us what job is <u>most</u> important <u>to begin</u>.
   4. I felt the pain too keenly <u>to sleep</u>; but <u>now</u> I feel <u>somewhat</u> better.
   5. To write poems <u>successfully</u> requires a <u>sufficiently</u> industrious effort, along with a worthwhile message to convey.
   6. Sitting <u>perfectly still</u>, the praying mantis <u>intently</u> watched the beetle <u>slowly</u> crawling across the leaf.
   7. Sparkling <u>brightly</u> in the sunlight, the <u>gently</u> rolling waves made an <u>especially</u> beautiful sight.
   8. The cows are coming to the barn <u>unusually early tonight</u>.
   9. How did those creatures know that the storm would strike <u>so severely</u>?
  10. God has <u>obviously</u> given animals the ability to detect <u>easily</u> some things that man can<u>not</u> perceive.

B. Copy each adverb, and write the word or words that it modifies.
   1. This drawing has extraordinarily fine details, and Lovina has almost finished it already.
   2. Clyde has been working fast; however, the bales are stacked quite neatly.
   3. The robin sat high above and soon filled the air with songs pleasant to hear.
   4. Communicating regularly will often solve misunderstandings before they seriously interfere with good relationships.
   5. Carol sat down to read, but just then the telephone rang loudly.
   6. Why do some people talk so indistinctly that they are hard to understand?
   7. Where can we find wood patterns that are easy to follow and are organized efficiently?
   8. We went inside to escape the rapidly growing clouds of mosquitoes.

Review Exercises

A. Identify each underlined item as a gerund (*G*), a gerund phrase (*GP*), an infinitive (*I*), an infinitive phrase (*IP*), or a noun clause (*NC*). If the underlined word group is not a noun, write *none*. [54]
   1. By <u>doing nothing</u>, we do ill.
   2. <u>To be washed white</u> and to be whitewashed are very different things.
   3. A man <u>who has no manors</u> may still have manners.
   4. Of hard striving comes <u>thriving</u>.
   5. People cannot repeat <u>what you never said</u>.

B. Tell whether each underlined item functions as a subject (*S*), a direct object (*DO*), an indirect object (*IO*), the object of a preposition (*OP*), or a predicate nominative (*PN*). [54]
1. Someone has well said <u>that the man without faith is a walking corpse</u>.
2. Our Lord's last will and testament is <u>excellent reading</u> for His heirs.
3. Contentment consists not in <u>having great wealth</u> but in having few wants.
4. <u>To remain silent</u> is a way for even a fool to appear wise.
5. The sword of revenge gives <u>whoever wields it</u> a bitter wound.

---

84. Recognizing Other Adverbs

In Lesson 83 you saw that adverbs modify verbs, adjectives, adverbs, and verbals. These are the most common functions of adverbs. This lesson covers less common functions of adverbs. In fact, the last two points of the lesson introduce functions of adverbs that you likely have never considered before.

1. *Adverbs introduce questions.* Such adverbs also modify the verb in the question.

<u>Why</u> have you written such brief answers?
<u>When</u> will Father return?

2. *Adverbs join independent clauses.* When adverbs function in this way, they are called conjunctive adverbs and always modify the verb of the second clause. You will study conjunctive adverbs further in Chapter 13.

Being snowbound for three days was exciting; <u>nevertheless,</u> the extra work and the power failure tempered our enjoyment. (*Nevertheless* connects two clauses and modifies *tempered,* the verb of the second one.)

3. *Adverbs modify prepositions and conjunctions.* Both prepositions and conjunctions show relationships between words. But sometimes a connecting word alone does not express the relationship accurately enough; a modifier is needed to show it more precisely. Then an adverb may be used to modify the conjunction or preposition. Observe how this is done in the following examples.

A large bear wandered <u>nearly</u> into our back yard.
(The preposition *into* is not precise enough because the bear did not actually wander into the yard. *Nearly* modifies *into* and helps to show the exact relationship between the wandering bear and the back yard.)

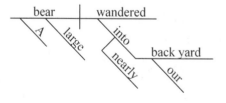

The truck stopped <u>just</u> before it hit the car.

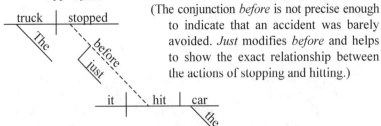

(The conjunction *before* is not precise enough to indicate that an accident was barely avoided. *Just* modifies *before* and helps to show the exact relationship between the actions of stopping and hitting.)

4. *Adverbs modify whole sentences.* An adverb does not always modify a specific word. Sometimes it modifies an entire sentence. Study the following example.

Clearly, the boys misunderstood each other.

(*Clearly* modifies the entire sentence, *the boys misunderstood each other,* by indicating that its idea is clear. To say that it modifies *misunderstood*—"misunderstood clearly"—would not be sensible.)

Here are some adverbs that can modify whole sentences.

certainly	providentially	surprisingly
clearly	regrettably	tragically
interestingly	sadly	understandably
obviously	strangely	

Note that when an adverb modifies a whole sentence, it is usually the first word. But an introductory adverb can also modify just the verb. How can you tell the difference? Here is a method that you should find helpful.

Change the introductory adverb to its adjective form, and use that form in the following expression: "It is ——— that…" Continue with the rest of the original sentence. If the resulting sentence means the same as the original, the introductory adverb modifies the entire sentence. If the meaning is different, the introductory adverb modifies only the verb.

Problem: Obviously, Absalom planned to seize the throne from David.
    Think: It is obvious that Absalom planned to seize the throne from David.
           (This sentence has the same meaning.)
Solution: *Obviously* modifies the entire sentence.

Problem: Sadly David departed from Jerusalem.
    Think: It is sad that David departed from Jerusalem.
           (This sentence has a different meaning.)
Solution: *Sadly* modifies the verb *departed.* (David departed sadly.)

Problem: Sadly, David himself had contributed to Absalom's rebellion.
    Think: It is sad that David himself had contributed to Absalom's rebellion.
           (This sentence has the same meaning.)
Solution: *Sadly* modifies the entire sentence.

Applying the Lesson

A. Copy each underlined adverb, and write whether it modifies a verb (*v.*), a preposition (*p.*), or a conjunction (*c.*).

1. If you waited <u>nearly</u> until class time to start, <u>how</u> did you expect to finish your assignment?
2. <u>Just</u> as our car passed a service station, the engine stopped; <u>however</u>, the station was closed.
3. Father did not know <u>exactly</u> where the owner lived, but he knew <u>almost</u> beyond a doubt that it was not far away.
4. <u>Soon</u> after Father called, the owner came; <u>still</u>, more than an hour passed before we were on our way again.
5. <u>Why</u> does this hole extend <u>deep</u> into the ground?
6. The hawk flew <u>directly</u> over the barn and then dived <u>straight</u> toward the ground.

B. Each sentence has two adverbs that modify prepositions or conjunctions. Copy those adverbs, and write *p.* or *c.* after each to tell what part of speech it modifies.

1. The children pulled weeds almost until sundown; and soon after they finished, Mother called them for supper.
2. Just as I stepped outside, two large planes flew right over our place.
3. One plane flew directly over my head, and the other flew somewhat to the side.
4. Though we were slightly behind schedule, we still arrived long before the sun set.
5. Jason found his coat far behind the house, exactly where he had left it.
6. The archer aimed straight at the mark, but the arrow landed far to the side.
7. Plunging deep into the water, the whale dived nearly to the bottom.
8. Right after we moved here, the people living directly across the road came for a friendly visit.

C. Write whether each underlined adverb modifies a *verb* or an entire *sentence*.

1. <u>Certainly</u>, the Bible will always stand in spite of man's unbelief and disobedience.
2. <u>Clearly</u> the minister's voice rang through the auditorium.
3. <u>Obviously</u>, we had no choice but to stand outside during the entire service.
4. <u>Interestingly</u>, the soldiers who guarded Jesus' tomb were not punished even though they reported that they had fallen asleep.
5. <u>Sadly</u> two of Jesus' disciples discussed His death as they walked toward Emmaus.
6. <u>Understandably</u>, they were greatly disappointed that He had been crucified.
7. <u>Soon</u> Jesus Himself explained the Old Testament prophecies to them.
8. <u>Tragically</u>, the very people that Jesus came to save have largely rejected Him.

Review Exercises

A. Name the punctuation that should follow each underlined word: *colon, semicolon, ellipsis points, dash,* or *none.* [4, 6]

1. The answers to all men's problems are found in only one <u>Book</u> the Bible.

2. "That salesman certainly knows the Bible," Father remarked, "<u>but</u>"

3. Clear Bible teachings that many people reject <u>include</u> nonresistance, nonconformity, the headship veiling, and the nonswearing of oaths.

4. The song on the back cover did not go very well the first time we sang <u>it</u> none of us students had ever heard it before.

5. "Did you hear <u>about</u> oh, I'm sorry; I don't want to gossip." Freda blushed as she spoke.

6. Uncle Roy's have been asked to move to <u>Guatemala</u> therefore, my older brother will move to their farm.

B. Write the letter of the sentence in which the boldface part is correct. [5, 6]

1. a. You may find some information in a reference book such as *Halley's Bible Handbook.*
   b. You may find some information in a reference book such as **Halley's Bible Handbook.**

2. a. Developing **self-discipline** is an important goal in life.
   b. Developing **self discipline** is an important goal in life.

3. a. "Was it Grandfather Stauffer who often said, 'The more you discipline yourself, the less others will need **to?'**" asked Brenda.
   b. "Was it Grandfather Stauffer who often said, 'The more you discipline yourself, the less others will need **to'?**" asked Brenda.

4. a. Jesus said, "In my Father's house are many mansions **(dwelling places):** if it were not so, I would have told you."
   b. Jesus said, "In my Father's house are many mansions **[dwelling places]:** if it were not so, I would have told you."

5. a. "I heard one of the boys shout, '**Fire!**'" gasped Sue Ann.
   b. "I heard one of the boys shout, '**Fire**'!" gasped Sue Ann.

6. a. The **"Savannah,"** the first ship to use steam power in crossing an ocean, sailed her maiden voyage in 1818.
   b. The *Savannah,* the first ship to use steam power in crossing an ocean, sailed her maiden voyage in 1818.

7. a. The enrollment in our school is **fortyfive** this year.
   b. The enrollment in our school is **forty-five** this year.

8. a. The Latin word from which we get the word **"pagan"** refers to country dwellers.
   b. The Latin word from which we get the word *pagan* refers to country dwellers.

9. a. Uncle Gilbert recounted his **not-to-be-forgotten** experiences on the mission field.
   b. Uncle Gilbert recounted his **not to be forgotten** experiences on the mission field.

10. a. This recipe calls for one and **one third** cups of milk.
    b. This recipe calls for one and **one-third** cups of milk.

85. Adverb Phrases and Clauses

Like adjectives, adverbs come not only as single words but also as phrases and clauses. Adverb phrases may be either prepositional or infinitive.

Prepositional Phrases

A prepositional phrase may be an adverb. When such a phrase modifies a verb or a verbal, it answers questions like *how, when, where,* and *why.*

> Jesus came to this earth for man's salvation. (*To this earth* tells *where* about the verb *came; for man's salvation* tells *why* about the verb *came.*)
> Jesus' blood, shed on the cross, is fully able to redeem man from sin.
> (*On the cross* tells *where* about the participle *shed; from sin* tells *from what* about the infinitive *to redeem.*)

A prepositional phrase that modifies an adjective or an adverb tells *to what degree, how,* or *how much.* It usually comes immediately after the word it modifies. Sometimes an adverb prepositional phrase modifies an adjective or an adverb unit like *too friendly* or *too quickly.*

> Our High Priest, responsive to our needs, intercedes marvelously beyond our comprehension. (*To our needs* tells *how* about the adjective *responsive; beyond our comprehension* tells *to what degree* about the adverb *marvelously.*)
> God's greatness is too vast for our feeble understanding. (*For our feeble understanding* tells *to what degree* about the adjective unit *too vast.*)

Some sentences have several prepositional phrases in succession. Sometimes these phrases are a series of adverb phrases, each modifying the same word independently of the others. Study the following sentence, in which arrows point from the underlined modifiers to the word modified.

> The girls went to Brother Carl's place on their bicycles for the milk.

At other times, the first preposition introduces the whole string of prepositional phrases, which work together as one adverb. Each of the other prepositional phrases is an adjective modifying the object in the previous phrase. When prepositional phrases occur in succession, you must think carefully about each one to decide whether it is an adjective or an adverb phrase.

> The boys are working with scrap lumber from Uncle Abe's sawmill across the river.

Infinitive Phrases

An infinitive phrase, consisting of an infinitive and its modifiers and complements, can be used as an adverb. (Infinitives can also function as substantives and as adjectives.) An infinitive that modifies a verb almost always tells *why.*

> Father has gone to town to buy some parts.
> (*To buy some parts* tells *why* about *has gone.*)

To watch the solar eclipse, we reflected the image of the sun onto white paper.
(*To watch the solar eclipse* tells *why* about *reflected.*)

An infinitive that modifies an adjective or an adverb tells *to what degree* or *how.* Usually, it immediately follows the word it modifies. Again, these infinitives sometimes modify a unit like *too startled.*

Mr. Evans seemed happy to help us.
(*To help us* tells *how* about the predicate adjective *happy.*)
This box, rather heavy to move by myself, will stay here for now.
(*To move by myself* tells *how* about the adjective unit *rather heavy.*)
The fire spread too slowly to cause major damage. (*To cause major damage* tells *to what degree* about the adverb unit *too slowly.*)

Adverb Clauses

An adverb clause is a dependent clause that modifies a verb, an adjective, or another adverb. An adverb clause begins with a subordinating conjunction. The following list contains some of the most common subordinating conjunctions.

after	even if	than	when
although	even though	that	whenever
as	how	though	where
as if	if	till	wherever
because	since	unless	whether
before	so that	until	while

Just like single-word adverbs and adverb phrases, adverb clauses can modify verbs, verbals, adjectives, or adverbs. Many adverb clauses answer the basic adverb questions *how, when,* and *where.* In addition, they can answer the questions *why, how long, how much, to what degree, in spite of what,* and *under what condition.* Adverb clauses can also modify adjective or adverb units like *as soon* or *so long.*

In these mountains, the temperature drops rapidly after the sun sets.
(*After the sun sets* tells *when* about the verb *drops.*)
A guilty person, acting as if he were innocent, compounds his wrongdoing.
(*As if he were innocent* tells *how* about the verbal *acting.*)
Content wherever God led him, the apostle Paul had learned a vital secret of true joy. (*Wherever God led him* tells *where* about the adjective *Content.*)
The stranger spoke English more clearly than I had expected. (*Than I had expected* tells *to what degree* about the adverb unit *more clearly.*)

When *as* or *than* introduces an adverb clause of comparison, the clause is often elliptical.

I mop the kitchen floor as often as the dining room floor.
(as often *as I mop the dining room floor*)
Anita has mopped the kitchen floor more often than I.
(more often *than I have mopped the kitchen floor*)

Punctuation With Adverb Phrases and Clauses

Use a comma after an introductory adverb phrase or clause (unless it is a short prepositional phrase). An adverb clause at the end of a sentence needs no comma. If an adverb clause comes in the middle of a sentence, use a comma before and after it. Only a short clause should occur in the middle; a long clause usually mars sentence coherence, as you saw in Chapter 10.

> Behind a stack of boxes in the attic, I found an old picture frame.
> To get the frame, we restacked the boxes in a different corner.
> Before we used the frame, we sanded and stained it.
> The wide wooden frame, when it was refinished, looked quite attractive.
> We worked quickly because Father's birthday was only a week away. (no comma)

Applying the Lesson

A. Copy each prepositional phrase used as an adverb, including any adjective phrase that may be in it. Write the word or word group that the phrase modifies.
1. With the light of God's Word, we can journey toward heaven in confidence.
2. To the child of God, this world is empty of strong attractions, for he counts heavenly things precious above all earthly things.
3. God is gracious beyond measure, yet we fail in many ways to partake of His grace.
4. In every culture, fleeing from temptation and following after righteousness are essential for victory over evil.
5. Founded in 1822 by American freedmen, Liberia became a republic independent from the United States in 1847.
6. In those early years, a livelihood came too hard for many of the poor settlers, and the colony could hardly have survived without help from charitable organizations.

B. Copy each infinitive phrase used as an adverb, and write the word or word group that the phrase modifies.
1. To appreciate others properly, we must recognize that we are not too good to need improvement.
2. However, some people think of themselves too highly to see the worth of others.
3. The development of Christlike character is a goal worthy enough to deserve our highest efforts.
4. To grow in grace, we must feed on the Bible sufficiently to gain definite inspiration.
5. The boys had been working too reluctantly to expect much help from the girls.
6. The small boy, eager to see the cows better, wandered out on the road.

C. Copy each adverb clause, and write the word or word group that the clause modifies.
1. When God created the eye, He designed a structure so wonderful that we marvel at His wisdom.

2. The lens of the eye, created so that it can change focus quickly, consists of living, transparent cells.
3. Most optical instruments change focus as one or more lenses are repositioned.
4. Whenever our eyes focus, the lenses change shape so smoothly that we hardly notice it.
5. Many adults' lenses, grown stiff because they are older, no longer change shape as readily as they did formerly.
6. Bifocal glasses, needed after the natural lenses do not work properly, prove so helpful that thousands of people use them.

D. Copy each word that should be followed by a comma, and add the missing comma. If no comma is needed, write *correct*.
1. To view the small mountain village we climbed the ridge behind our barn.
2. These old books since they were rebound are a pleasure to read.
3. We could easily see the trail home because a full moon shone brightly.
4. In Grandfather Brandt's cottage at the end of our lane we have spent many happy hours.
5. Although we sat quietly beside the stream we saw no deer.
6. We stood on the porch while a procession of antique cars drove by.
7. This tractor though it is more than forty years old still runs well.
8. Until we hear further news we shall simply wait and pray.
9. From the comfort of our warm house we watched the snow swirling and drifting.
10. To let us see the northern lights better Father turned off the porch light.

Review Exercises
Choose the words that are correct for the subjunctive mood. [68]
1. If the sun (was, were) shining, the grass would be dry by now.
2. A man, like a river, will become crooked if he (follow, follows) the path of least resistance.
3. If we (would have seen, had seen) the sign, we would have stopped for gas.
4. If Grandfather (was, were) here, we could ask his advice.
5. The instruction manual recommended that the owner (changes, change, changed) the engine oil every two thousand miles.
6. The neighbors have requested that my brother (be, is, was) responsible for their lawn for the next three weeks.
7. His new employer ordered that he (arrives, arrive, arrived) promptly every morning at 7:00.
8. Brendon would have gotten a better grade on his speech if he (would have looked, had looked) at the audience more often.
9. If it (be, is) practical, I would like to convert this old feed cart into a small chest.
10. If I (was, were) arrested for being a Christian, would there be enough evidence to convict me?

86. Forms of Comparison for Modifiers

Basic Definitions and Forms

Many adjectives and adverbs have three degrees of comparison: positive, comparative, and superlative. The following chart illustrates these three degrees.

Positive	Comparative	Superlative
short	shorter	shortest
big	bigger	biggest
early	earlier	earliest
faithful	more faithful	most faithful
beautifully	more beautifully	most beautifully

The positive degree describes without comparing. This is the simplest form of a modifier.

We have a <u>short</u> history lesson today.
I finished my chores <u>early</u> this evening.
Karen can draw kittens <u>beautifully</u>.

The comparative degree compares two items. For regular modifiers, it ends with *-er* or includes the word *more*. Use *-er* with most one-syllable and some two-syllable words. If necessary, double the final consonant or change a final *y* to *i* before adding *-er*. For most two-syllable words and for all longer words, use *more*. Use the word *less* for negative comparisons of all words.

We have a <u>shorter</u> history lesson today than we had yesterday.
I finished my chores <u>earlier</u> this evening than on Monday evening.
Karen can draw kittens <u>more beautifully</u> than I can.

The superlative degree compares more than two items. For regular modifiers, it ends with *-est* or includes the word *most*. Follow the same rules for using *-est* and *most* (or *least*) as those for the comparative degree.

Today we have the <u>shortest</u> history lesson that we have had all month.
Tonight I finished my chores the <u>earliest</u> of all the evenings this week.
Karen can draw kittens the <u>most beautifully</u> of anyone in our class.

Some common modifiers have irregular forms of comparison.

Positive	Comparative	Superlative
good, well	better	best
bad, badly, ill	worse	worst
far	farther	farthest
much, many	more	most
little (amount)	less	least
little (size)	littler	littlest

I tried to read the poem <u>well</u>, but Louise certainly read it <u>better</u>.
We enjoy <u>many</u> blessings from God's hand; few people have ever enjoyed <u>more</u> blessings.

Usage Guidelines

As you work with forms of comparison, observe the following guidelines.

1. *Avoid the common mistake of using the superlative form to compare only two items.*

Incorrect:
We tried to decide which of the two methods would be <u>most</u> practical.
Both James and Robert have progressed well, but Robert is <u>farthest</u> along.
Correct:
We tried to decide which of the two methods would be <u>more</u> practical.
Both James and Robert have progressed well, but Robert is <u>farther</u> along.

2. *Do not make a double comparison.*

Incorrect: Asa's early years were <u>more godlier</u> than his last years.
Correct: Asa's early years were <u>godlier</u> than his last years.

3. *A modifier that expresses an absolute quality cannot logically have degrees of comparison.* The following adjectives (and their adverb forms) are some examples of modifiers that may express absolute qualities: *square, straight, round, fatal, dead, perfect, true, unanimous, unique.*

Incorrect: Jolene's rectangles look <u>squarer</u> than mine.
The second vote was <u>more unanimous</u> than the first one.
Correct: Jolene's rectangles look <u>more nearly square</u> than mine.
The second vote was <u>more nearly unanimous</u> than the first one.

Some of the words listed above may express qualities that are not absolute, and then they may logically have degrees of comparison. For example, the phrase *more perfectly* is correct when it means "more fully" or "in greater detail." This is its meaning in the following verse.

"When Aquila and Priscilla had heard [Apollos], they took him unto them, and expounded unto him the way of God <u>more perfectly</u>" (Acts 18:26).

4. *When comparing one thing with a group of which it is part, do not omit the word* other *or* else. If you omit these words, you will say that something is bigger or better than itself.

Illogical: My sister Jane has darker hair than anyone in our family.
My pet rooster is more aggressive than any rooster on our farm.
Logical: My sister Jane has darker hair than anyone <u>else</u> in our family.
My pet rooster is more aggressive than any <u>other</u> rooster on our farm.

5. *Do not change an adverb to an adjective when using a comparative or superlative form.* This is something rather common that people do with *-ly* adverbs. Some tend to drop the *-ly* and add *-er* or *-est* to the *adjective* form of the word.

Incorrect: An eagle can fly <u>swifter</u> than a robin.
Correct: An eagle can fly <u>more swiftly</u> than a robin.

Applying the Lesson

A. Write the comparative and superlative degrees of these adjectives and adverbs.

1. little (size)	5. importantly	8. sorrowful
2. much	6. noisy	9. hilly
3. good	7. glad	10. dim
4. little (amount)		

B. Write the correct form of each modifier in parentheses.
1. Jezebel defied God (boldly) than did her husband Ahab.
2. But she was not (guilty) than he, for he was both king and head of the home.
3. For many years, Manasseh ruled the (badly) of all Judah's kings.
4. The account of the rich young ruler is one of the (sad) stories in the Gospel.
5. This old red oak is the (stately) tree on our property.
6. It is (good) for climbing than any of the other trees.
7. Of all the students, Clara is the (far) along with her drawing.
8. Tabby seems (contented) to drink milk than to catch mice.
9. You need a (hot) fire to kindle an oak log than an ash log.
10. The wind has been blowing (strongly) this afternoon than it did this morning.
11. Lisa has been showing herself (responsible) as she becomes older.
12. Which of the boys has the (many) chores this week?

C. Write one to three words to show how to correct the mistake in each sentence.
1. Both Isaiah and Jeremiah prophesied to Judah, but Jeremiah's prophecies came latest.
2. Peter was more outspoken than any disciple of Jesus.
3. Jacob proved himself a more godlier man than Esau.
4. After the Holy Spirit came, the disciples understood many things clearer than they could before.
5. Though the second bee sting was more fatal than the first one, the victim survived.
6. Sparkle is the most friendliest dog we have ever owned.
7. Brian is taller than anyone in his grade.
8. Of *World Book* and the *Encyclopedia International,* I think *World Book* is easiest to use.
9. The second of our two tomato plantings was most profitable.
10. Father can generally saw a board straighter than I can.
11. Lowell spread the paint more even on this side than on the other side.
12. We rent two alfalfa fields, but the one on Mr. Hackley's farm is best.

Review Exercises

A. For numbers 1 to 4, write the words that should be deleted from each sentence to improve its conciseness. For numbers 5 and 6, write a more concise phrase to replace the underlined parts. [77]
1. The book *Thrilling Escapes by Night* is a book that tells about William Tyndale's difficult struggles in translating the Bible into the English language.
2. I considered the idea carefully in my mind before I started sharing it with my friends.

3. In every test of earthly life, God can give His children a superabundance of grace that is more than sufficient for all their needs.

4. Though our visitor was a complete stranger whom I did not recognize, he grasped my hand in a warm, friendly, cordial handshake.

5. Due to the fact that the battery was dead, we initiated an assiduous quest for a pair of booster cables.

6. A car that was blue in color was sitting beside the large farm building that my grandfather uses to shelter his livestock.

B. Write the letter of the sentence in each set that has proper parallelism. [77]

1. a. Quickly and skillfully, Mother threaded her needle and hemmed the dress.
   b. Quickly and with great skill, Mother threaded her needle and hemmed the dress.

2. a. The leaden sky, the temperature that was falling rapidly, and the raw wind foretold a coming storm.
   b. The leaden sky, the rapidly falling temperature, and the raw wind foretold a coming storm.

3. a. After a person has had his personal devotions, they are ready for a meaningful day with God.
   b. After a person has had his personal devotions, he is ready for a meaningful day with God.

4. a. Our entire family has been and will be helping in the woodshop.
   b. Our entire family has and will be helping in the woodshop.

5. a. A miracle is when God overrides the laws of nature.
   b. A miracle is an event in which God overrides the laws of nature.

6. a. With little children who tend to forget, with adolescents who have new ideas, and with teenagers who push for freedoms, parents must be firm and consistent.
   b. With little children who tend to forget, adolescents who have new ideas, and teenagers who push for freedoms, parents must be firm and consistent.

87. Chapter 11 Review

A. Copy each underlined adjective. First label it *L* (limiting) or *D* (descriptive); then label it *AT* (attributive), *AP* (appositive), or *PR* (predicate).

1. God's gracious love, bountiful beyond our comprehension, inspires us to deep reverence.

2. Twenty kind friends came to help with our increasing work during Father's slow recovery.

3. The highest good to seek is spiritual and eternal, yet most people seek fulfillment in the paltry pleasures of this world.

4. Biblical principles to obey are precious to dedicated people who are seeking a safe way to heaven above.

5. Which verse reminds us that these trials are a normal part of human life?

B. Copy each adjective phrase or clause. If a phrase is part of a longer phrase or clause, include it with the longer item and also copy it separately. Label each item *prep.* (prepositional phrase), *part.* (participial phrase), *inf.* (infinitive phrase), or *cl.* (clause).
1. Turtles, living in most warm regions of the world, are the only reptiles to have shells.
2. Removing this shell, which is a definite part of the turtle's skeleton, will kill the turtle.
3. The upper shell, called the carapace, is attached directly to the ribs and to part of the backbone; the lower shell, named the plastron, is attached to the clavicle.
4. The place where these two shells meet is called the bridge.
5. Made of bony material, this bridge strengthens the turtle's house and also demonstrates the wisdom of God, who designed the turtle so well.

C. Copy the correct participle for each sentence.
1. (Living, Having lived) in Mexico as a child, Uncle Leon speaks Spanish.
2. Those boys (scrambling, having scrambled) up the bank are getting muddy.
3. (Melting, Melted) already, this six-inch snowfall will not last long.
4. These adobe bricks, (drying, dried) in the hot sun, have made a strong house.

D. Label each underlined phrase or clause *R* (restrictive) or *N* (nonrestrictive). Also copy each word that should be followed by a comma, and add the comma.
1. The Hellenistic Age [a]spanning the years from 323 to 30 B.C. marks the era [b]when Greek culture spread through the Mediterranean world.
2. The first date is the year [a]when Alexander the Great died, and the latter date marks the defeat of Egypt [b]which was the last survivor of Alexander's empire by the Romans.
3. The Lord [a]who has absolute sovereignty ordained that the language [b]spread by the Hellenists would be the Greek of the New Testament.

E. Copy each adverb (not counting phrases or clauses) and the word or word group that it modifies. Write *sentence* if it modifies the whole sentence.
1. Why does God daily bestow such bountiful blessings upon His people?
2. Actually, He continues to bless richly even those who stubbornly refuse to recognize Him.
3. Praising God regularly is easy to forget; therefore, praise becomes a sadly neglected activity.
4. Sometimes the Israelites fell deep into sin shortly after God provided miraculously for them.
5. Understandably, God's wrath was kindled because of their ingratitude.

F. Copy each adverb phrase or clause, including any that occurs within another phrase or clause. Also write the word or word group that the adverb modifies.
1. For many years, scientists believed that the heart drew blood into itself, as the Greek physician Galen had taught in the A.D. 100s.
2. Galen had likened the heart to a furnace because he thought the heart heated the blood.

3. According to Galen's theory, blood was used up by body organs and replaced by blood manufactured in the liver.
4. In the seventeenth century, William Harvey's observations produced conclusions that were different from Galen's.
5. When Harvey studied a beating heart, he noticed in its movement a significant fact.
6. The work of the heart was its contracting to expel blood, not its expanding to draw blood in.

G. Copy each word that should be followed by a comma, and add the missing comma. If no comma is needed, write *correct*.
1. To do more studies on the heart Harvey conducted a series of simple experiments.
2. When he tied a knot around a snake's main artery blood backed up in the heart.
3. He cut the artery between the knot and the heart to further test his ideas.
4. As he had expected the spurting blood kept time with the heartbeat.
5. To help other doctors understand the circulatory system Harvey wrote a book called *On the Motions of the Heart and Blood in Animals.*

H. Write the correct form of each modifier in parentheses.
1. Jonathan's bucket had the (little) dirt and leaves mixed with the berries.
2. The weather has become much (sultry) than it was yesterday.
3. After dark, the situation of the stranded men became (desperate) than before.
4. Donna has felt ill all week, but today she feels definitely (bad).
5. Anita has offered the (reasonable) suggestion of all.

I. Write one to three words to show how to correct the mistake in each sentence.
1. Violet used better figures of speech in her last poem than in any poem she has written.
2. The second tree looks the deadest of all the ones we planted.
3. Which of your grandfathers is oldest?
4. Eric's drawing is proportioned more realistic than I thought a six-year-old could do.

J. Write the missing words.
1. A triplet is a sentence with three expressions that have different ——— but similar ———.
2. A triplet is especially effective if the three parts show a distinct ——— of thought, or if they have ——— or ———.
3. Write suitable words to complete this triplet: We need hindsight to learn from the ———, insight to live in the ———, and foresight to plan for the ———.

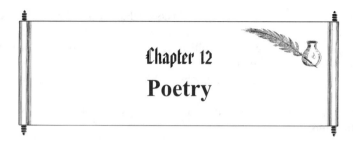

Chapter 12
Poetry

88. The Nature of Poetry

Broadly speaking, all literature falls into one of two main categories: prose or poetry. Prose includes essays, reports, and stories, and it represents the natural structure of language in sentences and paragraphs. Poetry, however, has the unique structure of lines and stanzas. Prose is concerned primarily with communicating our ideas; poetry deals much more with our feelings. Good poetry is language that expresses thoughts and emotions in a beautiful way.

Characteristics of Poetry

> Awake to worship with the morn,
> And consecrate thy day new-born.
> Again at eve in prayer be found
> As shadows curtain earth around.
> —*J. Sidlow Baxter*

What characteristics distinguish the lines above as poetry rather than prose? You will study a number of them in this lesson.

1. *Most poetry has rhyme and rhythm.* These are two of the most obvious and elementary characteristics of English poetry. *Morn* rhymes with *born,* and *found* with *around.* As you read the poem, you can also feel the regular beat of the rhythm.

Rhyme and rhythm, however, are not the only or even the most important distinguishing marks of poetry. You have learned that free verse is poetry with neither rhyme nor rhythm. On the other hand, mere verse—too shallow to qualify as true poetry—does have rhyme and rhythm, but it may lack the deeper qualities of true poetry. To further complicate the distinction between poetry and prose, we might label as poetic (though not as poetry) certain writings that have very little rhyme or rhythm. Why? Because poetry has other characteristics that we tend to overlook.

2. *Poetry appeals to the imagination and stimulates the thoughts.* This quality of poetry lifts words out of the intellectual realm and into the emotional. When language touches our emotions, it is likely to make a deeper impression than when it simply states a fact.

Consider the following example: "Begin each day with worship, and end each day with prayer." This sentence does not appeal to the emotions, and it is not likely to make a deep impression on anyone. Compare that sentence with the poem above.

The poetic lines appeal to your imagination and stimulate your thoughts in a way the sentence cannot do. For that reason, the message of the poetry will probably stick better.

3. *Good poetry delivers a wealth of meaning in a few words.* The structure of poetry allows the poet to condense his language much more than a prose writer can do. Many poems abound with elliptical sentences, communicating in a few words a whole unit of thought. The four lines of poetry below describe a nature scene.

> The hill-top, tip-toe cherry tree,
> Shouting with silver ecstasy;
> Wild birds blowing down the wind;
> Blue-brook music far and thinned;

A prose writer would say, "The faint, faraway music of the blue brook," but the poet says, "Blue-brook music far and thinned." Notice, too, how deftly the poet can sketch a scene with just a few words. Did you ever see a cherry tree on tiptoe, shouting with ecstasy? And what is *silver* ecstasy? Poetry can communicate vivid ideas that can hardly be expressed in any other way.

4. *Poetry often employs figurative language.* The figures of speech in poetry add a touch of creativity and beauty that fascinates and exercises the mind. For example, in the first sample poem, the words "thy day new-born" and "shadows curtain earth around" are figurative. In the example above, the tree is personified as standing on its tiptoes, shouting, and exulting in ecstasy. Suppose you were to rewrite those expressions without figurative language. Can you see how the quality of the poem would suffer?

5. *Poetry often employs repetition.* The sample above repeats beginning consonant sounds: <u>t</u>op, <u>t</u>ip, <u>t</u>oe, <u>t</u>ree; <u>b</u>irds, <u>b</u>lowing, <u>b</u>lue, <u>b</u>rook. It also repeats vowel sounds: h<u>i</u>ll, t<u>i</u>p, w<u>i</u>th, s<u>i</u>lver; bl<u>ue</u>, m<u>u</u>sic.

Now read the following stanza. What kind of repetition do you see?

> We shall do so much in the years to come,
>   But what have we done today?
> We shall give our gold in a princely sum,
>   But what did we give today?
> We shall lift the heart and shall dry the tear,
> We shall plant a hope in the place of fear,
> We shall speak the words of love and cheer;
>   But what did we speak today?
>   —*Nixon Waterman*

In these lines, the poet effectively repeats words and phrases with similar structures. Repetition of sounds, words, or phrases contributes richly to a poem's expression of thoughts and emotions in a beautiful way.

Advantages of Poetry

Poetry is a special form of communication with specific advantages. Which do you think would be easier to memorize—fifty words from Psalm 119 or fifty words from 2 Chronicles 6? The poetic structure of the psalm makes it easier to memorize than the prosaic structure of the historical passage. The rhyme, rhythm, and repetition found in most poetry also helps to make it easier to memorize.

In addition, poetry is a good way to express our emotions. As the apostle Paul wrote of the marvel of God's mercy extended to both Jew and Gentile, he burst out in a poetic expression of praise.

> "O the depth of the riches both of the wisdom and knowledge of God!
> How unsearchable are his judgments, and his ways past finding out!
> For who hath known the mind of the Lord? or who hath been his counsellor?
> Or who hath first given to him, and it shall be recompensed unto him again?
> For of him, and through him, and to him, are all things:
> To whom be glory for ever. Amen" (Romans 11:33–36).

When God answered Hannah's prayer for a son, she responded with a poetic prayer of thanksgiving and joy (1 Samuel 2). Upon receiving news of Saul's and Jonathan's deaths, David poured out his sorrow in a poetic tribute to them. The poetry in the Bible, in our hymnals, and in many other places constantly reminds us of the noble emotions that others have experienced.

A closely related advantage of poetry is its ability to uplift others' emotions. Whenever we put a poem on a scrapbook sheet, include a poem in a letter, or send a card with a poem, we are demonstrating this important value. Poetry is often more encouraging than prose because poetry is concise, it has strong emotional appeal, and its rhyme and rhythm make it appealing to read.

Poetry also can be a good way to teach. God specifically states this purpose: "Let the word of Christ dwell in you richly in all wisdom; teaching and admonishing one another in psalms and hymns and spiritual songs, singing with grace in your hearts to the Lord" (Colossians 3:16). By illustrating, explaining, and applying Scriptural truths, poetry can be a powerful means of indelibly impressing that truth upon our minds. The following stanza of poetry illustrates this purpose.

> If an impulse comes to say
> Some unthoughtful word today
> That may drive a friend away,
>   Don't say it.

Poetry is also valuable because it can be set to music to fill a vital role in our worship. By its unique expressions, poetry can convey eternal truths to us in a way that teaching and preaching cannot. Moreover, in an effective hymn the music so complements the words that the total effect on the emotions and on the spirit is powerful.

Types of Poetry

Most poetry belongs in one of three main classes. However, the distinctions between these classes are not sharply defined; some poems may fit in more than one group.

1. A *lyric* (lir'·ik) poem shows the poet's inner thoughts and feelings. Lyric poems

generally use first person pronouns. This is the type of poetry most often set to music.

> O Master, let me walk with Thee
> In lowly paths of service free;
>   Tell me Thy secret, help me bear
>   The strain of toil, the fret of care.

2. A *didactic* (dĭ·dak′·tĭk) poem presents specific instruction or moral teaching. Generally, a poet writes didactic poetry in the second person. This type of poetry is also often set to music.

>   Take time to be holy,
>   Speak oft with thy Lord;
>   Abide in Him always,
>   And feed on His Word;
>   Make friends of God's children,
>   Help those who are weak,
>   Forgetting in nothing
>   His blessing to seek.

3. A *narrative* poem tells a story. This type of poetry may occasionally be set to music. Narrative poems usually use the third person pronouns. They often contain many stanzas.

>   The stable boy had finished work that day,
>   The manger filled with new and fragrant hay,
>   Had fed the beasts, and usually would sleep
>   Snuggled for warmth among the placid sheep,
>   But not tonight, for he'd conceived a plan
>   To join a merchant's camel caravan
>   And travel to far places. He had heard
>   Exciting tales of cities which had stirred
>   His longing for adventures. He would go
>   Where things were happening; his friends would know
>   Why he had gone. He'd often said to them,
>   "Oh, nothing happens here in Bethlehem."
>   He looked back once, before they traveled far,
>   And wondered vaguely, "Why that brilliant star?"

Applying the Lesson

A. Write the letter of the best answer for each.

1. Which one of the following statements is true?
   a. Poetry has rhyme and rhythm, but prose has neither.
   b. Poetry appeals mainly to one's thoughts, and prose appeals mainly to one's emotions.
   c. Poetry can communicate the same thoughts as prose, but in fewer words.
   d. Prose tends to be more repetitive than poetry.

2. The main reason poetry is easier to memorize than prose is that
   a. poetry has rhyme, rhythm, and repetition.
   b. poetry appeals to emotions.
   c. poetry is generally shorter than prose selections.
   d. poetry employs figurative language.
3. Which of the following does *not* describe an advantage of poetry?
   a. Poetry is a good way to inspire noble emotions in others.
   b. Poetry can aid us in our worship.
   c. Poetry can express ideas beautifully and vividly.
   d. Poetry is easier to read than prose is.

B. Write the letter of the choice that best describes each selection.
   1. Tall was the cobbler, and gray, and thin,
      And a full moon shone where the hair had been.
      a. The figurative language describes a poor man who often worked late at night.
      b. The figurative language describes an older man who had lost much of his hair.
   2. Drop Thy still dews of quietness
          Till all our strivings cease.
      a. The soft /s/ sounds help to emphasize the idea of peace.
      b. The final /l/ sounds help to add musical appeal.
   3. Thy calmness bends serene above,
          My restlessness to still.
      a. The lines picture the peace of God as a parent calming a troubled child.
      b. The lines picture a troubled heart as a turbulent sea under a calm sky.
   4. Thy hand in all things I behold,
          And all things in Thy hand.
      a. The occurrence of "all things" in the middle of each line adds musical appeal.
      b. The reversed repetition emphasizes trust in God for any circumstance.
   5. Blow, bugles, blow, set the wild echoes flying;
      Answer, echoes, dying, dying, dying.
      a. The repeated words add musical appeal.
      b. The many commas help to improve the rhythm.
   6. God moves in a mysterious way,
          His wonders to perform.
      a. A wealth of meaning is packed into these short lines.
      b. The perfect rhythm adds strong appeal to these lines.
   7. Life is real! Life is earnest!
          And the grave is not its goal.
      a. The many short words help to make these lines impressive.
      b. The fervent language provides a strong emotional appeal.
   8. Over the mountain is gleaming and streaming the sunshine fair
      Loudly declaring to mortals that God is there!
      a. The long lines help to emphasize the message of this selection.
      b. The rhythm pattern and rhyming words help to give a feeling of joyous enthusiasm.

C. Write whether each selection is primarily *lyric, didactic,* or *narrative.*

1. Yes, leave it with Him; the lilies all do,
   And they grow;
   They grow in the rain, and they grow in the dew—
   Yes, they grow.
   They grow in the darkness, all hid in the night,
   They grow in the sunshine, revealed by the light—
   Still they grow.

2. If He should come today
   And find my hands so full
   Of future plans, however fair,
   In which my Saviour has no share,
   What would He say?
   —*Grace Troy*

3. I met God in the morning,
   When the day was at its best,
   And His presence came like sunrise,
   Like a glory in my breast.
   —*Ralph S. Cushman*

4. Then the pitying people hurried
   From their homes and thronged the beach;
   Oh, for power to cross the waters
   And the perishing to reach!
   Helpless hands were wrung in terror,
   Tender hearts grew cold with dread,
   And the ship, urged by the tempest,
   To the fatal rock-shore sped.

5. Read not this Book, in any case,
   But with a single eye;
   Read not, but first desire God's grace
   To understand thereby.

Review Exercises

Label each underlined verb *TA* (transitive, active voice), *TP* (transitive, passive voice), *IC* (intransitive complete), or *IL* (intransitive linking). [69]

1. We lessen the pain of suffering when we <u>learn</u> the lesson of gratitude.
2. The most important part of doctrine <u>is</u> the first two letters.
3. We <u>may linger</u> long at the looking glass of the Word with no fear of growing vain.
4. That which lies in the well of our thoughts <u>will be drawn</u> up in the bucket of our speech.
5. We <u>show</u> our character by the things at which we laugh.

89. The Rhyme of Poetry

Rhyming Patterns

Rhyme is probably one of the first elements of poetry you ever recognized. Poets use a variety of rhyming patterns, and they have developed a way to analyze the pattern of a particular poem by using a different small letter for each set of rhyming words. The three most common rhyming patterns in English poetry are shown below. Except for the *aabb* pattern, poetic lines are usually indented to show which ones rhyme.

Example 1:

Lives of great men all remind us	a
We can make our lives sublime,	b
And, departing, leave behind us	a
Footprints on the sands of time.	b

Example 2:

I met God in the morning,	a
When the day was at its best,	b
And His presence came like sunrise,	c
Like a glory in my breast.	b

Example 3:

God hath not promised skies always blue,	a
Flower-strewn pathways all our lives through;	a
God hath not promised sun without rain,	b
Joy without sorrow, peace without pain.	b

Of course, the possibilities of rhyming patterns are as varied as man's imaginations. Here are several patterns that are more challenging.

Example 4:

Softly I closed the Book as in a dream	a
And let its echoes linger to redeem	a
Silence with music, darkness with its gleam.	a

Example 5:

When storms arise,	a
And dark'ning skies	a
About me threat'ning lower,	b
To Thee, O Lord, I raise mine eyes,	a
To Thee my tortured spirit flies	a
For solace in that hour.	b

Example 6:

O Love that will not let me go,	a
I rest my weary soul in Thee;	b
I give Thee back the life I owe,	a
That in Thine ocean depths its flow	a
May richer, fuller be.	b

Sometimes you must read several stanzas or the entire poem to catch the full beauty of the rhyming pattern. In the following poem, the first line is repeated in each stanza, the second and third lines rhyme within the stanzas, and the fourth lines rhyme throughout the poem.

Example 7:

Heav'nly Father, hear our prayer	a
When the dawn is breaking,	b
And our souls are waking	b
To life's newborn day.	c
Heav'nly Father, hear our prayer	a
When the noon is blazing,	d
And our foe is raising	d
War along life's way.	c
Heav'nly Father, hear our prayer	a
When the day is ending,	e
And we're homeward wending:	e
Rest beyond life's fray.	c

Some poems also have internal rhyme, which is not shown by writing the letters of the rhyming pattern.

Example 8:

This is my Father's world;	a
And to my list'ning ears,	b
All nature <u>sings</u>, and round me <u>rings</u>	c
The music of the spheres.	b

Rules for Rhyme

The intended rhyming words should generally be true rhymes. Even experienced poets sometimes use imperfect rhymes like *known—done* and *Word—Lord*. However, such rhymes will mar the music of poetry if they are used carelessly or too frequently. The following four rules show what makes perfect rhymes.

1. *The vowel sounds of rhyming syllables must be the same.* Rhyme is a matter of sound, not spelling.

<u>Foot</u> and <u>put</u> rhyme; <u>foot</u> and <u>boot</u> do not.

2. *The final consonant sounds of rhyming syllables must be the same.*

<u>Wheat</u> and <u>fleet</u> rhyme; <u>wheat</u> and <u>weed</u> do not.

3. *The beginning consonants of rhyming syllables must be different.* If two different words sound exactly alike, they are homonyms, not rhymes.

<u>Rain</u> and <u>stain</u> rhyme; <u>rain</u> and <u>reign</u> do not.

4. *The rhyming syllables must be accented.*

<u>Contend</u> and <u>befriend</u> rhyme; <u>contend</u> and <u>opened</u> do not.

Masculine and Feminine Rhyme

Masculine rhyme involves only one syllable. Words of several syllables may have masculine rhyme, but the rhyme is only in the last syllable. By far, most rhymes fall into this category.

might—sight   guest—behest   behold—untold

Feminine rhyme, which involves more than one syllable, adds a special beauty to poetry. The rhyming part of the word must be an accented syllable that is not the last syllable. The accented syllables must truly rhyme, not be alike; the syllables following the rhyming syllables must have exactly the same sounds.

True feminine rhymes:	Not true feminine rhymes:
submission—contrition	sparingly—warily
brightening—lightening	contending—portending

Feminine rhyme sometimes involves syllables in two different words. Notice how this is true in the following example.

> Saviour, like a shepherd <u>lead us</u>,
> Much we need Thy tend'rest care;
> In Thy pleasant pastures <u>feed us</u>,
> For our use Thy folds prepare.

Applying the Lesson

A. Write the rhyming patterns for these stanzas. (Consider imperfect rhymes as rhymes.) In number 4, be sure to write the pattern for the whole poem.

1. I will not doubt, though all my ships at sea
       Come drifting home with broken masts and sails;
       I will believe the Hand which never fails,
    From seeming evil worketh good for me.
       And though I weep because those sails are tattered,
       Still will I cry, while my best hopes lie shattered:
       "I trust in Thee."
         —*Ella Wheeler Wilcox*

2. A garden is a lovesome thing, God wot!
       Rose plot,
          Fringed pool,
       Fern'd grot—
          The veriest school
          Of peace; and yet the fool
    Contends that God is not—
       Not God! in gardens! when the eve is cool?
    Nay, but I have a sign;
    'Tis very sure God walks in mine.
         —*Thomas Edward Brown*

3. Thy mighty arm
   Will let no harm
     Come near me nor befall me;
   Thy voice shall quiet my alarm
   When life's great battle waxeth warm—
     No foeman shall appall me.
                    —*Paul Laurence Dunbar*

4. Above the eastern mountain, see a fountain splash its hues
     Of purple, orange, pink, and red,
   In streaks and arches, blends and contrasts, shouting out great news!

   What news of such dimension earns attention boldly said?
     Why, nothing less than that the sun
   Is bursting with new energy to put the night to bed!

   The fountain spills those splashes; color crashes as if spun
     Across the floor of morning sky: a new day has begun!
   The dazzling splendor of the sun will reign till day is done.

5. Strong Son of God, immortal Love,
     Whom we, that have not seen Thy face,
     By faith, and faith alone, embrace,
   Believing where we cannot prove.
                    —*Alfred Tennyson*

B. From the selections above, write examples of the following things.
   1. One set of feminine rhymes found at the end of lines.
   2. Three sets of internal rhyming words.
   3. One set of imperfect rhymes.

C. Write words to complete these selections with perfect rhymes. The indents show
   which lines should rhyme.
   1. Triumphant was Christ! He arose!
        The Victor who broke death's strong ———;
        The work of the devil was vain.
        Forever Christ Jesus shall ———,
      For He has defeated all ———.
   2. Down the vast valley I view with keen ———
        Scenes of rich verdure our God has ———:
          Forests of hemlocks and firs grace its edges;
      Oaks and black walnuts abound beyond measure
      Down by the riverbed. I am elated,
        Beauty beholding while up on these ———.
   3. O Rooster Red, what do you ———
        To strut around the barnyard so?
      You flaunt your feathers' fancy sheen,
        Proclaim your highness with a ———.

4. Do you see this lovely apple in my ———?
    Smell its sweetness? feel its firmness? hear its ———
    As my teeth sink into mellow fruit for ———?
    Atheism I shall never ———!

D. Choose one of the following rhyming patterns, and write an original four-line stanza to match it.

   abcb   aabb   abab   abba

   Your stanza does not need to express a profound truth, but it does need to deal with a worthwhile topic. Since poetry often touches the emotions, the best topic to choose is probably one that you have strong feelings about. Here are a few suggestions.
   Your home
   Your birthday
   A beautiful spring day
   Your grandparents
   A worship service
   A cemetery
   A walk in the woods
   Your pet dog, cat, rabbit, or hamster
   A scenic view of a mountain, valley, lake, or river

---

90. Improving Your Editing Skills, Part 9

Many English words have a variety of meanings and uses. In most cases, we can combine words in more than one way to communicate our thoughts. But occasionally a certain word combination can produce an *ambiguous* sentence. Such a sentence may be seriously misleading—or embarrassingly humorous.

The following item once appeared as a headline in a newspaper.

SQUAD HELPS DOG BITE VICTIM

Did the squad actually help the dog to bite its victim? Of course not. The squad helped the *victim* who had received a dog bite. Common sense tells us which meaning to take, and no harm is done.

This time we can smile and pass on. But some ambiguous statements are confusing or misleading, so you need to make it your responsibility to detect and change such statements. A person should not need to be a detective to understand what he is reading.

In this lesson and in all your proofreading, make sure every sentence is clear and easily understandable.

Marks Used in Editing and Proofreading

$\vee$ or $\wedge$ insert (caret)	$\mathcal{J}$ delete	. . . . stet (let it stand)	⎯⎯⎯⎯⎯⎯ use italics
¶ begin new paragraph	no ¶ no new paragraph	*lc* change to lowercase (small letter)	*uc* change to uppercase (capital letter)
# insert space	⌣ delete space	← move (arrow)	⌐⌐⌐⌐⌐ transpose

Editing Practice

A. Use proofreading marks to correct the two errors in capitalization, punctuation, or the use of italics in each sentence.

1. The Imperial valley stretches from Southern California into northern Mexico.

2. One hundred miles long and forty to sixty miles wide this valley lies almost completely below sea level

3. The annual precipitation in this valley averages under four inches but the All-American Canal brings water from the Colorado river.

4. Irrigation has made the valley a productive farming region alfalfa, cotton and sugar beets grow in the summer and melons in the winter.

5. Iodine, a grayish black solid is one of the Elements.

6. The word iodine comes from a Greek word that means violet".

7. Although this element itself is not violet it does produce a violet vapor, when it is heated nearly to its melting point.

8. effective against a wide variety of bacteria and fungi iodine has long been a common antiseptic and disinfectant.

9. Iodine occurs in the human body in trace amounts (0.00004% by weight,) yet it is essential to the health of our bodies

10. Excess iodine in the body can cause tenseness and
    nervousness; iodine defi ciency produces lethargy and
    goiter (enlargement of the thyroid gland.

B. The paragraphs below use fifteen of the words or phrases whose standard usage you studied in Chapter 5. Use proofreading marks to correct the ones that are incorrect.

1.   Have you ever heard of *dihydrogen monoxide*? You had ought to know

2. about this chemical compound, for it has lots of harmful properties. For one

3. thing, the said compound is a principal component of acid rain. Beside that,

4. it has an erosive affect on soil. Every year dihydrogen monoxide renders

5. many tons of precious topsoil useless for farming.

6.   In its solid form, this compound can be altogether treacherous. Small

7. amounts have caused strong, healthy men to literally lose there equilibrium

8. and collapse. Its liquid form is found in cancerous tumors. And those who

9. use it in its gaseous state better be careful as well, for direct contact with

10. human skin produces painful burns. Farther investigation will reveal many

11. other ways in which this compound is harmful.

12.   Should the general public have access to a material with so many averse

13. characteristics? Should its use be controlled by local or federal statues?

14. Before credulous readers respond in rash excitement, they should consider

15. the common name of dihydrogen monoxide: water.

C. Use proofreading marks to correct all the errors in these paragraphs, including the ones that are specifically mentioned below. No line has more than one error.
    a. Use a transposition mark to improve the word order in line 4.
    b. Improve the last sentence of paragraph 2 by repositioning the phrase *like toothpicks.*
    c. In the last sentence of paragraph 3, change the position of *over a wide area* so that it clearly modifies *trees and wildlife.*

1.   One of the most powerful volcanic eruptions ever recorded

2. in North America occur at Mount Saint Helens in the state

3. of Washington. Having laid dormant since 1857, this mountain

4. on May 18, 1980 literally blew off its top. The tremendous

5. explosion scattered ash, stone and other debris more than

6. 12 miles (19 kilometers) out ward from the peak. It blew

7. away the top 1,300 feet (400 meters) of the mountain,

8. reducing its heigth to 8,364 feet (2,549 meters).

9.   Hot ash and rocks ignited forest fires and melted snow

10. on the sides of the mountain. As a result, flood's and mud-

11. slides rushed down the mountain slopes destroying build-

12. ings, roads, and bridges. Millions of trees toppled in

13. the terrible aftermath of the explosion like toothpicks.

14.   At least 60 people perished in the dissaster, and

15. damages ran into hundreds of millions of dollars. Trees

16. and wildlife died from the thick layer of ash deposited

17. after the blast over a wide area.

18.   Since its catastrophic Eruption in 1980, Mount Saint

19. Helens has erupted severaltimes and intermittently

20. spewed out ash and steam it stands today as a clear

21. testimony to the power of and almighty Creator.

---

91. The Rhythm of Poetry

God has created rhythm. Count the seconds ticking by. Consider the regular march of the sun across the sky, the regular phases of the moon, and the regular alternations of the seasons. Watch the waves washing ashore. The world that God has created is filled with rhythm.

God has created man with a sense of rhythm too. Feel the rhythm in your heartbeat and in your breathing. Watch someone walking, skipping, or running. Gently rock a baby to sleep. Sing "Onward, Christian Soldiers." Who can deny that our bodies possess both a rhythm of their own and the capacity to enjoy rhythm?

Poetic Feet

Rhythm is an important element of poetry. Rhythm in poetry is a pattern of accented and unaccented syllables. Each unit of rhythm, called a poetic foot, contains one accented syllable and the unaccented syllable or syllables associated with it. Marking the rhythm of the poetic feet is known as scansion. When you scan a line of poetry, you mark each accented syllable with a slanted line and each unaccented syllable with a breve. Below are two lines of poetry with the syllables marked.

<pre>
/ ˘ /   ˘   / ˘ / ˘
O my soul, bless thou Jehovah
/   ˘ ˘ / ˘ ˘ /
Wonderful story of love
</pre>

Most English poetry uses one of four common feet: *iambic, trochaic, anapestic,* or *dactylic.* Each of these is explained and illustrated below. The number after each line of poetry shows the number of feet in that line. This number is found by counting the accented syllables.

1. *The iambic foot consists of one unaccented syllable followed by one accented syllable.* This is the most commonly used pattern in English poetry. Perhaps this is true because the iambic pattern is the closest to the rhythm of our ordinary speech. The light, cheerful rhythm of the iambic foot is well suited to themes of praise, joy, and beauty.

<pre>
˘   /   ˘   /   ˘ / ˘   /
My God, how wonderful Thou art,   4
˘   / ˘ / ˘   /
Thy majesty how bright;   3
</pre>

2. *The trochaic foot consists of one accented syllable followed by one unaccented syllable.* Its heavier rhythm is well suited to sober, thoughtful themes. Lines written with trochaic rhythm often end with an incomplete foot. If an incomplete foot contains an accented syllable, it is counted as a foot.

<pre>
/   ˘   / ˘   /   ˘   / ˘
God, who touchest earth with beauty,   4
/   ˘   / ˘ /
Make me lovely too;   3
</pre>

3. *The anapestic foot consists of two unaccented syllables followed by one accented syllable.* This is a flowing, almost galloping rhythm that is well suited to themes of hope, joy, and earnestness. Lines written with anapestic rhythm often begin with an incomplete foot and occasionally end with an incomplete foot.

<pre>
˘ / ˘ ˘ / ˘ ˘   /   ˘ ˘ / ˘
His love has no limit, His grace has no measure,   4
˘ / ˘ ˘ / ˘ ˘   / ˘ ˘ /
His power no boundary known unto men;   4
</pre>

4. *The dactylic foot consists of one accented syllable followed by two unaccented syllables.* (A dactyl is a finger. The dactylic foot, like a finger, has one "longer" part—the accented syllable—followed by two "shorter" parts—the unaccented syllables.) Dactylic rhythm, like anapestic, is well suited to themes of hope, joy, and earnestness. Because a dactylic foot ends with two unaccented syllables, you will rarely find a complete foot at the end of a line.

<pre>
/ ˘ ˘   /   ˘   ˘   / ˘ ˘ / ˘
Under His wings, O what precious enjoyment!   4
/   ˘ ˘ / ˘ ˘   / ˘ ˘   /
There will I hide till life's trials are o'er;   4
</pre>

Poets may use combinations of these four basic poetic feet. Sometimes one foot clearly predominates in the poem, with a secondary foot placed at regular intervals. Occasionally the lines of a poem have alternating feet.

The following stanza illustrates a blend of dactylic and trochaic. The first three lines have two dactylic feet followed by two trochaic feet; the last line has three trochaic feet.

/ ˇ ˇ / ˇ ˇ / ˇ /
Down at the cross where my Saviour died,   4

/ ˇ ˇ / ˇ ˇ / ˇ /
Down where for cleansing from sin I cried,   4

/ ˇ ˇ / ˇ ˇ / ˇ /
There to my heart was the blood applied;   4
/ ˇ / ˇ /
Glory to His Name!   3

Some poetic lines have irregular rhythm for the simple reason that perfect rhythm is not always practical. Perhaps the only way to have perfect rhythm is to use an uncommon word or an unnatural word order. It is usually better to have slightly irregular rhythm than to use clumsy or obscure wording.

On the other hand, the musical appeal of a poem suffers if the rhythm is too uneven. When you write poetry, do not decide too quickly that a line with irregular rhythm must be left that way. Most likely, you simply need to do more work on that line. You should not be satisfied until the rhythm is perfect or very nearly perfect.

Meter

The word *meter* refers to the rhythm pattern of a poem. As you can see from the examples above, various meters are used in poetry. Specific names can be given to lines of poetry according to the number of feet they have. Each name consists of the word *meter* with a prefix representing a number. Study the following names and examples.

1. *A monometer* (mə·nom'·i·tər) *line has one foot.*

> Thus I
> Pass by
> And die:
>
> As one
> Unknown
> And gone.
> —*Robert Herrick*

2. *A dimeter* (dim'·i·tər) *line has two feet.*

> The hands of Christ
> Seem very frail,
> For they were broken
> By a nail.
> —*John Richard Moreland*

3. *A trimeter* (trim′·i·tər) *line has three feet.*

> Here's a hand to the boy who has courage
>   To do what he knows to be right;
> When he falls in the way of temptation,
>   He has a hard battle to fight.
> Who strives against self and his comrades
>   Will find a most powerful foe.
> All honor to him if he conquers.
>   A cheer for the boy who says "No!"
> > —*Phoebe Cary*

4. *A tetrameter* (te·tram′·i·tər) *line has four feet.*

> Happiness is like a crystal,
>   Fair and exquisite and clear,
> Broken in a million pieces,
>   Shattered, scattered far and near.
> Now and then along life's pathway,
>   Lo! some shining fragments fall;
> But there are so many pieces,
>   No one ever finds them all.
> > —*Priscilla Leonard*

5. *A pentameter* (pen·tam′·i·tər) *line has five feet.*

> Just stand aside, and watch yourself go by;
> Think of yourself as "he" instead of "I."
>   Note closely, as in other men you note,
>   The bag-kneed trousers and the seedy coat.
> Pick flaws; find fault; forget the man is you,
> And strive to make your estimate ring true.
>   Confront yourself, and look you in the eye—
>   Just stand aside, and watch yourself go by.
> > —*Strickland Gillilan*

Lines of six, seven, and eight feet also occur, but they are rare. The names for these longer lines are hexameter (hek·sam′·i·tər), heptameter (hep·tam′·i·tər), and octameter (ok·tam′·i·tər).

Many poems have lines of varying lengths. For example, the alternation of tetrameter and trimeter lines is quite common.

> I love to steal awhile away
>   From ev'ry cumb'ring care,
> And spend the hours of setting day
>   In humble, grateful prayer.
> > —*Phoebe H. Brown*

To give the complete name of the rhythm pattern in a stanza, we must name both the poetic foot and the meter of each line. Thus the example immediately above is iambic tetrameter and trimeter. The other examples above are as follows: (1) iambic monometer, (2) iambic dimeter, (3) anapestic trimeter, (4) trochaic tetrameter, and (5) iambic pentameter. The following stanza has a combination of anapestic and iambic rhythm, with trimeter, dimeter, and tetrameter lines.

O give ear to our cry, O Lord;   (3 feet)
Turn again unto us.   (2 feet)
For how long wilt Thou angry be?   (3 feet)
Turn again unto us.   (2 feet)
As a Shepherd kind, Thou hast led us on,   (4 feet)
Thou hast cared for all Thy flock;   (3 feet)
With the finest wheat Thou hast satisfied,   (4 feet)
And with honey from the rock.   (3 feet)

Applying the Lesson

A. Write the complete name of the rhythm pattern in each stanza. If several different feet or meters are used, be sure the name includes them all.

1. In vain do men of science seek to prove
    The hidden world that throbs behind the seen;
    The ever-present cause of things that move
    Eludes their searching sight, however keen.
    —*Angela Morgan*

2. Who Thou art I know not,
    But this much I know:
    Thou hast set the Pleiades
    In a silver row.
    —*Harry Kemp*

3. The gardens bring news of His glory,
    The forestlands, hoary with age;
    The years are aflame with His story,
    Each day is a luminous page.
    —*Thomas Curtis Clark*

4. Beauty is mine for today—
    Song that a passing bird sings,
    Fairness of fruit out of reach,
    Down of the butterfly's wings.
    —*Mary Brennan Clapp*

5. I heard a bird at break of day
    Sing from the autumn trees
  A song so mystical and calm,
    So full of certainties,
  No man, I think, could listen long
    Except upon his knees.
  Yet this was but a simple bird,
    Alone, among the trees.
        —William Alexander Percy

6. To the work! To the work! We are servants of God,
  Let us follow the path that our Master hath trod;
  With the balm of His counsel our strength to renew,
  Let us do with our might what our hands find to do.
        —Anonymous

7. Beautiful springtime when all is delight;
  Beautiful summer, so warm and so bright;
  Beautiful autumn, with fruits and with grain;
  Beautiful winter, with snowflakes again.
        —W. A. Bixler

8. Christian, seek not yet repose,
    Cast thy dreams of ease away;
  Thou art in the midst of foes;
    Watch and pray.
        —Charlotte Elliott

B. Improve the rhythm of the original stanza that you wrote for Lesson 89. The rhythm in your finished stanza should be perfect, with no irregularities.

C. Choose one of the following stanzas, and write a poem of your own to match its rhyme and rhythm patterns exactly. The second one is a special challenge. Can you write a stanza to match its anapestic rhythm and internal rhymes?

1. If you were busy being glad,
  And cheering people who are sad,
  Although your heart might ache a bit,
  You'd soon forget to notice it.

2. Though the cover is worn,
  And the pages are torn,
    And though places bear traces of tears,
  Yet more precious than gold
  Is this Book worn and old,
    That can shatter and scatter my fears.

Remember that the topic of your poem must be worthwhile, and that it should probably be something that you have strong feelings about.

D. Begin looking for a poem (not used in this chapter) that you would enjoy reading aloud to your classmates in Lesson 95. Show it to your teacher for his approval by the time you reach Lesson 94.

---

92. Other Elements of Poetic Music

Poetry and music have much in common. Not only is poetry often set to music in songs, but it also has a music of its own. The music of poetry depends largely on repeated words and sounds.

Alliteration

Alliteration is the repetition of beginning consonant sounds. This is especially effective when the alliteration links words with related meanings or words in related grammatical structures.

> <u>B</u>ane and <u>b</u>lessing, <u>p</u>ain and <u>p</u>leasure,
>   By the cross are sanctified.

Alliteration produces various effects. Generally, it tends to speed up a poetic passage. Repeating soft sounds like *s, f,* and *w* adds a tone of softness, tenderness, weariness, or suchlike. Repeating harsh sounds like *b, d,* and *k* suggests things like sharpness, harshness, and power. Notice the difference of effect in the following examples.

> <u>S</u>ilently <u>s</u>nowflakes are <u>s</u>ifting to earth,
>   <u>S</u>oftening <u>s</u>ounds in their <u>s</u>weeping embrace.

> <u>B</u>oldly the <u>b</u>lizzard is <u>b</u>lasting the earth,
>   <u>B</u>linding the travelers <u>b</u>raving its gales.

Assonance

Assonance is the repetition of similar vowel sounds in accented syllables. Assonance can affect the speed of a poetic passage in opposite ways. The repetition of the /a/, /e/, and /i/ sounds tends to speed up a poem because these are the most clipped of English vowel sounds. The repetition of most other vowel sounds, however, tends to slow down a poetic passage because those sounds are more drawn out. Assonance is most effective, of course, when its effect on speed relates to the meaning of the passage.

Study the following sets of lines. See if you can feel the slowing-down effect in the first and the speeding-up effect in the second. In the first stanza, the slow assonance matches the somber tone; and in the second stanza, the faster assonance matches the hopeful tone.

> O Lord, sustain us thr<u>ough</u> this day!
>   Del<u>u</u>sion br<u>oo</u>ds o'er h<u>u</u>man souls:
> The f<u>oo</u>ls who hated tr<u>u</u>th have gone astray.

> And yet our blessed Master, Friend,
>   Sends us each morn a message blest;
> If men but hear, what joys their way attend!

Note that all the underlined vowels are in accented syllables. The vowels in *who* (line 3) and *Sends* (line 5) do not illustrate true assonance, because they are in unaccented syllables.

Natural Words and Word Order

Natural, familiar words and word order add to the music of poetry. As much as possible, avoid unnatural words such as *e'en* and *'twixt*. Arrange the words in the most normal word order possible. Although good poems do occasionally transgress these ideals, poetry is at its best when it has a smooth, natural sound.

Read the following two stanzas of poetry. The two versions express the same thoughts, but the unnatural words and word order in the first detract from the music of the poetic expressions.

> Life's troubled sea I'm daily sailing o'er,
>   Winds fiercely blow and waves are rising high;
> But fear I'll not, for Jesus goes before,
>   And me He'll lead to mansions in the sky.

> I'm sailing over life's tempestuous sea;
>   Though winds blow wild and waves are rising high,
> I will not fear, for Christ doth pilot me—
>   He'll lead me to those mansions in the sky.

Refrains

Occasionally, poets use refrains for special effect. The refrain is a short phrase, one or two lines, or an entire stanza repeated throughout the poem. Often the refrain is repeated in a very regular pattern, but it may also be repeated at random.

The following poem illustrates a refrain at the end of each stanza. Notice that the word order is changed slightly for the middle three stanzas.

Voyagers

> O Maker of the mighty deep
>   Whereon our vessels fare,
> Above our life's adventure keep
>   Thy faithful watch and care.
> In Thee we trust, whate'er befall;
> Thy sea is great, our boats are small.

> We know not where the secret tides
>   Will help us or delay,
> Nor where the lurking tempest hides,
>   Nor where the fogs are gray.
> We trust in Thee, whate'er befall;
> Thy sea is great, our boats are small.

When outward bound we boldly sail
  And leave the friendly shore,
Let not our hearts of courage fail
  Before the voyage is o'er.
We trust in Thee, whate'er befall;
Thy sea is great, our boats are small.

When homeward bound we gladly turn,
  O bring us safely there,
Where harbor lights of friendship burn
  And peace is in the air.
We trust in Thee, whate'er befall;
Thy sea is great, our boats are small.

Beyond the circle of the sea,
  When voyaging is past,
We seek our final port in Thee;
  O bring us home at last.
In Thee we trust, whate'er befall;
Thy sea is great, our boats are small.
                              —*Henry van Dyke*

When certain lines are used as a refrain, their last words are considered rhyming words even though they are the same each time. For example, if the rhyme pattern of the poem above were shown with small letters, the first stanza would be labeled *ababcc*. The second stanza would be marked *dedecc*, and all the other lines ending with *befall* or *small* would also be marked *c*.

Applying the Lesson
A. Read these poems, and do the exercises that follow each one.

Above the Trembling Elements
Above the trembling elements,
  Above life's restless sea,
Dear Saviour, lift my spirit up,
  Oh, lift me up to Thee!

Great calmness there, sweet patience, too,
  Upon Thy face I see;
I would be calm and patient, Lord,
  Oh, lift me up to Thee.

I am not weary of Thy work,
  From earth I would not flee;
But while I walk, and while I serve,
  Oh, lift me up to Thee!

1. Copy a set of words with assonance.
2. Copy a set of words with alliteration.
3. Copy the words used as a refrain throughout these stanzas.

Love at Home
There is beauty all around,
    When there's love at home;
There is joy in every sound,
    When there's love at home;
Peace and plenty here abide,
Smiling sweet on every side,
Time doth softly, sweetly glide,
    When there's love at home.

Kindly heaven smiles above,
    When there's love at home;
All the earth is filled with love,
    When there's love at home;
Sweeter sings the brooklet by,
Brighter beams the azure sky;
Oh, there's One who smiles on high
    When there's love at home.

4. From stanza 1, copy two sets of words with alliteration. One set should include more than two words.
5. From stanza 2, copy two sets of words with alliteration. One set should include more than two words.
6. Copy the words used as a refrain throughout these stanzas.

B. From below, choose one poetic line that illustrates alliteration and one that illustrates assonance. Write another line for each one to continue the alliteration or assonance. Your lines do not need to rhyme with the ones given, but they should match in rhythm.
1. The sacred Scriptures speak
2. Christ is abiding with presence divine
3. Do you fondly enjoy all these fine feathered friends
4. Silver wisps of cirrus clouds

Review Exercises

A. Copy the correct participle for each sentence. [81]
1. Grandfather Williams, (recovering, recovered) from his recent stroke, is starting to walk again.
2. These delicious oranges, (growing, grown) in California, have been shipped across the country by truck.
3. (Teaching, Having taught) school for fifteen years, Brother Allgyer has influenced many homes in our community.
4. The students, (printing, having printed) the school newspaper, expect to be finished soon.

B. For each underlined word, write *yes* or *no* to tell whether it should be followed by a comma. [81, 85]
1. Formed with amazing characteristics the lowly woodpecker testifies to the wisdom of his Creator.

2. Since he must be able to hold to vertical tree <u>trunks</u> God has given him short <u>legs</u> and powerful claws.
3. A beak slamming into <u>wood</u> as often as a hundred times a <u>minute</u> must be harder than the beaks of other birds.
4. The woodpecker's head can withstand this tremendous <u>banging</u> because God has placed a special shock-absorbing <u>tissue</u> between his beak and his skull.
5. Where does he store his <u>tongue</u> which is about four times <u>longer</u> than his beak?
6. As you may <u>know</u> the lower part of his tongue is <u>looped</u> around the back of his skull!

C. Write enough words to show how to correct the mistake in each sentence. [86]
1. I have always found this old recliner comfortabler than most newer chairs.
2. In his sermons, I have heard Brother Earl recite more Bible verses than anyone I know.
3. Brother Paul's cornfield looks more perfect than any other that I know of.
4. Though this drill costs five dollars more than that one, its quality makes it the best buy.
5. Today we have had numerous interruptions, but we expect things to go smoother tomorrow.
6. Visitors have a way of showing up at the most inopportunest times!

93. The Descriptive Language of Poetry

What distinguishes poetry from prose? You have studied rhyme, rhythm, alliteration, and assonance as devices for making poetry musical. In addition to those methods, poets choose words carefully to make their poems colorful and appealing. The following poem illustrates many of the specific ways in which poets use descriptive language.

Farmyard Song

Over the hill the farm boy goes;
His shadow lengthens along the land,
A giant staff in a giant hand;
In the poplar tree, above the spring,
The katydid begins to sing;
The early dews are falling.
Into the stone heap darts the mink,
The swallows skim the river's brink,
And home to the woodland fly the crows,
When over the hill the farm boy goes,
Cheerily calling—
"Co', boss! co', boss! co'! co'! co'!"
Farther, farther over the hill,
Faintly calling, calling still—
"Co', boss! co', boss! co'! co'!"

Into the yard the farmer goes;
    With grateful heart at the close of the day,
    Harness and chain are hung away;
In the wagon shed stand yoke and plow,
The straw's in the stack, the hay in the mow;
    The cooling dews are falling.
The friendly sheep his welcome bleat,
The pigs come grunting to his feet,
    The whinnying mare her master knows,
    When into the yard the farmer goes,
        His cattle calling—
        "Co', boss! co', boss! co'! co'! co'!"
While still the cowboy, far away,
Goes seeking those that have gone astray—
        "Co', boss! co', boss! co'! co'!"

Now to her task the milkmaid goes;
    The cattle come crowding through the gate,
    Lowing, pushing, little and great;
About the trough, by the farmyard pump,
The frolicsome yearlings frisk and jump,
        While the pleasant dews are falling.
The new milk heifer is quick and shy,
But the old cow waits with tranquil eye,
    And the white stream into the bright pail flows,
    When to her task the milkmaid goes,
        Soothingly calling—
        "So, boss! so, boss! so! so! so!"
The cheerful milkmaid takes her stool,
And sits and milks in the twilight cool,
        Saying, "So, boss! so, boss! so! so!"

To supper at last the farmer goes;
    The apples are pared, the paper read,
    The stories are told, then all to bed.
Without, the crickets' ceaseless song
Makes shrill the silence all night long;
        The heavy dews are falling.
The housewife's hand has turned the lock,
Drowsily ticks the kitchen clock,
    The household sinks to deep repose,
    But still in sleep the farm boy goes,
        Singing, calling—
        "Co', boss! co', boss! co'! co'! co'!"
And oft the milkmaid, in her dreams,
Drums in the pail with the flashing streams,
        Murmuring, "So, boss! so!"
                        —*J. T. Trowbridge*

Appeal to the Five Senses

Good poets use many words that appeal to the five senses. This is especially true of nature poems; however, appeal to the five senses contributes to the interest and the appeal of any poem. Do you see this kind of descriptive language in the poem above? Here are a few examples.

Sight:
Into the stone heap darts the mink,
The cattle come crowding through the gate,
The frolicsome yearlings frisk and jump,

Sound:
"Co', boss! co', boss! co'! co'! co'!"
The friendly sheep his welcome bleat,
The pigs come grunting to his feet,
The whinnying mare her master knows,
Without, the crickets' ceaseless song
Makes shrill the silence all night long;

Touch:
The cooling dews are falling.
And sits and milks in the twilight cool,

The following lines of poetry develop a moral or religious theme, but they too have words that appeal to the five senses. Those words are underlined so that you can readily recognize them.

Beware the stinging gibe and quip,
Think twice;
Lest you yourself may feel the whip,
Think twice.

He takes the sound of the dropping nuts
And the scent of the wine-sweet air

Belshazzar is king! Belshazzar is lord!
And a thousand dark nobles all bend at his board:—
Fruits glisten, flowers blossom, meats steam, and a flood
Of the wine that man loveth, runs redder than blood:

Denotation and Connotation

Good poets are careful to choose words with exactly the right meanings for their poems. The *denotation* of a word is its strict, exact meaning. Several different synonyms may have very similar denotations, and sometimes a poet could use them interchangeably. However, very few synonyms, if any, are perfectly interchangeable in every context. One reason is that words have not only denotations but also *connotations.* The connotation of a word is its "personality"—the feeling that the word conveys beyond its denotation.

A poet describing some tall, graceful trees might write about their *slender* trunks because the word *slender* has just the right "feel" for this context. The poet might also consider *slim* or *thin,* but he almost certainly would not use *spindly* if he wanted a word with a pleasant connotation.

In "Farmyard Song," Trowbridge demonstrates a mastery of the connotations of words. Consider the following two examples.

> Into the stone heap *darts* the mink,
>> (*Darts* is an excellent word for describing the fast movement of a mink. Words like *bustles* and *scoots* would not fit as well.)
> But the old cow waits with *tranquil* eye,
>> (*Tranquil* describes well the calm appearance of the old cow. Words like *peaceful* and *docile* would not make good substitutes.)

Figurative Language

Poets often use figurative language to express ideas that plain language cannot convey effectively. You should be familiar with four common figures of speech: similes, metaphors, personification, and hyperbole.

A *simile* makes a figurative comparison by using *like* or *as.* Notice the simile in the last line of the following stanza.

> The sea! the sea! the open sea!
> The blue, the fresh, the ever free!...
>> It plays with the clouds; it mocks the skies;
>> Or like a cradled creature lies.
>>> —*Bryan Waller Procter*

What word picture is painted by this simile? A baby in a cradle suggests calmness and peacefulness. Likewise, the sea is often calm and peaceful.

A *metaphor* makes a figurative comparison without using *like* or *as.* Some metaphors contain a form of *be* and say that one thing is another thing when that is not literally true. Other metaphors use literal terms to describe something that happens only in a figurative sense. Notice the two kinds of metaphors in the following lines of poetry.

> I am my neighbor's Bible,
>> He reads me when we meet;
> Today he reads me in my home—
>> Tomorrow, in the street.

In *personification,* a thing or quality is pictured as if it had the characteristics of a living creature. One example of personification occurs in the above stanza about the sea: "It plays with the clouds; it mocks the skies." The following example is from the poem at the beginning of the lesson.

> Drowsily ticks the kitchen clock,

Of course, the kitchen clock did not feel any drowsiness. But in the context of a household becoming sleepy and going to bed, *drowsily* fits well to describe the clock's soft, steady ticking.

A *hyperbole* might be called an artistic exaggeration—something which everyone knows is not literally true but which makes a vivid picture in the mind. The following lines of poetry consist almost entirely of hyperbole.

> Bowed by the weight of centuries he leans
> Upon his hoe and gazes on the ground,
> The emptiness of ages in his face,
> And on his back the burden of the world.
> —*Edwin Markham*

Onomatopoeia

Onomatopoeia (on′·ə·mat′·ə·pē′·ə) is the use of words having an imitative sound, such as the *rattle* of empty wagons, the *rumble* of distant thunder, and the *honk* of geese. Below are some examples from the poem "Farmyard Song."

> The friendly sheep his welcome <u>bleat</u>,
> The pigs come <u>grunting</u> to his feet,
> The <u>whinnying</u> mare her master knows,
> Drowsily <u>ticks</u> the kitchen clock,
> And oft the milkmaid, in her dreams,
> <u>Drums</u> in the pail with the flashing streams,

A more subtle kind of onomatopoeia does not involve the sound of the object being described. Rather, the sound of the word itself has an imitative character that suggests something about its meaning. Expressions like the *yawning* canyon and the *sting* of a smitten conscience are examples of this kind of onomatopoeia. Here are two other examples from the poem "Farmyard Song."

> <u>Drowsily</u> ticks the kitchen clock,
> Drums in the pail with the <u>flashing</u> streams,

Applying the Lesson

A. From each selection, copy the words that appeal to the senses, and write which of the senses each word or word group appeals to.
1. "My men grow mutinous day by day;
   My men grow ghastly wan and weak."
   The stout mate thought of home; a spray
   Of salt wave washed his swarthy cheek.
2. Now fades the glimmering landscape on the sight,
   And all the air a solemn stillness holds,
   Save where the beetle wheels his droning flight,
   And drowsy tinklings lull the distant folds;
3. I paused last eve beside the blacksmith's door,
   And heard the anvil ring, the vesper's chime,
4. Lord, Thou hast suffered; Thou dost know
   The thrust of pain, the piercing dart,
   How wearily the wind can blow
   Upon the tired heart.

5. He takes the scent of the softening ground
   Where the first green blade pricks through

6. "Barley bread, barley bread! Who will buy my barley?
   Sweet and crisp as any from the oven in the square,

B. In each stanza, choose the word with the best connotation to match the context.

1. Gazing on the eastern sky, I contemplate,
   With a (tremble, quiver, shiver) of delight, "My Lord might come today!"

2. Fearsome indeed the chief captain's appearance so grim;
   Eyes full of malice made hopes of relief appear dim.
      "(Tremble, Quiver, Shiver) before me! Recant your perverseness!" he
      roared.
   Calmly the saints replied, "Nay, for we trust in the Lord."

3. As he sang to his sheep through the lonely black night,
   David found in the (silent, solemn, sullen) stars' warm, friendly light
   A reminder of God's watchful care.

4. These whelming griefs I failed to meet by faith, and soon
   Self-pity's (silent, solemn, sullen) fog hung o'er my soul.

5. Feebly the feverish man tossed and turned;
   None of his (cackling, jabber, prattle) could we understand.

6. A little boy with eyes of blue
   Sat and (cackled, jabbered, prattled) to his toys.

C. Write which kind of figurative language is found in each selection.

1. "Show me your God!" the doubter cries.
   I point him to the smiling skies;

2. Who can be lonely on a hill
   If it is God's windowsill?

3. Up the vaulted dome of heaven,
   Like a great inverted bowl.

4. The winds my tax collectors are,
   They bring me tithes divine.

5. The night was long—so long it seemed at last
   That years had gone and life was nearly past.

6. I've anchored my soul in the haven of rest,
   I'll sail the wide seas no more.

D. From each set of lines, copy one word that makes use of onomatopoeia.

1. Doth conscience now prick thee with sharp needle point?
   Do memories painful condemn thee?

2. O let me hear Thee speaking in accents clear and still,
   Above the storms of passion, the murmurs of self-will.

3. As a mother stills her child,
   Thou canst hush the ocean wild.

4. When at last I near the shore,
   And the fearful breakers roar.

5. In the rustling grass I hear Him pass,
   He speaks to me everywhere.
6. Under the stars of the heavens,
   Alone with his bleating sheep.

Review Exercises

A. For each pair, write the letter of the selection that has better unity or coherence. [74]

1. a. The early Mennonites of Pennsylvania did not, since they came from Germany and Switzerland, have a good grasp of English.
   b. The early Mennonites of Pennsylvania did not have a good grasp of English, since they came from Germany and Switzerland.
2. a. They admitted that they were "not Exquisite in the English Language," and their lack of understanding caused them trouble.
   b. They admitted that they were "not Exquisite in the English Language," and it caused them trouble.
3. a. Indian uprisings stirred the colonists to armed resistance in the 1750s, this brought a test of the Mennonites' nonresistance.
   b. Indian uprisings stirred the colonists to armed resistance in the 1750s. This brought a test of the Mennonites' nonresistance.
4. a. The test came because of the words that the Mennonites had used when they promised to always faithfully support the king of England.
   b. The test came because of the words that the Mennonites had used when they promised to be faithful in always supporting the king of England.

B. Write the letter of the method used to produce emphasis in each selection. You will not use all the letters. [75]
   a. direct quotations
   b. unusual word order
   c. periodic sentence
   d. balanced sentence
   e. repetition of key words
   f. short sentence after several longer ones
   g. series arranged from least important to most important
   h. series of similar questions, commands, or short statements

1. Loyalty to their king the Mennonites had willingly pledged.
2. But they discovered that something was wrong. Their people had wrongly translated the promises they had made when they were naturalized. The Mennonites had ignorantly promised to support the king with heart, hands, and life—and that was terribly wrong.
3. The more the Indians attacked the colonists, the more the Mennonites faced military pressures.
4. One colonial leader had the ability to express his ideas eloquently and persuasively. He did not appreciate the nonresistant stand of the simple Mennonites. He argued that since all the people would benefit from defending the colony, it was not fair that only some of them should bear the burden of its defense. That leader was Benjamin Franklin.

5. In contrast to the skilled rhetoric of Benjamin Franklin, who could argue so convincingly that few people could refute his logic, the Mennonites seemed ignorant and tongue-tied.

6. Finally in 1755, the Mennonites wrote a letter to the Pennsylvania Assembly. They explained that they had not understood English well when they made their earlier promise. They affirmed that they still recognized King George as their rightful king. They stated that they would cheerfully pay any taxes levied by Great Britain. But they made it clear that they could not take up arms to defend themselves or their country.

7. Never think your efforts in studying English are worthless. Skilled use of English will help to prevent misunderstandings with friends, with business people, and with government authorities.

---

94. Special Types of Poetry

The world of poetry contains rich variety. The poet may choose one of the four poetic feet or a combination of them for his rhythm. He may choose any of the common rhyming patterns, or he may write a poem with an original rhyming pattern. He may employ a variety of means to add music and description to his poetry. In this lesson you will study a variety of special types of poetry.

Bible Poetry

Bible poetry does not have rhythm and rhyme, but it does contain many of the other qualities of poetry discussed in Lesson 88. It appeals to the imagination and stimulates the thoughts. It delivers a wealth of meaning in a few words, and it employs figurative language and repetition. In fact, these qualities often shine more brightly from Bible poetry than from much modern poetry.

We can find poetic passages throughout the Bible; however, we find most Biblical poetry concentrated in a set of five books, commonly called the Books of Poetry: Job, Psalms, Proverbs, Ecclesiastes, and the Song of Solomon.

Job consists primarily of the poetic discourses and philosophic arguments of five different men. The book climaxes with God Himself composing several chapters of poetry.

> Gavest thou the goodly wings unto the peacocks?
> Or wings and feathers unto the ostrich? (Job 39:13)

Psalms is a collection of hymns used in public worship by the Jews.

> Bless the LORD, O my soul:
> And all that is within me,
> Bless his holy name. (Psalm 103:1)

Proverbs is a book of wise sayings in poetic form.

> Hearken unto thy father that begat thee,
> And despise not thy mother when she is old. (Proverbs 23:22)

Ecclesiastes teaches about the shortness and insecurity of life, the vanity of earthly men and earthly things, and man's responsibility on earth.

Vanity of vanities, saith the Preacher,
Vanity of vanities; all is vanity. (Ecclesiastes 1:2)

The *Song of Solomon,* also called Canticles, contains several poems dealing with the marriage relationship. It speaks figuratively of the love between Christ and the church.

I am my beloved's,
And my beloved is mine. (Song of Solomon 6:3)

One of the most outstanding qualities of Bible poetry is its use of parallelism, the repetition of related ideas in similar grammatical structures. Parallelism comes in three basic forms: synonymous, antithetic, and synthetic.

Synonymous parallelism occurs when parallel lines express similar thoughts. The word *synonym* comes from two Greek word elements meaning "to name along with." This describes exactly what synonymous parallelism does: it restates a thought, thus giving it greater emphasis. The following example is a set of four lines with synonymous parallelism.

The law of the LORD is perfect, converting the soul:
The testimony of the LORD is sure, making wise the simple.
The statutes of the LORD are right, rejoicing the heart:
The commandment of the LORD is pure, enlightening the eyes. (Psalm 19:7, 8)

Antithetic parallelism occurs when parallel lines express opposite thoughts. The word *antithetic* comes from two Greek word elements meaning "to set against." That is what antithetic parallelism does: it sets down a line with a thought contrasting to the previous line. The Book of Proverbs contains scores of verses with antithetic parallelism.

It is as sport to a fool to do mischief:
But a man of understanding hath wisdom. (Proverbs 10:23)

Synthetic parallelism occurs when parallel lines express thoughts that build one upon another. The word *synthetic* comes from two Greek word elements meaning "to put together." Synthetic parallelism does that by putting two or more lines together in a progression of thought.

The LORD is my strength and my shield;
My heart trusted in him, and I am helped:
Therefore my heart greatly rejoiceth;
And with my song will I praise him. (Psalm 28:7)

Blank Verse and Free Verse

Blank verse has rhythm but no rhyme, and free verse has neither. Yet both are classed as poetry because they have the deeper qualities of poetry. You may think these kinds would be easier to write than metrical, rhyming poetry, for one does not need to deal with the restrictions of rhyme and rhythm. But remember that in blank or free verse, the natural beauty of rhyme and rhythm is not present to camouflage any lack in the deeper qualities of poetry. Therefore, meaningful blank or free verse may actually be more difficult to write than poetry with rhyme and rhythm.

The following examples illustrate these two kinds of poetry.

Blank verse:

Begin the Day With God

Every morning lean thine arms awhile
Upon the windowsill of heaven
And gaze upon thy Lord.
Then, with the vision in thy heart,
Turn strong to meet thy day.

—Author unknown

Free verse:

Fog

The fog comes
On little cat feet.

It sits looking
Over harbor and city
On silent haunches,
And then moves on.

—Carl Sandburg

Ballad

A ballad (bal'·ǝd) is a special narrative poem that usually contains many stanzas. It follows a traditional form, having four-line stanzas alternating between iambic tetrameter and iambic trimeter. The rhyming pattern is generally *abcb*. A ballad usually tells a moving story that deals with a theme such as death, war, friendship, bereavement, or homesickness.

The following example shows the beginning and ending stanzas of a ballad. Since the whole poem contains thirty-four stanzas, the middle stanzas are summarized.

The Unbarred Door

1 When on America's eastern plain
    Still roamed her forest child,
And the new homes of Europe's sons
    Were rising in the wild,

2 Upon a clearing in a wood,
    Amos had built his cot;
He tilled his little farm and lived
    Contented with his lot.

3 A just, peace-loving man was he,
    Kind unto all, and true;
And well his ever-open door
    The wandering Indian knew.

4 But often were the settlers' lands
    By force or fraud obtained,
And to the Red man dispossessed,
    Revenge alone remained.

5 And 'round the blazing fire of logs,
    When winter nights were cold,
To shuddering listeners, dreadful tales

Of Indian raids were told.

6   But Amos feared not, though his home
    All undefended lay,
    And still his never-bolted door
    Was open night and day.

Stanzas 7–24 tell how a neighbor warned Amos that the Indians were about to attack. Though Amos still wanted to leave the door unlocked, his wife finally persuaded him to bar the door. They went to bed, and his wife soon fell asleep; but Amos could not sleep until he had gotten up and unbarred the door.

25 That night a painted warrior band
    Through the dark forest sped,
    With steps as light upon the leaves
    As panthers' stealthy tread.

26 They reached the farm; "We make no war
    With good and faithful men,"
    The foremost Indian turned and said.
    "Here dwells a son of Penn."

27 "But, brother, if still his heart is right,
    How shall we surely know?"
    Answered another, "Time brings change,
    And oft turns friend to foe."

28 Said the first one, "I will go,
    And gently try the door;
    If open still, it proves his heart
    Is as it was before."

29 It yielded and they entered in.
    Across the room they stepped,
    And came where Amos and his wife
    Calm and unconscious slept.

30 With tomahawk and scalping knife,
    They stood beside the pair.
    A solemn stillness filled the room;
    An angel guard was there.

31 The eye sought eye and seemed to say,
    "How sound the good man sleeps!
    So may they rest, and fear no ill,
    Whom the Great Spirit keeps."

32 Then noiselessly they left the room
    And closed the door behind,
    And on their deadly war trail passed,
    Some other prey to find.

33 And horror shrieked around their steps,
And bloodshed marked their way;
And many homes were desolate,
When rose another day.

34 But Amos with a thankful heart
Greeted the morning light,
And knew not until after years
How near was death that night.

—Author unknown

Quatrain

The quatrain (kwät′·rān′) develops a theme in one four-line stanza. Although writing a four-line poem may sound appealing, it takes careful thought and skill to write a truly complete, worthwhile quatrain. Here is one example.

The moving finger writes, and having writ,
Moves on; nor all your piety nor wit
Shall lure it back to cancel half a line,
Nor all your tears wash out a word of it.

—Translated from The Rubáiyát of Omar Khayyám

Sonnet

The sonnet (son′·it) is a fourteen-line poem written in iambic pentameter. Sonnets come in a variety of rhyming patterns. They may appear as two stanzas of eight lines and six lines respectively, or they may appear as one long stanza. One of the special appeals of the sonnet is its ability to deal with a theme in only fourteen lines. Read the following example.

Work

Let me but do my work from day to day
In field or forest, at the desk or loom,
In roaring marketplace or tranquil room;
Let me but find it in my heart to say,
When vagrant wishes beckon me astray,
"This is my work; my blessing, not my doom;
Of all who live, I am the one by whom
This work can best be done in the right way."

Then shall I see it not too great, nor small,
To suit my spirit and to prove my powers;
Then shall I cheerful greet the laboring hours,
And cheerful turn, when the long shadows fall
At eventide, to play and love and rest,
Because I know for me my work is best.

—Henry van Dyke

Applying the Lesson

A. Write which of the three kinds of parallelism is used in each of these selections of Bible poetry.

1. Psalm 9:8
2. Psalm 20:7
3. Psalm 25:4
4. Psalm 34:11
5. Proverbs 14:29
6. Proverbs 15:11
7. Proverbs 23:24
8. Ecclesiastes 12:1

B. Write a short stanza of blank or free verse on one of these subjects or another approved by your teacher.

1. A Bible promise
2. Reverence at church
3. God's greatness
4. A gray squirrel
5. The beauty of a spring morning
6. The pleasure of hard work

C. Write a quatrain on one of these subjects or another approved by your teacher.

1. Contentment
2. Faith
3. Eating a crisp, juicy apple
4. Watching a deer dash into the woods

Review Exercises

A. Write the six key words that help us remember the six basic listening skills. (Remember, these words start with the letters *A–F.*) [10]

B. Tell whether each statement about outlining is true or false. [25–26]

1. Outlining what we read helps us to comprehend it better.
2. Each item in a topical outline should begin with a capital letter and end with a period.
3. In outlining a Bible passage, we must determine the primary truth it is teaching.
4. The main headings of an outline should not overlap in thought.
5. We should try to keep the points of an outline parallel with each other.
6. There may be several different ways to outline the same Bible passage.

---

95. Appreciating Poetry

Good poetry, you learned in Lesson 88, appeals to the imagination and stimulates the thoughts. You will realize the full value of a poem, however, only as you turn the jewel this way and that to see its luster from many angles. This lesson should help you to reflect on poems so that you can gain a fuller appreciation of their beauty.

1. *Take time to understand the message of a poem.* Many poems come alive only after you have read them several times and meditated on the wealth of meaning packed into those few words. Read the following poem.

A Prayer to the God of Nature

1 God of the roadside weed,
  Grant I may humbly serve the humblest need.

2 God of the scarlet rose,
  Give me the beauty that Thy love bestows.

3 God of the hairy bee,
  Help me to suck deep joys from all I see.

4 God of the spider's lace,
  Let me, from mine own heart, unwind such grace.

5 God of the lily's cup,
  Fill me! I hold this empty chalice up.

6 God of the sea gull's wing,
  Bear me above each dark and turbulent thing.

7 God of the watchful owl,
  Help me to see at midnight, like this fowl.

8 God of the antelope,
  Teach me to scale the highest crags of hope.

9 God of the eagle's nest,
  Oh, let me make my aerie near Thy breast!

10 God of the burrowing mole,
  Let cold earth have no terrors for my soul.

11 God of the chrysalis,
  Grant that my grave may be a cell of bliss.

12 God of the butterfly,
  Help me to vanquish death, although I die.

—Frederic Lawrence Knowles

The first stanza indicates that a roadside weed serves a "humblest need." What need could be served by a weed? Well, weed seeds provide food for birds, and the roots of weeds help to hold soil in place. Their leaves take in carbon dioxide and give off oxygen, and they also release moisture into the air. All these are humble but important services that weeds provide.

Stanza 7 refers to the owl and speaks of seeing "at midnight, like this fowl." What does this line mean? It could refer to waking up in the middle of the night and still being able, by faith, to see God and His goodness. Or the poet may be speaking of the darkness of sin and deception in this world, and asking for spiritual vision to find his way through.

Other stanzas bring many similar thoughts. Stanza 2 mentions the scarlet rose, which glows with inner beauty and gives off a sweet fragrance (as our lives should do). In stanza 4 we find the spider, patiently spinning its web with a substance that comes from within its being (like the grace of God flowing through us to others). Stanza 6 speaks of the sea gull, always flying swiftly and effortlessly above the dark and turbulent sea but never overcome by it. And stanzas 10–12 refer to the mole and the butterfly, creatures that teach valuable lessons about death. What a treasury of ideas we find in this one poem!

2. *Read poetry aloud to better appreciate its music and its message.* The musical beauty of the rhyme and rhythm comes alive only as we actually hear it. This is even more true of the music of any alliteration, assonance, and onomatopoeia that may be present. Hearing that music will often impress the message of the poem more forcefully upon us than a silent reading can do.

In reading or reciting poetry to others, be sure to speak slowly and clearly enough to convey the message effectively. This is especially important with a memorized poem, which is so familiar to you that you may tend to rattle it off with little expression. Be careful not to spoil the profound message of a poem by giving a careless recitation.

3. *Notice any unusual rhyme and rhythm patterns.* Many excellent poems have rhyme and rhythm patterns that are very common. However, the skillful use of unique patterns makes a definite contribution to the richness of a poem. Even if these patterns do not improve the musical sound, the reader has a sense of pleasure just in seeing the poet's skill with words.

Consider again the following stanza from Lesson 91. If you thought at first that the rhythm was quite uneven, that idea probably changed when you saw what the pattern is—a combination of anapestic and iambic rhythm.

> O give ear to our cry, O Lord;
> Turn again unto us.
> For how long wilt Thou angry be?
> Turn again unto us.
> As a Shepherd kind, Thou hast led us on,
> Thou hast cared for all Thy flock;
> With the finest wheat Thou hast satisfied,
> And with honey from the rock.

4. *Read a poem by thoughts, not merely by lines.* This is especially important when sentences or clauses end elsewhere than at the ends of lines. The following poem illustrates this point.

> Use me, God, in Thy great harvest field,
> Which stretcheth far and wide like a wide sea;
> The gatherers are so few; I fear the precious yield
> Will suffer loss. Oh, find a place for me!
> A place where best the strength I have will tell:
> It may be one the older toilers shun;
> Be it a wide or narrow place, 'tis well
> So that the work it holds be only done.
> —*Christina Rossetti*

5. *Learn to recognize figures of speech.* The figurative language in a poem may be veiled. Unless you analyze it, you will neither understand nor appreciate it as

fully as you might. Perhaps you have sung these words from the song "O Love That Will Not Let Me Go."

> O Light that followest all my way,
>   I yield my flickering torch to Thee;
> My heart restores its borrowed ray,
> That in Thy sunshine's glow, its day
>   May brighter, fairer be.

Why does the author write of a "flickering torch"? This metaphor emphasizes that the best that man can be or do is like a feeble light ready to burn out. And why does the author write of restoring a "borrowed ray"? Even that feeble, flickering light has its source in God, not in ourselves.

6. *Consider the poet's choice of words.* See, hear, and feel the descriptions. Observe how the denotations and connotations of the words complement the message of the poem. Read the following stanza.

> There's a song in the air!
> There's a star in the sky!
> There's a mother's deep prayer
>   And a baby's low cry!
> And the star rains its fire while the beautiful sing,
> For the manger of Bethlehem cradles a King!

Do you enjoy the descriptiveness of the words "a mother's deep prayer" and "a baby's low cry"? *Deep* and *low* are synonyms. Could the poet have interchanged these words freely in these lines? Notice that he wrote "the star *rains* its fire." Words like *pours* or *dumps* would not be nearly as suitable for this context.

Applying the Lesson

A. Read aloud the poem that you have selected to read to your class.

B. Read the following poem, and do the exercises below.

Prayer

1   Lord, what a change within us one short hour
2   Spent in Thy presence will prevail to make!
3   What heavy burdens from our bosoms take,
4   What parched grounds refresh as with a shower!
5   We kneel, and all around us seems to lower;
6   We rise, and all, the distant and the near,
7   Stands forth in sunny outline brave and clear;
8   We kneel, how weak! we rise, how full of power!
9   Why, therefore, should we do ourselves this wrong,
10   Or others, that we are not always strong,
11 That we are ever overborne with care,
12   That we should ever weak or heartless be,
13 Anxious or troubled, when with us is prayer,
14   And joy and strength and courage are with Thee!
15   —*Richard Chenevix Trench*

1. Write answers to the following exercises on the structure of the poem.
   a. Give the complete name for the rhythm pattern of these lines.
   b. How many lines does the poem have?
   c. Which of the types of poetry described in Lesson 94 is this?
2. Copy words for the following things.
   a. Two examples of alliteration.
   b. One example of assonance from line 12.
3. The poem shows a number of sharp contrasts between a person's experience before and after an hour of prayer. Before prayer, a person bears (a) ———, his soul is like (b) ———, his surroundings have the feel and appearance of a coming (c) ———, and he is (d) ———. After prayer, a person's burdens have been (e) ———, his soul has become (f) ——— as with a (g) ———, his surroundings have become (h) ———, and he has become (i) ———.
4. It is not hard to understand how failing to pray does ourselves harm. But according to lines 9 and 10, it also harms others. How might this be possible?
5. We need never be weak, afraid, or anxious; for we can (a) ———, and God has (b) ———, (c) ———, and (d) ——— to give to us.

Review Exercises

Identify the form of each underlined verb as simple (*S*), progressive (*P*), or emphatic (*E*). [70]

1. I have never seen so many blackbirds before.
2. Brother Lamar and his family will be serving in the Bahamas for two years.
3. Though we had a flat tire, we did manage to get to church before the service began.
4. When the dogs began barking, Brian knew that he had been seen.
5. Mother is planning to invite Sister Brenda to spend the evening with us.
6. The colors do match, but they are a bit too bright.

---

96. Writing Poetry

Can every person be a poet? Or is poetry writing a special skill conferred on a select few? The answers are both yes and no. Every normal person can write some lines that others will recognize as poetry. But not everyone will write top-quality poems, nor will everyone enjoy writing poetry.

Inspiration for Poetry Writing

Because of the emotional involvement of poetry, you cannot write truly effective poetry simply by following a set of mechanical rules. You need to be inspired with a message that you want to communicate. And how can you become inspired if you do not feel so already? One important source of inspiration is the Bible, with its rich treasures of thoughts and themes that poetry can explore. For example, Psalm 87:3 says, "Glorious things are spoken of thee, O city of God." John Newton wrote the following poem from this inspiration.

Glorious things of thee are spoken,
    Zion, city of our God;
He whose word cannot be broken
    Formed thee for His own abode:
On the Rock of Ages founded,
    What can shake thy sure repose?
With salvation's walls surrounded,
    Thou mayst smile at all thy foes.

Another good source of inspiration is nature. Behold the loveliness of wildflowers on an otherwise drab scene. Ponder the grandeur of the ocean or a mountain range. It was the beauty of God's creation that inspired Maltbie D. Babcock to write the following words.

This is my Father's world;
    And to my list'ning ears,
All nature sings, and round me rings
    The music of the spheres.

You might also find inspiration for poems in the experiences of people you know or read about. "The Landing of the Pilgrim Fathers," by Felicia D. Hemans, is one well-known poem of this kind. Here are the first two stanzas.

The breaking waves dashed high
    On a stern and rock-bound coast,
And the woods against a stormy sky
    Their giant branches tossed:
And the heavy night hung dark
    The hills and waters o'er,
When a band of exiles moored their bark
    On the wild New England shore.

The following poem is a tribute to the author's father.

The years have been many, and the years have been long,
    But at last I'm returning to Daddy at home;
        My daddy's out watching, though he can hardly see,
        But I'm thankful that Daddy has recognized me.
He walks with a cane as he hurries along,
    Coming to meet me and welcome me home;
        His shoulders are stooped with the weight of the years,
        And I hardly can hold back the flood tide of tears.
There's snow in his hair,
    And I helped put it there—
    A halo of worry and care.
        As my daddy grows old,
        He's more precious than gold,
For I cherish the snow in his hair.
                —Ray E. Martin

Even common, everyday things can be a source of inspiration for poems. Poets find inspiration in things that others have seen or heard dozens of times without paying special attention to them. The following poem describes a very common object.

Bread

Be gentle
  When you touch bread.
Let it not lie
  Uncared for—unwanted.
So often bread
  Is taken for granted.
Be gentle
  When you touch bread.

There is so much beauty
  In bread—
Beauty of sun and soil,
Beauty of patient toil.
Winds and rains have caressed it,
Christ often blessed it.
Be gentle
  When you touch bread.

         —Author unknown

Mechanics of Poetry Writing

The message of a poem is its most important feature. Lines may have perfect rhyme and rhythm; but without a worthwhile message, they have no real value. Still, good mechanics greatly enhance a worthwhile theme. Review the following points.

1. Capitalize the first letter of each line, and capitalize otherwise as you would in prose.
2. Punctuate as you would in prose. Some lines may have no punctuation at the end, and some may have punctuation in the middle.
3. Leave a space between each stanza and the next.
4. Indent according to the rhyming pattern. Four patterns are shown below, with rhyming words from familiar hymns to illustrate. Lesson 89 shows the method of indenting for a number of other rhyming patterns.

prayer ......a	cross ......a	way ....a	King ....a
care ....a	died...b	perform...b	sing ....a
throne.......b	loss.........a	sea...............c	praise ...b
known.......b	pride..b	storm.......b	glorious c
			victorious...c
			over us.......c
			Days......b

5. Choose the kind of rhythm that matches the theme of the poem. Iambic and trochaic meters are well suited for natural, serious subjects; dactylic and anapestic meters are better suited for themes of joy and enthusiasm.
6. Use perfect rhymes as much as possible. Frequent and careless use of imperfect rhymes will mar the musical beauty of a poem.
7. Arrange the words in a smooth pattern. Avoid using awkward, unnatural word order to make the rhyme and rhythm come out.
8. Try to avoid words not used in common language, even if you find them in a published poem.
9. Avoid overworked words. Be original.

10. Make sure the figures of speech are appropriate. Some figures fit one poem but not another.
11. Choose words with the right connotation. If a word does not quite fit, keep looking for a better word, or rewriting the line, until you succeed.

Applying the Lesson

Write a poem of four to six stanzas, with at least four lines in each stanza. Follow the rules for mechanics given in this lesson. Choose descriptive words. Include at least one figure of speech, one example of alliteration, one example of assonance, and one example of onomatopoeia. Your teacher will give you a date when the poem is due.

---

97. Chapter 12 Review

A. Write the term that fits each description.
 1. The kind of poem that gives specific instruction or moral teaching.
 2. The kind of poem that shows the poet's inner thoughts and feelings.
 3. The kind of poem that tells a story.
 4. Rhyme involving more than one syllable.
 5. Repetition of similar vowel sounds in accented syllables.
 6. Repetition of beginning consonant sounds.
 7. A phrase, a line, or an entire stanza repeated throughout a poem.
 8. The unit for analyzing rhythm.
 9. The marking of the rhythm in poetry.
10. The rhythm pattern of a poem.
11. The "personality" of a word.
12. The strict, exact meaning of a word.
13. Speaking of a thing or quality as having the characteristics of a living creature.
14. A figurative exaggeration for the purpose of emphasis.
15. A figurative comparison that uses *like* or *as*.
16. The use of literal terms to describe something that happens only in a figurative sense.
17. The use of words having an imitative sound.
18. Poetry without rhyme or rhythm but with frequent use of parallelism.
19. Poetry with rhythm but not rhyme.
20. A fourteen-line poem in iambic pentameter.
21. A poem that develops a theme in four lines.
22. A narrative poem that contains many stanzas.

B. Write whether each stanza comes from a *lyric, didactic,* or *narrative* poem.
 1. Oh, worship the King all-glorious above,
   And gratefully sing His wonderful love;
    Our Shield and Defender, the Ancient of Days,
    Pavilioned in splendor, and girded with praise.

2. The thought of God is like the tree
    Beneath whose shade I lie,
And watch the fleet of snowy clouds
    Sail o'er the silent sky.
'Tis like that soft, invading light
    Which in all darkness shines,
The thread that through life's somber web
    In golden pattern twines.
           —*Frederick W. Faber*

3. In the garret under the sloping eaves
    Stood Grandmother Granger's old hair trunk,
With battered bureaus and broken chairs,
    And a spinning wheel and similar junk.
The hirsute cover was worn in spots;
    'Twas once the hide of a brindle cow,
That grazed of yore in the meadows green
    Where Harlem flats are towering now.
           —*Minna Irving*

4. You never can tell when you send a word
    Like an arrow shot from a bow
By an archer blind, be it cruel or kind,
    Just where it may chance to go.
           —*Ella Wheeler Wilcox*

C. Write the rhyming pattern for each stanza. In number 4, be sure to write the pattern for the whole poem.

1. God of our strength, enthroned above,
The source of life, the fount of love:
    O let devotion's sacred flame
    Our souls awake to praise Thy Name.

2. Praise to the Lord, the Almighty, the King of creation!
O my soul, praise Him, for He is thy health and salvation!
    All ye who hear,
    Now to His temple draw near;
Join me in glad adoration!

3. The praises we sing of Jesus our King,
    As onward through life we may go,
With joy we proclaim His wonderful name,
    Till all His salvation shall know.

4. Silently another day   Lord, how pleasant is Thy care,
    Glides on rosy wings away.   Free from danger, free from fear.
    Father, be our constant stay,   May we trust Thee, Saviour dear,
        Hear our humble plea.   Thou wilt faithful be!

D. From the stanzas in Part C, copy words to illustrate the following things.
  1. Two examples of alliteration.   4. Two pairs of internal rhymes.
  2. One example of assonance.   5. One example of imperfect rhyme.
  3. One set of feminine rhymes.

E. Write the complete name of the rhythm pattern in each stanza. Numbers 4 and 5 each have two different kinds of meter.

  1. If you hear a kind word spoken
        Of some worthy soul you know,
     It may fill his heart with sunshine
        If you only tell him so.

  2. Light after darkness,
        Gain after loss,
     Strength after weakness,
        Crown after cross;
     Sweet after bitter,
        Hope after fears,
     Home after wandering,
        Praise after tears.
              —*Frances R. Havergal*

  3. Talk happiness. The world is sad enough
     Without your woes. No path is wholly rough;
        Look for the places that are smooth and clear,
        And speak of those, to rest the weary ear
     Of Earth, so hurt by one continuous strain
     Of human discontent and grief and pain.
              —*Ella Wheeler Wilcox*

  4. When the road seems so long, and I don't have a song,
        And my footsteps are dragging and slow;
     Then I cry to my Lord and I feast on His Word,
        In the Rock I am safe from the foe.
              —*Rachel Martin*

  5. The camel, at the close of day,
        Kneels down upon the sandy plain
     To have his burden lifted off,
        And rest to gain.
              —*Anonymous*

F. Read these poems, and do the exercises that follow.

May My Faith Be Firmly Anchored

Like a strong and stately oak tree,
    That withstands the stormy gale,
May my faith be firmly anchored
    On the Lord who cannot fail.

Although storms of deep frustration,
    Storms of sorrow rush and rage,
May my faith be firmly anchored,
    Strong in God and unafraid.
              —*Ruth Groff*

Fierce Raged the Tempest

Fierce raged the tempest o'er the deep,
Watch did Thine anxious servants keep,
But Thou wast wrapped in guileless sleep,
    Calm and still.

"Save, Lord, we perish," was their cry,
"O save us in our agony!"
Thy word above the storm rose high,
    "Peace, be still."

The wild winds hushed; the angry deep
Sank, like a little child, to sleep;
The sullen billows ceased to leap,
    At Thy will.

So, when our life is clouded o'er,
And storm-winds drift us from the shore,
Say, lest we sink to rise no more,
    "Peace, be still."
                        —*Godfrey Thring*

1. From the second poem, copy two expressions that appeal to the sense of sight, and two that appeal to the sense of hearing.
2. The first poem refers to *stately* oak trees. The following words are synonyms of *stately: noble, eminent, princely, elegant, august, dignified, imposing.* Without regard to rhyme and rhythm, choose two of these synonyms having a suitable connotation to fit that line of poetry.
3. Copy one simile from each of the two poems.
4. The second poem is an extended metaphor. To what is the storm figuratively compared? Be sure to read stanza 4 carefully.
5. Copy three expressions from the second poem that are examples of personification.
6. Copy a word from the second poem that illustrates onomatopoeia.

G. Write whether each verse illustrates *synonymous, antithetic,* or *synthetic* parallelism.
1. "Surely thou didst set them in slippery places: thou castedst them down into destruction" (Psalm 73:18).
2. "O come, let us worship and bow down: let us kneel before the Lord our maker" (Psalm 95:6).
3. "Before I was afflicted I went astray: but now have I kept thy word" (Psalm 119:67).
4. "Deliver me, O Lord, from mine enemies: I flee unto thee to hide me" (Psalm 143:9).

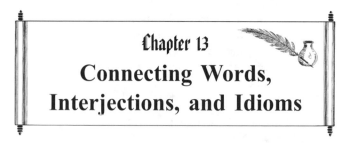

Chapter 13

Connecting Words, Interjections, and Idioms

98. Prepositions and Prepositional Phrases

We use many prepositions to show relationships between substantives and other words in sentences. Prepositions express relationships so precisely that changing a preposition can completely change the meaning of a sentence. Talking *to* someone is quite different from talking *about* someone. And a fire *in* the house is quite different from a fire *near* the house! A study of these simple but useful words will help you to express your ideas in a clear and meaningful way.

1. *A preposition is a word that shows the relationship between its object and some other word in the sentence.* The following tables show the prepositions used most commonly.

Common Prepositions

aboard	at	by	inside	outside	under
about	before	concerning	into	over	underneath
above	behind	despite	like	past	until
across	below	down	near	since	unto
after	beneath	during	of	through	up
against	beside	except	off	throughout	upon
along	besides	for	on	till	with
among	between	from	onto	to	within
around	beyond	in	out	toward	without
as	but				

Common Compound Prepositions

according to	by means of	in spite of	out of
along with	due to	instead of	owing to
aside from	in addition to	next to	prior to
as of	in front of	on account of	with regard to
because of	in place of		

2. *A prepositional phrase includes the preposition, its object, and any modi-fiers of the object.* The object of a preposition is the substantive that the preposition relates to another word. You can find it by saying the preposition and then asking *whom* or *what.* If two substantives answer the question, the preposition has a com-pound object.

The following sentences contain three underlined prepositional phrases. The second one has a compound object, and the third has a compound preposition.

> While Moses was <u>in the mount</u>, God showed him the plans <u>for the tabernacle and its furnishings</u>. Later Moses built these things <u>according to those plans</u>.

3. *A preposition normally precedes its object, except when the object is an interrogative or a relative pronoun or is modified by one of these.*

> Which <u>room</u> shall we girls sit <u>in</u> to visit? (The object *room* is modified by the interrogative pronoun *Which. In which room* modifies *shall sit.*)
> We can use the room <u>that</u> Susanna just stepped <u>into</u>.
> (The relative pronoun *that* is the object of the preposition *into. Into that* modifies *stepped.*)

4. *The object of a preposition is usually a noun or pronoun, but it may also be a verbal, a verbal phrase, or a noun clause.*

> <u>Besides washing the dishes</u>, I have several school lessons to finish. (The object of the preposition *Besides* is the verbal phrase *washing the dishes.*)
> I must work hard <u>for whatever I learn</u>.
> (The object of the preposition *for* is the noun clause *whatever I learn.*)

5. *Prepositional phrases can function as adjectives, adverbs, or nouns.* An adjective prepositional phrase usually comes right after the substantive it modifies.

> The book <u>on the table</u> contains a true story <u>about Grandfather's old mill</u>.

When an adverb prepositional phrase modifies a verb, it can often be placed at different locations without changing the meaning of the sentence. A phrase that modifies an adjective, an adverb, or a verbal usually comes right after the word it modifies.

> <u>By God's grace</u> we can live faithfully <u>in spite of temptation</u>.
> (The underlined phrases can be moved to other positions.)
> <u>Filling our minds</u> <u>with good thoughts</u> is essential <u>to a victorious life</u>.
> (The underlined phrases cannot be moved to other positions.)

A noun prepositional phrase names a place or a thing and is usually the subject of a sentence with a linking verb.

> <u>In your book</u> is a good place to find the answer. (*In your book* names a place to find the answer; it is the subject of the sentence.)
> <u>Before five o'clock</u> would be a good time to start. (*Before five o'clock* names the time for starting; it is the subject of the sentence.)

6. *Several prepositional phrases in succession can be either a series of independent phrases or one unit of phrases.* In a series of independent phrases, each phrase modifies the same word. In a unit of phrases, each successive phrase is actually

part of the first phrase, modifying the object in the previous prepositional phrase. Study the following examples.

> Several sisters met <u>at Grandmother's house</u> <u>for a cleaning day</u>.
> (*At Grandmother's house* and *for a cleaning day* are independent modifiers of *met.*)

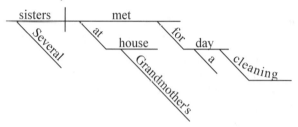

> The children played <u>with the kittens in the basket on the porch</u>.
> (*With the kittens in the basket on the porch* is a unit modifying *played; in the basket* modifies *kittens; on the porch* modifies *basket.*)

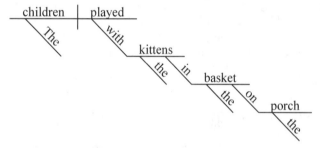

7. *Do not confuse prepositions with adverbs.* If the word is used alone to tell *when* or *where,* it is an adverb. It can be a preposition only if it has an object.

Adverbs:
We climbed <u>up</u> to get a good view of the fire.
The refugees hurried <u>over</u> before the river rose higher.

Prepositions:
We climbed <u>up the silo</u> to get a good view of the fire.
The refugees hurried <u>over the bridge</u> before the river rose higher.

8. *Do not confuse prepositional phrases beginning with* to *with infinitives. To* is part of an infinitive when a verb form follows it. *To* is a preposition when a substantive follows it.

> We turn <u>to</u> the Bible <u>to</u> find encouragement. (*To the Bible* is a prepositional phrase; *to find encouragement* is an infinitive phrase.)

Applying the Lesson

A. Copy each prepositional phrase. If a phrase is part of a longer phrase, include it with the longer phrase and also copy it separately. Label each phrase *adj., adv.,* or *n.*

1. In spite of ample revelation in nature and the Bible, many men refuse to acknowledge God as Creator and Lord.
2. Within human hearts is the primary scene of the battle between God and Satan.
3. Below twenty dollars is quite cheap for a bicycle in this condition.
4. Along with my regular chores, I must help with Brendon's chores because of his injured back.
5. Due to her arthritis, we help Grandmother Wise regularly by doing her cleaning and laundry.
6. Which book are you looking for?
7. What did the pioneer builders raise these heavy logs with?
8. After a brief rest, we returned to our work with renewed zeal.
9. The city of Amsterdam began as a small fishing village during the thirteenth century.
10. Built on a dike of the Amstel River, the city was originally named Amsteldam.
11. Religious warfare throughout the late sixteenth century brought a dramatic increase in the population of the city.
12. The city reached its golden age of wealth and commerce in the second half of the seventeenth century.
13. A treaty signed in 1648 took trade away from Antwerp, a rival to Amsterdam's trade.
14. During this era of rapid growth, Amsterdam's merchants founded many companies for trade with the Indies.

B. Copy each underlined word, and label it *adv.* or *prep.*
1. I thought the shovel should be hanging <u>on</u> the shop wall, but when I looked <u>inside</u>, I found it <u>beneath</u> the worktable.
2. Standing <u>near</u> the summit, we gazed on the fertile valleys lying <u>below</u> and the rugged mountains stretching far <u>beyond</u>.
3. Pea picking is <u>over</u> for this year, and tomorrow I plan to mow the vines <u>off</u>.
4. The board meeting was held <u>across</u> the road from Grandmother Risser's house, so we went <u>along</u> and visited while Father walked <u>over</u> to the church.

Review Exercises

Write whether each underlined adverb modifies a *verb*, a *verbal*, an *adjective*, an *adverb*, a *preposition*, a *conjunction*, or an entire *sentence*. [83–84]
1. Job <u>meekly</u> submitted to the hardships he did not understand.
2. Speaking <u>accusingly</u>, his three friends offered their opinions.
3. They were <u>entirely</u> too harsh in their judgment.
4. <u>Clearly</u>, they did not understand.
5. Methuselah lived <u>longer</u> than any other man named in history.
6. He died <u>just</u> before the Flood.
7. Even when facing a den of lions, Daniel remained <u>completely</u> faithful to his God.

8. The Israelites discovered that they had been deceived <u>soon</u> after the Gibeonites left.

---

99. Coordinating Conjunctions

Coordinating conjunctions usually are small words, but they may join major sentence parts together. The joined parts are *coordinate;* that is, they have a definite equality. Coordinating conjunctions join sentence parts so that they can work unitedly together.

1. *Coordinating conjunctions join sentence parts and show the relationships between those parts.* The common coordinating conjunctions are *and, but, or, for, nor, yet,* and *so. And* shows addition or continuing thought; *but* and *yet* show contrast or unexpected outcome; *or* and *nor* show choice or option; *for* and *so* show cause and effect.

2. *Coordinating conjunctions join sentence parts of parallel structure and function.* Parallel structure means that the joined parts are both words, prepositional phrases, gerund phrases, dependent clauses, and so forth. Parallel function means that the joined parts both function as subjects, verbs, predicate nominatives, adverbs, and so forth.

> *Trials* <u>and</u> *temptations* cause a saint to seek the Lord.
> (*And* joins single words used as subjects.)
> The Christian should not be unwilling *to endure trials* <u>or</u> *to face temptations.*
> (*Or* joins infinitive phrases used as adverbs.)
> *Victory is possible in any circumstance,* <u>for</u> *God's grace is always sufficient.*
> (*For* joins independent clauses.)

Sometimes writers or speakers use a coordinating conjunction to join a word to a phrase or a phrase to a clause. This is improper because the structure of the two parts is different. Correct the mistake either by making the joined parts parallel or by rewriting the sentence.

> **Incorrect:** Mother sang *softly* <u>and</u> *in soothing tones* to the sick baby.
> (word joined to phrase)
> **Correct:** Mother sang *softly* <u>and</u> *soothingly* to the sick baby.
> In soothing tones, Mother sang softly to the baby.

3. *When a coordinating conjunction joins the clauses in a compound sentence, a comma is usually needed before the conjunction.* If the two clauses are very short and closely related, you may omit the comma. If one or both of the clauses already have several commas, you may need to use a semicolon to show clearly the division between the clauses. Study the following sentences.

> The Christian faces many temptations, but he does not need to fall.
> (normal compound sentence)

God's grace is sufficient and we can overcome.
(short clauses; no comma needed)
Even though we are tested severely, we can be victorious; for God's grace,
which He freely makes available, is always sufficient.
(other commas; semicolon used)

4. *Correlative conjunctions are coordinating conjunctions that work in pairs.*
Like the common coordinating conjunctions, correlative conjunctions show how the
joined items are related. *Both—and* shows addition or continuing thought; *not only—
but also* shows addition, with greater emphasis on the second item; *either—or,
neither—nor,* and *whether—or* show choice or option.

5. *Be careful to place correlative conjunctions just before the sentence parts
that they join.* If you put them in the wrong place, they will appear to join unparallel parts.

Incorrect:
We <u>both</u> *need* more helpers in the kitchen <u>and</u> *at the produce stand.*
<u>Either</u> the *boys* misunderstood <u>or</u> *ignored* Father's instructions.
Correct:
We need more helpers <u>both</u> *in the kitchen* <u>and</u> *at the produce stand.*
The boys <u>either</u> *misunderstood* <u>or</u> *ignored* Father's instructions.

6. *When using* not only—but also, *be careful not to omit the word* also.

Incorrect: We should <u>not only</u> *read* the Bible <u>but</u> *obey* its precepts.
Correct: We should <u>not only</u> *read* the Bible <u>but also</u> *obey* its precepts.

7. *With the correlative conjunction* whether—or, *the second item is often elliptical.* Because of the missing words, the joined sentence parts may appear to have
unequal structure when in fact they are parallel.

I hardly knew <u>whether</u> *to choose the cookies* <u>or</u> *the pie.*
(Meaning: <u>whether</u> to choose the cookies <u>or</u> to choose the pie)
<u>Whether</u> *you choose cookies* <u>or</u> *pie,* you must take a helping of fruit.
(Meaning: <u>whether</u> you choose cookies <u>or</u> you choose pie)

8. *Conjunctive adverbs function as both conjunctions and adverbs.* The following
words are often used as conjunctive adverbs.

accordingly	furthermore	likewise	otherwise
afterward	hence	meanwhile	still
also	henceforth	moreover	then
anyway	however	namely	therefore
besides	indeed	nevertheless	thus
consequently	instead		

Conjunctive adverbs join independent clauses and show specific relationships
between the clauses. A semicolon always precedes the conjunctive adverb, and a
comma often follows it. If the sentence reads smoothly without a pause after the

conjunctive adverb, you may omit the comma.

> We had a long warm spell in January, followed by bitter cold; <u>consequently</u>, the apple trees will bear no fruit this year.
> The sun shone brightly all morning; <u>then</u> a cold north wind drove the temperature below freezing.

Conjunctive adverbs are not considered true conjunctions, for they can be moved to different positions in a sentence. (True conjunctions must come between the sentence parts they join.) In one sense, a sentence with a conjunctive adverb simply has two clauses joined by a semicolon, with the conjunctive adverb modifying the verb in the second clause. Consider the following examples.

> Achan had sinned, <u>so</u> the Israelites suffered defeat at Ai.
> (*So* cannot be moved; it is a true conjunction.)
> Achan had sinned; <u>therefore</u>, the Israelites suffered defeat at Ai.
> Achan had sinned; the Israelites, <u>therefore</u>, suffered defeat at Ai.
> (*Therefore* can be moved; it is not a true conjunction. It modifies *suffered*.)

Applying the Lesson

A. Copy the conjunctions, and label them *CC* (common coordinating conjunction), *Cor* (correlative conjunction), or *CA* (conjunctive adverb).
1. An abrasive is a hard material used for grinding or polishing various materials.
2. Abrasives commonly appear in many forms of both grains and powders.
3. Harder abrasives are often mixed with other materials and used to make either grinding wheels or cutting tools.
4. Medium abrasives, bonded to paper or cloth, produce polishing belts and disks.
5. Mild abrasives are mixed with both pastes and liquids to produce polishing agents; moreover, they are often mixed with solvents to produce cleaning powders.
6. Not only the students but also the teacher had heard the fire sirens; however, no one could see any smoke.
7. The electricity went off late in the afternoon; consequently, Mother could not finish the meal she had started, and we ate a cold supper.
8. We are praying that God would send rain, for the crops are suffering severely; nevertheless we trust the Lord, who controls the weather.

B. Write enough of each sentence to show how to correct the mistake in it.
1. A godly person lives righteously and in holiness.
2. Your very thoughts must be right or you cannot do right.
3. God will surely both provide strength and wisdom for His children.
4. Seek the Lord in hard times and when things go well.
5. Every young person should develop good habits and godly character, indeed, such development sharply affects one's entire life and eternal destiny.
6. I either misunderstood the question, or the book has a mistake.

7. We hiked through the woods quietly and with great attentiveness.
8. This time we saw not only the usual deer but several foxes.
9. This poem neither has consistent rhythm nor good rhyme.
10. Father preached at Lyonsville Mennonite Church, then we went to Grandfather Rohrer's place for dinner.
11. We worked hard all morning yet the work seemed to keep piling up.
12. Eugene has both washed our van and Grandfather's car.
13. The girls made not only a large batch of bread but several dozen filled doughnuts.
14. Not only did we study the book thoroughly, but Brother Henry used a small circuit board to illustrate the lesson.

Review Exercises
Choose the words that are correct for the subjunctive mood. [68]
1. How I wish that the sun (was, were) shining today!
2. If we (would have read, had read) the instructions, we would have avoided quite a few difficulties.
3. It is extremely important that the roof (is, be) replaced before winter.
4. Mother insists that the dishes (are, be, were) washed before we may read or play.
5. If Jesus Himself (was, were) in our classroom, would we behave any differently?
6. If this wind (was, were) cold, we would need heavy coats.
7. The Lord (be, is) with you in your mission work in South America.
8. Jeremy would have come sooner if he (would have known, had known) that you were here.
9. If the outlook (be, is) dark, try the uplook.
10. All of Thomas's friends recommended that he (persist, persists) for a few more weeks.

---

100. Subordinating Conjunctions and Interjections

A subordinating conjunction joins clauses of unequal rank. The clause it introduces is *subordinate* to the rest of the sentence; that is, its function is less important than that of the main clause. The clause that a subordinating conjunction introduces cannot stand alone but has meaning only in relation to the rest of the sentence.

Subordinating Conjunctions
1. *A subordinating conjunction joins a dependent adverb clause to the independent clause in a complex sentence.* The following list shows a number of the most common subordinating conjunctions. Many of these words may also be used

as adverbs or prepositions. They are subordinating conjunctions only when they introduce dependent clauses.

after	even if	so that	when
although	even though	than	whenever
as	how	that	where
as if	if	though	wherever
as though	in order that	till	whether
because	provided	unless	while
before	since	until	

2. *A subordinating conjunction shows a specific relationship between the dependent clause and the independent clause.* These relationships include *when, where, how, why, under what condition, in spite of what,* and *to what degree.*

> Some people act <u>*as though*</u> *they always have the right to the last word.*
> (*As though* links the dependent clause to the independent clause by telling *how* about *act.*)
> <u>*If*</u> *you find yourself insisting on the last word,* check your attitudes.
> (*If* links the dependent clause to the independent clause by telling *under what condition* about *check.*)
> We often see faults in others more readily <u>*than*</u> *we see them in ourselves.*
> (*Than* links the dependent clause to the independent clause by telling *to what degree* about *more readily.*)

3. *A subordinating conjunction often provides a more effective link between clauses than does the coordinating conjunction* and. The word *and* provides a quick and handy way to join words and word groups. But *and* merely indicates one idea added to another, whereas subordinating conjunctions allow you to express a great variety of more specific relationships.

> **Vague:** Merely adds one idea to another
> The sun broke through the clouds, <u>and</u> the temperature soared.
> **Specific:** Shows exact time relationship
> <u>After</u> the sun broke through the clouds, the temperature soared.

4. *When a dependent clause comes at the beginning of a complex sentence, a comma separates it from the independent clause.* Two commas are used if the dependent clause comes in the middle. But if the clause comes at the end of the sentence, no comma is needed.

> <u>If you have time</u>, please stop at the store and get some bread.
> Please stop at the store, <u>if you have time</u>, and get some bread.
> Please stop at the store and get some bread <u>if you have time</u>.

Interjections

1. *An interjection is a word that expresses strong feeling.* The cry or exclamation of an interjection may express pleasure, admiration, adoration, surprise, pain, or any other feeling. The following list shows some common interjections.

ah	behold	ho	ouch	what
aha	good	hurrah	say	whew
alas	ha	lo	well	why
amen	hallelujah	oh		

<u>Behold</u>, God's presence shall always sustain us.
<u>Why</u>, we hardly knew what to do next!
<u>What</u>! You haven't heard about Uncle Lloyd's accident?

Words that represent sounds also frequently serve as interjections. Such a word is followed by an exclamation point or a period, depending on the intensity of the sound. Also, the word is italicized because it is "quoting" a sound. No italics are needed when such a word simply names a sound, as in the fourth example below.

Crash! The lamp plunged to the floor, breaking into hundreds of pieces.
Tap, tap, tap. A soft knocking sounded at the door.
Honk! Honk! Grandpa's geese announced our arrival.
We heard the <u>honk</u> of Grandpa's geese.
(a noun that names a sound; no italics needed)

Actually, almost any word can function as an interjection if it is used as an independent exclamation. But if a verb gives a one-word request or command, it is a complete sentence, not an interjection.

<u>Tea</u>! That certainly would taste good now. (interjection)
<u>Listen</u>! How could I listen with all the other distractions? (interjection)
<u>Listen</u>! What is that noise? (one-word command; a complete sentence)

2. *The use of commas and exclamation points with interjections depends on the degree of emotion intended by the writer.* Exclamation points mark strong interjections. The words *amen, hallelujah, hurrah, ouch, what,* and *whew* are usually strong exclamations, and so are words that represent sounds. If you use an exclamation point, capitalize the next word. Commas mark mild interjections. Many interjections can be used either way.

<u>Oh,</u> I don't believe I want any juice right now.
<u>Oh!</u> We were greatly alarmed when we saw the fire.

If the whole sentence shows strong feeling, you may use a comma after the interjection and an exclamation point at the end of the sentence. You may also use two exclamation points as in the second example below. But you must not overdo this in writing, for exclamation points should be used sparingly.

Well<u>,</u> I certainly did not expect this much help<u>!</u>
Well<u>!</u> I certainly did not expect this much help<u>!</u>

If an interjection comes in the middle of a compound sentence, set it off with commas.

I went to the barn to feed the heifers; and<u>,</u> behold<u>,</u> Stephen had already finished the job.

3. *Use interjections cautiously and sparingly.* They can easily become idle words of which we must give an account, and they can even fall into the category of profanity. Avoid the following kinds of interjections.

a. The name of God or any alteration of it.

b. Words that refer to characteristics of God.

c. Words that refer to hell, Satan, or any part of his kingdom.

d. Common words used as interjections that have nothing to do with their normal meanings. Words such as *boy, man,* and *rats* are sometimes used in that way.

Even interjections that are proper in themselves can be used in a wrong way. For example, it is improper to use *amen* and *hallelujah* in a light or carnal way. Also, the Bible commands us to control our emotions and our words. We need to avoid any exclamation of anger or disgust, no matter how acceptable the word itself may be.

Applying the Lesson

A. Copy each dependent clause, and underline the subordinating conjunction.

1. The tiny country of Andorra is so small that it appears as a mere speck on a map of Europe.

2. In fact, New York City contains twice as many square miles as Andorra has.

3. Even though Andorra is very small, its population density is fairly high so that its 2000 population was estimated at 67,000.

4. Because it is located within the Pyrenees Mountains, it consists wholly of mountains and mountain valleys.

5. Luxuriant pastures cover these mountain valleys while the summer sun shines warmly on them; however, deep snow covers them when the long, severe winters set in.

6. While snow covers those steep mountain slopes for many months, many people come to ski; indeed, tourism brings more income to the country than any other industry does.

7. Andorra became an independent nation after Charlemagne granted it independence in the ninth century.

8. Although the nation governs itself, it is not wholly independent if we define independence in the normal way.

9. Theoretically, its two co-princes—a Spanish bishop and the French president—could wield as much authority as any despot could.

10. In practice, the co-princes exert little real authority, and the people govern themselves as they wish through an elected legislature.

B. Rewrite each sentence, joining the clauses with a suitable subordinating conjunction instead of with *and.* Be sure to use commas correctly. You may change the order of the clauses if you wish.

1. The Bible is the Word of the sovereign God, and it never changes.

2. We have taken our burdens to the Lord in prayer, and we should leave them there.

3. We cannot overpower evil in our own strength, and we can conquer through Christ.

4. Jesus ascended into heaven, and the disciples watched.

5. We had several heavy showers, and the skies suddenly cleared.
6. Grandpa Snyder sat on the porch, and the sun shone warmly this afternoon.
7. This book is quite interesting, and I have read it several times.
8. We widened the driveway, and the milk truck can get in better.

C. Copy each interjection, the word before it (if there is one), and the word after it. Use correct capitalization and punctuation, and underline any word that should be italicized.
  1. Behold our God reigns over all.
  2. In spite of our best efforts, we still have great needs; but lo the Lord richly provides for us.
  3. Hallelujah praise the Lord for His great glory and goodness!
  4. What you are not afraid to speak evil of the Lord!
  5. Since God's name is sacred, we should honor it highly; but alas many take it in vain.
  6. Spiders they give me the chills.
  7. Thud another hay bale landed on the barn floor.
  8. Whew that was surely a vicious-looking dog!
  9. Say are you almost finished with your chores?
  10. Buzz a bumblebee flew right past my nose.

Review Exercises

A. For numbers 1 to 4, write the words that should be deleted from each sentence to improve its conciseness. For numbers 5 and 6, write a more concise word or phrase to replace the underlined parts. [77]
  1. Every day we must implore God's daily direction and guidance in our lives.
  2. At an early age in his life, Ronald showed a natural inborn aptitude for working with numbers.
  3. The Empire State Building is a building that may absorb up to as many as twenty bolts of lightning during the time of a single storm.
  4. The view that we could see from the summit of the mountaintop inspired our inner hearts with the greatness of God.
  5. When circumstances are <u>such that they are counter to our liking</u>, we must not <u>lapse into pensive melancholy</u>.
  6. I hope you <u>are aware of the fact</u> that the meeting tonight will <u>make a punctual commencement</u> at 7:00.

B. Write the letter of the sentence in each set that has proper parallelism. [77]
  1. a. You should have asked and still can ask your parents for permission to go along.
     b. You should have and still can ask your parents for permission to go along.
  2. a. To query is the asking of a question.
     b. To query is to ask a question.
  3. a. If you cannot understand a test question, if you need additional scratch paper, or if you have any other difficulty, please ask me for help.
     b. If you cannot understand a test question, you need additional scratch paper, or you have any other difficulty, please ask me for help.

4. a. Easily and with confidence, Brian shifted the old pickup into first gear and headed out the back lane.
   b. Easily and confidently, Brian shifted the old pickup into first gear and headed out the back lane.
5. a. Mother sighed as she looked at the box of mending, the stack of unlaundered clothing, and the sink full of dirty dishes.
   b. Mother sighed as she looked at the box of mending, the clothing that needed laundering, and the dirty dishes filling the sink.
6. a. Stephen pulled on the doorknob, and it comes right off in his hand!
   b. Stephen pulled on the doorknob, and it came right off in his hand!

---

101. Improving Your Editing Skills, Part 10

Editing Skills

"And the house, when it was in building, was built of stone made ready before it was brought thither: so that there was neither hammer nor axe nor any tool of iron heard in the house, while it was in building" (1 Kings 6:7). This verse speaks of the amazing skill of the men who built Solomon's temple. They cut the stones so precisely that no further shaping was needed at the temple site. According to Josephus, the stones were so well polished that no sign of any working tool could be discerned on them.

How did those workers develop that kind of skill? Certainly they did not attain it in one day or one month. These men must have had long years of practice in their trade. As the familiar saying goes, "Practice makes perfect."

You have worked through nine lessons on editing skills. You have practiced your proofreading skills on various composition lessons. Perhaps you have also used these skills on other occasions. Do you now qualify as an expert proofreader? Probably not. But like the builders of Solomon's temple, you have practiced and your ability has improved. This editing lesson will be a final test of the skills you have developed.

Marks Used in Editing and Proofreading

∨ or ∧ insert (caret)	◡ delete	. . . . stet (let it stand)	_____ use italics
¶ begin new paragraph	no ¶ no new paragraph	*lc* change to lowercase (small letter)	*uc* change to uppercase (capital letter)
# insert space	⌒ delete space	← move (arrow)	⌐⌐⌐ transpose

Editing Practice

A. Use proofreading marks to correct all the errors in these sentences. Watch especially for errors in the use of conjunctions and interjections.

1. Hallelujah! what a a wonderful God we serve!

2. Our God is perfect not only in majesty but in grace and goodness.

3. God neither will carelessly forget nor purposely ignore anyone who's heart is set on Him.

4. Oh how foolish are poeple who are proud and concieted!

5. Some times people seem quite ignorant of there responsibility to God and his Word.

6. Jehu was neither loyal to Baal nor nor to God.

7. What did your nieghbor fall off of the same roof?

8. Well I'll be glad for an occassion to visit my Uncle Leonard.

9. Father would sure be glad to find not only a power sander but a lathe at the auction.

10. To be pending means when something is hanging in uncertianty.

B. Use proofreading marks to correct all the errors in these sentences. Watch especially for errors in general usage.

1. The word hydraulics comes form the greek word hydor, which refers to water.

2. Although the word formally referred only to water in motion, to day it is used for the study of any liquid at rest or in motion.

3. One important principal of hydraulics was invented by Blaise Pascal (blez pa·skal'), who lived in the 1600s.

4. Pascal's law states that a presurized liquid exerts an equal force in all directions and at right angels to the surface of its container.

5. You can't hardly fail to understand this law if one sees the affect of water pressure on a flat fire hose.

6. Irregardless of how flat the hose has been, under high pressure it becomes round and taunt in such a short time.

7. You have got to understand Pascal's law in order to understand the working of hydraulic presses, hydraulic jacks, hydraulic brakes, and etc.

8. An intresting hydraulic phenomenon that occurs in water pipes called water hammer.

9. If a valve in a pipe is closed quickly, it causes a sudden pressure wave inside of the pipe being as inertia tends to keep the water moving forward.

10. That pressure wave, surging back and forth threw the pipe, causes a noise that sounds incredulously like a hammer blow on the pipe.

C. Use proofreading marks to correct all the errors in these paragraphs.

1. Mount Kilimanjaro (kil'·ə·mən·jär'·ō) is a Volcanic

2. mountain in northern Tanzania. It has two peaks, of which

3. the taller one (called Kibo) raises to an altitude of 19,340

4. feet (5,895 meters). This is the most highest point on the

5. continent of Africa. The other peek is called Mawensi.

6. Though Kibo lays only 3 degrees south of the equator.

7. It is always covered with about 200 feet (61 meters) of

8. snow and ice. Their are several glaciers on the sides of

9. this peak, Mawensi has none. People living on the lower

10. slopes the of volcano raise bananas, millet, and coffee.

11. Cattle also graze on the side's of the mountain.

12. In 1848 some German missionaries became the first

13. europeans to see Mount Kilimanjaro. When they told about

14. a snow-covered peak so near the equator, hardly any one

15. believed their story rightaway. Two mountain climbers, a

16. German and an Austrian, first reached the top of Kibo in

17. the 1889.

---

102. Idioms

Have you ever said, "I am going to stay at home"? What did you mean? Where are you *going* if you intend to *stay*? This expression is quite familiar to any fluent speaker of the English language, and it is a perfectly acceptable English construction. Yet if you analyze it word by word, you will find that it makes no sense. Welcome to the fascinating study of idioms.

An *idiom* is an expression that cannot be explained grammatically or logically, yet it is an established part of a language. We learned English idioms naturally as we learned to speak the language. In fact, if a person makes errors in the use of common idioms, it is a sign that he does not know the language well.

Many idioms contain common words like *go, get, up,* and *down.* These words provide a handy way to communicate ideas that may require clumsy or unnatural wording to express in any other way. Read the examples below, with special attention to the natural, everyday tone of the sentences in the first group.

Sentences with idioms:	Sentences without idioms:
What are you <u>going to</u> do?	What do you intend to do?
Is it <u>going to</u> rain today?	Will it rain today?
Grandfather <u>got</u> sick last night.	Grandfather became sick last night.
Lloyd is <u>getting</u> ready to go.	Lloyd is preparing to go.
I just <u>got</u> finished with my chores.	I just finished my chores.
Hurry <u>up</u> and come downstairs.	Come downstairs quickly.
It is <u>up</u> to her.	The decision is hers.
Did you look <u>up</u> the new word?	Did you find the new word?
Write <u>down</u> these words.	Write these words on paper.
Slow <u>down</u> (*or* slow <u>up</u>) for these bumps.	Go more slowly because of these bumps.

The illogical nature of many idioms is illustrated especially well by the last pair of examples. Both "slow down" and "slow up" mean exactly the same thing! There are dozens of other idioms that are no more logical than these. Here are just a few of the many that you use in your everyday speaking and writing.

Other idiomatic expressions:
I can't <u>lay my eyes on</u> it now. (see it)
Did you <u>catch</u> a cold? (become sick with a cold)
<u>All of a sudden</u>, the heifers ran off. (suddenly)
The extra helper <u>came in handy</u>. (served in a handy way)

Idiomatic Usage

The proper use of prepositions is often a matter of correct idioms. In other words, certain prepositions are "correct" or "incorrect" not because of their meanings but simply because of what is established as proper usage. This is the basis for a number of rules in the "Glossary of Usage" (Chapter 5). Here are three examples.

We agree <u>to</u> a plan and agree <u>with</u> a person.
We part <u>from</u> a person and part <u>with</u> a thing.
We wait <u>for</u> a person if we await his coming. We wait <u>on</u> a person if we serve him.

Use the dictionary when you are not sure about an expression. Many advanced dictionaries have run-in entries that show established idioms. For example, the entry for *put* may include the following run-in entries at the end.

— **put across,** to state so as to be understood clearly: *put across his point of view.*
— **put down,** (1) to record on paper. (2) to repress: *put down a rebellion.*
— **put off,** to delay; procrastinate: *put it off until tomorrow.*
— **put out,** to extinguish: *put out a fire.*

Applying the Lesson

A. Each of these sentences contains an expression that is not in natural, everyday language. Copy that phrase, and after it write an idiom with a form of *get,* which could replace it.
1. At what time do you arise from your bed in the morning?
2. We could not achieve an entrance because the door was locked.
3. Lisa was so surprised that she could hardly recover from it.
4. Roy dismounted from his bicycle and parked it in the garage.
5. The two selfish neighbors could not have peaceful associations with each other.
6. Our horse achieved an escape because the gate was left open.

B. Write the meaning of each underlined expression. You may use a dictionary.
1. Though Job was sorely tested, he would not <u>give up</u> his faith.
2. He <u>kept on</u> trusting in God regardless of his losses and sufferings.
3. Gehazi <u>made up</u> a story to obtain some of Naaman's rewards.
4. I could not finish mowing the lawn because the mower was <u>acting up</u>.
5. The cannon <u>went off</u> with a thunderous boom.
6. Use of the telephone <u>caught on</u> quickly after people recognized its advantages.
7. Be careful not to let the bucket <u>run over</u>.
8. We had thought that Spot was gone <u>for good</u>, but yesterday he returned.

C. Rewrite each sentence so that it expresses the same thought without an idiom.
1. Put out the light.
2. I was taken in by the salesman's smooth words.
3. How did the barn catch fire?

4. I tried to catch your eye.
5. Audrey certainly takes after her mother.
6. On the whole, this market has good produce.
7. I was about to say that.
8. Mother is going to make a dress.
9. Wake up and get going to the barn!
10. If it's going to rain, we must round up the cattle.

Review Exercises

A. Copy the correct participle for each sentence. [81]
   1. Samuel and Stanley, (growing, having grown) so much during the summer, found that their winter coats were too small for them.
   2. The ice on the pond, (melting, melted) slowly but surely, will soon be completely gone.
   3. (Breaking, Broken) during the night, the window must now be replaced.
   4. (Entering, Having entered) the front door, I tripped over the threshold.

B. For each underlined word, write *yes* or *no* to tell whether it should be followed by a comma. [81–85]
   1. Scattered across the yard leaves and branches caused an untidy clutter after the storm.
   2. While you were washing the dishes we were dusting the furniture and the woodwork.
   3. You can purchase a book containing all this information for only $13.95.
   4. The Anabaptists in Europe faced severe persecution before some came to America.
   5. The parents as well as the children enjoyed watching the monkeys whose actions were almost human.
   6. If this rain continues the lawn and the garden will soon be flooded.

C. Write enough words to show how to correct the mistake in each sentence. [86]
   1. Cousin Sandra has a most unique way of describing the things she saw in Guatemala.
   2. He examined the two apples, took the smallest one for himself, and gave the other to his friend.
   3. Boys, you must enter the room quieter than that.
   4. Those who are more richer in natural possessions must beware lest they be poorer in spiritual matters.
   5. Though Albert speaks less than anyone in his family, he usually says more than the others!
   6. During the night Lyndon's cold grew worse, and in the morning he spoke even hoarser than yesterday.

103. Improving Your Writing Style, Part 6: Review

In your previous writing style lessons, you have studied five elements of an effective writing style. This lesson reviews those elements.

1. Originality

You should not always use the first wording that comes to your mind. Rather, look for fresh, creative ways of expressing yourself—ways deliberately designed to add appeal. Sprinkle your creativity like salt throughout your writing, always remembering to keep your imagination within proper bounds. The added life in your compositions will be well worth the extra time and effort.

In your pursuit of originality, beware that you do not merely use clichés—expressions that once were clever but that now have lost their sparkle through too much use. Surely you do not want your writing to become *as cold as ice* because you have written everything *off the cuff*!

2. Exact Words

Exact words paint clear, colorful pictures in a reader's mind. So eliminate vague nouns, verbs, and modifiers. *Get* them out of your writing, and *make* room for better ones. While you are doing that, remember to watch out for *make* and *get*! For example, you should not write about *pets* that are *getting into things* when *naughty little puppies* are *digging holes in Mother's flower beds.*

3. Active Voice

Deliberately use verbs in the active voice. Passive verbs produce dull writing because they turn living, active people into passive subjects that do nothing. Verbs in the passive voice *can be eliminated* from almost every one of your sentences—but that will happen only if *you eliminate* such verbs.

4. Figurative Language

The careful use of similes, metaphors, personification, and hyperboles can take a dormant paragraph and set it abloom with color and fragrance. Devising an effective simile may seem *as difficult as drilling through rock,* but figurative expressions are *gems* that add *luster* to your writing.

5. Triplets

Writing a set of three similarly constructed expressions adds a sense of completeness to a sentence. It allows addition of just enough details to add force but avoid clutter. A skillful use of triplets will *reinforce your sentences, refine your writing, and refresh your readers.*

Work hard to incorporate these devices as you write. They will help you to produce compositions that others enjoy reading.

You studied modifiers in Chapter 11. The use of exact, descriptive adjectives and adverbs (as you saw in the second writing style lesson) will definitely improve your writing style. This is especially true of descriptive writing. Notice the contribution made by modifiers in the following descriptive composition.

Clinch Mountain Lookout

The atmosphere boiled with heat that morning in northeastern Tennessee. The brazen ball of the sun sent heat waves shimmering upward from each place struck by the flaming rays. From the high elevation atop Clinch Mountain in the Appalachians, the murky haze of the sky knew no relief from the burning brilliance.

To the left of the narrow plaza perched on the brow of the giant hill, a four-lane superhighway snaked its way down the mountainside. On one side of the weaving road, a straight cliff rose to the heavens, and on the opposite side a sheer precipice dropped to the depths below. In the distance, the highway wound itself out of sight among the trees huddled at the base of the steep mountain.

Beyond the low stone wall surrounding the lookout, the mountain dropped rapidly downward. Small ridges furrowed the valley far below us. These ridges and the narrow valleys between them wore a dense blanket of dark green trees. This rich veil of forest broke only to surround a humble dwelling or to permit a ribbon of road to pass through its midst. On these minute paths, tiny vehicles crept along at a snail's pace. Farther on, the vast Cherokee Lake spread its fingers through the valleys, reducing the ridges to mere islands enclosed in its encompassing grasp. An occasional boat disturbed the stillness of the lake, casting up sparkling, dancing waves in its wake.

The haze of the horizon hid the full extent of the lake. The distant scenes faded into obscurity, hidden by the heated atmosphere of that day when we paused on Clinch Mountain.

—Written by a tenth grader

Applying the Lesson

Write a descriptive composition of 150–200 words. Put special effort into applying the five elements of effective writing style that you have studied. Evaluate your first draft by checking it with each of the following questions.

1. Have I used fresh, creative expressions and avoided clichés?
2. Have I used specific nouns, verbs, and modifiers?
3. Have I used active verbs rather than passive verbs?
4. What figures of speech could I use to make the essay more colorful?
5. What triplets could I use to add extra appeal?

104. Chapter 13 Review

A. Copy each prepositional phrase. If a phrase is part of a longer phrase, include it with the longer phrase and also copy it separately. Label each phrase *adj., adv.,* or *n.*
1. By the word of His power, God created the earth and everything that is on the earth.
2. Due to man's limited understanding, scientists remain unable to fully explain many principles about how creation functions.
3. For my thirteenth birthday, my grandparents gave me that book with the dark blue cover.
4. Above one hundred degrees is uncomfortably warm for working in the garden!
5. For a short time, we rested under the maple tree near the garden.

B. Copy the conjunctions, and label them *CC* (common coordinating conjunction), *Cor* (correlative conjunction), *SC* (subordinating conjunction), or *CA* (conjunctive adverb).
1. A seismograph both measures and records tremors in the ground.
2. Seismographs are important wherever earthquakes are common, for tremors usually increase before a major earthquake strikes.
3. These tremors vary widely; therefore, an observing station has several seismographs so that the geologists can collect precise measurements.
4. The main components of a seismograph are a rigid pier, a weight suspended on a weak spring, and a recording drum.
5. Ground tremors shake not only the pier but also the recording drum; however, the weight stays relatively motionless.
6. Since a pen is attached to the stationary weight, the movement of the rest of the equipment, and of the ground, is marked on the recording drum.

C. Write enough of each sentence to show how to correct the mistake in it.
1. We must both exercise simple faith in God and personal diligence.
2. God can see us equally well in the daytime and when it is black midnight.
3. God daily pours out rich blessings, nevertheless many people fail to acknowledge Him as the giver.
4. We owe God not only words of thanksgiving but deeds of commitment.
5. A willingness to share reflects a thankful heart but selfishness indicates an unthankful heart.

D. Rewrite each sentence, joining the clauses with a suitable subordinating conjunction instead of with *and.* You may change the order of the clauses if you wish.
1. The tornadoes developed with little warning, and many people were unprepared.
2. Father was at a meeting, and a severe thunderstorm damaged our house.
3. The road crews worked steadily all night, and the snow fell too rapidly for them to keep all the roads open.

4. We lived on Uncle Benjamin's farm, and several years of drought made farming difficult.

5. We learned the new song well, and we sang it frequently.

E. Copy each interjection, the word before it (if there is one), and the word after it. Use correct capitalization and punctuation.

1. I had felt that everything was going wrong, but behold later I could see how God was working out His perfect will.

2. Alas we find it too easy to forget that God is in full control.

3. Ah but God is worthy of all praise and honor.

4. Why of course the Bible is God's message to man!

5. What you mean that Mr. O'Brien declares the Bible to be a hoax!

F. Rewrite each sentence so that it communicates the same idea without an idiom.

1. The girls' help surely came in handy today.

2. Nathaniel was taken in by the stranger's story.

3. Alice takes after her older sister in many ways.

4. Timothy is going to make a bookcase for Father.

5. You must get rid of the trash that is cluttering your desk.

6. The grease in the frying pan caught fire.

7. We put the fire out with baking soda.

8. Gerald soon found out what the problem was.

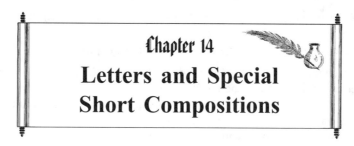

Chapter 14
Letters and Special Short Compositions

105. Book Reports

All books are placed in one of two main categories: fiction and nonfiction. Stories that are not factual belong in the fiction category, and books of factual information belong in the nonfiction category. When you gave book reports in earlier grades, you probably reported on books of fiction or biography (which is one category of nonfiction). For this lesson you will write a report on a book of nonfiction other than a biography. Because books of fiction and nonfiction have different purposes, reports on the two kinds follow different patterns.

The following sample book report illustrates the points that you will study in this lesson. The boldface words name its various parts.

Title	**Learning From the Book of Nature**
Basic facts	This book was written by William Child and copyrighted in 1996 by Rod and Staff Publishers.
Purpose	In the introduction, the author indicates his purpose in writing this book. He points out that God created nature for several reasons: to provide for man's needs, to inspire man, and to teach man spiritual lessons. This book develops that third point. At the beginning of most chapters, William Child very interestingly presents some facts about nature. In the latter part of each chapter, he parallels those nature facts to spiritual concepts and draws some lessons for us to consider.
Summary of several main points **First main point**	In the second chapter, the author discusses the problem of parasites. Many have wondered, "Why did God create parasites?" Or at least they have wondered, in the words of the author's daughter, "Why did God make mosquitoes?" The *Psithyrus* bumblebee, for example, is a parasite to the *Bombus* bumblebee. Instead of building its own colony and gathering its own pollen, the *Psithyrus* queen lays her eggs in a *Bombus* nest, where the host species takes care of them. Cowbirds and some kinds of cuckoos lay their eggs in the nests of smaller birds. Since the fledgling cowbirds are bigger than the host fledglings, they compete with them for food and care. Yet God did create these parasites for a purpose: they help to keep a healthy balance in the populations of various species.

Although God created a balanced world, the Fall of Man and the curse it brought have produced an imbalance in nature. These imbalances remind us to be humble because the curse on nature resulted from man's sin. The curse also helps man to see that he needs God's help for his salvation. Dealing with troublesome parasites reminds us that we are weak. And these parasites, along with the thorns and thistles, give us reason to long for the future when the curse will be removed.

Second main point

Chapter 3 describes the struggle of the Monterey pine to survive in its adopted home of New Zealand. In years with normal precipitation, the Monterey pine does quite well. In wet years, however, fungi in the soil destroy the tiny feeder roots of the trees, weakening their ability to absorb water and minerals. If a dry year follows the wet year, the weakened tree is especially vulnerable to wood wasps, which lay their eggs in the tree. The wood wasp larvae eat the living tissue of the tree, thus killing the tree.

This succession of stresses that can kill the Monterey pine reminds us of Job, who experienced several intense stresses one after another. But because he maintained a strong faith in God, these stresses could not destroy Job's spiritual life.

Third main point

The author writes about watersheds in Chapter 11. A watershed is the area of land from which any particular stream or river receives water drainage. A knowledge of watersheds is useful to engineers designing a dam, farmers planning field terraces and farm ponds, and home buyers choosing a house near a stream. Watersheds vary greatly in size, in terrain, and in moisture content.

As the author points out, our lives can be compared to watersheds. If we are just living naturally, without God's power, what we are and think simply reflects what our surrounding circumstances have influenced us to be and think. But if we allow God to transform us and the Holy Spirit to control our lives, the watershed works in reverse. Then, as the author writes, "We are no longer the affected-by-the-world but the effective-for-Christ."

Stimulating
questions

What caused thirty-ton rocks to rise twenty feet out of Jim Walker's pasture in the spring of 1973? What lessons can we learn from these rocks? Did you know that forest fires are actually helpful in various ways? And can you name several ways in which "fires" benefit our spiritual lives? This fascinating book will answer these questions and probably many other questions that may never even have occurred to you.

Evaluation   Although *Learning From the Book of Nature* deals with some technical scientific information and some deep spiritual truths, it is written in an easy-to-read style. The author consistently employs specific, descriptive language. One good example is the first sentence of the second paragraph in Chapter 1: "From within the first stretch of woods along the road, we heard an occasional series of slaps and rattles as acorns of white and chestnut oaks fell to the earth through layers of leaves and branches." The author uses plenty of figurative language too. He writes of "seedpods ready to catch a ride on any passing furry or clothed creature." He writes of red-headed woodpeckers that "used an oak stump near their elm snag as a table and cutting board. There they butchered and processed their provisions, saving only digestible parts for their young." I am sure you will enjoy this interesting, informative book.

[809 words]

Contents of a Book Report

A report on a book of nonfiction should include four or five kinds of information. First, you must state the basic facts about the book. Name the title, the author, the publisher, and the copyright date. You might include any significant information about the author that would help your reader to understand the book.

Second, give a statement of the overall purpose of the book. Often the author directly states that purpose in his introduction or foreword to the book. Sometimes, however, you may need to formulate for yourself what that purpose is.

In the main part of the book report, you should summarize several of the main points that the author uses to develop his overall purpose. Devote at least one entire paragraph to each main point that you choose to highlight. State the main point, and give some of the supporting details that the author uses to prove or illustrate that point. A good way to conclude this central part of the report is to ask several stimulating questions that the book answers.

Your book report may sometimes include a fourth kind of information—any weaknesses or errors that you find in the book. Naturally, this section should generally be brief; for if the book has too many objections, it is not worthwhile enough to report on. Be sure to present your criticisms with courtesy and dignity. Along with the criticism, you should give a positive statement of what constitutes a right view of the matter.

Finally, your report should include your own evaluation of the book. You might describe a certain part or a special feature of the book that you enjoyed in particular. Is the author's style especially appealing? Does he use figures of speech that are exceptionally fresh and descriptive? Does he employ alliteration or use triplets? Give a few noteworthy examples.

Steps in Writing a Book Report

As with any other composition, writing a book report requires planning and organization. The first step, of course, is to read an approved book. And reading for a book report calls for careful, thorough reading. Discipline your mind to find information for your report.

Second, you should list details for the different kinds of information that you will include in the report. For best results, this step may well overlap the first. As you read, note on paper the main supporting points that will serve well in developing your report. You should definitely note any weaknesses or errors that your report will mention.

After you have your list of details, you are ready to write the report. Stick to the main points you have listed; do not attempt to describe the whole book. Write the report in your own words. Direct quotations should be kept few and short. If you do quote directly from the book, remember to use quotation marks.

The final step is to proofread your report. Check the sentence structure; look for usage errors; scrutinize the mechanics. Consider the elements of writing style that you have learned in the writing style lessons. And be sure to evaluate the content of your report. Do you have the four or five different kinds of information that you should have? Have you included several of the author's main points? Do you have sufficient supporting details for each of those points? Strive to make your report as nearly perfect as you can.

Applying the Lesson

A. Write a report on an approved book of nonfiction that you have read recently. Your report should have at least 400 words.

B. Proofread and revise your book report.

---

106. Friendly Letters

Letters fill an important place in our lives. In fact, the Bible includes a number of letters (epistles) that are inspired by God. Several of these—Philemon, 2 John, and 3 John—are personal letters. All the epistles contain expressions of admonition, encouragement, and concern for the receivers. Though these letters were written centuries ago, God also intended them for us. They share with us the good things of God, and they give practical instructions for Christian living.

Letters today may also bring us nearer to God and to our loved ones. They keep us in touch with our friends. Letters of appreciation and encouragement are a blessing to anyone. Letters of sympathy give comfort and courage to friends who experience death or hardship in the family. Letters of apology help to keep our interpersonal relationships clear.

Since letters are so valuable, it is important to write them in an interesting and correct manner. Here is a sample for your reference as you review the parts of a friendly letter.

<table>
<tr><td>**Heading**</td><td>227 Jefferson Street
Seaford, NY 11783
June 26, 20—</td></tr>
<tr><td>**Greeting**</td><td>Dear Mildred,</td></tr>
<tr><td rowspan="2">**Body**</td><td>"Great is the Lord, and greatly to be praised." This verse entered my mind last evening when our family visited Aunt Sharon. As we admired her dark red, velvety roses, I remembered that you had asked if we had seen them. I looked at those lovely blooms very closely for you because I knew you won't be able to see them this year. Isn't it marvelous to see God's greatness even in something as small as flowers? God put special care into making a rose, but how much greater is the concern and effort He put forth to make us, His children.

I spent last Saturday with the Keener family. Dorothy needed help.</td></tr>
<tr><td>The night before, a new calf was born at their farm. "It's brown," five-year-old Kurt quickly told me. Then after dinner we had time to go and see it. But guess what? The calf was black.

"Why, Kurt," I said in surprise, "the calf is black."

"I know it looks black," he informed me, "but it is really brown because Mama said so."

How puzzling! But Dorothy solved the mystery when I asked her about it. She had not even had time to see the calf yet. She had just taken for granted the calf would be brown because the cow was. We both laughed over the incident, but she decided that she had better know what she is talking about the next time. Which reminded me again of how easy I find it to talk without thinking through what I am saying. But I'm thankful that we can trust God to help us to overcome this problem as well as give victory in every other area.</td></tr>
<tr><td>**Closing**
Signature</td><td>I'll look forward to hearing from you before long.
Sincerely,
Linda</td></tr>
</table>

Friendly Letter Content

A friendly letter should have worthwhile content. Use the following checklist to help you in writing your letters.

1. Begin with a fitting Scripture verse, a few lines of poetry, or some other inspirational thought.

2. Move directly into the body of your letter. Avoid meaningless sentences like "Well, how are you?" or "I'm finally getting around to writing again."
3. Answer any questions that your friend asked in a previous letter.
4. Share interesting and profitable information. Before you begin, make a list of specific ideas that you want to include.
5. Show an interest in the person to whom you are writing. Think of things you would ask your friend if you were talking to him, and ask those questions in your letter.
6. Use correct grammar, mechanics, and usage. Although the style may be informal, it should not be careless or slangy.
7. Write a worthwhile conclusion, such as "I hope to hear from you soon" or "I'm looking forward to your visit."
8. Write an appropriate closing. Here are some good closings for a friendly letter.

Sincerely,	Your friend,
Sincerely yours,	With love and prayers,
Your son,	In Christian love,

Friendly Letter Form

A friendly letter should follow standard form. Include the five parts of a friendly letter, and make the general appearance of your letter neat and attractive.

1. The heading, written in the upper right-hand corner, includes the writer's address and the date of the letter. Follow the normal rules of capitalization and punctuation in the heading.
2. The greeting, written at the left margin, addresses the person to whom the letter is written. Capitalize the first word and all nouns in the greeting, and place a comma after it.
3. The body, which is the message of the letter, should be written in proper paragraph form.
4. The closing should appear below the last line of the body. Place its left edge directly below that of the heading. Capitalize only the first word.
5. The signature, always handwritten, should be directly below the closing.

Social Notes

Social notes are special kinds of friendly letters. They include thank-you notes, invitations, replies to invitations, notes of apology, and notes of sympathy.

1. *Thank-you notes.* A thank-you note should express sincere gratitude for a gift or for an expression of hospitality. Even if we have had opportunity to say "Thank you," taking time to write a note of thanks can show deeper appreciation. Always be completely honest in your expressions of thanks. Do not write flowery phrases just to make your friend feel good. If a gift itself is not particularly useful, express appreciation for the person's thoughtfulness. Do be careful not to hurt the person's feelings.

Route 2, Box 26
Greenville, AL 36037
June 21, 20—

Dear Aunt Lois,

As I sit here in my sweltering bedroom and listen to the insects outside my window, I think longingly of the cool nights when we slept at your house in the Kentucky hills. When you have hot days such as we are experiencing now, you can remember that nighttime will be much better. But here the nights are only slightly cooler than the days.

Even though it is uncomfortably warm here, I'm glad to be back home. We are also glad that we stopped at the caverns you mentioned, even though it took us longer than we expected to get home. We surely enjoyed that tour.

Thank you very much for the sincere welcome you gave to us during our visit in Kentucky and for the place you provided for our weary bodies to rest. I'm sure that God has already blessed you, and I'm praying that He will continue to do so.

Your niece,
Mary Lou

2. *Invitations.* Most invitations that you make will be spoken, but sometimes you may have occasion to write one. Be sure to specify the three W's of an invitation: *what, when,* and *where.* Include any important information about special plans so that the receiver can prepare properly.

Route 3
Hanover, MD 21076
June 2, 20—

Dear Eldon,

Father and Mother are inviting you to come to our house after the Witmer reunion on June 18. You could stay the whole week afterward, and Father could take you home again the next Saturday. He plans to take several calves to the livestock auction in your home town. You would be back home by noon on June 25.

Please bring old clothes along because Father said we may paint the garage. And don't forget the fishing hole, the tree house, and that cave we discovered on the ridge last summer.

Happy days ahead! I'm looking forward to seeing you.

Sincerely,
Maynard

3. *Replies to invitations.* When you reply to an invitation, whether accepting or declining, you should write in a warm and friendly manner. Express appreciation for the thoughtfulness of the one who extended the invitation. To avoid any misunderstanding, you should also repeat the details of the invitation.

15 Canal Bridge Road
Pleasant Hill, NC 27866
June 10, 20—

Dear Maynard,

Thank you for the invitation to spend a whole week at your place in the mountains. Father and Mother say I may come. I am really excited. I'll bring old clothes for the painting job and be prepared to work in the garden or anything else you will have for me to do.

I'm not forgetting my fishing rod either. I can hardly wait to enjoy all the things you have mentioned.

Your cousin,
Eldon

If you must decline, courtesy calls you to explain why you cannot accept the invitation.

15 Canal Bridge Road
Pleasant Hill, NC 27866
June 10, 20—

Dear Maynard,

Thank you for the invitation to spend a whole week at your place in the mountains. I was really excited when I received your letter. As it happens, we have a bumper crop of blueberries this year, and that week will probably be in the middle of the harvest. My job is to show the customers where to pick and to keep them supplied with baskets—besides running countless other errands that will keep me hustling from morning till night. Father says we won't make it to the reunion either.

I'm really disappointed about not being able to spend that week with you. Father says maybe something else will work out later. I hope it does!

Your cousin,
Eldon

4. *Notes of apology.* A note of apology should be a sincere expression of regret for a wrong you have done to another person. Sometimes it serves as a way of expressing what is difficult to say in person. Be specific enough that the person understands what you are referring to. Do not make excuses or blame other people or circumstances. Simply acknowledge your wrong, and ask for forgiveness. If the wrong involved some damage that you can pay for or otherwise make right, offer to do so.

523 River Road
West Liberty, KY 41472
August 23, 20—

Dear Joan,

I'm sorry for my unkind words to you on Sunday after the service. I know that I tend to speak too sharply, but I do want to overcome this bad habit. Please forgive me, and pray for me. By God's grace, I intend to control my tongue better in the future. I'm also writing to Carol and Anita because they heard those ugly words too.

Sincerely,
Wilma

5. *Notes of sympathy.* A note of sympathy should be a sincere expression of your sympathy for a person experiencing grief or hardship. Do not write about how terrible the person's experience is. You probably should not attempt to explain why God may have allowed the experience. Do let the person know that you are sharing his grief, and also write something inspirational: Bible verses, lines of poetry, or sentences of your own that will encourage the person to trust in the Lord. It is always fitting to assure your friend that you are praying for him. A note of sympathy should be brief and to the point. If you have other interesting things to share, write a friendly letter soon afterward.

Route 1
Tilley, AB T0J 3K0
December 18, 20—

Dear Gwendolyn,

I was deeply sorry to hear of the passing of your little sister. Although we shall be unable to attend the funeral, our thoughts and prayers are certainly with you and your family. How wonderful it is to know that Jesus cares for us in every circumstance, no matter how difficult or sorrowful.

Does Jesus care when I've said "good-bye"
To the dearest on earth to me,
And my sad heart aches till it nearly breaks—
Is it aught to Him? Does He see?

Oh, yes, He cares, I know He cares!
His heart is touched with my grief;
When the days are weary, the long nights dreary,
I know my Saviour cares.

In Christian love,
Mary Alice

Of course, you may also send a sympathy card when a friend has experienced the loss of a loved one. Such a card usually bears its own message of sympathy; yet no matter how well it states your feelings, you should also write a note of your own. A personal expression of sympathy is more meaningful than a factory-printed message.

The Envelope

An envelope should include a return address and a mailing address. Place the return address in the upper left-hand corner with standard capitalization and punctuation. Place the mailing address about in the center, but a bit lower and farther right. Type or neatly print the mailing address with all capital letters and no punctuation so that the postal service can handle the letter most efficiently.

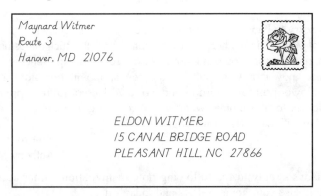

You should fold the letter and place it into the envelope correctly. For a large envelope, first fold the bottom third of the paper up; then fold the top third down. For a small envelope, first fold the lower half of the paper up; then fold it in thirds. Always place the letter in the envelope with the last fold line at the bottom.

To use a large envelope:

fold paper in thirds   ready for
                              large envelope   insert like this

To use a small envelope:

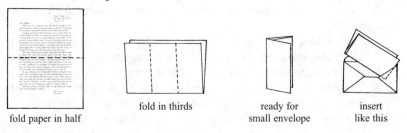

fold paper in half   fold in thirds   ready for   insert
                                                      small envelope   like this

Applying the Lesson
A. Write a friendly letter to a friend, a relative, or a missionary. Address an envelope, and place your letter in it.

B. Rewrite the following note of sympathy, which has some of the weaknesses mentioned in the lesson. Use your home address and today's date in the heading.

Dear Roger,

I was sorry to hear about the bad car accident your family had. Isn't it awful that five of you are in the hospital at the same time? But such things happen for a reason, and I'm sure you can learn a lesson from this experience.

Did you know that we're putting up a new shop with two stories? We plan to use the lower part for a garage and woodworking area. The upper part will be nice to use for those times when all the cousins get together.

I'll close with best wishes for your recovery.

Your friend,
Anthony

C. Write Gladys's reply to the following note of invitation, either accepting or declining it. Use your home address and today's date.

265 Sawmill Road
Washington Boro, PA 17582
April 18, 20—

Dear Gladys,

I am looking forward to seeing you and your family at Grandfather Showalter's place on Sunday, April 29. Father and Mother have given me permission to ask you to stay at our place from Sunday evening through early Wednesday afternoon. Father is scheduled to have a prayer meeting topic at Grand View Wednesday evening, and our family plans to be at Brother Laban Horst's place for supper. So we would be going almost past your farm at about 1:30 Wednesday afternoon.

If it suits for you to come, bring an extra set of good clothes along, for our congregation will hold a service at the Goldenrod Home on Tuesday evening. Hope to see you soon!

Your cousin,
Rita

Review Exercises

Tell whether each of these statements about an argumentative essay is true or false. [45–49]

1. The introduction is like bait to attract readers to the essay.
2. The thesis statement tells exactly what the argument is about.
3. Dealing with counter arguments helps to strengthen your position.
4. You must use details, reasons, and illustrations to validate your points.
5. You should usually give your strongest supporting reason first.
6. Nothing in an argument carries as much force as a well-grounded opinion.
7. In your conclusion, you should restate the thesis in different words.
8. If your points are presented clearly enough, your conclusion need not summarize them.

107. Business Letters

The older you grow, the more responsibility you will likely assume in business-related interests. Do you need to place an order by mail? Must you inform a business that an order was filled unsatisfactorily? Do you wish to know what products or services a business offers? For these and many other situations, a clear understanding of what makes a good business letter will be a definite asset in communicating effectively and in receiving good customer service.

The following example illustrates proper business letter form. Refer to this example as you study the lesson.

Heading	`24 Amstead Road`
	`Manchester, WI  53946`
	`February 9, 20—`

Inside address	`Rod and Staff Publishers, Inc.`
	`P.O. Box 3`
	`Crockett, KY  41413-0003`

Salutation	`Dear Sirs:`
Body	`I have recently read several copies of the `<u>`Christian Example`</u>`. Please send me subscription prices for this periodical and any others that you print. Thank you.`

Closing
Signature
	`Very truly yours,`
	Alfred McCrea
	`Alfred McCrea`

Business Letter Form and Content

The form of a business letter differs slightly from that of a friendly letter. In addition to the five parts of a friendly letter, a business letter has an *inside address.* The inside address is the name and address of the receiver, and it is placed lower than the heading but at the left-hand margin. The greeting of a business letter is usually called a *salutation;* it is followed by a colon rather than a comma. Both the salutation and the closing should be more formal than those of a friendly letter. The signature of a business letter should be written twice, once by hand and once in type or printing. A blank line should separate each part of a business letter from the next part.

Business letter salutations:

Dear Sir: (Use this if the name of the businessman is unknown.)
Dear Mr. Landis: (Use the name if it is known.)
Dear Sirs: *or* Gentlemen: (Use this when writing to a company.)

Business letter closings:

Very truly yours,   Yours truly,   Sincerely yours,

Cordially yours, (Use this for a business acquaintance.)

Respectfully yours, (Use this for very formal letters.)

The body should illustrate the three C's of business letters: *courteous, clear,* and *concise.* God's people should always be courteous, even when pointing out a problem. Courtesy helps to build good business relationships. Expressions like "please," "I would appreciate," and "at your convenience" help to give the letter a courteous tone.

A business letter is clear when it gives specific information about the order, the request for information, or the problem. Clarity spares the business person the frustration of trying to decipher what you mean. It is important for prompt, satisfactory service.

A business letter is concise when it states its purpose simply and frankly. Since time is valuable to a business person, keep your letter free from details unrelated to the point of the letter.

A business letter should have a neat, formal appearance. Type the letter on unlined white paper, or write it neatly in black or blue ink on lined white paper. Keep margins of about one inch along the left and right edges, and try to center the letter vertically on the paper. Businesses often put their letters on letterheads, which are pages with the business name and address printed at the top. Because the letterhead shows the name and address, the writer of the letter needs to add only the date at the place where the heading normally occurs.

Smith Stone and Brick

112 Commerce Parkway, Bellaire, OH 43906
740-676-7869

Face Brick	Flue Liners	Natural Stone
Fire Brick	Flue Caps	Eldorado Stone

April 12, 20—

Sunrise Construction
2435 Maple Avenue
Barnesville, OH   43713

Dear Sirs:

   Thank you for your interest in our products.
Enclosed you will find a brochure that shows

Business Letter Purposes

A business letter has a specific business purpose. If the letter is written to place an order, it should include specific details. Give clear information about each item: catalog number, size, color, and quantity. Write each item on a separate line, and include the price. If practical, put all the money figures in a neat column so that they can be added easily. Specify how the order is to be shipped if the method of delivery is important to you. If payment is enclosed, state the exact amount and the method of payment.

                                    3620 Coseytown Road
                                    Greencastle, PA   17225
                                    March 9, 20—

Holmes Seed Company
2125 46th Street N. W.
Canton, OH   44709

Dear Sirs:

    Please send the following items advertised in your 1997 Vegetable Growers Price List.

    #0204 Blue Lake Bush Beans, 5 lb. at $1.90 each...$9.50
    #1205 Argent Sweet Corn 10 lb. at $5.55 each....55.50
    #1446 Straight 8 Cucumber, ¼ lb. for $3.35 ....3.35
    Shipping and handling............................5.47
                                            $73.82

    Please do not substitute if for any reason you cannot fill the above order. I am enclosing a check for $73.82. Thank you.

                                    Sincerely yours,

                                    Amos Petre

                                    Amos Petre

A request for adjustment should be courteous and specific. State precisely why the product or service was unsatisfactory. Summarize clearly what adjustments you would like the business to make. Do you want a refund or a replacement? Would you like a serviceman to return and make further repairs? Never stoop to sarcasm, insulting language, or unfair demands. Not only are those things poor business ethics, but they also reflect unchristian attitudes.

Route 4, Box 713
Amelia, VA   23002
January 25, 20—

Northern Hydraulics Catalog, Inc.
P.O. Box 1499
Burnsville, MN   55337-1499

Gentlemen:

On January 5, I ordered from you one #15766-F509 3/8" Air Impact Wrench. Unfortunately I received today a #1577-F509 1/2" Air Impact Wrench. I would like to return the item I received in exchange for the one I ordered.

I will appreciate your adjusting this matter for me. I await your further instructions.

Sincerely yours,

Jerry Schrock

Jerry Schrock

A letter requesting information should state clearly what you want. Such a letter is illustrated at the beginning of this lesson. Be sure to say precisely what information you want; a business may be unable to answer your request if it is too general. Use a tone that is courteous, not demanding. Aim to be just as considerate in a business letter as you would want to be in person.

Applying the Lesson

A. Improve the form and content of these business letters. You may need to supply imaginary information.

1.   Star Route Box 3
      Freeburg, PA   17827

      The Glacier Book Company
      340 Vine Street
      Denver, Colorado   80206

      Dear Sir,
          Send me one copy of <u>Amazing Life in the Desert</u> by Wanda Ackerman for $7.95 and two copies of <u>Deserts of North America</u> by Michael Smith for $8.50 each. I have enclosed a check to cover the costs of these books and the $4.75 postage and handling.

          Yours truly,

          Lee Martin

2.   March 18, 20—

Dear Mr. Larson:

I ordered two pairs of 18-inch work boots. Imagine my
disgust when I opened the package and found two pairs of
10-inch dress boots! I demand immediate attention to this
problem.

Sincerely yours,

Barry Flory

Barry Flory

B. Write a business letter to order the following materials. Assume that there are no charges for shipping and handling.

Two copies of #2117 *The Anguish of Love* for $8.20 each; one copy of #2308 *The Lim Family of Singapore* for $10.25; and two copies of #2467 *Where No One Stands Alone* for $6.20 each. The receiver's name and address is Rod and Staff Publishers, Inc., P.O. Box 3, Crockett, Kentucky 41413-0003. Use your home address and today's date in the heading.

C. Write a business letter to request an adjustment for the following situation.

Instead of receiving one copy of #2308 *The Lim Family of Singapore* (see Part B), you received one copy of #6308 *Martinko*.

D. Write a request for information, using the details below.

You would like information about Bible correspondence courses available from Lamp and Light Publishers, Inc., 26 Road 5577, Farmington, New Mexico 87401. Ask specifically for a list of titles and descriptions of these courses and for information on the cost of enrolling in a course.

Review Exercises

Tell whether each statement about paragraph writing is true or false. [61–63]
1. The construction of a paragraph is very similar to the construction of an essay.
2. Some main points of an essay can be developed in one paragraph; other points need more than one paragraph.
3. We establish the truth of a topic sentence by giving meaningful details.
4. General facts are more persuasive than specific ones.
5. In giving reasons to support a topic sentence, you must be sure that they are sound.
6. Few details carry as much force as pertinent illustrations.
7. Paragraphs, like essays, must be tied together coherently.
8. Repetition of key ideas tires readers and dampens their interest.

108. Explanation of a Process

Have you ever explained to a friend how to do your chores, how to make a certain dessert, or how a hay baler works? In giving such an informal explanation, you need not take great care to have perfect order and clarity because your listeners can ask questions or prompt you for additional details. For a formal written explanation, however, you cannot depend on readers' responses; you must prepare much more thoroughly beforehand.

Planning and Organizing

An explanation of a process requires careful planning and organization. Outline the steps of the explanation in a logical order, taking care that you do not omit any basic steps. If your explanation describes how to do something, you will use chronological order; if it describes how something works, you may use either spatial order or chronological order. Occasionally you might use a general-to-specific order, first describing the process in a general way and then describing certain parts of the process. And sometimes you might use a combination of these orders. The important thing is to use an order that enables the reader to picture the whole process clearly.

Include visual aids when practical. If you are explaining how to do something, a simple diagram illustrating the finished product or several stages in making the item goes a long way in making your explanation clear. If you explain how something works, a diagram illustrating the parts of a machine is much more helpful than a multitude of words. For this lesson, you will be assigned to give an explanation of 400–500 words.

Writing

Read the following sample explanation.

Cooking With Microwaves

1   If you are familiar with a microwave oven, you have probably wondered about the working of this appliance. How does it heat a sandwich all the way through in less than a minute? Even more amazing, how can it heat food on a paper plate without scorching or burning the plate? Understanding how a microwave oven works will help to answer these questions.

2   The heart of a microwave oven is a magnetron (mag'·ni·tron') tube, an electronic device that produces radiation in the form of microwaves. These waves are the same as light rays except that they are too long to be visible. Microwaves pass through paper and glass with little effect, but they cause water molecules to vibrate rapidly, thus producing heat.

3   When you use a microwave oven, you turn on a switch that sends electricity to the magnetron tube. This tube generates a stream of microwaves and sends them into the oven cavity, where the food is. On the way, the microwaves strike a spinning metal fan that distributes the rays for even heating of the food. Rays striking the walls of the oven are also reflected into the food, like light bouncing off a mirror. Thus very little energy in the microwaves is lost;

almost all of it goes into heating the food. The following diagram illustrates the process.

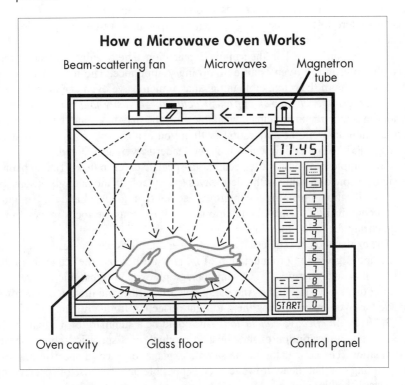

How a Microwave Oven Works

Beam-scattering fan   Microwaves   Magnetron tube

Oven cavity   Glass floor   Control panel

4   When heating a casserole in a microwave oven, you will often find that one part becomes quite hot while another part stays completely cold. This can happen even if a turntable rotates the dish during the heating process. The heating is uneven because the liquid in such a food is distributed unevenly. For this reason, it is often better to remove and stir the food several times as it heats, rather than heating it in a single stretch. Heating is more even in foods like soup and gravy because the liquid is distributed more evenly.

5   A microwave oven can be operated at different power levels for various purposes. For example, when you put frozen strawberries into a microwave oven, you do not usually want to cook them; you simply want to defrost them. You do this by operating the oven at a lower level of power so that the frozen fruit is heated more slowly.

6   The microwave oven is such a convenient appliance that it has become a standard feature in many kitchens. Let us remember that this device is possible only because of the special properties of microwaves that God has established.

[416 words]

Use the following steps to write an explanation of a process.

1. *Write an effective introductory paragraph.* A thought-provoking question or an interesting statement often makes a good opening sentence because it catches the reader's interest. Round the paragraph out by expanding or illustrating the idea introduced in the opening sentence.

Look at paragraph 1 in the sample explanation. The opening sentence suggests that the microwave oven is an extraordinary appliance. The next two sentences describe some of the remarkable things that a microwave oven can do.

2. *Describe each step in sufficient detail to be easily understood.* Keep your reader in mind. Try to anticipate what questions he may have, and be sure that your explanation answers those questions. Often you can clarify an unfamiliar item by comparing it to something with which the reader is well acquainted.

The sample explanation uses general-to-specific order in that it first explains the basic principle of heating with microwaves (paragraph 2) and later gives some practical details about operating the microwave oven (paragraphs 4 and 5). Paragraph 3 uses a combination of spatial and chronological order as the focus moves from the magnetron tube to the food in the oven cavity.

The explanation also gives details to answer questions that the reader might have. Paragraph 2 gives the pronunciation of *magnetron* because the reader is probably not familiar with that word. The same paragraph explains what microwaves are by relating them to visible light. And paragraph 3 describes the motion of microwaves inside the oven by comparing them to light reflecting from a mirror.

3. *Write an effective conclusion.* This could be a summary of the main steps in the process, a description of the finished product, or a specific impression of the explanation. The conclusion in the sample explanation gives a specific impression by pointing out that the microwave oven is possible only because of special properties established by God.

4. *Proofread and revise your explanation.* Make sure that your explanation has proper sentence structure, usage, and mechanics. In addition to these basic areas, check especially for clarity and completeness in presenting the steps of the process.

Applying the Lesson

A. Choose one of the following topics for an explanation.
1. How to make cheese
2. How to build a doghouse
3. How to start a strawberry patch
4. How to organize a family garden
5. How a jet pump works
6. How the digestive system works
7. How an electric generator works
8. How paper is made

B. Plan and write an explanation of 400–500 words.

C. Proofread and revise your explanation.

109. Character Sketches

An artist gazing over a beautiful scenery may decide to do one of several things. He may paint the scene in full color. He may draw it in fine detail with a pencil. Or he may sketch it rather briefly, highlighting only the most outstanding features of the scene.

The word-artist sometimes makes sketches too. Much descriptive writing falls into this category. The storywriter does not write about every detail in a scene; he writes just enough to make the setting clear. The essay writer who uses description to illustrate a point in his argument likewise writes merely enough to make his point.

In this lesson you will review another kind of sketch—the character sketch. The purpose of a character sketch is to show one distinctive impression about a person. Read the following sample character sketch, and refer to it as you study this lesson.

Always on the Go

1   She was actually my great-aunt, but we always called her Aunt Eva. When this lady suddenly passed away last fall, the world certainly lost an energetic person. A few years ago at a family gathering, one of Mother's sisters said, "Aunt Eva, you seem to be always on the go." I vividly remember Aunt Eva's silvery laugh as she answered, "Oh, no. I regularly sleep at least seven hours a night, and I spend at least half an hour in Bible study every morning and evening."

2   I was only five years old when her husband, Uncle Grant, died of a heart attack. Aunt Eva was then already sixty years old. Although she had never before driven a car, she soon got her driver's license. She wanted to be free to go to the sewing circle, to help wherever she was needed, and to visit her children and grandchildren.

3   Even when she was approaching seventy-five, she would not sit around and let the younger ones do the work. At family gatherings, as noted before, she kept herself busy. She was one of the most efficient organizers in setting out the meal. And after the meal, she was almost always one of the first on her feet, with "Well, the work won't go away by itself."

4   Three years ago, when Mother had her appendix removed, Aunt Eva spent a month in our home. Her energy seemed almost boundless as she cared for Mother and took charge of the housework. She baked bread and pies every Saturday. She even spent some time working in the garden. Often she repeated the saying, "Many hands make light work."

5   Aunt Eva's passing has left an empty spot in many lives, but her influence surely lives on. Often when I am tempted to be lazy or to resent a busy schedule, memories of Aunt Eva's energetic ways come back to inspire me. By God's grace, I want to be a willing worker like Aunt Eva.

The following steps explain how to write a character sketch.

1. *Choose to write about a person whose life teaches a worthy lesson.* Consider what specific characteristic you will emphasize about that person. No doubt there are several noble character traits that you could choose, but you must choose *one* to develop. That one characteristic will be the theme of your sketch. In the sample character sketch, the theme is Aunt Eva's energetic ways.

Be sure to follow the Golden Rule. You will not want to write anything that embarrasses, insults, or belittles another. On the other hand, you should not use empty flattery. Not every person you know will be a suitable subject for a character sketch. Choose someone that you can honestly describe as a worthy example.

2. *List details that illustrate the characteristic you have chosen to emphasize.* What specific events or actions illustrate your theme? This list will constitute the framework of your composition, so be sure to list enough details to draw a meaningful word sketch. You should have at least three specific points to develop. Paragraphs 2, 3, and 4 in the sample character sketch develop three illustrations of Aunt Eva's energetic ways: her effort at getting a driver's license at the age of sixty, her busyness at family gatherings, and her helpfulness and diligence in the author's home.

3. *Write a brief, appealing introduction.* You could place the character in a setting that either reflects or contrasts the trait you want to emphasize. To reflect a trait, you may give an incident in which the person clearly displays the characteristic in focus. To contrast a trait, you might show how outstanding the trait is in relation to a disadvantage in the person's life (such as a non-Christian home). You could also give a first impression, followed by a description of how different the person is when one learns to know him better. Or you may simply make an interesting observation that relates to the theme you will develop. The sample character sketch begins with this last method and then places the character in a setting that reflects the trait to be emphasized.

4. *Write the body of your character sketch in a way that shows, not merely tells, the person's character.* Make the person live for your readers by having him say and do things. Use specific words and picturesque language to draw a clear word picture.

5. *Write a conclusion that summarizes the main emphasis.* One way to conclude would be to show how the character trait in focus has been a blessing to the person you are describing. You might also conclude by stating your desire to follow the person's noble example.

Applying the Lesson

Write a character sketch of a person with whom you are well acquainted.

110.   Improving Your Speaking Style, Part 3: Enthusiasm

What do effective public speakers have in common? Good eye contact with the audience, for one thing. They establish eye contact early in their discourse and maintain it throughout their talk. Good voice control also characterizes effective speakers. They pronounce their words clearly, use a comfortable volume, and speak at a pitch and speed appropriate to what they are saying.

The ability to convey a sense of *enthusiasm* is another important part of an effective speaking style. Your enthusiasm definitely affects both the quality of your speech and the attention of your audience. On the one hand, a proper sense of enthusiasm helps you to put your best efforts into the speech. On the other hand, it will help to stimulate in your audience an enthusiasm that enables them to listen and understand you more easily. It even enhances their willingness to agree with you.

Developing Enthusiasm

Enthusiasm is not something that you can put on whenever you want it; rather, it must grow and develop within you. How can you cause it to grow? Can everyone attain this? You should be able to develop an enthusiasm for communicating with others if you do the following things.

1. *Choose a subject that interests you.* This is of utmost importance. How could you talk with enthusiasm about raising rabbits if you despise the daily routine of feeding them and keeping their pens clean? By contrast, someone who thoroughly enjoys taking care of rabbits will be in an excellent position to give a talk about his rabbit project.

Sometimes a subject for your speech will come easily. You may just *know* what you want to talk about as soon as you receive the assignment. At other times you must explore numerous possibilities before you find something that appeals to you. Beware lest you throw out every idea you encounter, just because it fails to strike you with great force. Students often find that after a bit of study, a subject is much more interesting than they had thought it would be.

2. *Become thoroughly familiar with your subject.* You can hardly speak with enthusiasm about a subject that you do not know well. You become familiar with a subject by personal experience, by discussing it with others, and by reading about it. Do not cheat yourself. Study your subject until you know it well, until you find an enthusiasm for it growing within you.

3. *Organize your material.* It is essential that you plan your talk carefully. How will you begin? What main points will you present, and in what order will they come? How will you close? Few things dampen enthusiasm more effectively than standing before a group with only a vague idea of what you will say and how you plan to say it.

Make your plans carefully, and then practice giving your talk. As you do this, you will feel a growing confidence about your talk, and your enthusiasm will grow with it. You will actually begin looking forward—though perhaps still with apprehension—to sharing your information with the group. But if you still feel absolutely no spark of enthusiasm, you are doing something wrong! You must make a change somewhere, either in your subject or in your preparation. For as long as a subject fails to stir your own enthusiasm, it has no chance of stirring the enthusiastic attention of your listeners.

Expressing Enthusiasm

Having gained a genuine enthusiasm for your subject, your next challenge is to communicate it to your listeners. To a degree this will happen automatically because enthusiasm in your heart will show on your face and in your actions. However, you as a speaker should pay deliberate attention to the following things, which help to add life and force to your words.

1. *Eye contact.* You will find it easier to look your listeners in the eye if you have an enthusiastic interest in your subject. This is true because you will be thinking more about your subject than about yourself. You will be confident that your subject is worthwhile and that your audience will also find it interesting. Meeting your listeners eye to eye will help you to communicate effectively as you move through the talk.

2. *Voice inflection.* What you feel will show in your voice. Remember the little boy who has just come home after receiving a lollipop from the doctor. You can hear his voice even now as he exclaims excitedly, "Father, look! A lollipop!" Contrast that with the same boy when he finds a not-so-cherished food on his plate. You can hear his voice again, can't you, as he says, "Mother, must I eat all this?"

Be assured that your own enthusiasm or lack of it shows through just as clearly when you give a talk. Seek to develop a strong enthusiasm, and then let your voice naturally convey that feeling to your audience.

3. *Facial expression.* You need to show your enthusiasm by looking that way. Again, this is not a matter of putting something on, but of showing on the outside what you feel on the inside. Gain an enthusiastic interest in your subject, and then let it show on your face.

4. *Gestures.* The gestures you use help to express your enthusiasm. If you are not interested, you probably will use few if any gestures. If you are too self-conscious, you may use some gestures but they will not reinforce the points you make. But if you are truly interested in your speech, your gestures will take on life and meaning. They may indicate size, shape, or direction. They may help to emphasize a major point. Or they may simply reinforce what you are saying.

Of course, gestures can be overdone. You do not need to act out a story in order to tell it effectively. But appropriate gestures, used with reserve and discretion, will definitely add appeal to your presentation.

5. *Posture.* Enthusiasm will motivate you to stand up straight as you speak before the class. It will keep you from shuffling your feet and slouching your body. It will prompt you throughout your speech to maintain the dignity of standing with your weight evenly balanced on both feet and your shoulders straight. Your posture definitely communicates the degree of your enthusiasm.

Your assignment in this lesson will be to describe an interesting animal, plant, or place that you have seen. In order to do this in a fresh, appealing way, you must do more than talk about the item in a humdrum manner. You will need to think of specific reasons why the item is interesting to you. If it is an animal, are you impressed by its size? its appearance? its actions? Exactly what makes it impressive and interesting? You may need to do a little research to find exactly how tall, how long, or how heavy it is, or what purpose is served by its spots or other unusual features.

After you have considered the details themselves, you must decide how you will present them. Think of appealing ways to portray the thing you are describing. Did the spider monkeys remind you of real spiders as they scampered about their cages? Did the seals make you think of barking dogs? Remembering exactly what you saw, heard, and felt will help you to describe your subject with interest and enthusiasm.

Applying the Lesson

A. Choose an interesting animal, plant, or place that is familiar to your class. On the board, list specific details that would be included in a description of it. Then work together at thinking of ways to present those details in fresh, creative ways.

B. Think of something interesting to describe, and prepare to give a talk of four to six minutes about it. Your talk should be based mainly on your personal knowledge, though you may use reference sources to obtain specific facts. The following ideas may stimulate your thinking.

1. An interesting animal
2. An unusual plant
3. A place your family has visited

4. A hobby
5. A family project
6. A summer project of your own

Try to develop and show a genuine enthusiasm for your topic. Also remember to practice eye contact and voice control as you studied in earlier lessons.

Review Exercises

Write the letter of the item that gives the best direction for each element of voice control. [76]

1. Articulation
   a. Open your mouth wide, forming all words with precise deliberateness.
   b. Pronounce each word distinctly.
2. Volume
   a. Speak loudly enough so that everyone can hear you without straining.
   b. Your voice should ring loudly and clearly over the entire audience.
3. Pitch
   a. Raise and lower the pitch of your voice to match what you are saying.
   b. Relax and try to use the higher tones in your voice range.
4. Speed
   a. Vary your speed, and use *uh*'s and *ah*'s to fill awkward pauses.
   b. Speak at approximately the same rate that you use in normal conversations.

111. Chapter 14 Review

A. Do these exercises on letter writing.
1. Name the five parts of a friendly letter in order.
2. List three ways in which the form of a business letter differs from that of a friendly letter.
3. Write the letter of the closing that would be appropriate for a business letter but not for a friendly letter.
   a. Your friend,
   b. Sincerely yours,
   c. Respectfully yours,
   d. Good-bye for now,
   e. In Christian love,
   f. With love and prayers,
4. What are the three C's of business letter content?
5. Explain how to fold a letter for a small envelope and for a large envelope.
6. How should the mailing address appear on an envelope?
7. How can you write a worthwhile thank-you note for a gift that you do not really like?
8. What are the three W's of a note of invitation?
9. What two basic things should you include in a note of apology?
10. Name several things that are appropriate in a note of sympathy.

B. Answer these questions about writing a report on a book of nonfiction.
1. What basic information should you give at the beginning of the report?
2. Where in the book might you find the author's purpose in writing the book?
3. What should be the main part of the report?
4. How should you develop this main part of the report?
5. What unfavorable points might be mentioned in a book report?

C. Answer these questions about writing an explanation of a process.
1. What three orders may be used in giving an explanation of a process?
2. What are two good ways to introduce your explanation?
3. What are two good ways to conclude your explanation?
4. What should you do as you write the body of the explanation to help make sure you include enough details?

D. Answer these questions about character sketches.
1. What is the purpose of a character sketch?
2. What are several things you must avoid when planning and writing a character sketch?
3. What are three good ways to introduce a character sketch?
4. How can you write your character sketch so that it shows rather than tells the character trait?
5. What are two good ways to conclude a character sketch?

E. Answer these questions about speaking style.
1. What are three ways to develop enthusiasm before you speak to a group?
2. What are five things that help to express enthusiasm while you speak to a group?

But to do good

and to communicate forget not:

for with such sacrifices

God is well pleased.

Hebrews 13:16

Year-end Reviews

112. Final Review 1 (Chapters 1–5)

A. Write correctly each word that has an error in capitalization. For errors in punctuation, write the word before the error and add or omit the mark involved. Each sentence contains three mistakes. (A set of commas or a title counts as one item.)

1. When David became King over all Israel the Canaanites and the Philistines controlled significant areas of Palestine

2. One Canaanite tribe the Jebusites occupied Jerusalem, however they called it Jebus.

3. Thinking their city was perfectly safe the Jebusites mocked David but he took the city, and made it his capital.

4. God gives the following commentary in his Word "And David grew great, and the LORD God of hosts was with him" (2 Samuel 5:10).

5. Well the Philistines you can be sure did not appreciate David's amazing God-given victories.

6. In a vain challenge to David's power the philistines gathered against David's Kingdom.

7. How faithfully the lord strengthened David, directed him in his battles and gave him victory

8. As David claimed God's promises o youth so you should claim the promises of the gospel.

9. Leonard E. Smith Jr operates a large hatchery near Williamsport Maryland.

10. His hatchery which serves farms over a four-state Region specializes in the Rhode Island Red, a brown egg layer; the Leghorn, a white egg layer, and the Plymouth Rock, a good meat chicken.

11. In History class we studied the influence of greek thinking on the west.

12. In our school books marked with an *R* may not be taken home Glenda without special permission from the Teacher.

13. Have you heard that uncle Wilmer plans to teach our Bible School class

14. If the Living Waters bookstore has the book *The Way Down is the Way up*, i want to buy a copy.

B. Each sentence below contains three errors in the use of quotation marks (and related capitalization), italics, dashes, parentheses, brackets, apostrophes, or hyphens. Write enough of each sentence to show the corrections. (A set of marks counts as one item.)

1. Putting the Lord first He will take no other place is essential to self control, stated Brother Clyde.

2. "Your great grandfather was thirty three," commented Father, "When he was first introduced to the Mennonite Church."

3. Is that why hed often ask us to sing People of the Living God? asked Clayton.

4. Blessed are they that mourn in repentance: for they shall be comforted Matthew 5:4.

5. Grandmother sat on the sun warmed porch she loves to be outside when its warm enough! and knitted for several hours.

6. After a bumpy, two hour ride on a bus called the Silver Coach, we arrived at a bus stop near Uncle Lloyds home.

7. On that never to be forgotten visit, our uncle took us to weather beaten houses many with broken windows in an area where churches are practically nonexistent.

8. Are there two cs in occasion?

9. When I read the book Bernese Anabaptists, I especially enjoyed the chapter Bernese Anabaptist Settlements in America; after all, my ancestor's were among those settlers.

10. In the winter of 92, we had a week of very unJanuary weather with several fifty and sixty-degree days.

C. Do these exercises on listening and speaking skills.

1. What is the relationship between hearing and listening?

2. List three attitudes essential to good listening.

3. List the six points that summarize good listening skills, as given in Lesson 10. (The key words start with the letters *A–F.*)

4. Why must you put forth special effort to have an active mind while listening?

5. List three things that you can do to keep your mind active.

6. List three things that you can do to block out distractions as you listen.

7. Why is it a good idea to think about the main ideas you will develop in a report before you begin researching for information?

8. Give three reasons why you should gather information from more than one source.

D. Label each numbered word group *S* (complete sentence), *F* (fragment), *R* (run-on error), or *E* (elliptical sentence).

[1]"Oh, look, everyone!" exclaimed Dennis. [2]"There must be dozens of hungry birds. [3]Flocking to the new feeder I put up!"

[4]"Sure are. [5]Some of those birds I haven't seen for months," commented Freda. [6]"Let's try to identify each kind, maybe we can keep a record all winter."

E. Label each underlined word, using the following abbreviations.

S—subject   IO—indirect object
V—verb   OC—objective complement
PA—predicate adjective   AP—appositive
PN—predicate nominative   DA—noun of direct address
DO—direct object

1. For nearly three hundred years, settlers pushed the ᵃfrontier, the ᵇedge of the country's occupied area, steadily westward.
2. Yes, ᵃCharles, in 1890 the ᵇdirector of the census announced that a distinct frontier line no longer existed.
3. In the middle 1600s, the western edge of Massachusetts ᵃwas a ᵇfrontier.
4. By the late 1800s, everyone considered the ᵃFar West the ᵇfrontier.
5. The first white men to cross the frontier made themselves no permanent homes.
6. These hunters and fur traders were generally friendly with the Indians.

F. Label each underlined word group *prep.* (prepositional phrase), *vb.* (verbal phrase), *ps.* (phrase of a single part of speech), *D* (dependent clause), or *I* (independent clause). Also label the part of speech for each item (except independent clauses).

1. ᵃAs they returned to settled areas, the hunters and traders often gave glowing reports of the beautiful, promising lands ᵇthat they had seen.
2. ᵃPushing into these wilderness areas, the frontier farmers ᵇwould clear small patches of land ᶜto plant their first crops.
3. These frontier farmers rarely stayed long ᵃin one place, but ᵇthey helped others to locate good land.
4. ᵃBeyond the frontier was the goal ᵇof these sturdy adventurers.
5. ᵃAfter their departure, newcomers ᵇwho brought better equipment would start ᶜestablishing more permanent farmsteads.

G. Label each sentence according to its use (*dec., int., imp., exc.*) and its structure (*S, CD, CX, CD-CX*). End punctuation has been omitted.

1. Purpose in your heart to always live a faithful, consistent life
2. If you want your life to please God, you must develop wholesome interests
3. Do you love the pure, simple ways of godliness, or do earthly fame and pleasure appeal to you
4. How foolish are those who try to mix worldliness and godliness
5. A friend of the world is an enemy of God, but one who humbles himself before God experiences God's grace

H. Label the word order of each sentence *N* (natural), *I* (inverted), or *M* (mixed).

1. In his natural state, man is helpless and hopeless.
2. Into this sin-cursed world came One who can meet man's need.
3. The Lord Jesus Christ gave His life to redeem man from sin.
4. Gratefully we give ourselves to Him.

I. Label the style of each sentence L (loose), P (periodic), or B (balanced).
   1. After a long, hard winter with three blizzards and several weeks of severe cold, spring has finally arrived.
   2. The more severe the winter is, the more intensely we long for spring.
   3. I always anticipate working up the garden soil and planting those first seeds.
   4. A wise man thinks all he speaks; a foolish man speaks all he thinks.

J. Copy this outline correctly. Each starred line has at least one mistake.

Christ's Crowns
*I. The Crown of Mockery (Matt. 27:29)
  A. Callous rejection (vv. 22–25)
  *B. cruel sufferings (vv. 26–30)
    *C. Contemptuous blasphemy (vv. 39–43)
*II. The majestic crown (Heb. 2:9)
  *A. in vindication of His absolute authority (vv. 7, 8)
  B. By virtue of His redeeming death (v. 9)
  *C. As we view His suffering perfection (v. 10)
III. The crowns of monarchy (Rev. 19:12, 16)
  A. His authoritative names
    1. "Faithful and True"
    *2. He is called "The Word of God"
    *3. "King of Kings"
  *B. He has authoritative works
    *1. directing the armies of heaven
      *a. Which involves judging the world
    *2. He will be disposing of the powers of evil

K. Do these exercises on outlining and on Bible reference books.
   1. How does outlining a lesson compel a student to analyze it thoroughly?
   2. What long-term benefits does outlining have?
   3. Why does a concordance require less caution than do other Bible reference books?
   4. Why is a modern dictionary not always a good source for finding the meanings of Bible words?
   5. Read the following entry from *Strong's Concordance,* and do the exercises that follow.

   > *1258.* (διάλεκτος) **dialĕktŏs,** *dee-al'-ek-tos;* from *1256;*
   > a (mode of) *discourse,* i.e. *"dialect"*:—language, tongue.

     a. What English word is derived from this Greek word?
     b. What is the actual definition of this Greek word?
     c. List the different ways in which this Greek word is translated in the King James Bible.
     d. What does the number *1256* in this entry tell you?
   6. What danger could a commentary pose even if it contained no errors?
   7. Name several doctrines that many commentaries do not uphold.
   8. Name several examples of false teaching that commentaries may contain.

L. Choose the standard expressions in parentheses.

1. Many people (reckon, think) that they can ignore God, (who's, whose) holy being calls for man's worship; but they (better, had better) consider (their, there, they're) ways.

2. The ungodly live with the (incredible, incredulous) (allusion, illusion) that they can transgress the (principals, principles) of truth and still get to heaven (sometime, some time).

3. We (have got to, must) keep our minds free from wrong thoughts, or we (will, won't) hardly grow any (farther, further) in our spiritual (statue, stature, statute).

4. (Being as, Since) each person is (altogether, all together) dependent on the Lord, he (had ought, ought) to pray every day, (irregardless, regardless) of how well things are going.

5. Man's (ability, capacity) to recognize God makes him far superior (than, to) animals; that (exalted, exulted) privilege, of course, is accompanied (by, with) great responsibility.

6. Father was never (formally, formerly) (learned, taught) algebra in school, but he has applied himself (mighty, quite) hard and has (affected, effected) a good degree of skill in it.

7. Since we could not help (but wonder, wondering) about the report, we waited (for, on) a more (credible, credulous) source of information before agreeing (to, with) the children.

8. Father (suspects, suspicions) (as, that) mice have chewed (in, into) the electrical wires and caused a short circuit in (the same, them).

9. (Beside, Besides) being my cousin, Sue Ann is my closest friend; it was hard to part (from, with) her when Uncle John's family (emigrated, immigrated) from the United States, but I am glad we can correspond (to, with) each other by mail.

10. Although Benigno's upbringing was quite different (from, than) ours, his friendly ways (complement, compliment) our school, and we want (him to feel, that he feels) (really, completely) welcome.

---

113. Final Review 2 (Chapters 6–9)

A. Answer these questions about argumentative essays.

1. What is the basic purpose of an argumentative essay?
2. What is the thesis statement, and where should it be stated?
3. If a thesis statement is poor, what are four possible ways of improving it?
4. What three elements does the full thesis have?
5. Why should an argumentative essay deal with counter arguments?
6. How should the introductory paragraph of an argument be like a funnel?
7. In what order should the supporting points be arranged?

8. What is a good way to determine whether a statement expresses a fact or an opinion?

9. How should the concluding paragraph compare with the introductory paragraph?

10. What are three things that help to make titles appealing?

B. Copy each noun, and label it *concrete* or *abstract.* Also label its gender (*M, F, N, C*).

1. The five ewes and the ram are enjoying their freedom in the back pasture of Uncle Eldon's farm.

2. We children enjoyed the privilege of feeding them during our visit.

3. The lambs are a special pleasure to watch as they enjoy the sunshine and warm breeze.

C. Write the plural form of each noun. Use the foreign plural spellings for numbers 8–12.

1. board of directors
2. life
3. donkey
4. trout
5. tariff
6. ratio
7. goose
8. nova
9. codex
10. diagnosis
11. phenomenon
12. bacillus

D. Rewrite each expression, using possessive forms. If it is better not to use a possessive form, write *X* after the number.

1. the plans of the teachers
2. the covers of the book
3. the kingdom of Xerxes
4. the growth of larvae
5. the questions of Clair and Dennis (joint ownership)
6. the maps of Paula and Norma (separate ownership)

E. Copy all the pronouns, including possessive pronouns. Label each one *P* (personal), *CP* (compound personal), *D* (demonstrative), *ID* (indefinite), *IR* (interrogative), or *R* (relative).

1. Whom shall we fear but our Lord, who rules over all?

2. Every promise in the Bible should remind you of your responsibility to do those things that are right and to please the One who loves us.

3. God has revealed Himself sufficiently so that all people can understand this if they will only give themselves to the truth.

F. Copy each substantive in these sentences, and label it *N* (one-word or compound noun), *pron.* (pronoun), *G* (gerund or gerund phrase), *I* (infinitive or infinitive phrase), *prep.* (prepositional phrase), *C* (clause), *T* (title), or *S* (subject of discussion). If a substantive is within a substantive phrase or clause or within a title, do not list it separately.

1. The school board approved the book *The Valley Between* for our library.

2. Watching that magnificent sunrise inspired me with God's glory.

3. In the kitchen is not a good place for whatever you have in that smelly box!

4. To check the proper spelling of *sagacious,* we needed to get the dictionary.

G. Write each underlined item correctly. If an item has no error, write *correct.*
1. The neighbors <u>who</u> Father asked all said that the stray dog was not <u>their's</u>.
2. The load on <u>that there</u> wheelbarrow was too heavy for Floyd to move by <u>hisself</u>.
3. Abigail and <u>myself</u> usually have more homework than <u>she</u>.
4. Lightning struck <u>Loren's and Linda's house</u>, so <u>me and Father</u> went there right away.
5. I do not know <u>whom</u> the boys on the steps are, but <u>them</u> on the porch are my cousins.
6. The <u>puppys' yipping</u> was quite disturbing until the boys <u>which</u> are responsible for their feed and water came home from school.

H. Answer these questions about paragraphs.
1. What two things may mar the unity of a paragraph?
2. How should a paragraph in the body of an argument resemble a miniature essay?
3. When should you use several paragraphs to develop one main point in your thesis?
4. What are three kinds of details that you might use in developing an argumentative paragraph?
5. What are the three general methods for building coherence into paragraphs and essays?

I. Choose the correct expressions in parentheses.
1. Jesus has (rose, risen) from the dead.
2. Each of His faithful followers (find, finds) security in His intercession.
3. (Don't, Doesn't) His promise to be with His people encourage us?
4. In contrast to eternity, seventy years (is, are) a short span of time.
5. The person who has (took, taken) a serious look at eternity will hardly misuse time.
6. Neither temptation nor hardships (need, needs) to discourage us.
7. Phonics (is, are) not much help in pronouncing *colonel* and *victual.*
8. Almost two-thirds of the orchard (have, has) been sprayed.
9. The family (have, has) taken their places around the table.
10. The family (have, has) succeeded in its goal for the day's project.
11. Fuzzy is the only one of the pups that (have, has) long, shaggy fur.
12. Either Alice or Minerva (is, are) responsible to wash the dishes this evening.
13. Father has often (went, gone) to help Mr. Bailey with his wood splitting.
14. The bacon and the eggs (is, are) still in the refrigerator.
15. The bacon and eggs that Grandmother made for breakfast (was, were) delicious.
16. Brother Alvin, along with his two boys, (was, were) helping to clean up after the storm.
17. Kevin Penner (did, done) my chores while I was sick.
18. Most of the eggs (was, were) broken when I fell with the full basket.

19. In that sentence, *gods* (need, needs) a lowercase letter.
20. The tweezers (belong, belongs) in this drawer.

J. Copy each underlined verb, and name its tense. Also label it *TA* (transitive, active voice), *TP* (transitive, passive voice), *IC* (intransitive complete), or *IL* (intransitive linking).
   1. This tree <u>has been growing</u> here since Grandfather Hostetter was a boy.
   2. Mother <u>opened</u> a jar of pickles for dinner.
   3. The meal <u>will be served</u> in a few minutes.
   4. If Uncle James is ordained tomorrow, all of Grandfather Lehman's sons <u>will have become</u> ministers.
   5. This tea certainly <u>had tasted</u> better before it sat in the pot half a day.
   6. That dog <u>barks</u> too much at night.

K. Write the correct subjunctive verb for each sentence.
   1. Dr. Hornbill urged that Grandfather (is, be) taken to a specialist.
   2. If I (would have watched, had watched) the cake better, it would not have burned.
   3. Suppose the car (was, were) to run out of gas on this lonely stretch of road!
   4. Sister Mary requested that everyone (pray, prays) for her wayward son.
   5. Glory (is, be) to the Father, who is worthy of all praise.

---

114. Final Review 3 (Chapters 10–14)

A. Write enough of each sentence to show how to improve the unity and coherence.
   1. Every young person must set high standards for his life. If he expects to mature in a godly manner.
   2. We should pray every day because it is vital to our spiritual survival, we can only overcome our enemy by keeping in touch with God.
   3. We must learn to, in spite of interruptions, enter our closet and pray.
   4. Considering the special temptations that would likely confront me, I even prayed with greater intensity than usual.

B. Rewrite these sentences, improving the emphasis by the methods indicated in parentheses.
   1. While Jesus ministered to men's souls, He also healed their bodies. (main idea in the main clause)
   2. These rulers utterly rejected the Good News of the kingdom. (unusual word order)
   3. As the throngs more freely proclaimed Jesus as the Messiah, the Jewish rulers sought more earnestly to kill Him. (balanced sentence)
   4. As Jesus' presence enhanced the assembly and His gracious words came forth, the lovingkindness of God was clearly evident. (repetition of *grace* in three forms)

C. Rewrite these sentences, improving the conciseness and parallelism.
1. On days when it is raining, we do not walk to school on foot.
2. Our beloved mother transports us to school by automobile when the weather is too inclement for us to travel on foot.
3. When one sees a rainbow arching beautifully and with impressive majesty across the sky, you have witnessed again a token of God's sure promise.
4. Our family has and will be operating a poultry business, orchard, and produce farm.

D. Copy each underlined adjective. First label it *L* (limiting) or *D* (descriptive); then label it *AT* (attributive), *AP* (appositive), or *PR* (predicate).
1. <u>Three</u> <u>stately</u> oaks still stand in the <u>front</u> lawn.
2. We often watch the deer <u>feeding</u>, and <u>this</u> evening was an <u>excellent</u> time <u>to come</u> here.
3. This <u>Italian</u> dressing, <u>smooth</u> and <u>spicy</u>, is <u>delicious</u>.

E. Copy each underlined adverb and the word or word group that it modifies. Write *sentence* if it modifies the whole sentence.
1. We saw an <u>amazingly</u> large woodchuck <u>just</u> inside the garden gate, <u>greedily</u> devouring the young bean plants.
2. <u>Why</u> did you folks come <u>to help</u> when you are <u>almost</u> <u>too</u> busy yourselves?
3. <u>Clearly</u>, the parents were <u>greatly</u> relieved to hear <u>so</u> <u>soon</u> that their son's operation appeared <u>completely</u> successful.

F. Label each underlined word group *prep.* (prepositional phrase), *part.* (participial phrase), *inf.* (infinitive phrase), or *cl.* (clause). Also label each *adj.* or *adv.*
1. Can you cut [a]<u>through a solid object</u> and have one piece [b]<u>when you are finished</u>?
2. [a]<u>Using ice, bare wire, and a brick</u>, you can perform this operation, [b]<u>which sounds impossible</u>.
3. Tie one end [a]<u>of the wire</u> to the brick, loop the other end around the ice [b]<u>to be cut</u>, and let the brick hang from the wire.
4. The pressure [a]<u>exerted on the ice by the weight</u> generates heat sufficient [b]<u>to melt a narrow strip of the ice</u>.
5. The place [a]<u>where the wire has passed through the ice</u> freezes again; therefore, the ice remains one solid chunk [b]<u>although the wire had cut through it</u>.

G. Label each underlined phrase or clause *R* (restrictive) or *N* (nonrestrictive). Also copy each word that should be followed by a comma, and add the comma.
1. A wooden bat has a spot [a]<u>called the center of percussion</u>, and hitting the ball there best uses the energy [b]<u>that the moving bat possesses</u>.
2. Find this center of percussion [a]<u>which is important for the best hit</u> by using a rubber mallet to tap your bat [b]<u>held loosely by its handle</u>.
3. The only place <u>where you feel no vibrations</u> is the center of percussion.

H. Write enough of each sentence to show how to correct the errors in using forms of comparison.
1. A solid hit at the center of percussion will sting your hands less than a hit on any part of the bat.

2. To someone intent on hitting a home run, making a good hit is probably more importanter than avoiding unpleasant vibrations.
3. Hitting at the center of percussion is better than hitting elsewhere because the ball will travel fartherest when you do.
4. This is true because littler of the energy of the bat is wasted in useless vibrations.
5. Hitting at the right spot is also important because strong vibrations can cause the bat to crack quicker than when it is used properly.
6. My younger brother can draw circles more round than I can.
7. My throat hurt this morning, and this evening it has become worser.
8. Which of these two buckets can hold the most water?

I. Write the term that fits each description.
   1. The kind of poem that tells a story.
   2. The kind of poem that gives specific instruction or moral teaching.
   3. The kind of poem that shows the poet's inner thoughts and feelings.
   4. Rhyme involving more than one syllable.
   5. Repetition of beginning consonant sounds.
   6. Repetition of similar vowel sounds in accented syllables.
   7. A phrase, a line, or an entire stanza repeated throughout a poem.
   8. The unit for analyzing rhythm.
   9. The marking of the rhythm in poetry.
   10. Inspired poetry without rhyme or rhythm but with frequent use of parallelism.
   11. Poetry with rhythm but not rhyme.
   12. A fourteen-line poem in iambic pentameter.
   13. A poem that develops a theme in four lines.
   14. A narrative poem that contains many stanzas.

J. Read the following stanzas, and do the exercises that follow.
   Poem 1:
   > A king might miss the guiding star,
   >   A wise man's foot might stumble;
   > For Bethlehem is very far
   >   From all except the humble.
   >   *—Louis F. Benson*

   Poem 2:
   > On a moss-covered log in the woods, I sit in solitude
   > While the warm summer breeze wafts its scents in wondrous multitude:
   >   From the rain-dampened earth rise the musty smells of rotting leaves
   > And the mushrooms that stand like small sentinels upon the moss;
   > In sweet contrast the fragrance of flowers fair now floats across
   >   From the stream; and the pine forest fresh, clean smells among them weaves.

   1. What is the rhyme pattern of poem 1? of poem 2?
   2. Copy the pair of words that is a feminine rhyme.
   3. Write the complete name of the rhythm pattern in both stanzas. If several different feet or meters are used, be sure the name includes them all.

4. From poem 2, copy an example of alliteration including at least four words.
5. Copy an example of assonance from poem 2.
6. Copy a figure of speech from poem 2, and write which kind of figure it is.

K. Label each underlined word *prep.* (preposition), *CC* (coordinating conjunction), *Cor* (correlative conjunction), *SC* (subordinating conjunction), or *CA* (conjunctive adverb).
   1. ^a<u>If</u> there are two rugs in your room, one ^b<u>before</u> the mirror and one before the bed, which one will be worn out first? (D. L. Moody)
   2. Common sense is the knack of seeing things ^a<u>as</u> they are, ^b<u>and</u> doing things as they ought to be. (C. E. Stowe)
   3. The humblest individual exerts some influence, ^a<u>either</u> for good <u>or</u> for evil, ^b<u>upon</u> others. (Henry Ward Beecher)
   4. The unsoundness of a vessel is not seen when it is empty; ^a<u>however</u>, when it is filled with water, then we shall see ^b<u>whether</u> it will leak <u>or</u> no. (old proverb)

L. Write enough of each sentence to show how to correct the errors in using conjunctions.
   1. We shall either plant the peas or the onions in this part of the garden.
   2. Yesterday was a warm day for May, indeed, it felt more like July than May.
   3. Duchess has been limping all day yet we cannot find any sores on her feet.
   4. Delmar often whistles when he is working and at play.
   5. Father not only tilled the garden but made the furrows for the seeds.

M. Copy each interjection, the word before it (if there is one), and the word after it. Use correct capitalization and punctuation, and underline any word that should be italicized.
   1. Men often seek the meaning of life in material things, but lo it is found only in a right relationship with the Lord.
   2. Hallelujah the Lord Jesus has risen from the dead.
   3. Doughnuts how good those fresh doughnuts smell!
   4. Well these filled doughnuts are my favorite.
   5. Splash the duck landed on the pond.

N. Rewrite each sentence so that it communicates the same idea without the underlined idiom.
   1. How are you <u>getting along</u> since your accident?
   2. <u>Look up</u> each unfamiliar word in the dictionary.
   3. I could not <u>come up with</u> the right answer.
   4. Daniel <u>made up his mind</u> that he would be faithful.

O. Do these exercises on letter writing.
   1. Name the five parts of a friendly letter in order.
   2. List three ways in which the form of a business letter differs from that of a friendly letter.
   3. What are the three C's of business letter content?
   4. How can you write a worthwhile thank-you note for a gift that you do not really like?

5. What two basic things should you include in a note of apology?
6. Name several things that are appropriate in a note of sympathy.

P. Answer these questions about writing a report on a book of nonfiction.
1. What basic information should you give at the beginning of the report?
2. Where in the book might you find the author's purpose in writing the book?
3. What should be the main part of the report?
4. How should you develop this main part of the report?
5. What unfavorable points might be mentioned in a book report?

Q. Answer these questions about writing an explanation of a process.
1. What three orders may be used in giving an explanation of a process?
2. What are two good ways to introduce your explanation?
3. What are two good ways to conclude your explanation?
4. What should you do as you write the body of the explanation to help make sure you include enough details?

R. Answer these questions about character sketches.
1. What is the purpose of a character sketch?
2. What are several things you must avoid when planning and writing a character sketch?
3. What are three good ways to introduce a character sketch?
4. How can you write your character sketch so that it shows rather than tells the character trait?
5. What are two good ways to conclude a character sketch?

Index